# ZATCH BELL!

## 21

STORY AND ART BY

### MAKOTO RAIKU

# ZATCH BELL!

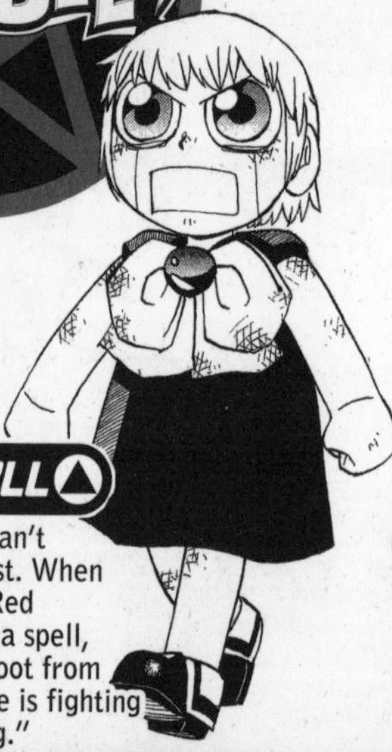

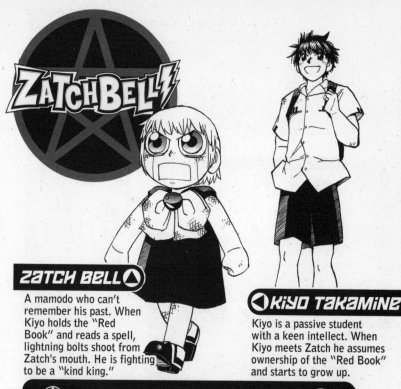

## ZATCH BELL

A mamodo who can't remember his past. When Kiyo holds the "Red Book" and reads a spell, lightning bolts shoot from Zatch's mouth. He is fighting to be a "kind king."

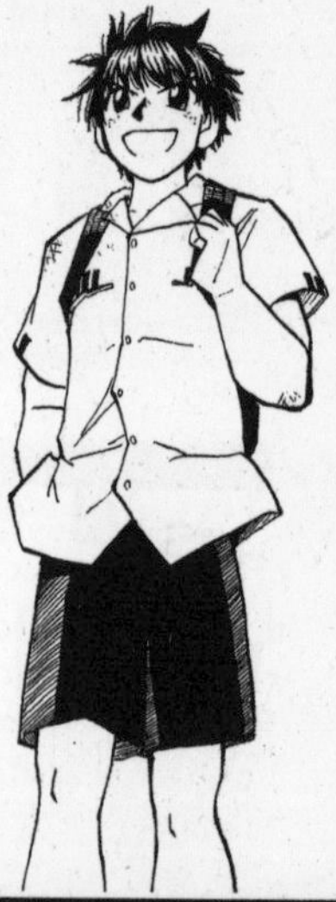

## KIYO TAKAMINE

Kiyo is a passive student with a keen intellect. When Kiyo meets Zatch he assumes ownership of the "Red Book" and starts to grow up.

## THE STORY THUS FAR

The battle to determine who will be the next king of the mamodo world takes place every 1,000 years in the human world. Each mamodo owns a "book" which increases its unique powers and they must team up with a human in order to fight for their own survival. Zatch is one of 100 mamodo chosen to fight in this battle, and his partner is Kiyo, a junior high school student. The bond between Zatch and Kiyo deepens as they continue to survive through many harsh battles. Zatch swears, "I will fight to become a kind king."

Only a few mamodo are left, and the battles are getting tougher. Zatch and his friends are shocked when TV news reporters reveal that a mysterious mamodo world structure has appeared in a remote location on Earth. Our heroes' surprise turns to horror when they discover that Faudo, the structure, is not a structure at all...it's a giant mamodo! To stop Faudo from being released, the heroes fly to New Zealand and parachute onto Faudo's body. But once they get there, they are attacked by Faudo's mysterious controllers...!

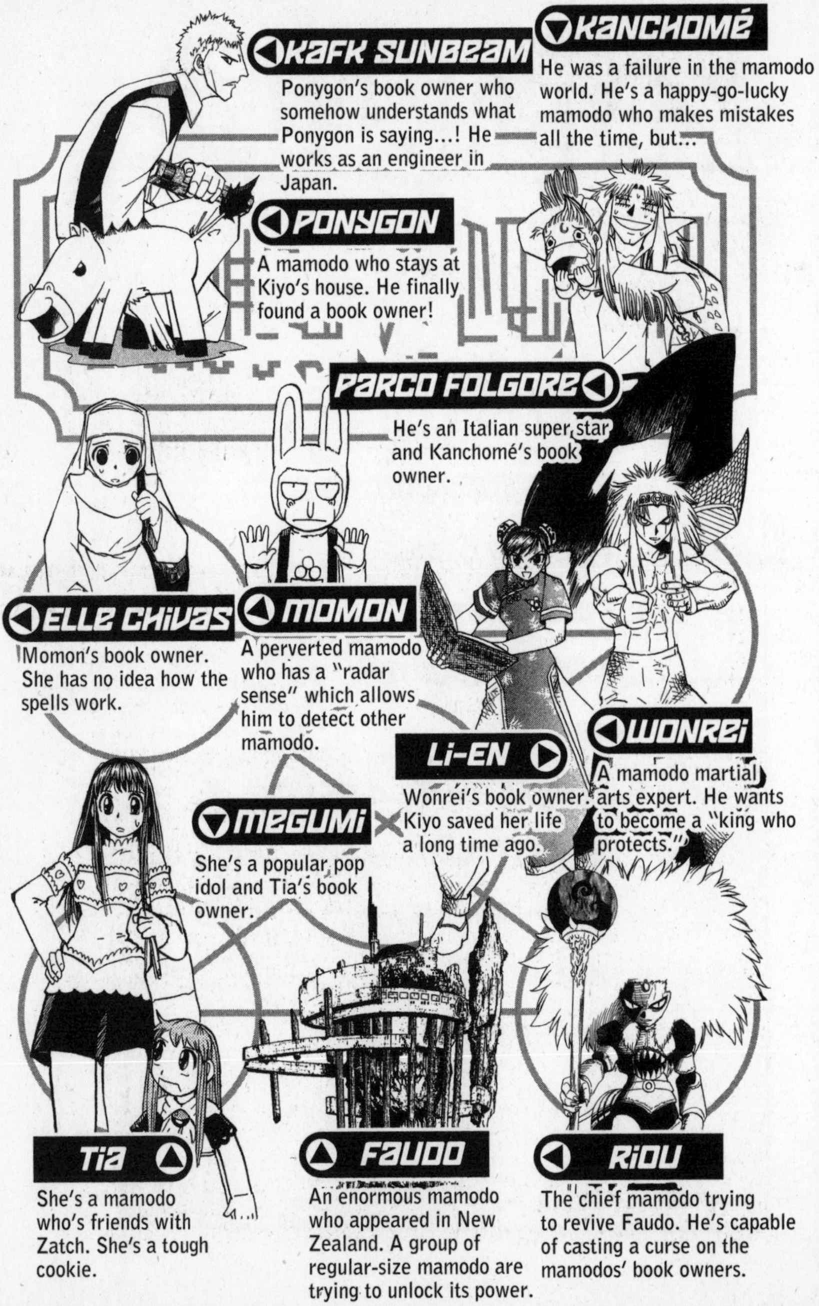

KANCHOMÉ
He was a failure in the mamodo world. He's a happy-go-lucky mamodo who makes mistakes all the time, but...
KAFK SUNBEAM
Ponygon's book owner who somehow understands what Ponygon is saying...! He works as an engineer in Japan.
PONYGON
A mamodo who stays at Kiyo's house. He finally found a book owner!
PARCO FOLGORE
He's an Italian super star and Kanchomé's book owner.
MOMON
A perverted mamodo who has a "radar sense" which allows him to detect other mamodo.
ELLE CHIVAS
Momon's book owner. She has no idea how the spells work.
WONREI
A mamodo martial arts expert. He wants to become a "king who protects."
LI-EN
Wonrei's book owner. Kiyo saved her life a long time ago.
MEGUMI
She's a popular pop idol and Tia's book owner.
RIOU
The chief mamodo trying to revive Faudo. He's capable of casting a curse on the mamodos' book owners.
FAUDO
An enormous mamodo who appeared in New Zealand. A group of regular-size mamodo are trying to unlock its power.
TIA
She's a mamodo who's friends with Zatch. She's a tough cookie.

# ZATCH BELL! 21

# CONTENTS

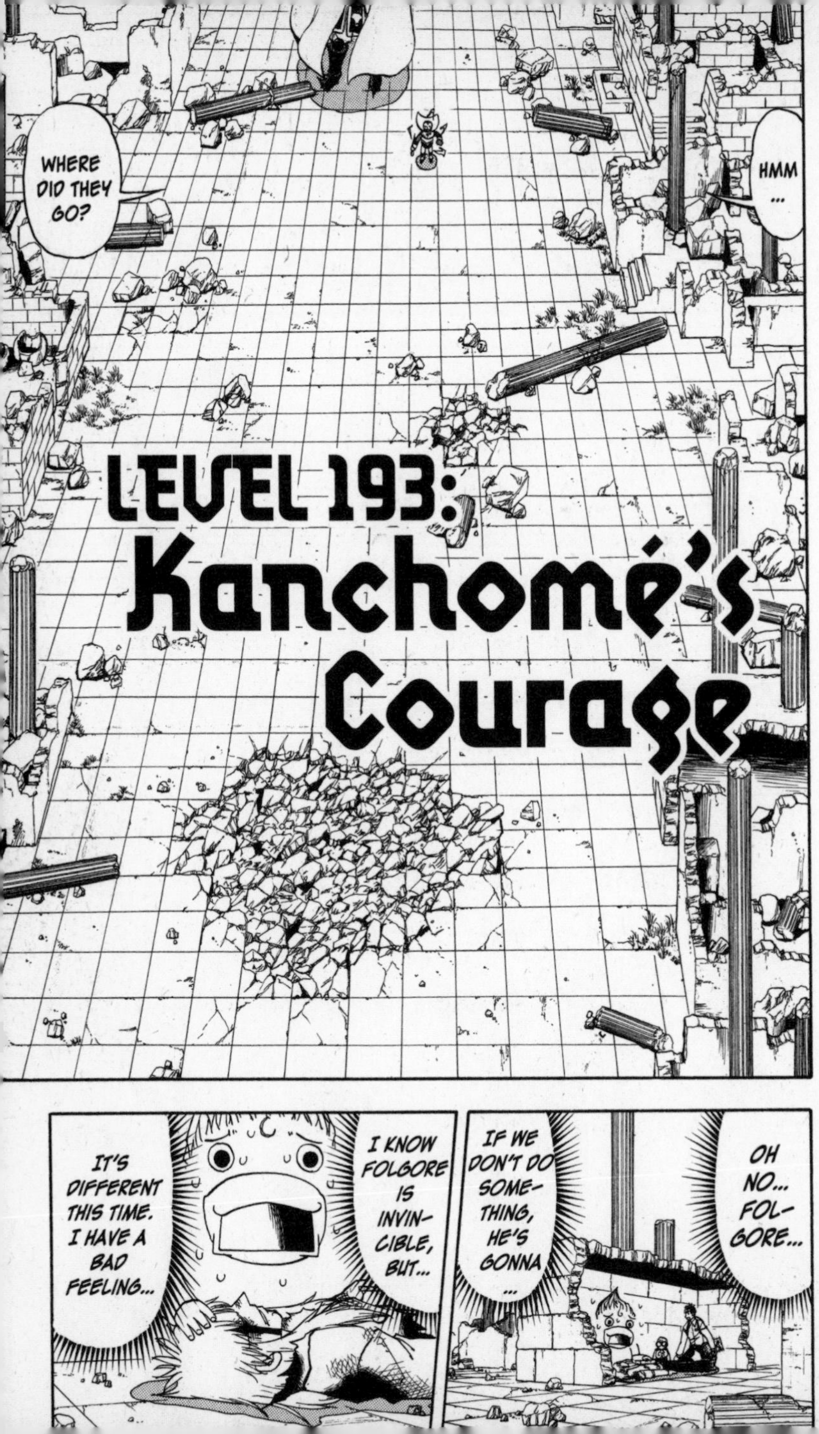
HMM ...
WHERE DID THEY GO?
LEVEL 193: Kanchomé's Courage
OH NO... FOLGORE...
IF WE DON'T DO SOMETHING, HE'S GONNA ...
I KNOW FOLGORE IS INVINCIBLE, BUT...
IT'S DIFFERENT THIS TIME. I HAVE A BAD FEELING...

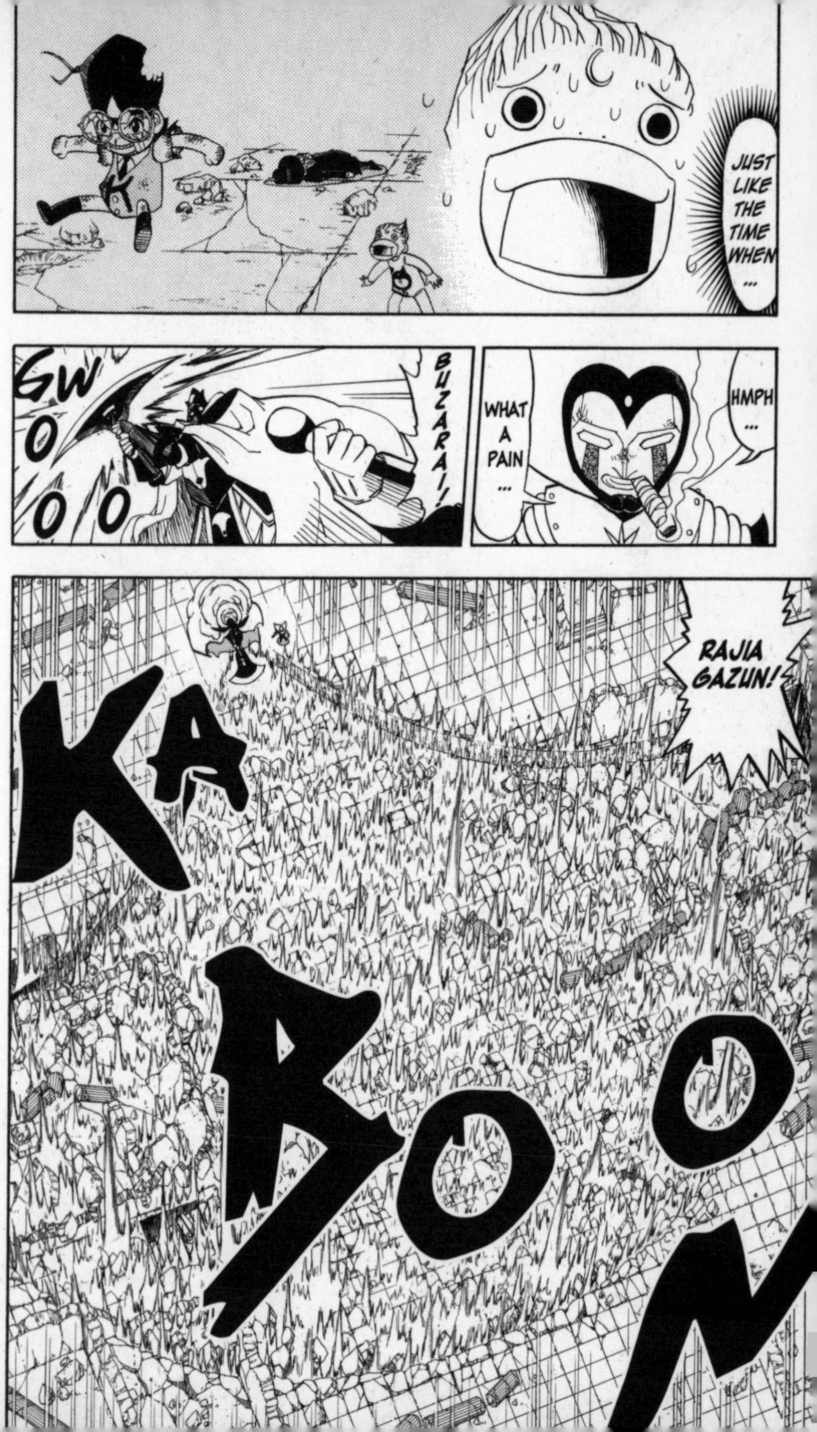

JUST LIKE THE TIME WHEN ...
HMPH ...
WHAT A PAIN ...
BUZARAI!!
GWOOOO
RAJIA GAZUN!
KA
KABOOM

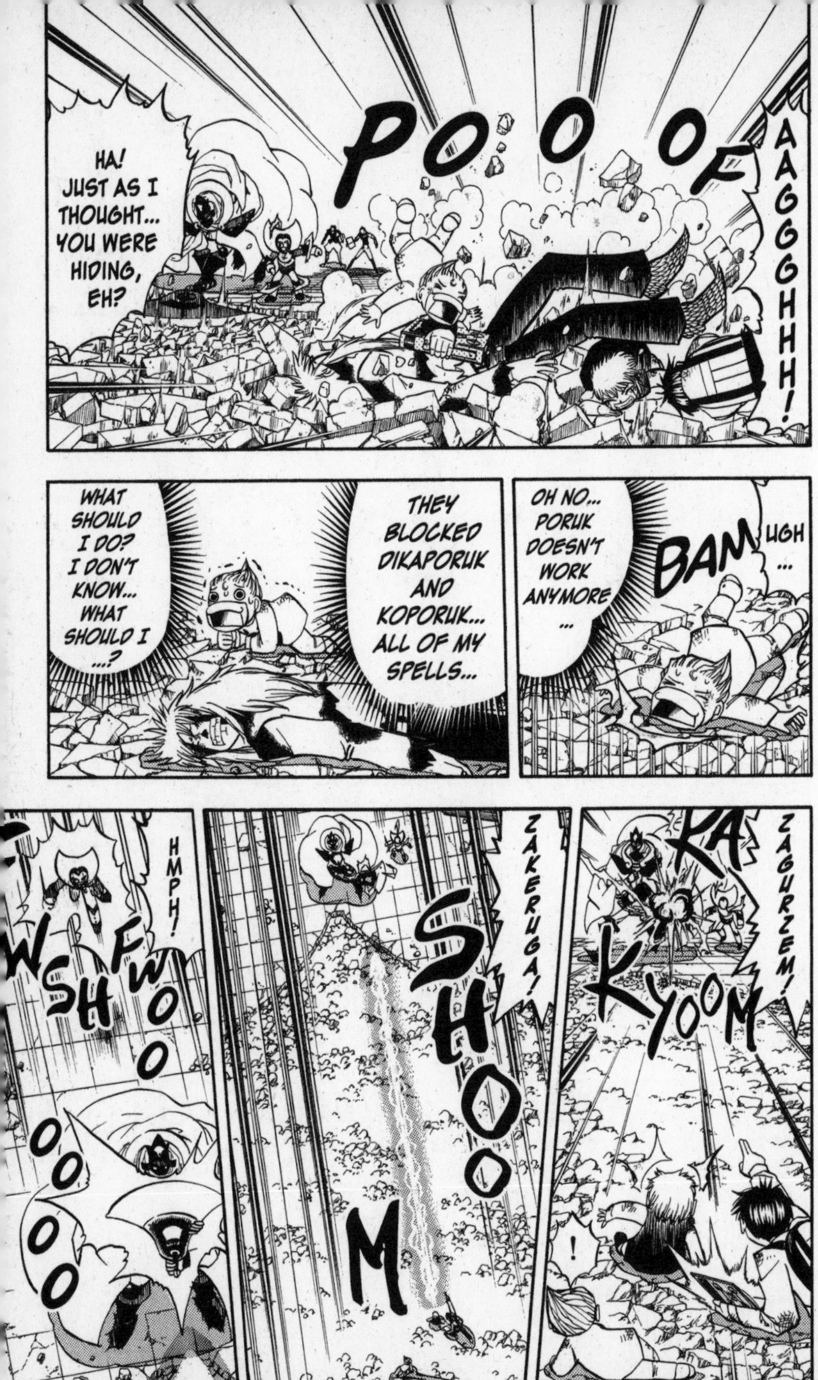
AAGGGHHHH!
POOOF
HA! JUST AS I THOUGHT... YOU WERE HIDING, EH?
UGH...
BAM
OH NO... PORUK DOESN'T WORK ANYMORE...
THEY BLOCKED DIKAPORUK AND KOPORUK... ALL OF MY SPELLS...
WHAT SHOULD I DO? I DON'T KNOW... WHAT SHOULD I ...?
ZAGURZEM!
KA
KYOOM
!
ZAKERUGA!
SHOOOM
HMPH!
FWOOOOOOOO
WSH

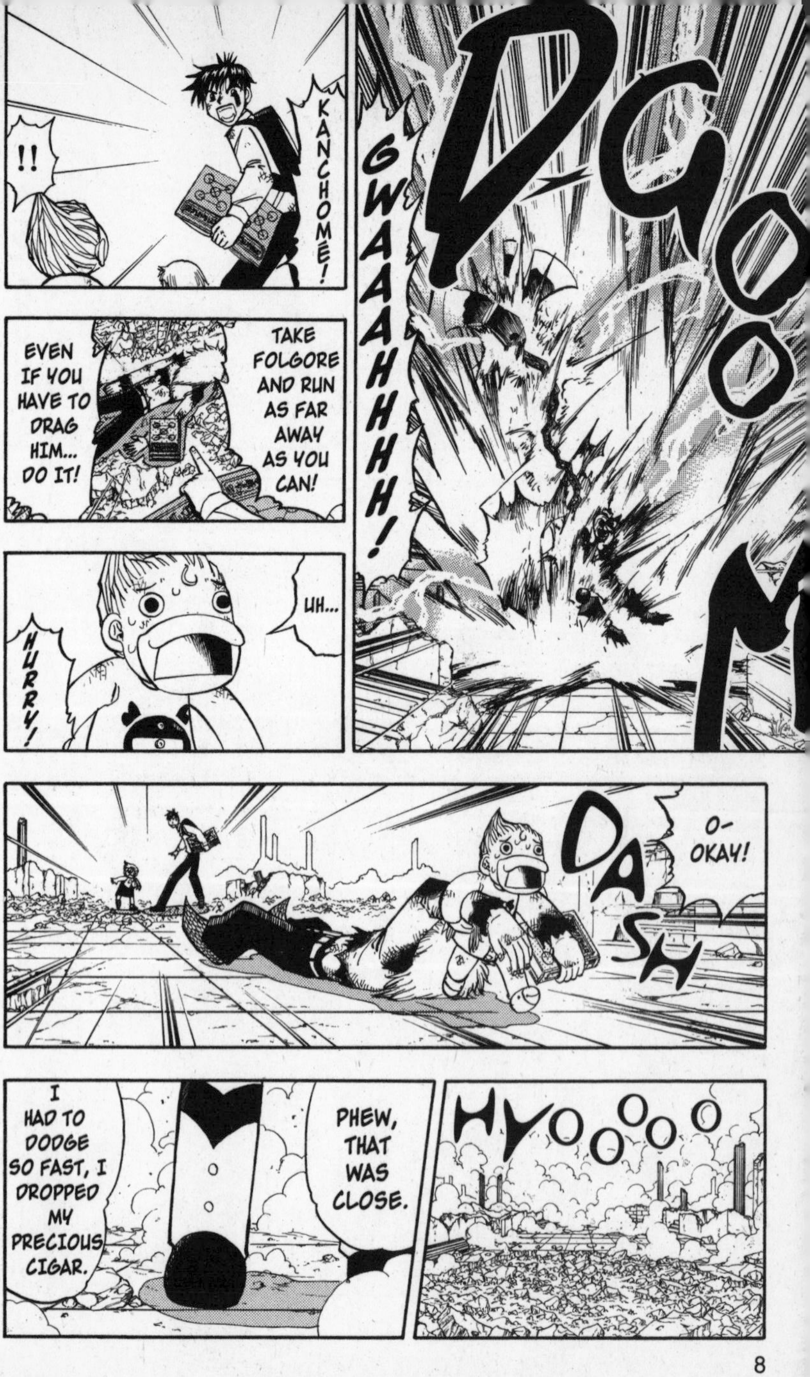
DGOOOM
GWAAAAHHHHH!
KANCHOMÉ!
!!
TAKE FOLGORE AND RUN AS FAR AWAY AS YOU CAN!
EVEN IF YOU HAVE TO DRAG HIM... DO IT!
UH...
HURRY!
O-OKAY!
DASH
HYOOOOO
PHEW, THAT WAS CLOSE.
I HAD TO DODGE SO FAST, I DROPPED MY PRECIOUS CIGAR.

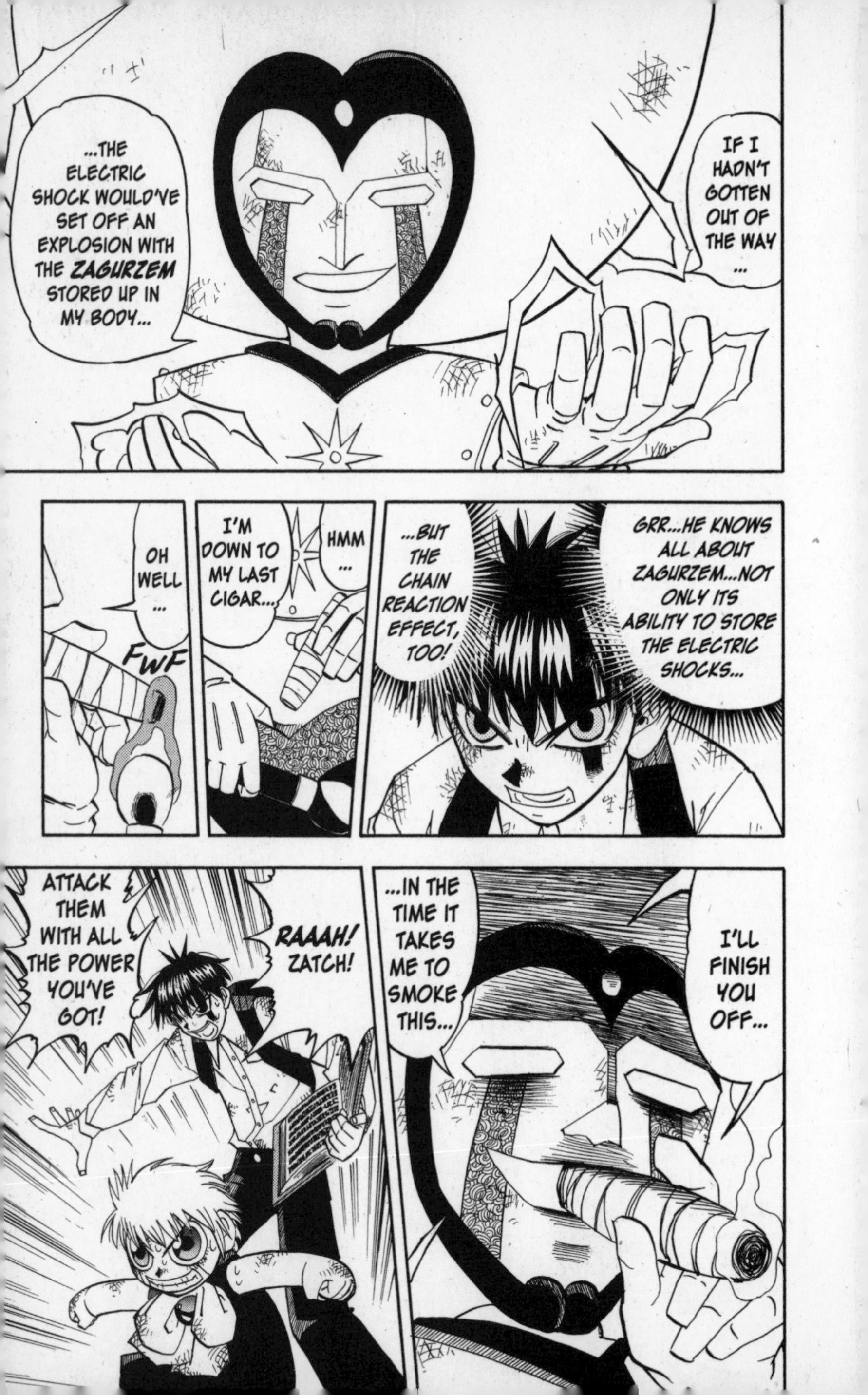
IF I HADN'T GOTTEN OUT OF THE WAY ...
...THE ELECTRIC SHOCK WOULD'VE SET OFF AN EXPLOSION WITH THE *ZAGURZEM* STORED UP IN MY BODY...
GRR...HE KNOWS ALL ABOUT ZAGURZEM...NOT ONLY ITS ABILITY TO STORE THE ELECTRIC SHOCKS...
...BUT THE CHAIN REACTION EFFECT, TOO!
HMM ...
I'M DOWN TO MY LAST CIGAR...
OH WELL ...
FWF
I'LL FINISH YOU OFF...
...IN THE TIME IT TAKES ME TO SMOKE THIS...
RAAAH! ZATCH!
ATTACK THEM WITH ALL THE POWER YOU'VE GOT!

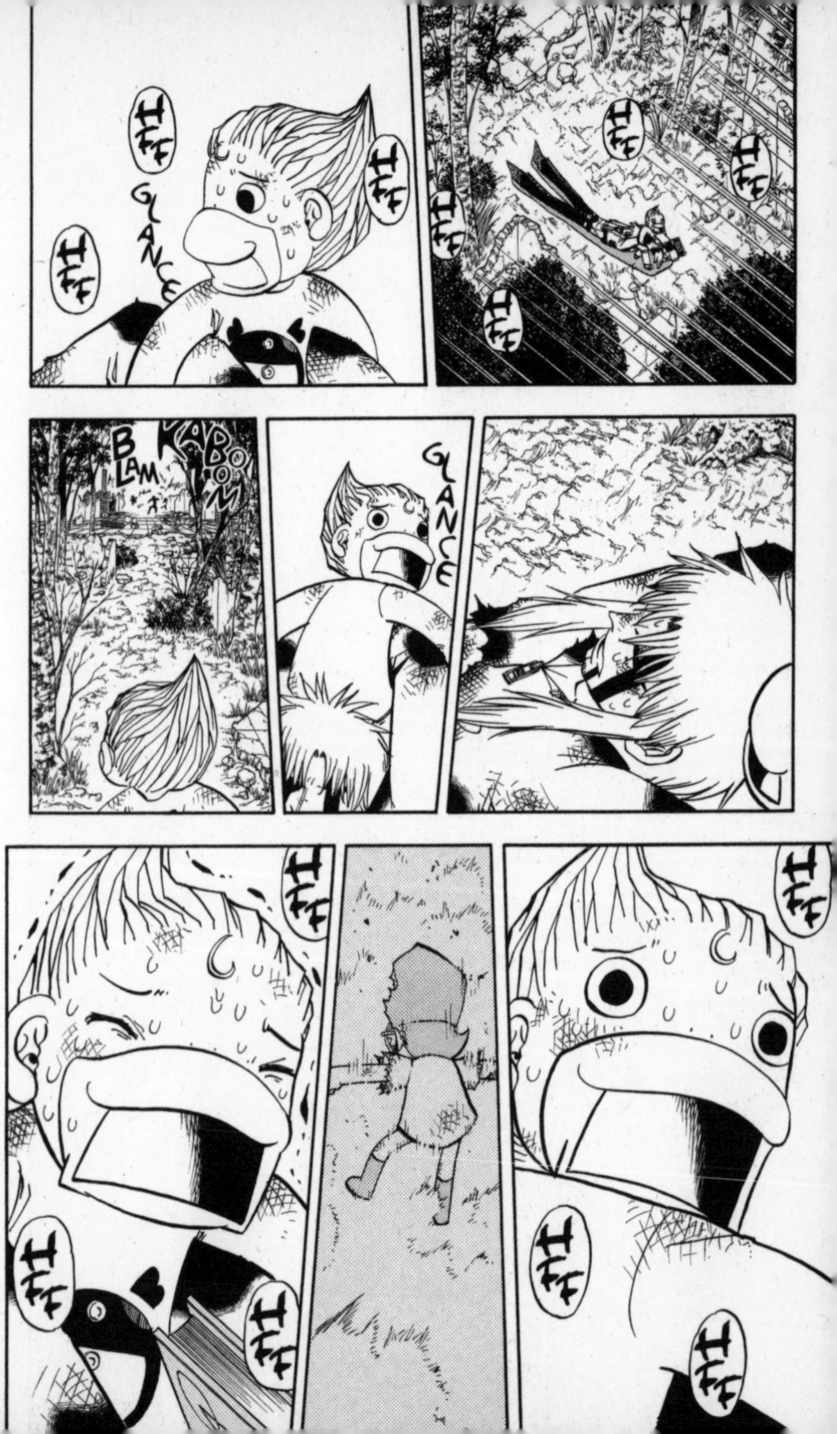
HFF
HFF
HFF
HFF
HFF
HFF
GLANCE
HFF
GLANCE
KABOOM
BLAM
HFF
HFF
HFF
HFF
HFF
HFF

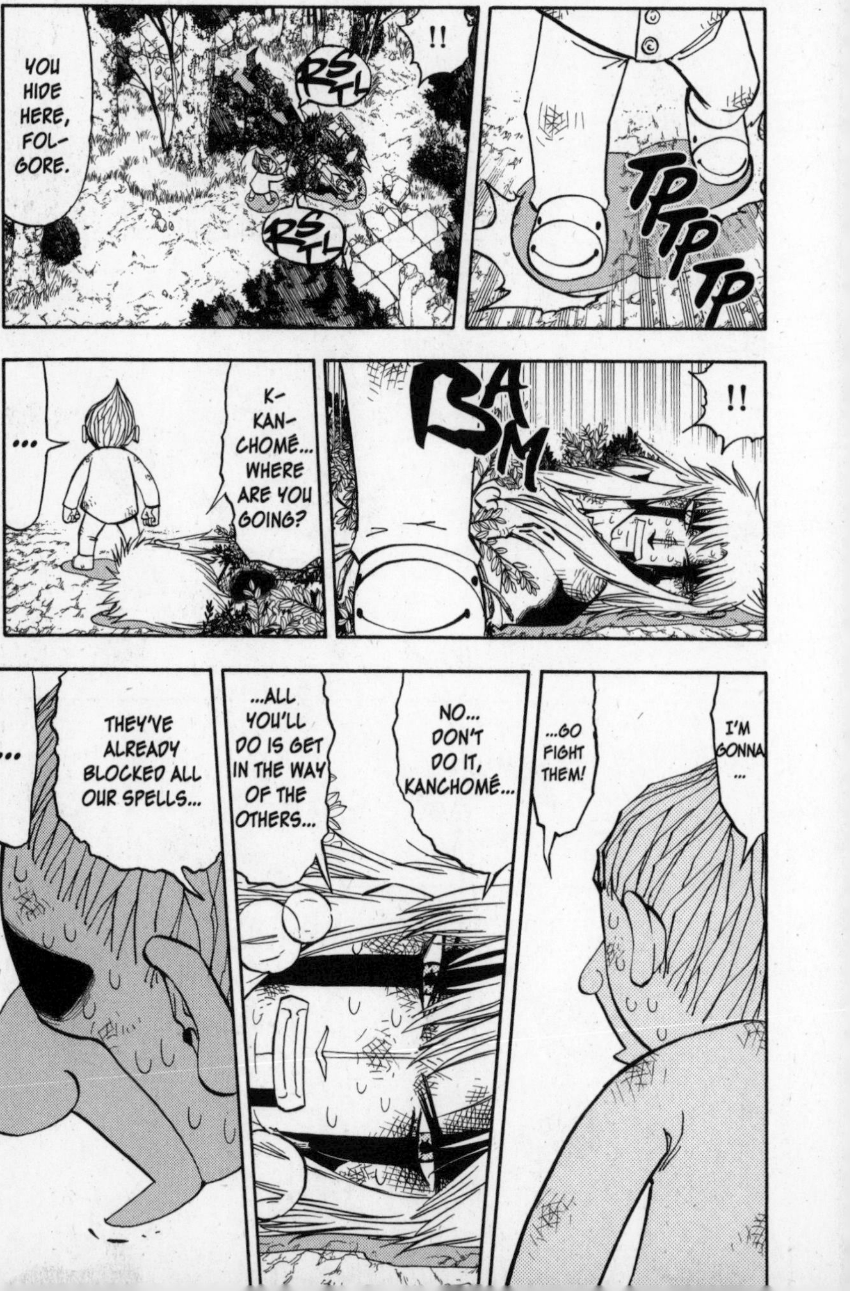
TP TP TP TP
!!
RSTL
RSTL
YOU HIDE HERE, FOLGORE.
!!
BAM
K-KANCHOMÉ... WHERE ARE YOU GOING?
...
I'M GONNA...
...GO FIGHT THEM!
NO... DON'T DO IT, KANCHOMÉ...
...ALL YOU'LL DO IS GET IN THE WAY OF THE OTHERS...
THEY'VE ALREADY BLOCKED ALL OUR SPELLS...
...

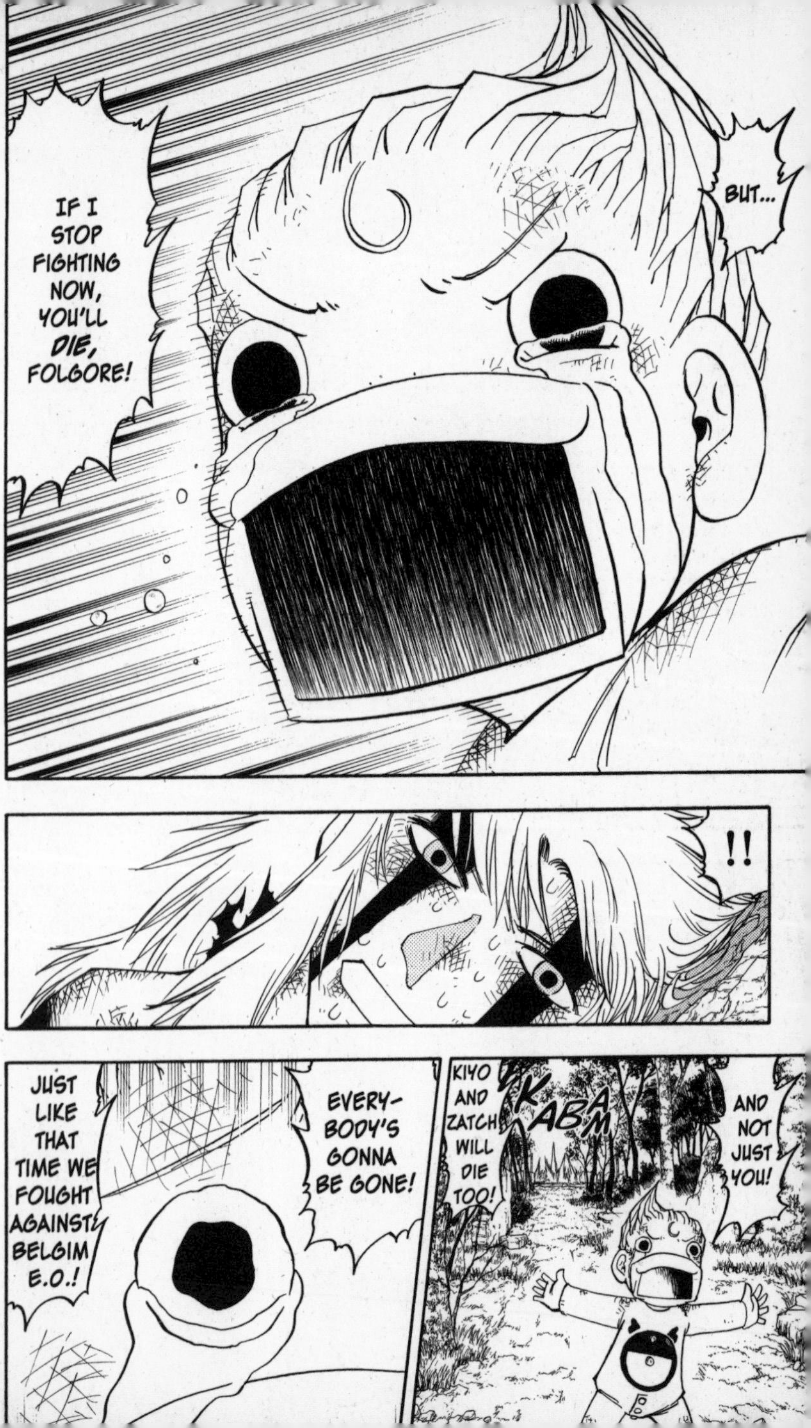
BUT...
IF I STOP FIGHTING NOW, YOU'LL *DIE*, FOLGORE!
!!
AND NOT JUST YOU!
KABAM
KIYO AND ZATCH WILL DIE TOO!
EVERY-BODY'S GONNA BE GONE!
JUST LIKE THAT TIME WE FOUGHT AGAINST BELGIM E.O.!

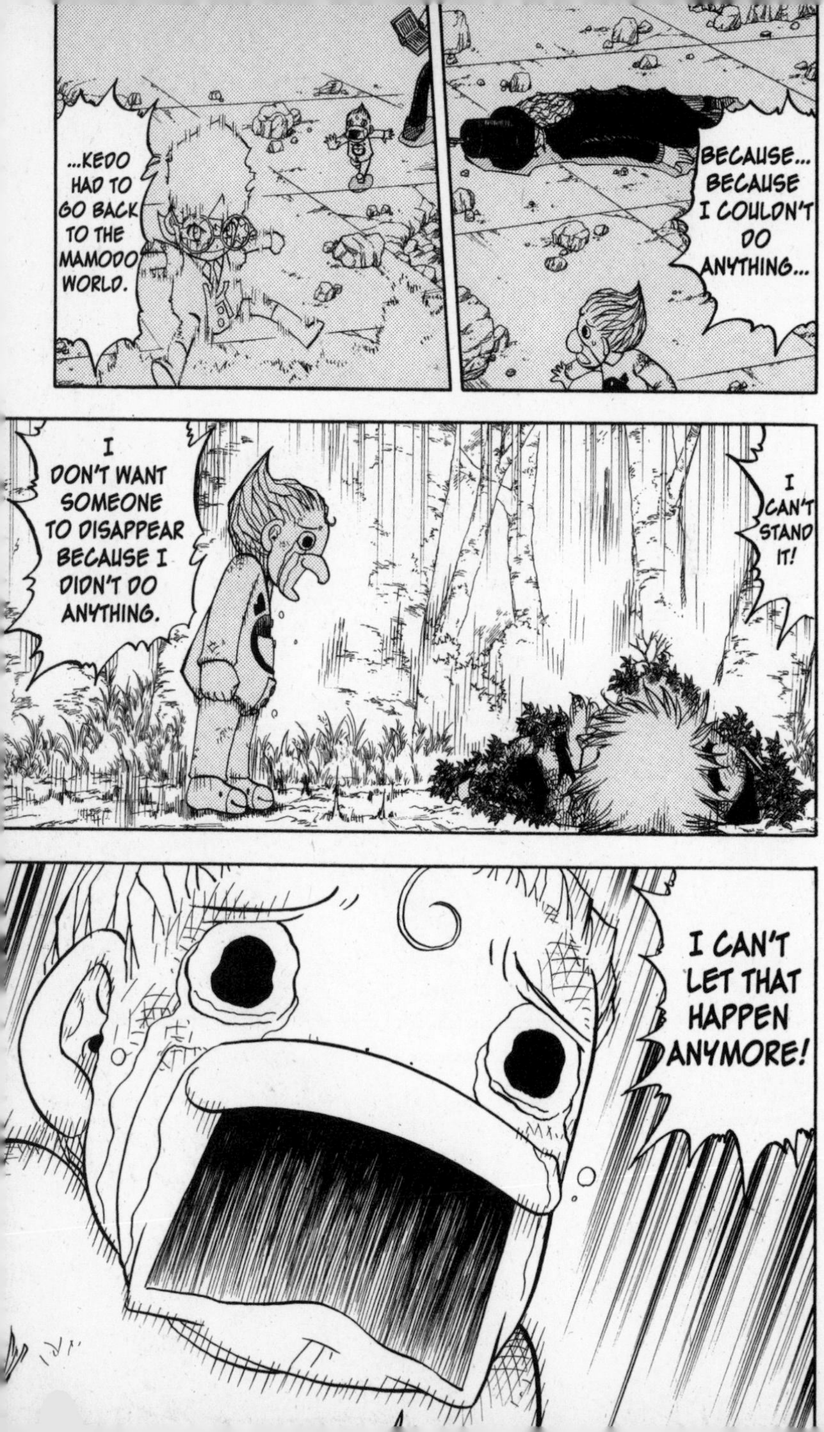
BECAUSE... BECAUSE I COULDN'T DO ANYTHING...
...KEDO HAD TO GO BACK TO THE MAMODO WORLD.
I CAN'T STAND IT!
I DON'T WANT SOMEONE TO DISAPPEAR BECAUSE I DIDN'T DO ANYTHING.
I CAN'T LET THAT HAPPEN ANYMORE!

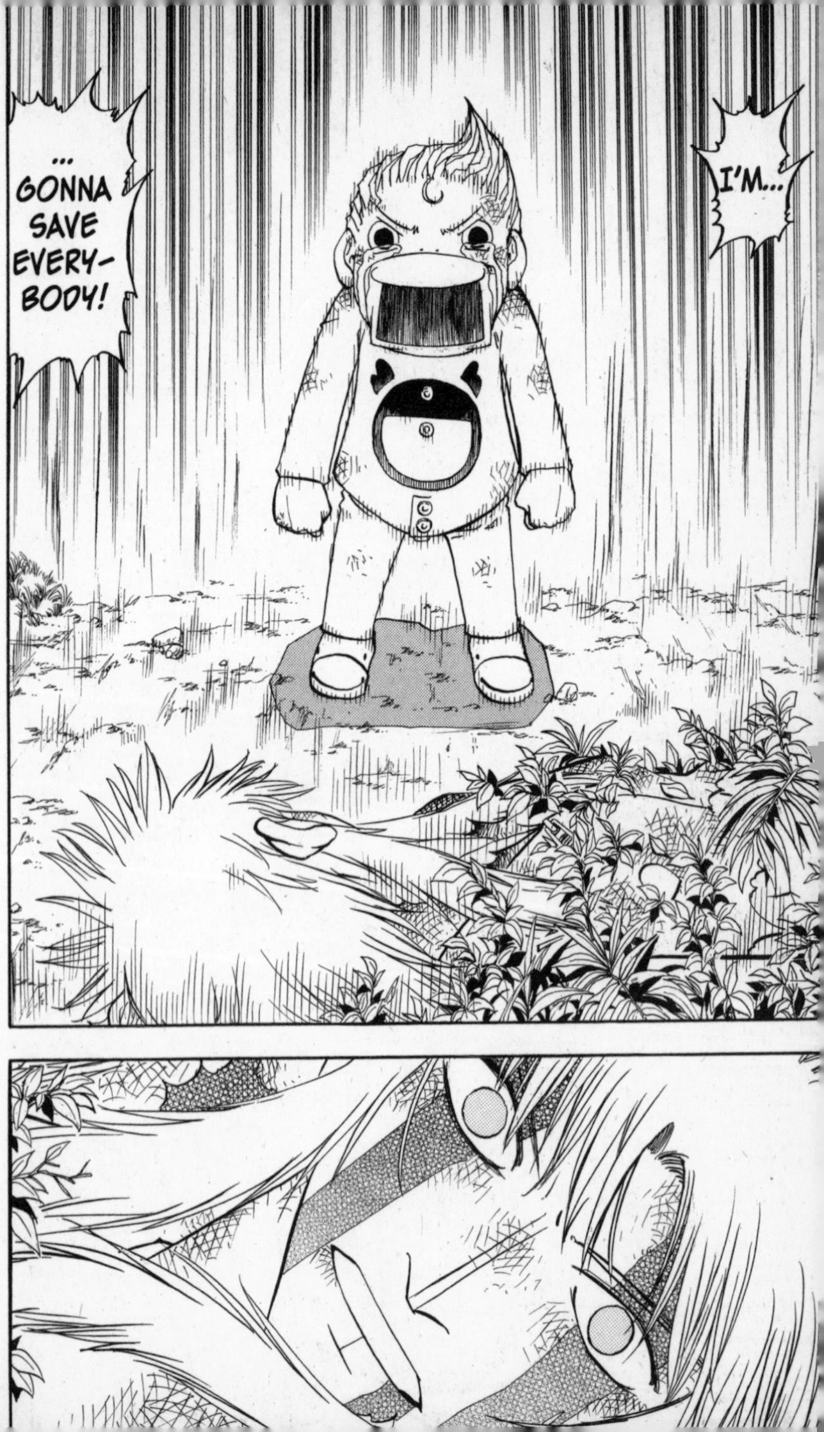
I'M...
... GONNA SAVE EVERY-BODY!

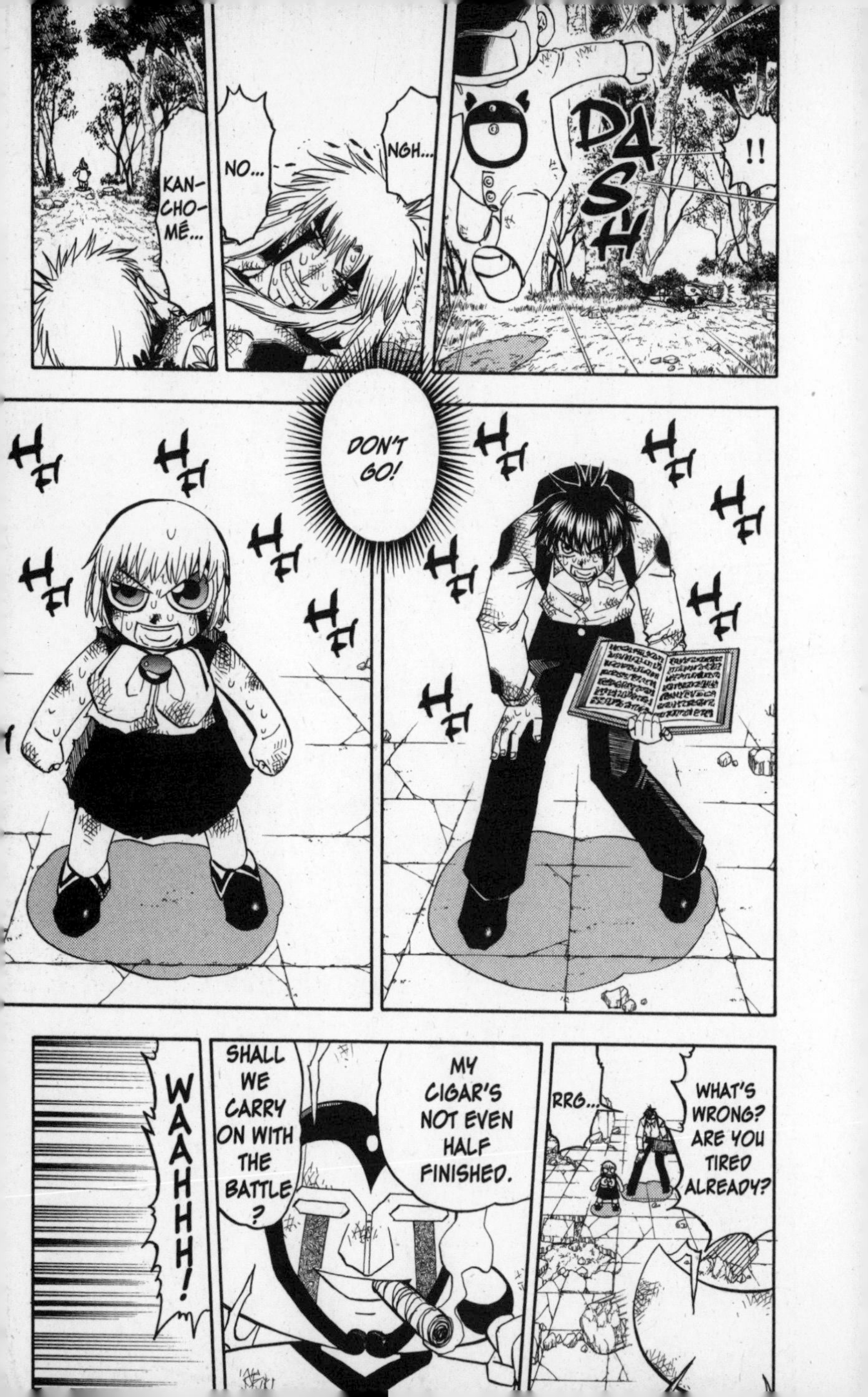
DASH
!!
NGH...
NO...
KAN-CHO-MÉ...
HF
HF
HF
HF
HF
HF
DON'T GO!
HF
HF
HF
HF
HF
WHAT'S WRONG? ARE YOU TIRED ALREADY?
RRG...
MY CIGAR'S NOT EVEN HALF FINISHED.
SHALL WE CARRY ON WITH THE BATTLE?
WAAHHH!

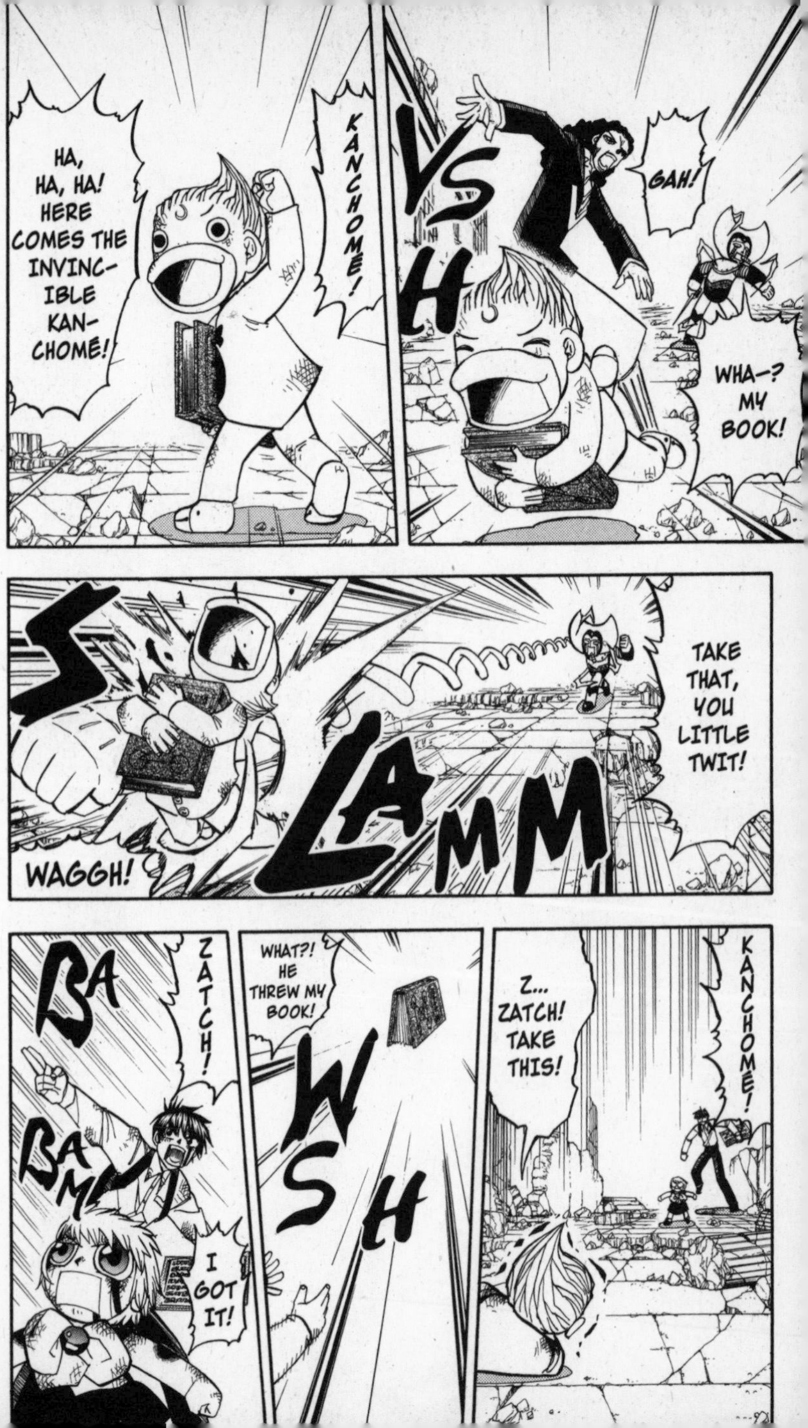
GAH!
VSH
WHA-? MY BOOK!
KANCHOME!
HA, HA, HA! HERE COMES THE INVINCIBLE KANCHOME!
TAKE THAT, YOU LITTLE TWIT!
SLAMM
WAGGH!
KANCHOME!
Z... ZATCH! TAKE THIS!
WHAT?! HE THREW MY BOOK!
WSH
ZATCH!
BA
BAM
I GOT IT!

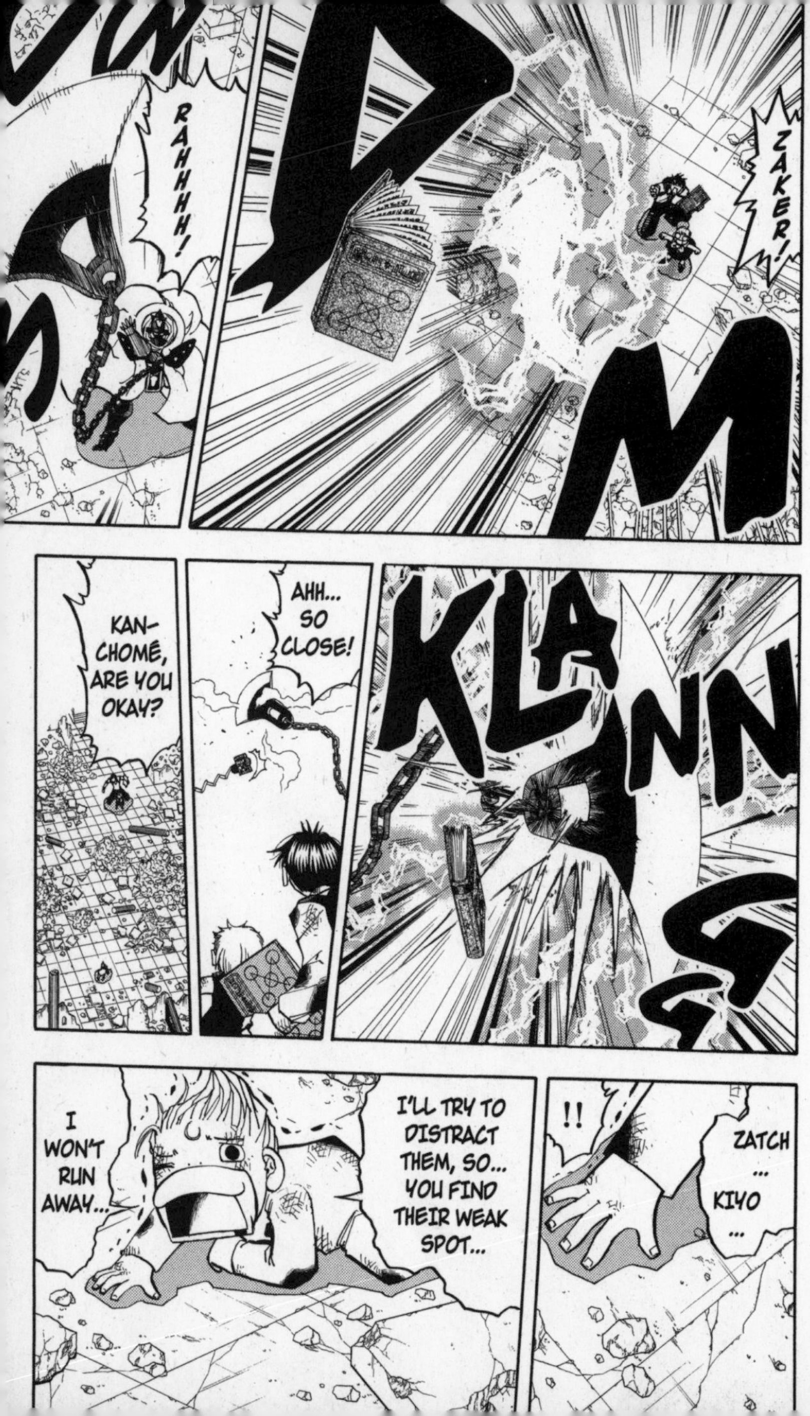
ZAKER!
RAHHHHH!
KLANNG
AHH... SO CLOSE!
KAN-CHOME, ARE YOU OKAY?
!!
ZATCH ... KIYO ...
I'LL TRY TO DISTRACT THEM, SO... YOU FIND THEIR WEAK SPOT...
I WON'T RUN AWAY...

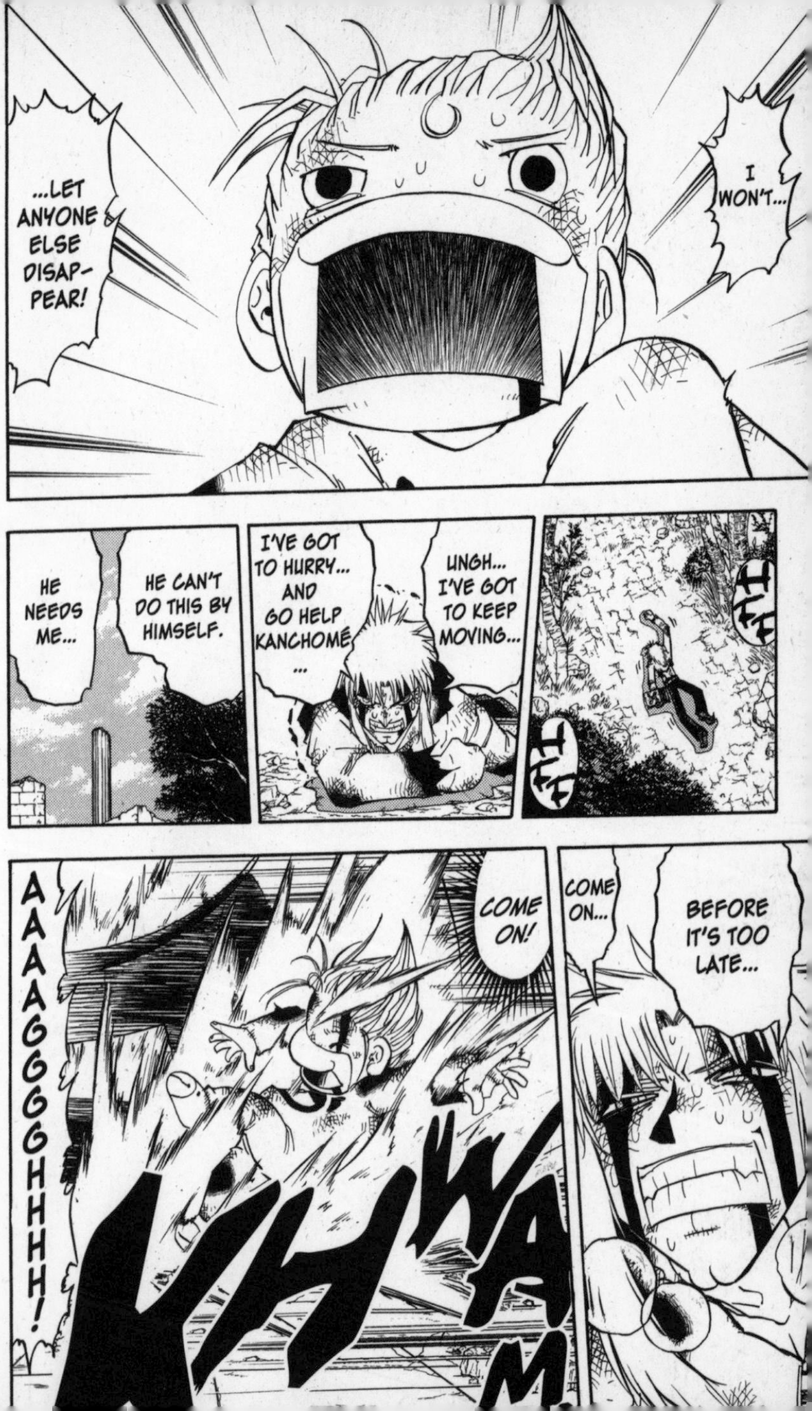
I WON'T...
...LET ANYONE ELSE DISAP-PEAR!
HFF
HFF
UNGH... I'VE GOT TO KEEP MOVING...
I'VE GOT TO HURRY... AND GO HELP KANCHOMÉ ...
HE CAN'T DO THIS BY HIMSELF.
HE NEEDS ME...
BEFORE IT'S TOO LATE...
COME ON...
COME ON!
AAAAGGGGHHHHH!

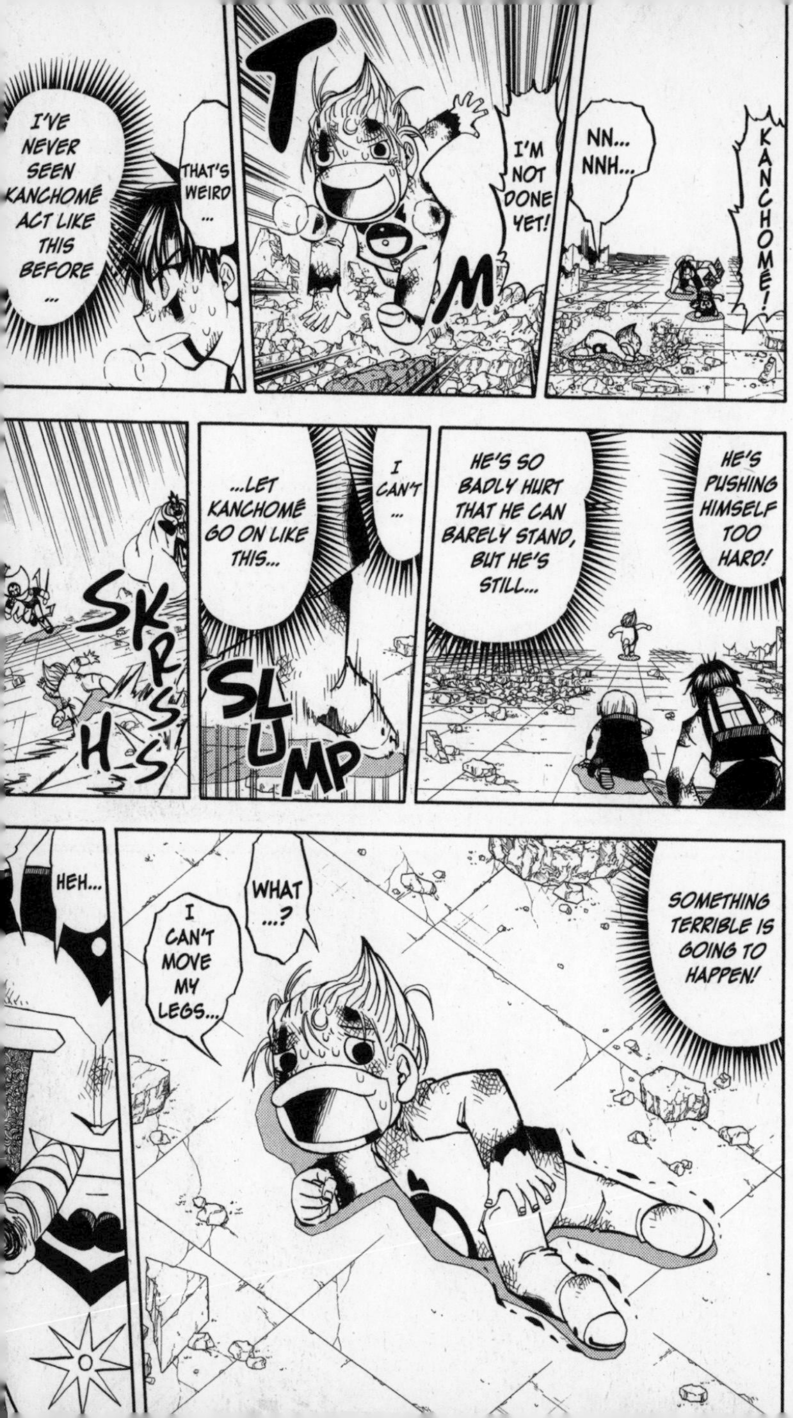
KANCHOMÉ!
NN... NNH...
I'M NOT DONE YET!
T
M
THAT'S WEIRD ...
I'VE NEVER SEEN KANCHOMÉ ACT LIKE THIS BEFORE ...
HE'S PUSHING HIMSELF TOO HARD!
HE'S SO BADLY HURT THAT HE CAN BARELY STAND, BUT HE'S STILL...
I CAN'T ...
...LET KANCHOMÉ GO ON LIKE THIS...
SLUMP
SKRSHS
SOMETHING TERRIBLE IS GOING TO HAPPEN!
WHAT ...?
I CAN'T MOVE MY LEGS...
HEH...

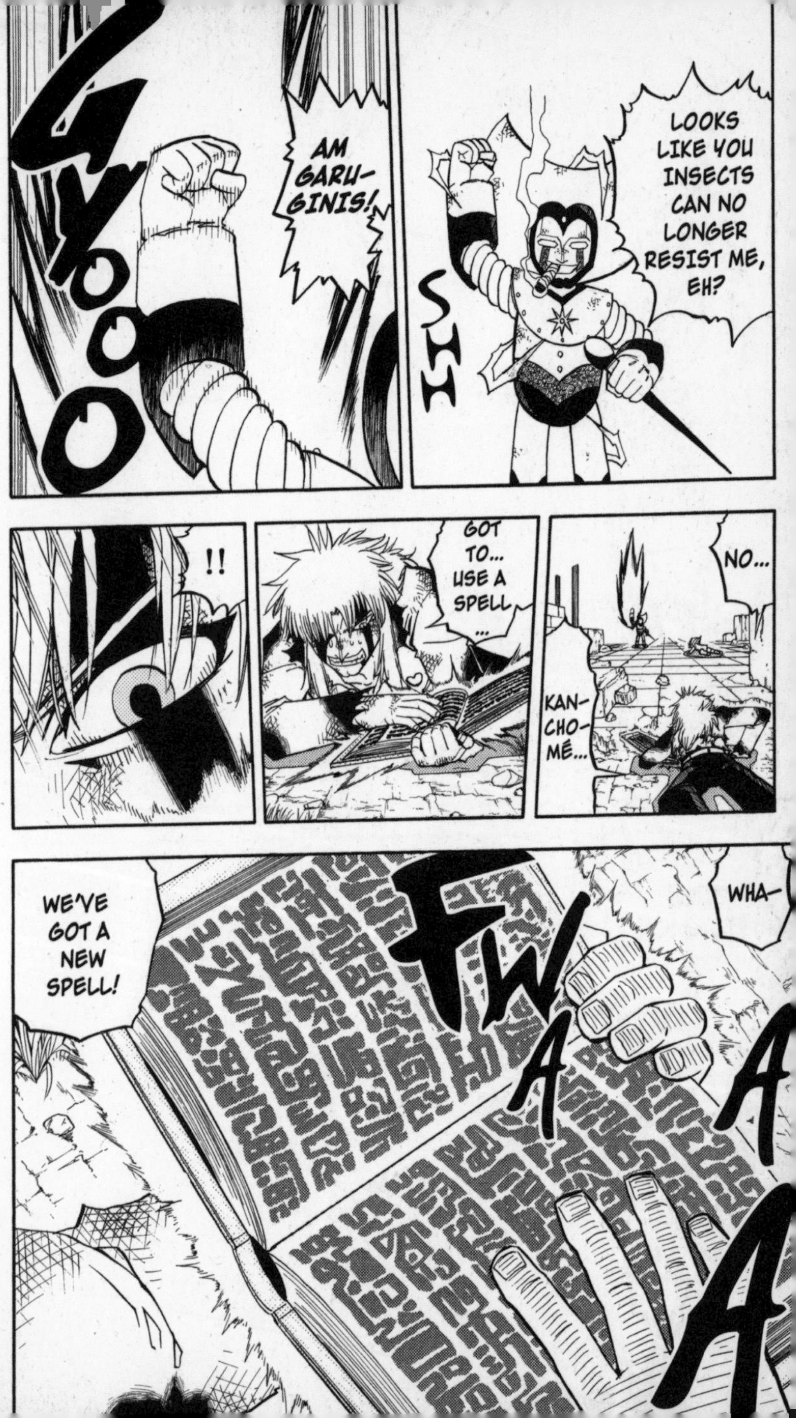
LOOKS LIKE YOU INSECTS CAN NO LONGER RESIST ME, EH?
AM GARU-GINIS!
NO...
KAN-CHO-MÉ...
GOT TO... USE A SPELL ...
!!
WHA-
WE'VE GOT A NEW SPELL!

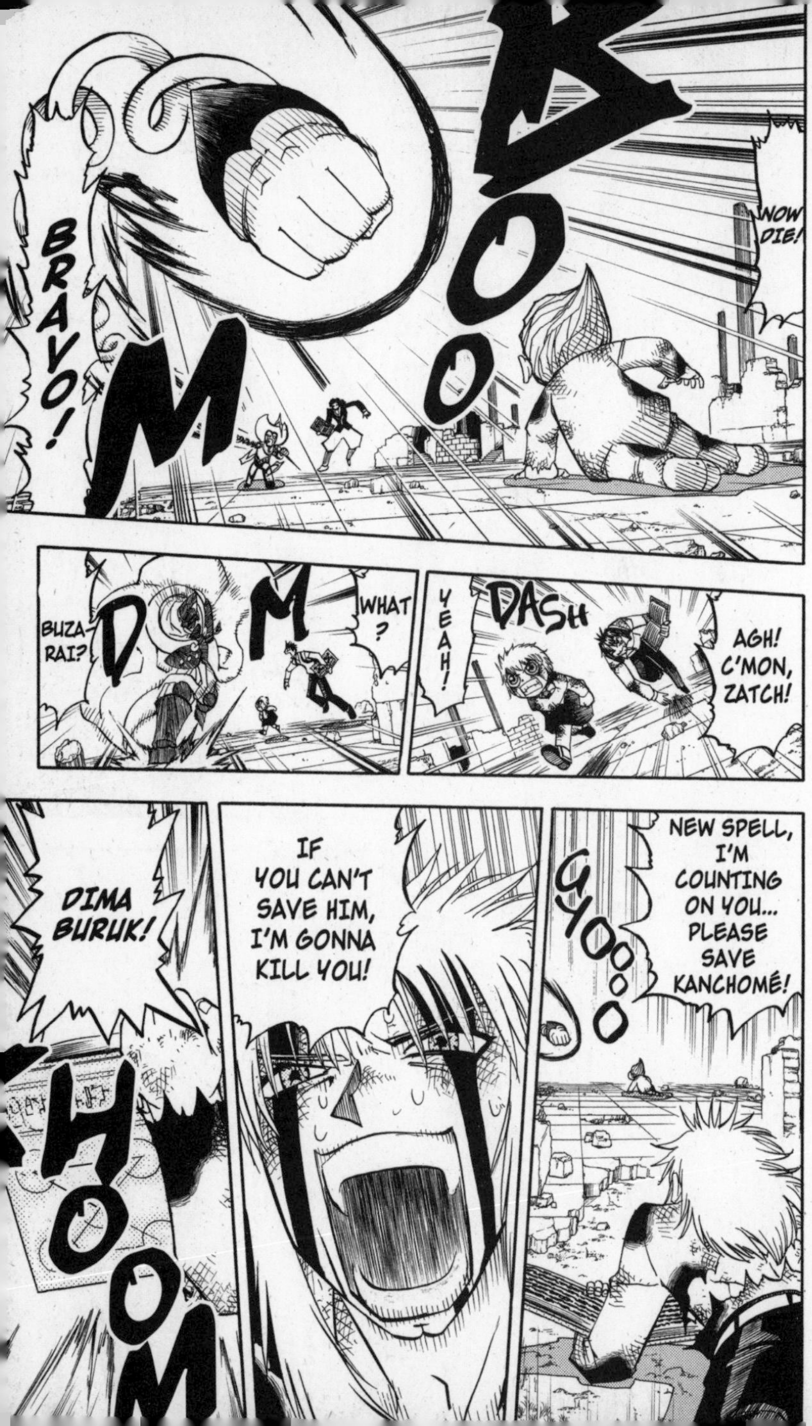
NOW DIE!
KOOM
BRAVO!
AGH! C'MON, ZATCH!
DASH
YEAH!
WHAT?
DM
BUZARAI?
NEW SPELL, I'M COUNTING ON YOU... PLEASE SAVE KANCHOMÉ!
GYOOOO
IF YOU CAN'T SAVE HIM, I'M GONNA KILL YOU!
DIMA BURUK!
HOOM

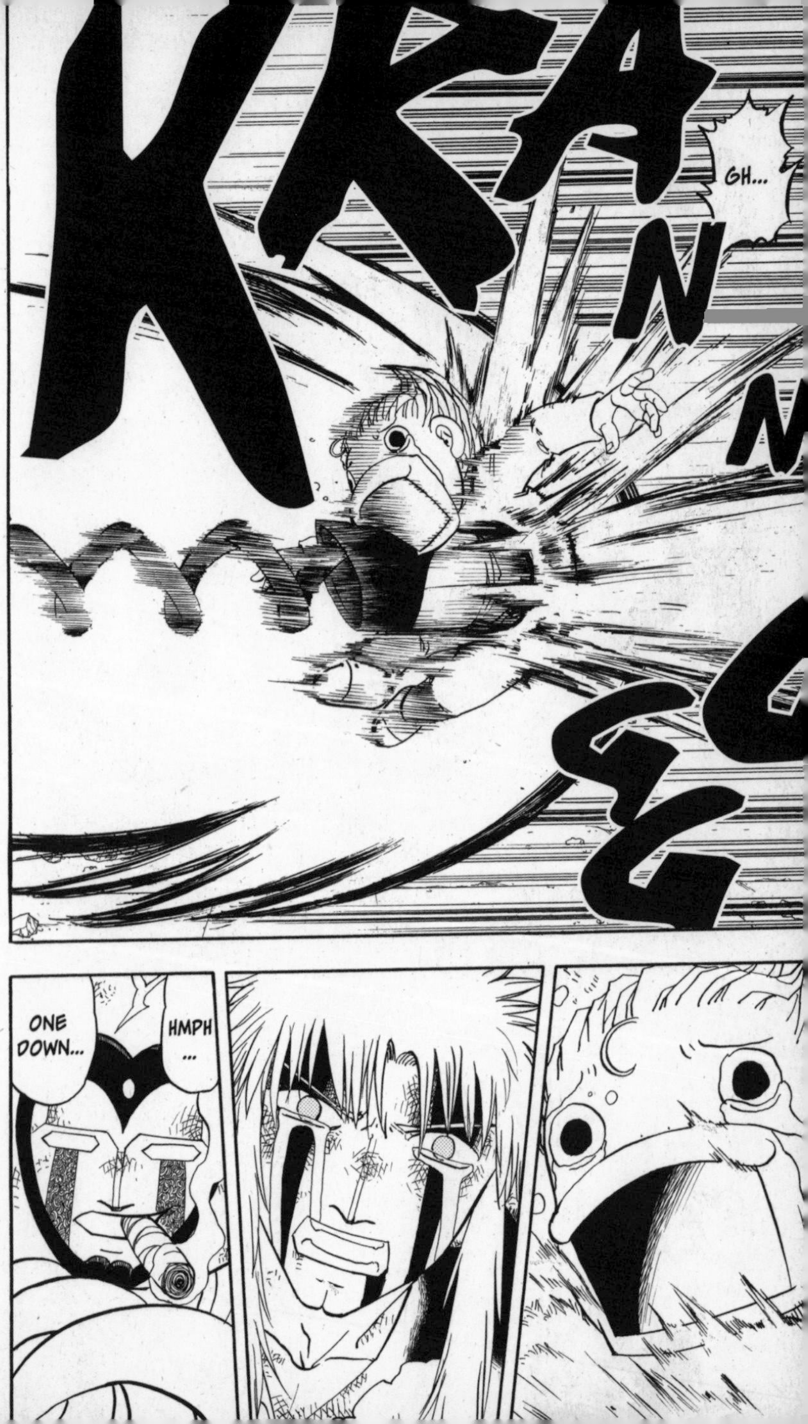
GH...
HMPH ...
ONE DOWN...

# LEVEL 194: A Strong Desire

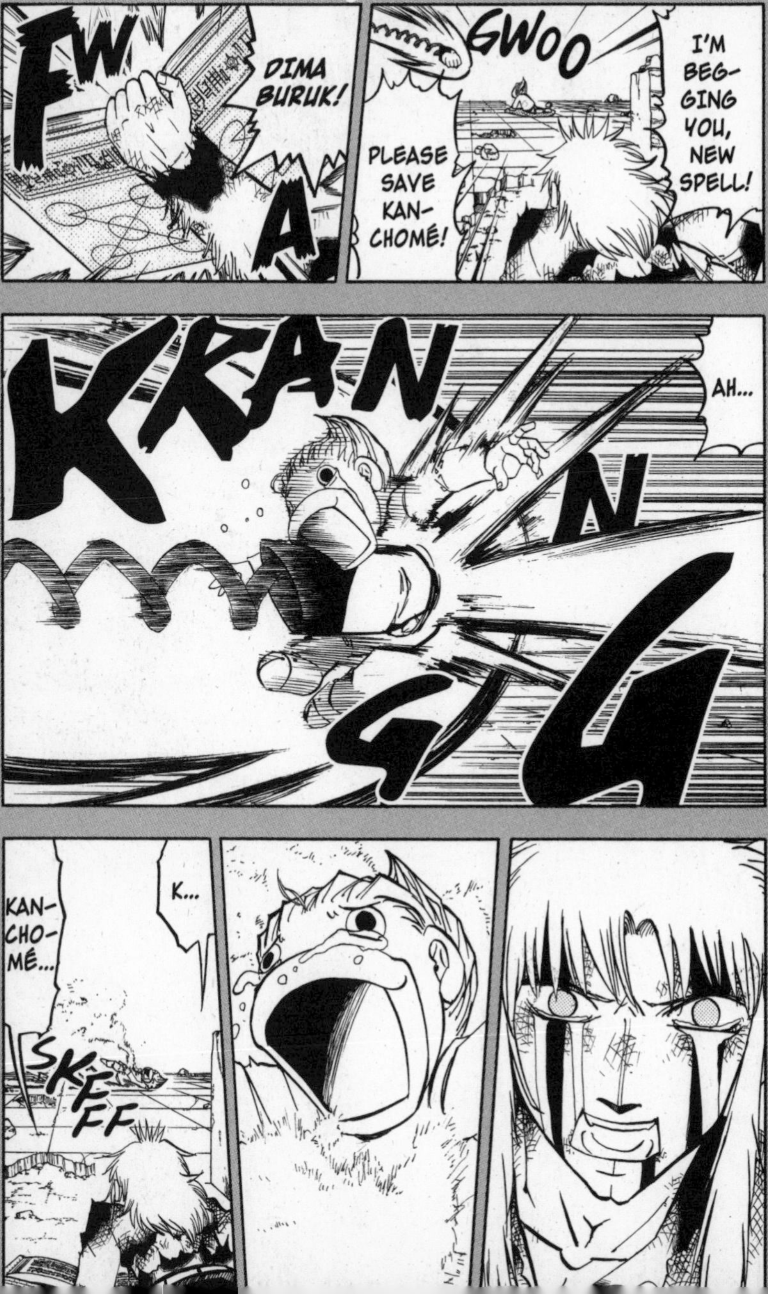
I'M BEG-GING YOU, NEW SPELL!
GWOO
PLEASE SAVE KAN-CHOMÉ!
DIMA BURUK!
FWA
AH...
KRAN
NG
K...
KAN-CHO-MÉ...
SKFFF

# LEVEL 194: A Strong Desire

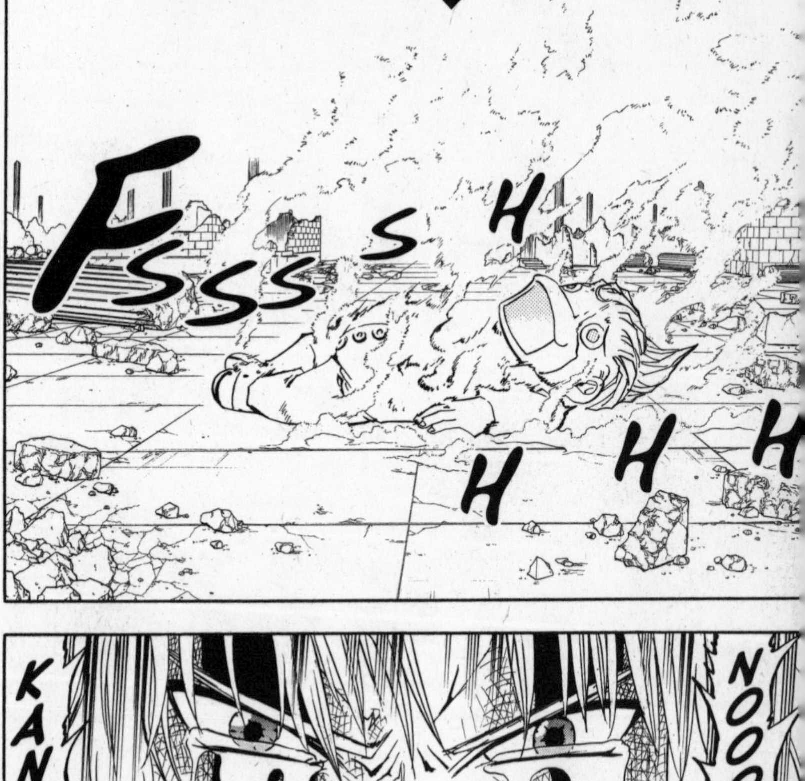
FSSSSS
HHHH

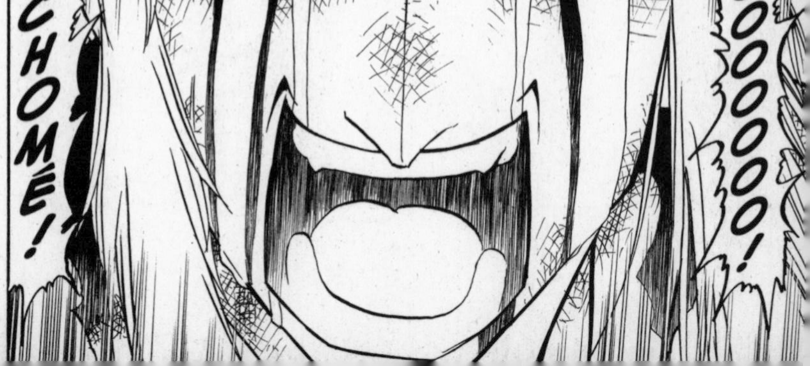
NOOOOOOOOOOOO!
KANCHOMÉ!

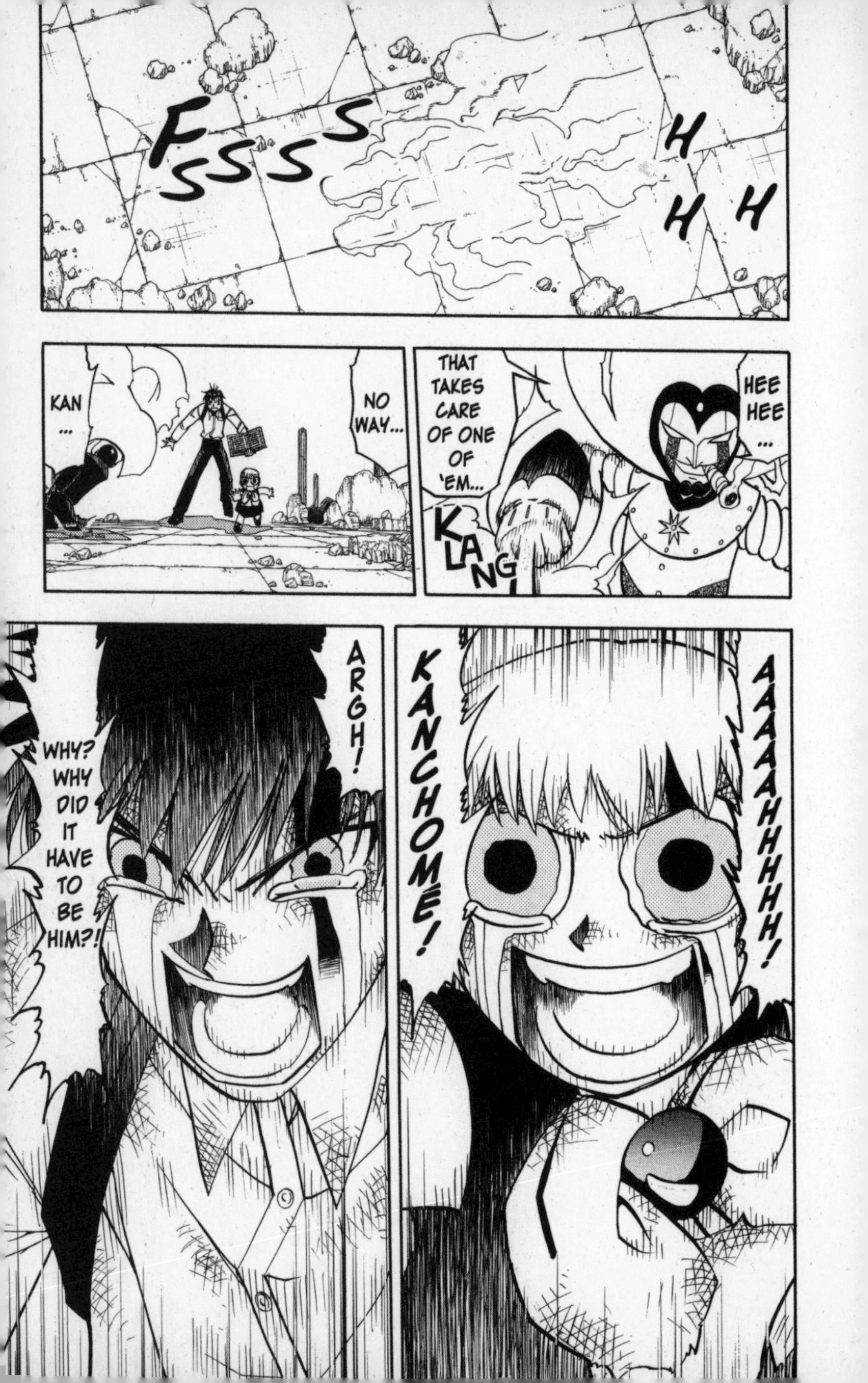
FSSSSS
HHHH
HEE HEE ...
THAT TAKES CARE OF ONE OF 'EM...
KLANG
NO WAY...
KAN ...
KANCHOMÉ!
AAAAAHHHHHH!
ARGH!
WHY? WHY DID IT HAVE TO BE HIM?!

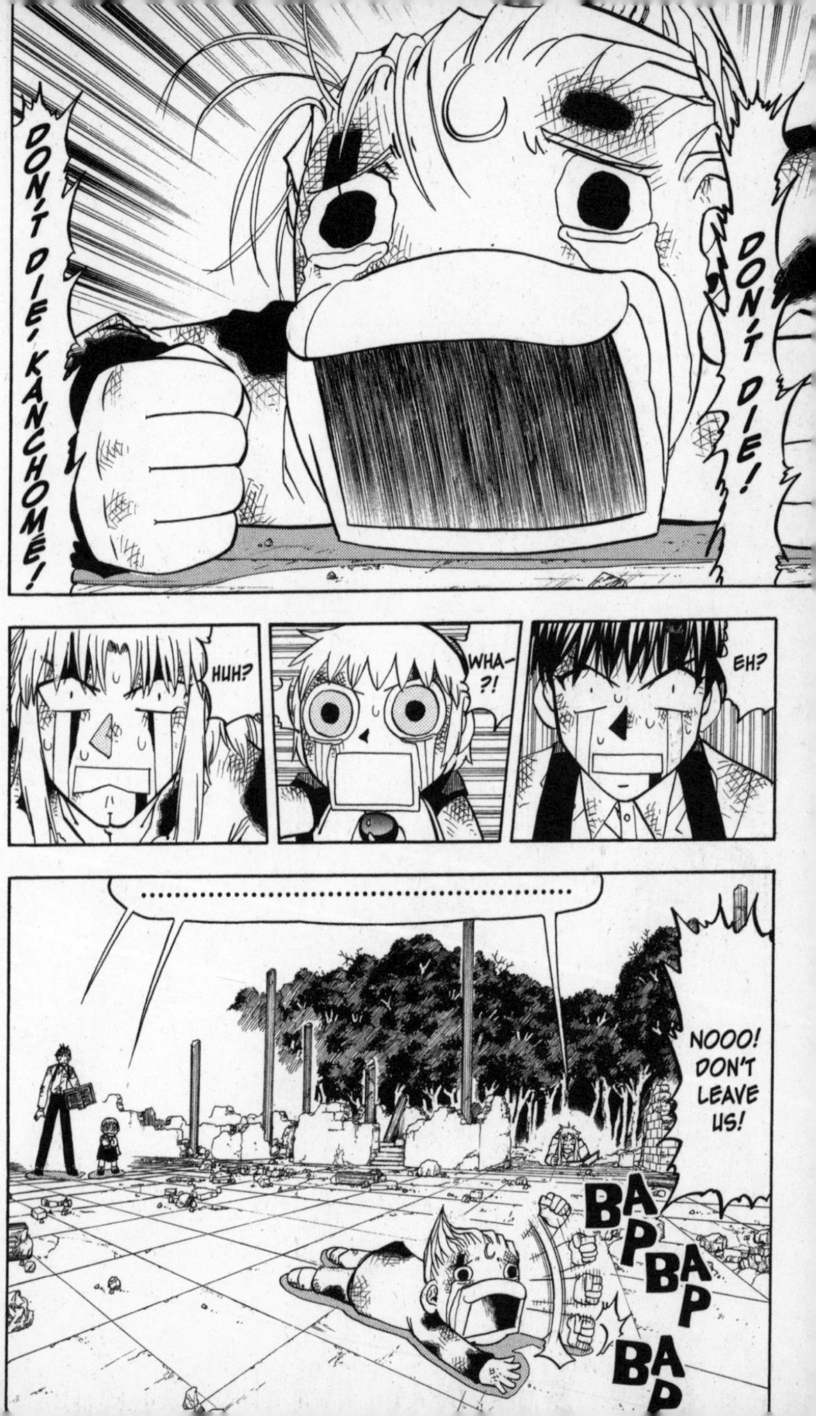
DON'T DIE!
DON'T DIE, KANCHOMÉ!
EH?
WHA-?!
HUH?
..............................................
NOOO! DON'T LEAVE US!
BAP
BAP
BAP
BA

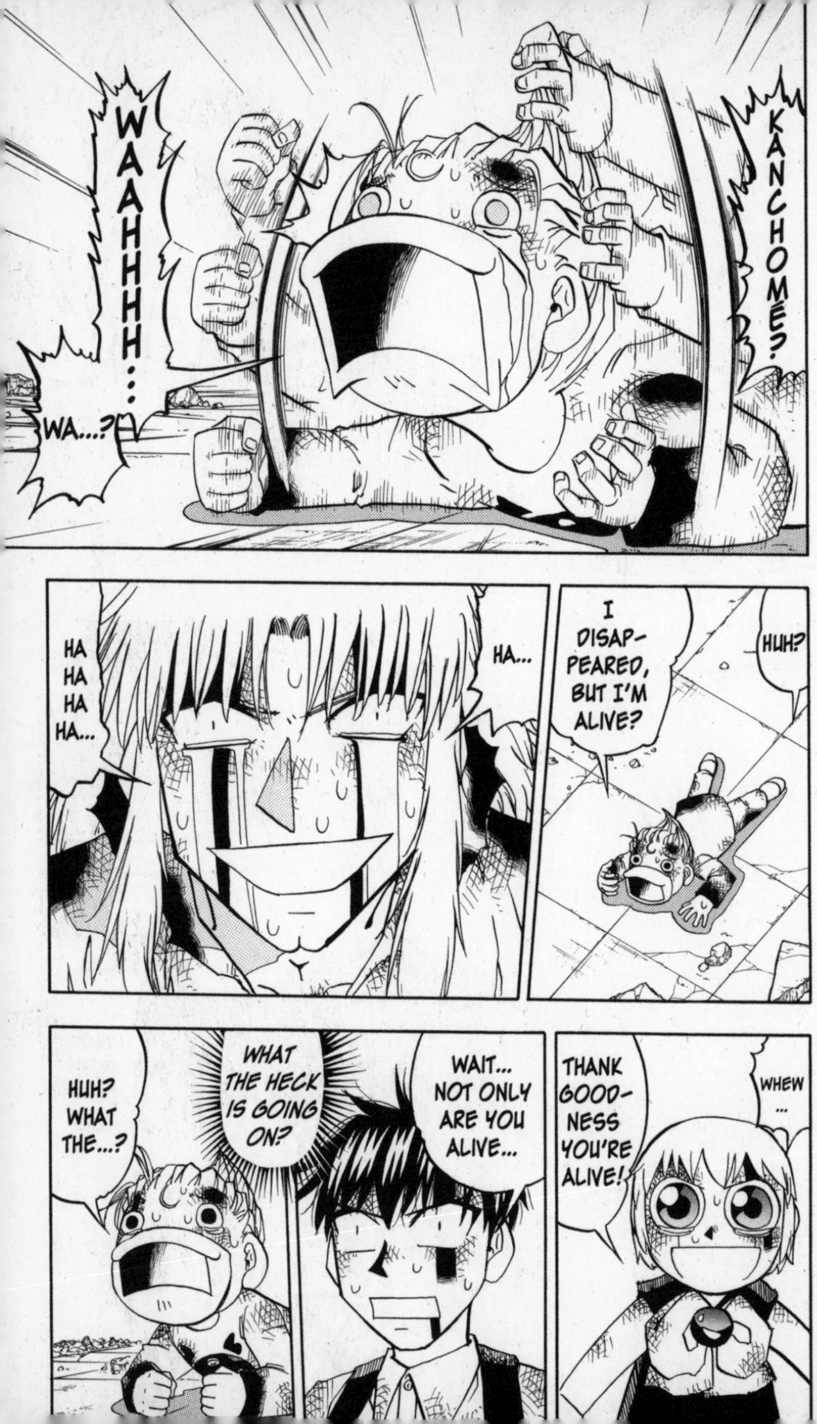
KANCHOME?
WAAHHHH...
WA...?
HUH?
I DISAP-PEARED, BUT I'M ALIVE?
HA...
HA HA HA HA...
WHEW...
THANK GOOD-NESS YOU'RE ALIVE!
WAIT... NOT ONLY ARE YOU ALIVE...
WHAT THE HECK IS GOING ON?
HUH? WHAT THE...?

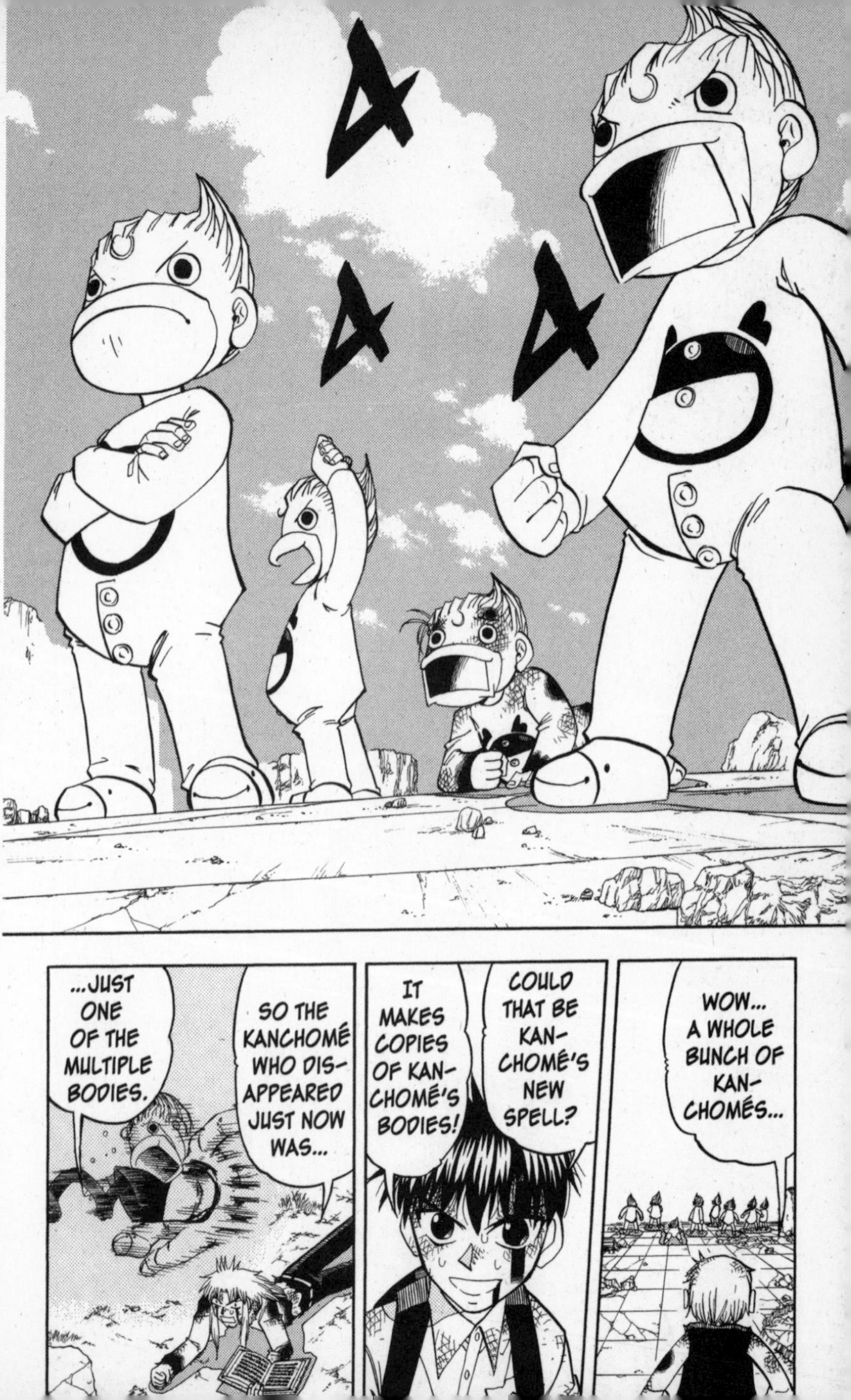
WOW... A WHOLE BUNCH OF KAN-CHOMÉS...
COULD THAT BE KAN-CHOMÉ'S NEW SPELL?
IT MAKES COPIES OF KAN-CHOMÉ'S BODIES!
SO THE KANCHOMÉ WHO DIS-APPEARED JUST NOW WAS...
...JUST ONE OF THE MULTIPLE BODIES.

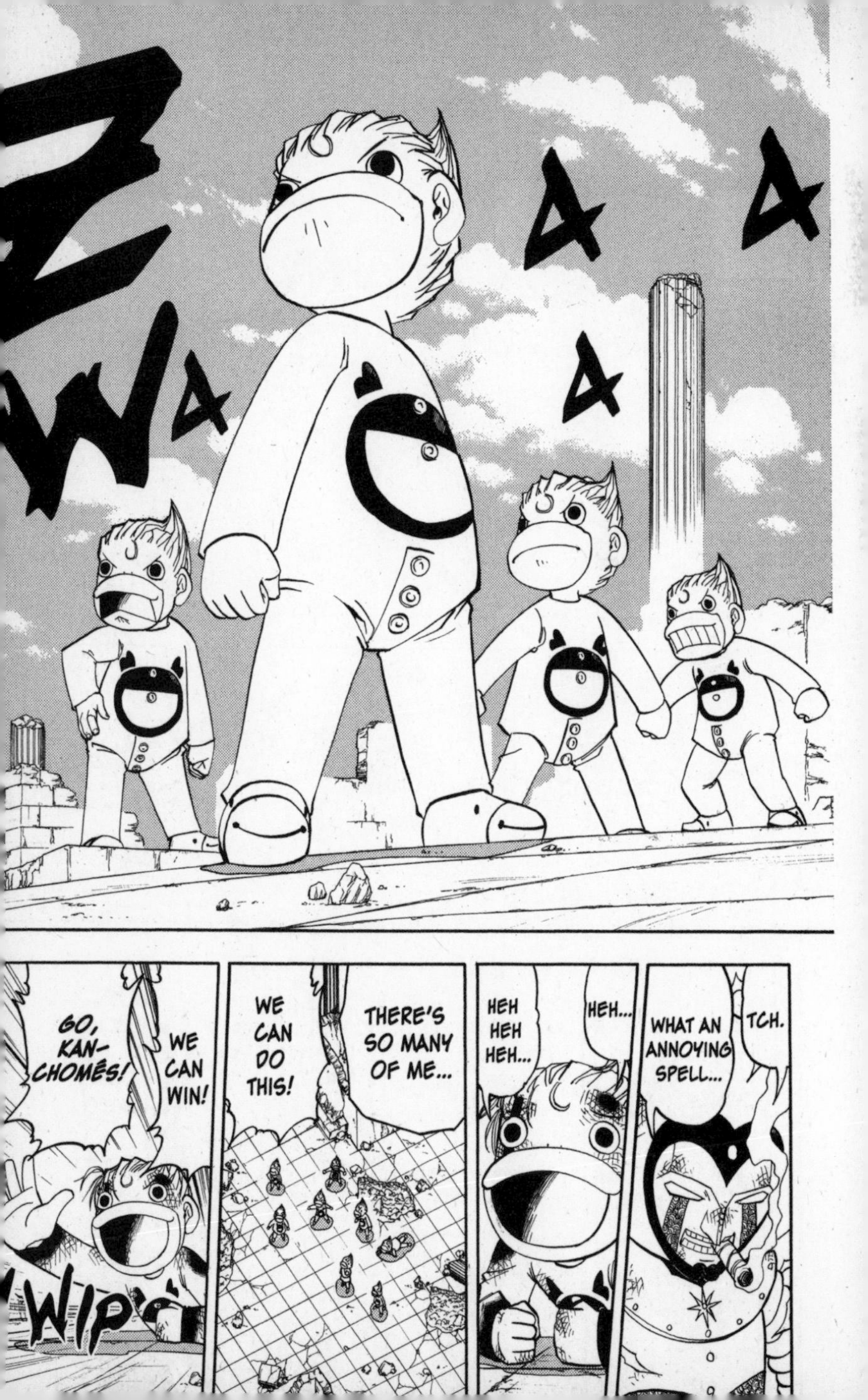
ZWAAAA
TCH.
WHAT AN ANNOYING SPELL...
HEH...
HEH HEH HEH...
THERE'S SO MANY OF ME...
WE CAN DO THIS!
WE CAN WIN!
GO, KAN-CHOMÉS!
WIP

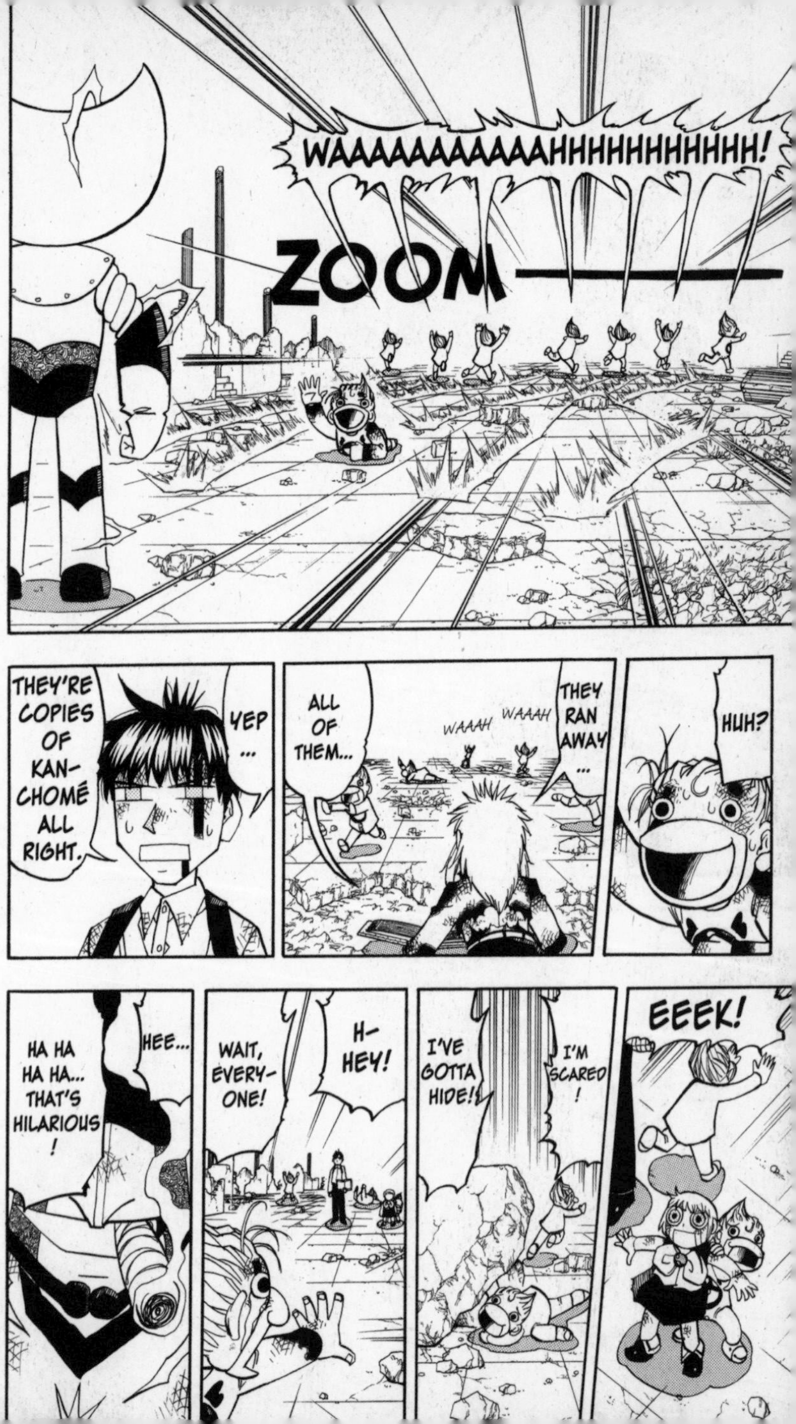
WAAAAAAAAAAAHHHHHHHHHHHH!
ZOOM
HUH?
THEY RAN AWAY...
WAAAH
WAAAH
ALL OF THEM...
YEP...
THEY'RE COPIES OF KANCHOMÉ ALL RIGHT.
EEEK!
I'M SCARED!
I'VE GOTTA HIDE!
H-HEY!
WAIT, EVERYONE!
HEE...
HA HA HA HA... THAT'S HILARIOUS!

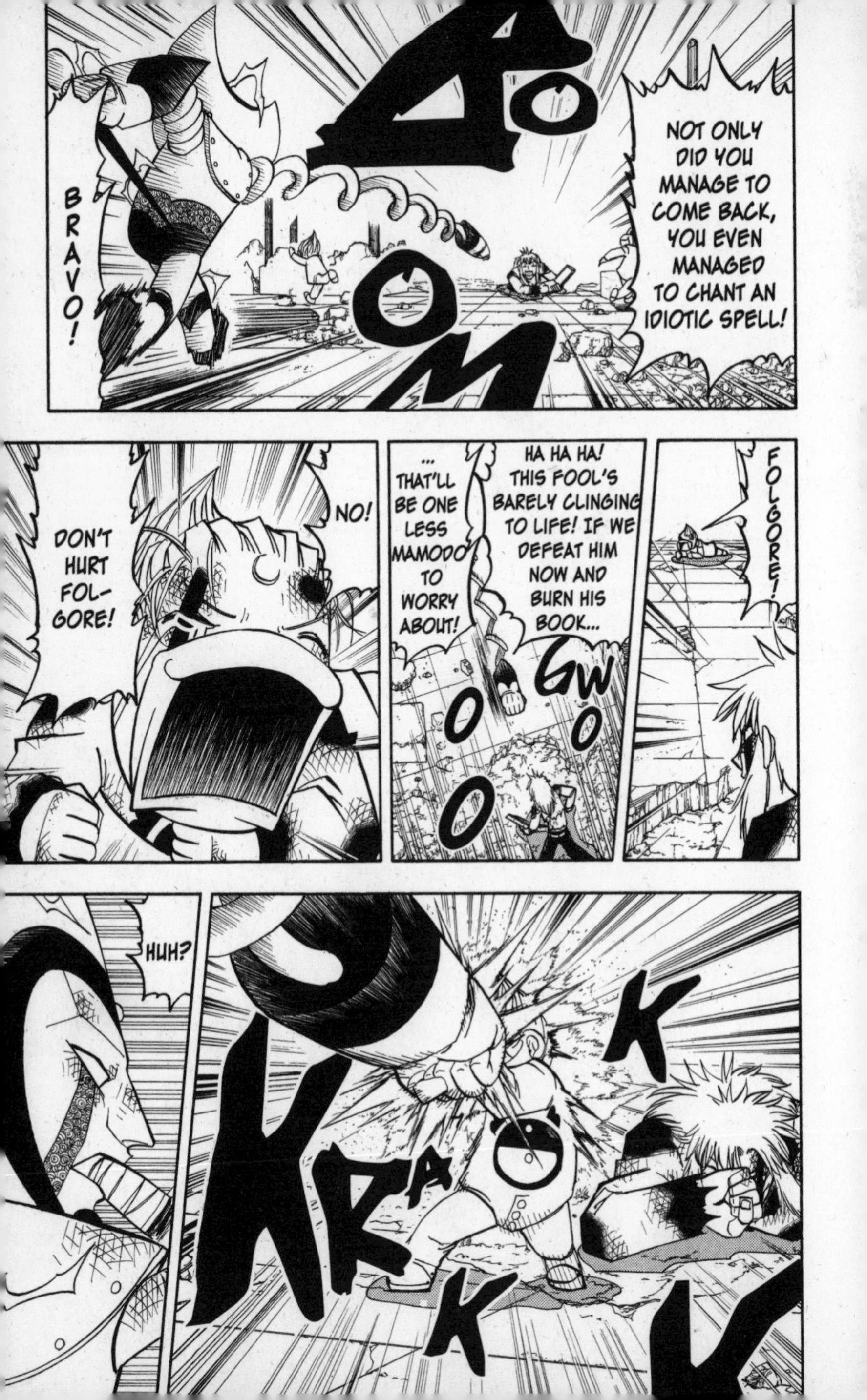
BOOM
NOT ONLY DID YOU MANAGE TO COME BACK, YOU EVEN MANAGED TO CHANT AN IDIOTIC SPELL!
BRAVO!
FOLGORE!
HA HA HA! THIS FOOL'S BARELY CLINGING TO LIFE! IF WE DEFEAT HIM NOW AND BURN HIS BOOK...
... THAT'LL BE ONE LESS MAMODO TO WORRY ABOUT!
GWOOOO
NO!
DON'T HURT FOL-GORE!
HUH?

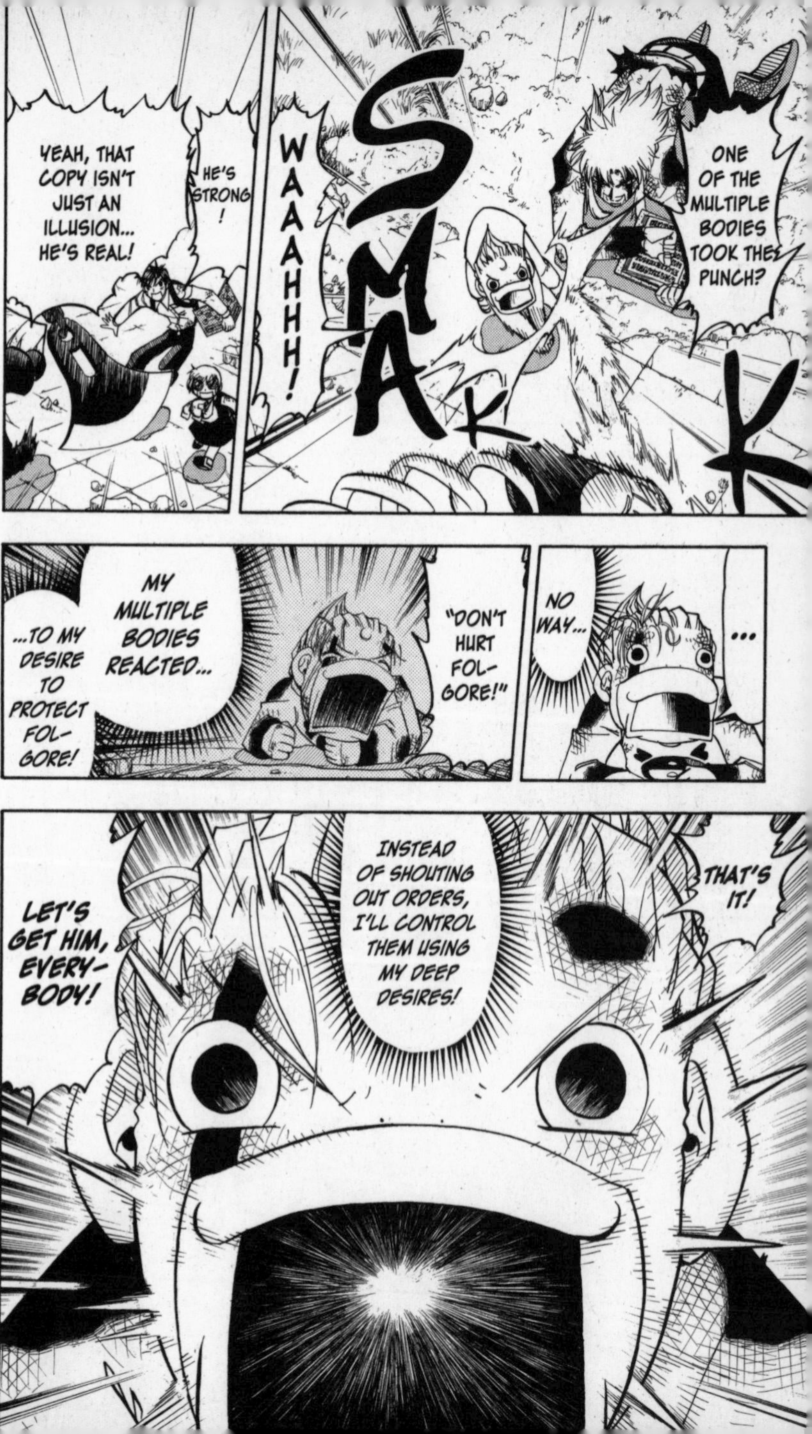
ONE OF THE MULTIPLE BODIES TOOK THE PUNCH?
SMAKK
WAAAAHHH!
HE'S STRONG!
YEAH, THAT COPY ISN'T JUST AN ILLUSION... HE'S REAL!
...
NO WAY...
"DON'T HURT FOL-GORE!"
MY MULTIPLE BODIES REACTED...
...TO MY DESIRE TO PROTECT FOL-GORE!
THAT'S IT!
INSTEAD OF SHOUTING OUT ORDERS, I'LL CONTROL THEM USING MY DEEP DESIRES!
LET'S GET HIM, EVERY-BODY!

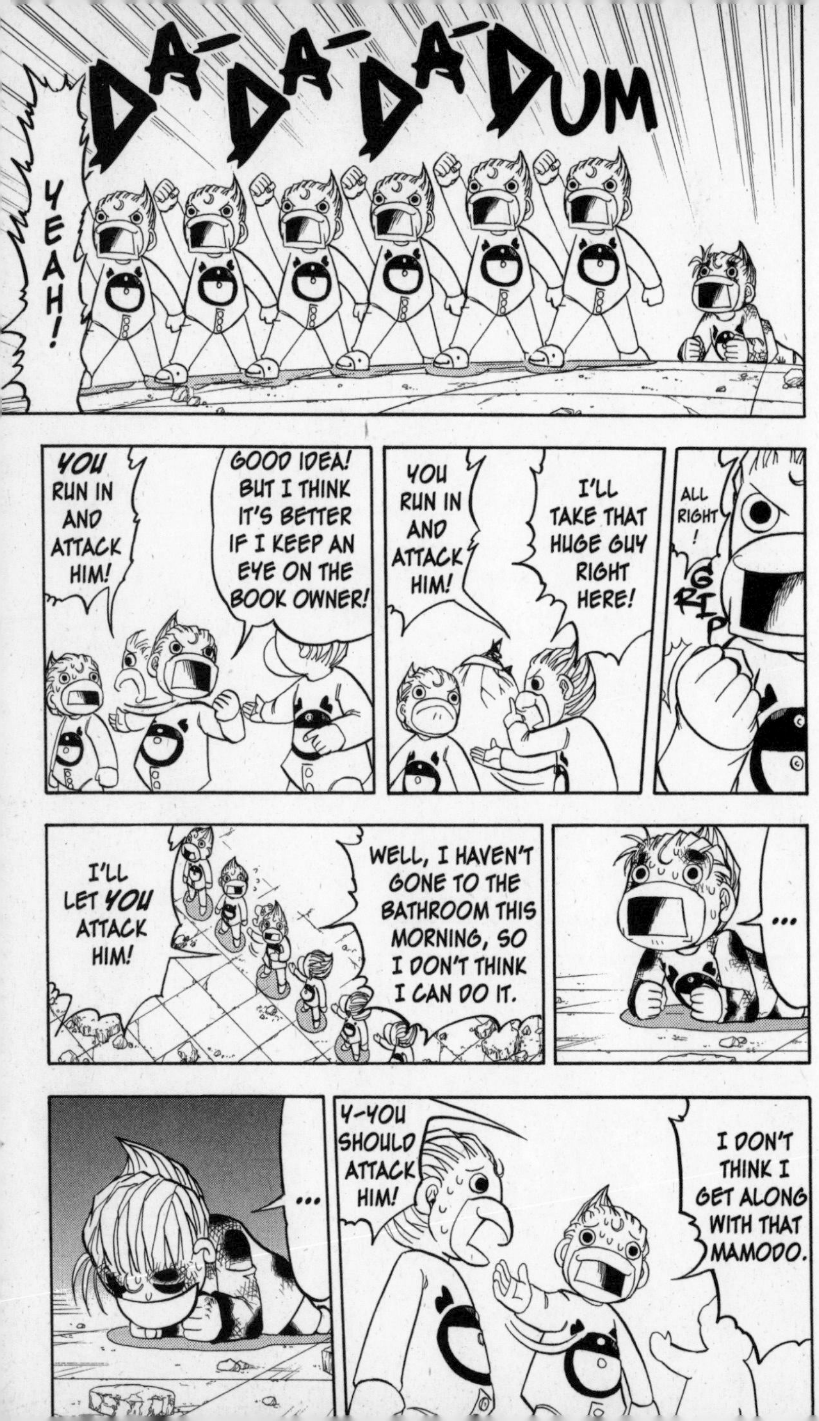
DA-DA-DA-DUM
YEAH!
ALL RIGHT!
GRIP
I'LL TAKE THAT HUGE GUY RIGHT HERE!
YOU RUN IN AND ATTACK HIM!
GOOD IDEA! BUT I THINK IT'S BETTER IF I KEEP AN EYE ON THE BOOK OWNER!
YOU RUN IN AND ATTACK HIM!
...
WELL, I HAVEN'T GONE TO THE BATHROOM THIS MORNING, SO I DON'T THINK I CAN DO IT.
I'LL LET YOU ATTACK HIM!
I DON'T THINK I GET ALONG WITH THAT MAMODO.
Y-YOU SHOULD ATTACK HIM!
...

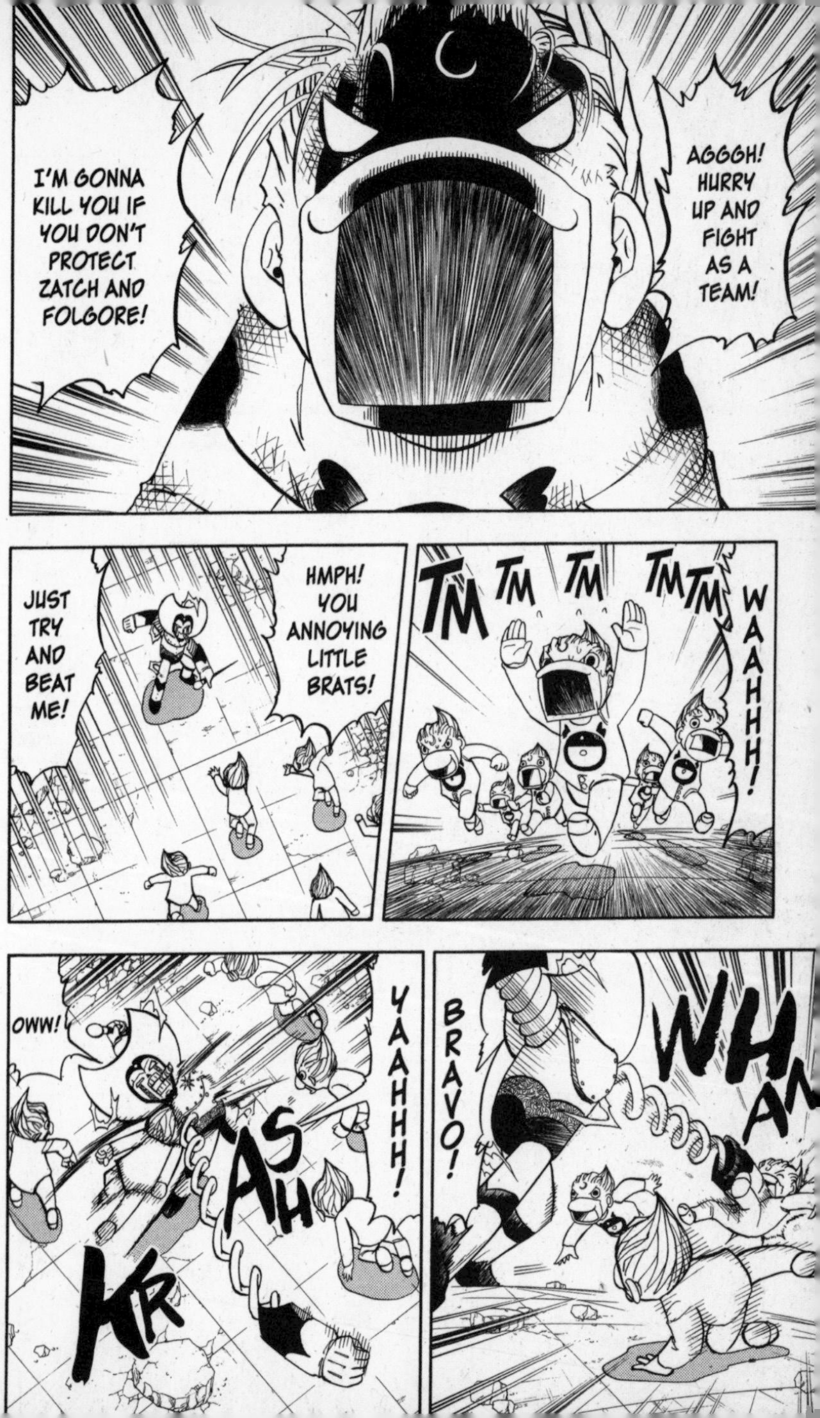
AGGGH! HURRY UP AND FIGHT AS A TEAM!
I'M GONNA KILL YOU IF YOU DON'T PROTECT ZATCH AND FOLGORE!
TM TM TM TMTM
WAAHHH!
HMPH! YOU ANNOYING LITTLE BRATS!
JUST TRY AND BEAT ME!
WHAM
BRAVO!
YAAHHH!
OWW!
KRASH

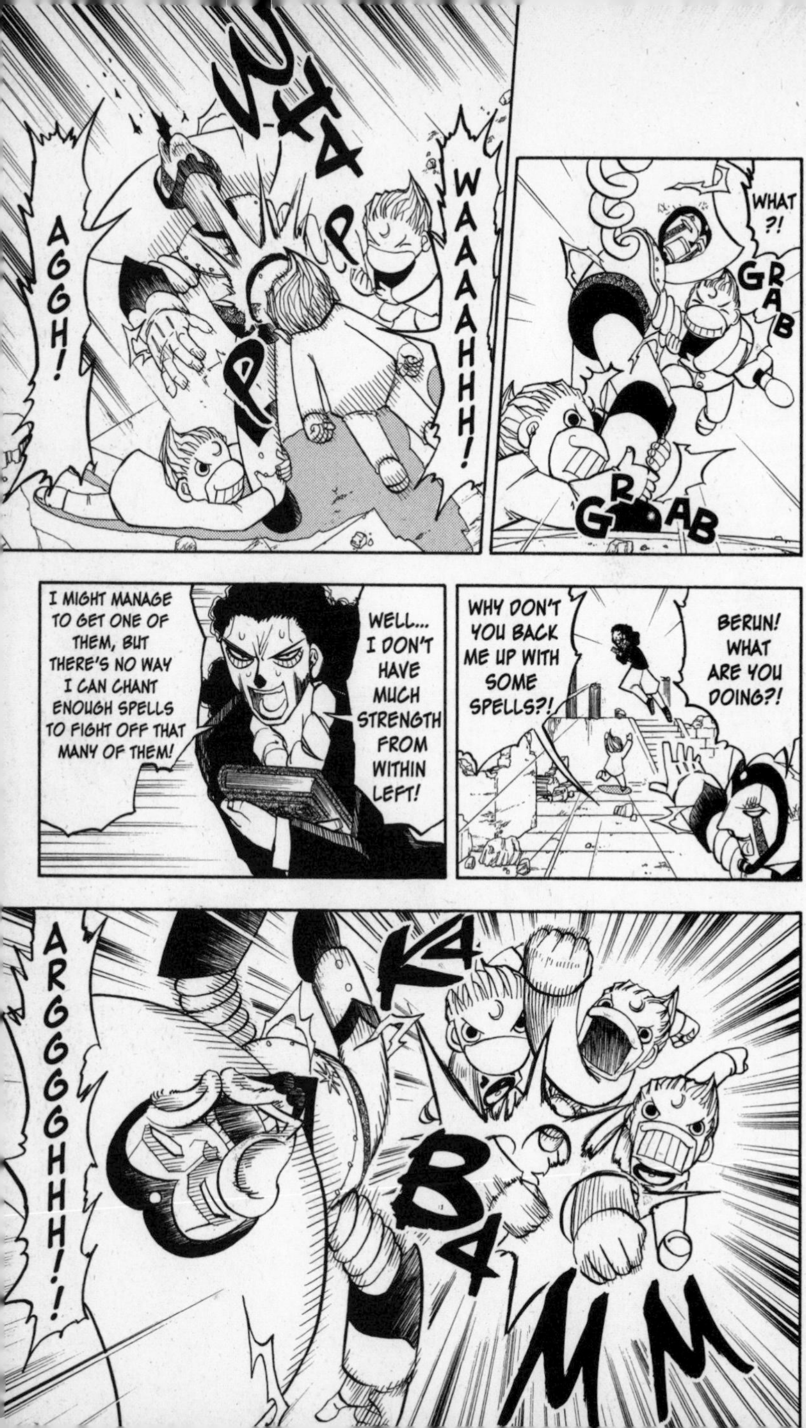
WHAT?!
GRAB
GRAB
WHAPP
WAAAAAHHH!
AGGH!
BERUN! WHAT ARE YOU DOING?!
WHY DON'T YOU BACK ME UP WITH SOME SPELLS?!
WELL... I DON'T HAVE MUCH STRENGTH FROM WITHIN LEFT!
I MIGHT MANAGE TO GET ONE OF THEM, BUT THERE'S NO WAY I CAN CHANT ENOUGH SPELLS TO FIGHT OFF THAT MANY OF THEM!
KABAMM
ARGGGGHHH!!

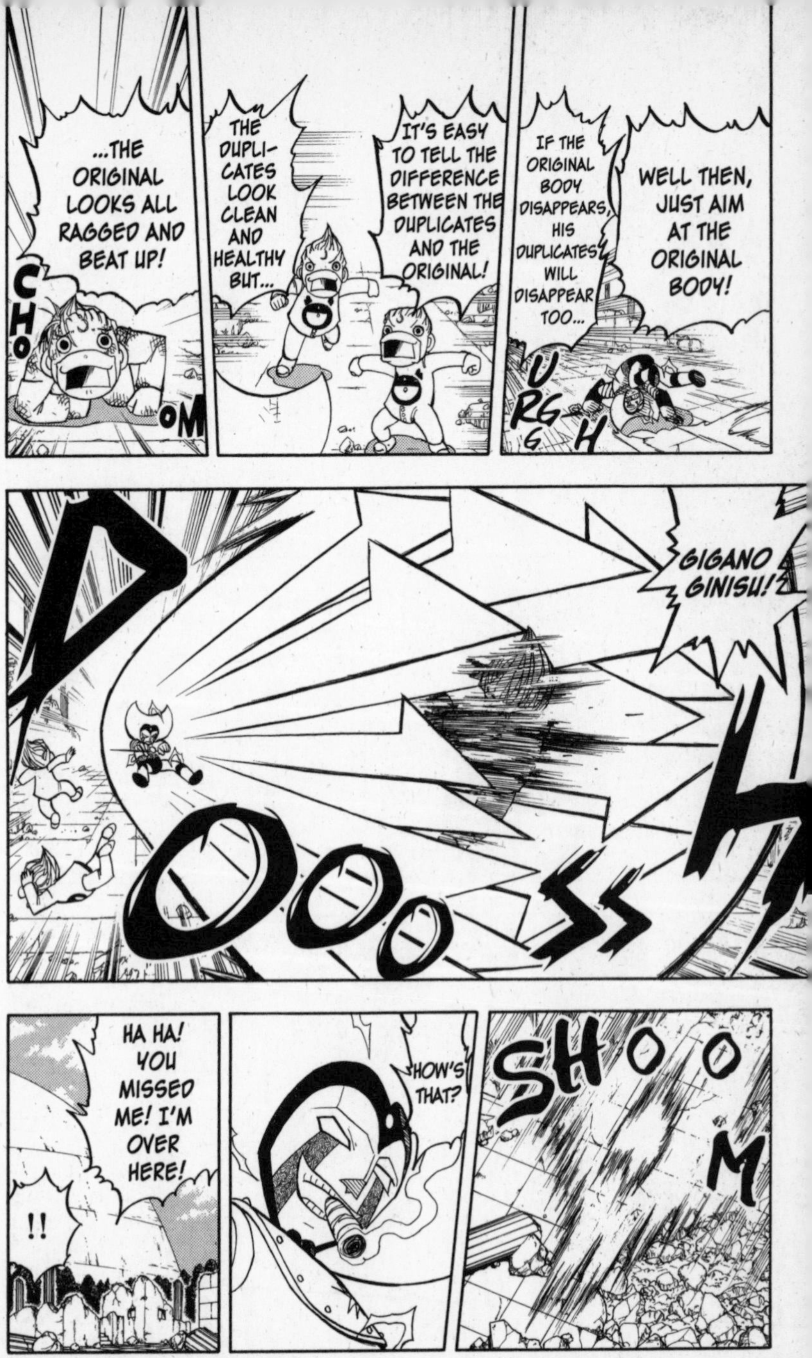
WELL THEN, JUST AIM AT THE ORIGINAL BODY!
IF THE ORIGINAL BODY DISAPPEARS, HIS DUPLICATES WILL DISAPPEAR TOO...
URGGH
IT'S EASY TO TELL THE DIFFERENCE BETWEEN THE DUPLICATES AND THE ORIGINAL!
THE DUPLICATES LOOK CLEAN AND HEALTHY BUT...
...THE ORIGINAL LOOKS ALL RAGGED AND BEAT UP!
CHOMP
GIGANO GINISU!
DOOOSSH
SHOOOM
HOW'S THAT?
HA HA! YOU MISSED ME! I'M OVER HERE!
!!

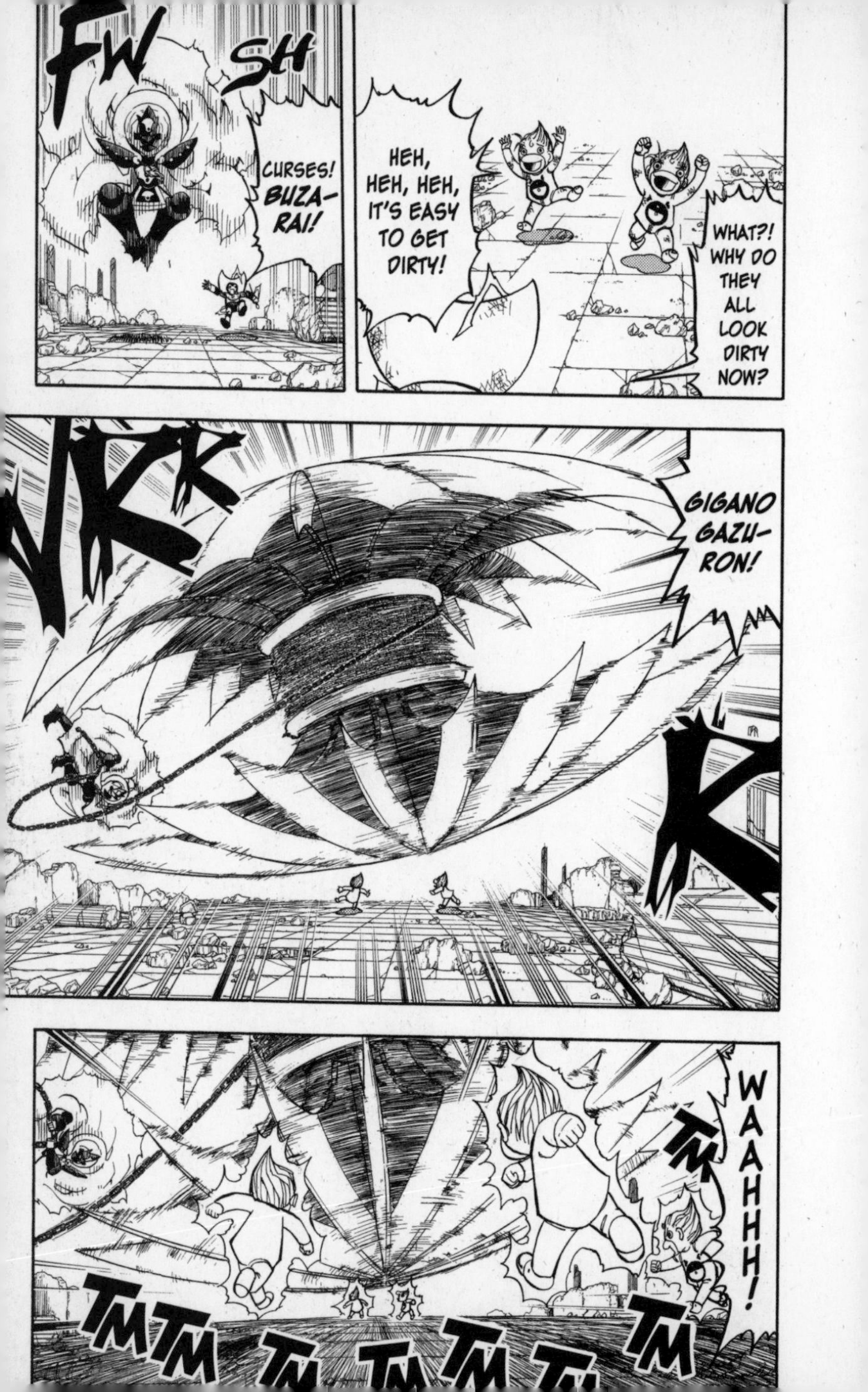
WHAT?! WHY DO THEY ALL LOOK DIRTY NOW?
HEH, HEH, HEH, IT'S EASY TO GET DIRTY!
FWSH
CURSES! BUZARAI!
GIGANO GAZURON!
KRK
K
WAAHHH!
TM
TM TM TM TM TM TM TM TM

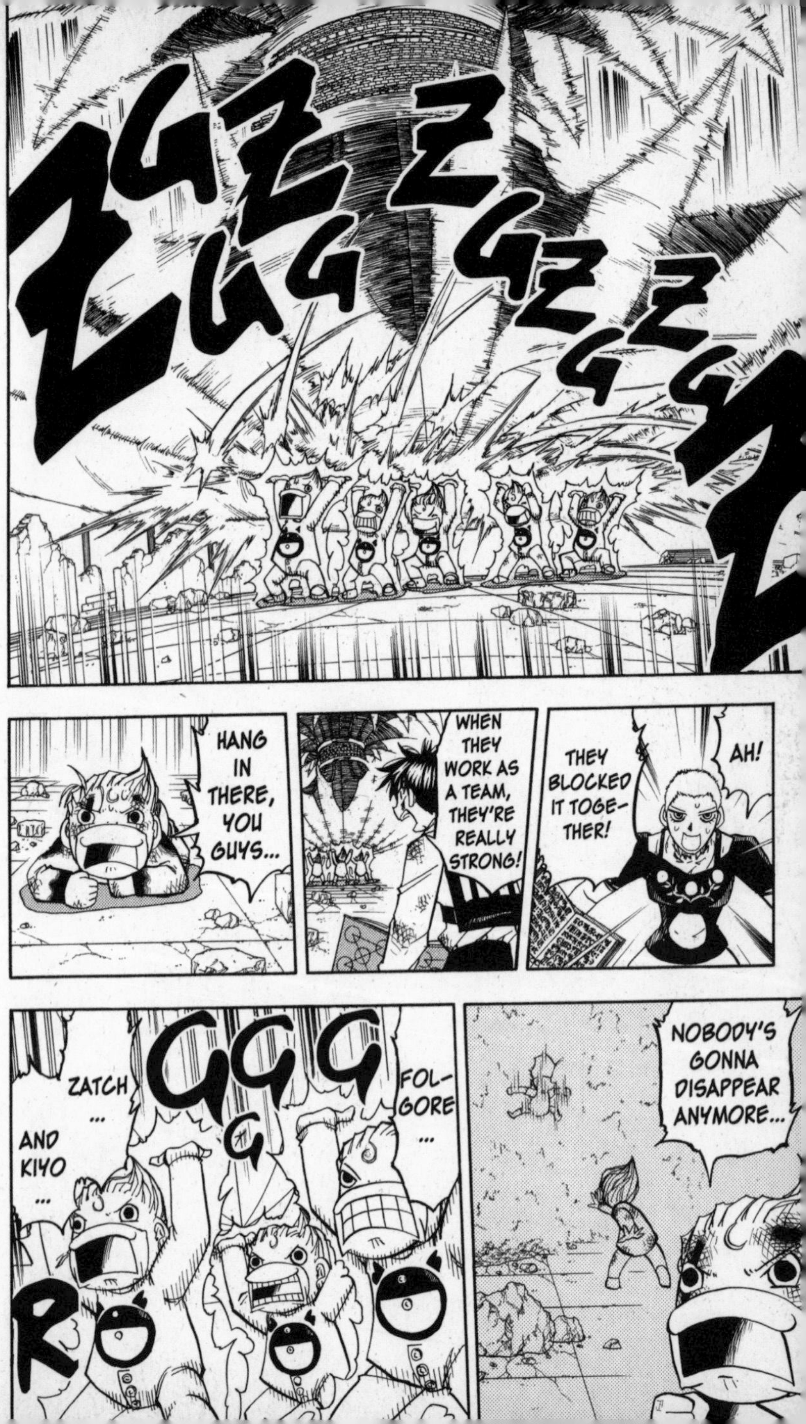
AH!
THEY BLOCKED IT TOGE-THER!
WHEN THEY WORK AS A TEAM, THEY'RE REALLY STRONG!
HANG IN THERE, YOU GUYS...
NOBODY'S GONNA DISAPPEAR ANYMORE...
FOL-GORE ...
GGGG
ZATCH ...
AND KIYO ...
ROOO

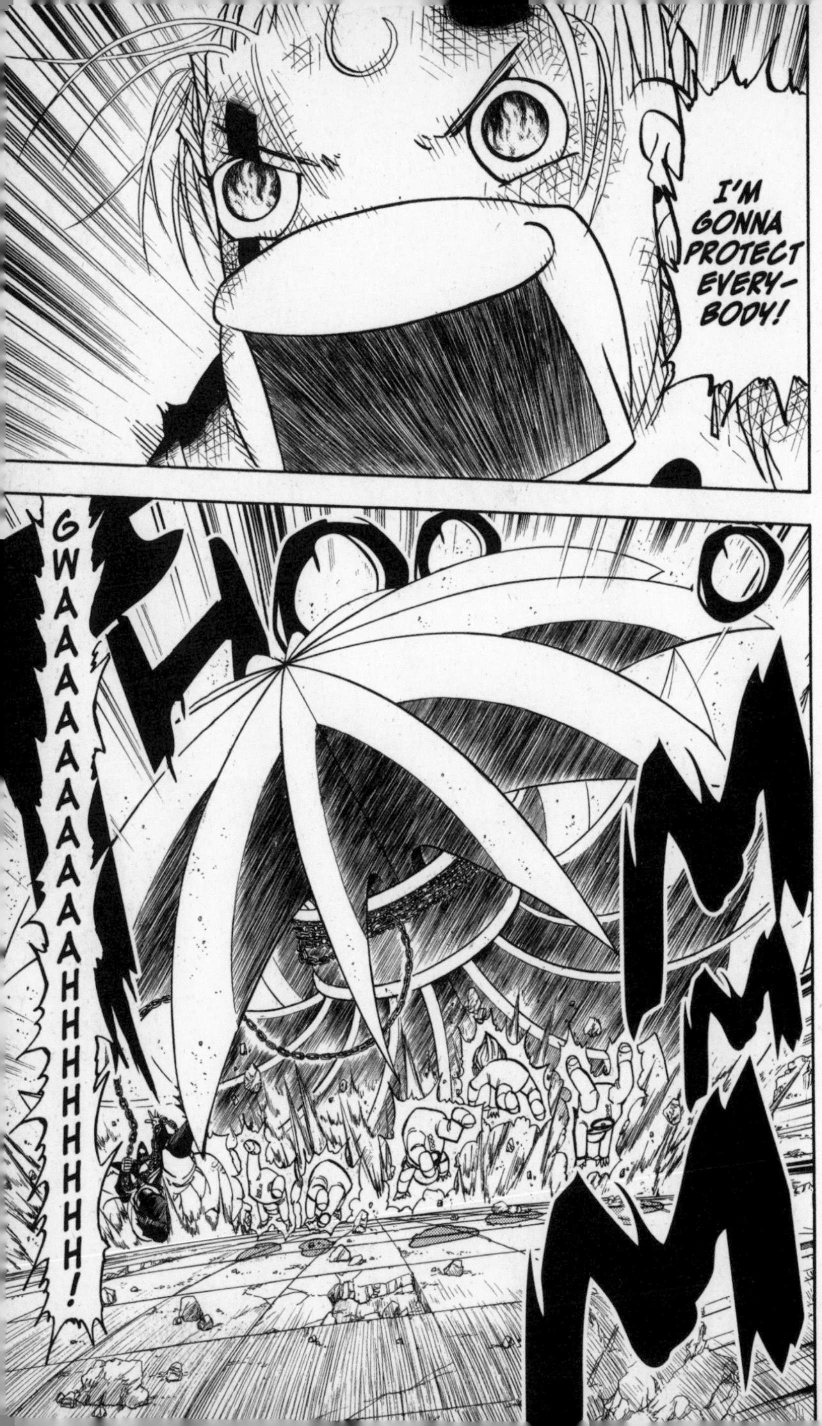
I'M GONNA PROTECT EVERY-BODY!
GWAAAAAAAAAAAAHHHHHHHHH!

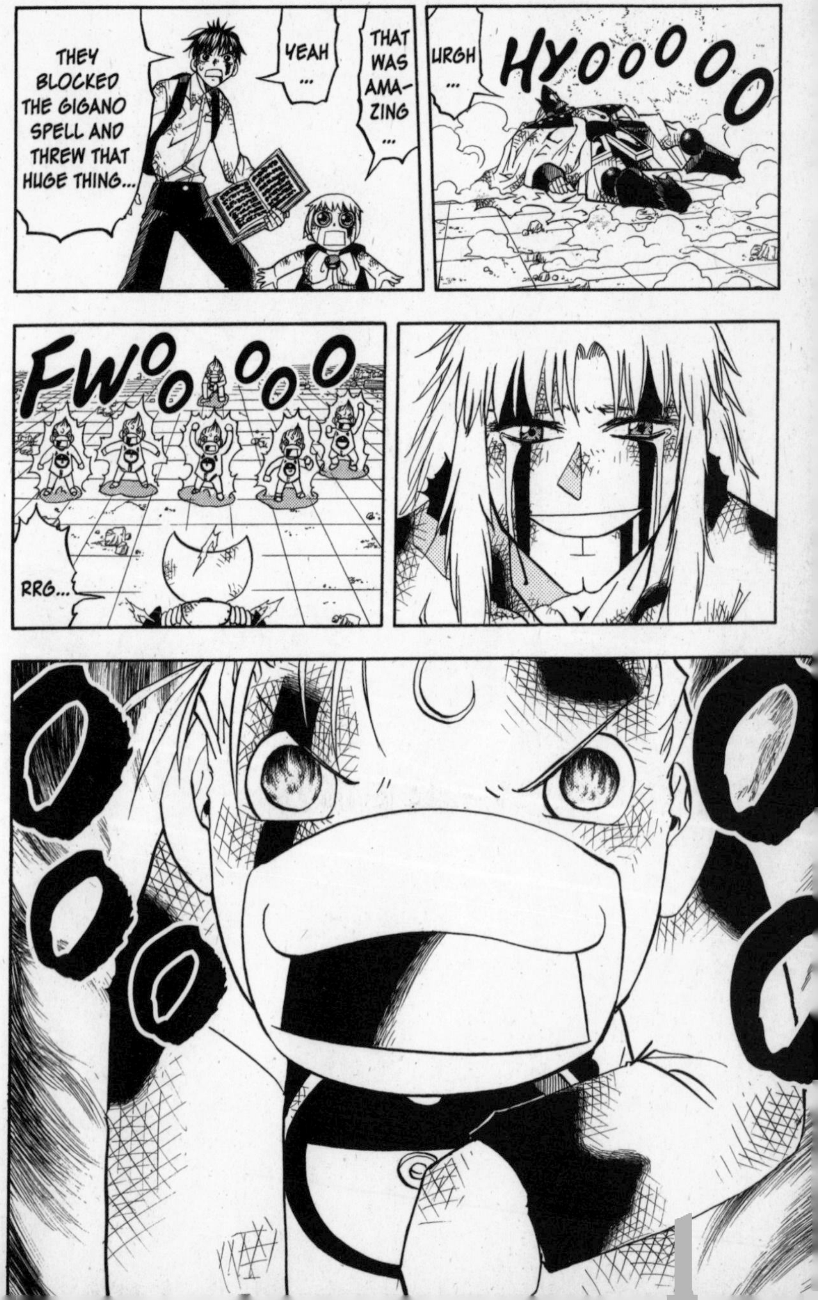
URGH ...
HYOOOOOO
THAT WAS AMA-ZING ...
YEAH ...
THEY BLOCKED THE GIGANO SPELL AND THREW THAT HUGE THING...
FWOOOOOO
RRG...

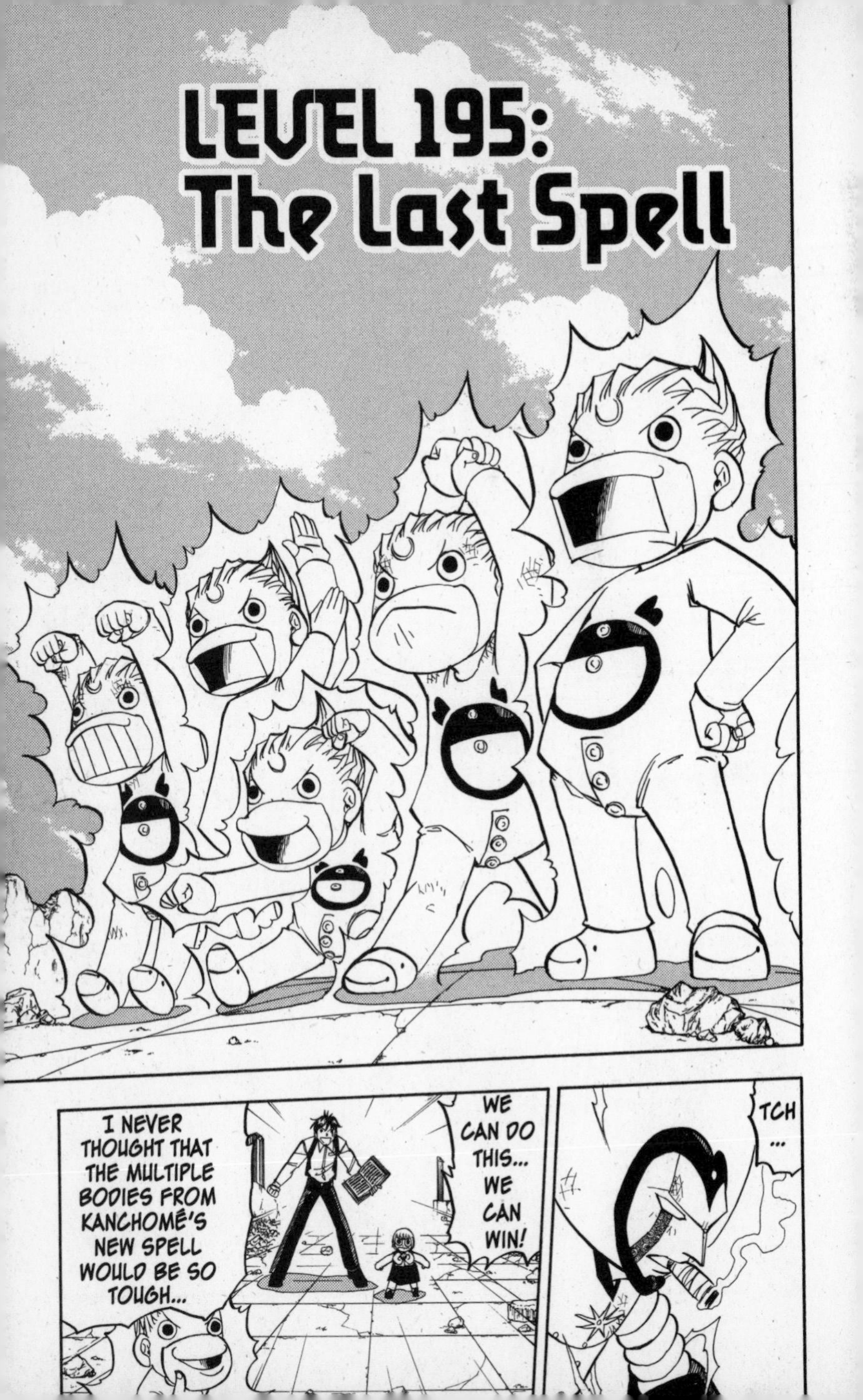
LEVEL 195:
The Last Spell
TCH...
WE CAN DO THIS... WE CAN WIN!
I NEVER THOUGHT THAT THE MULTIPLE BODIES FROM KANCHOMÉ'S NEW SPELL WOULD BE SO TOUGH...

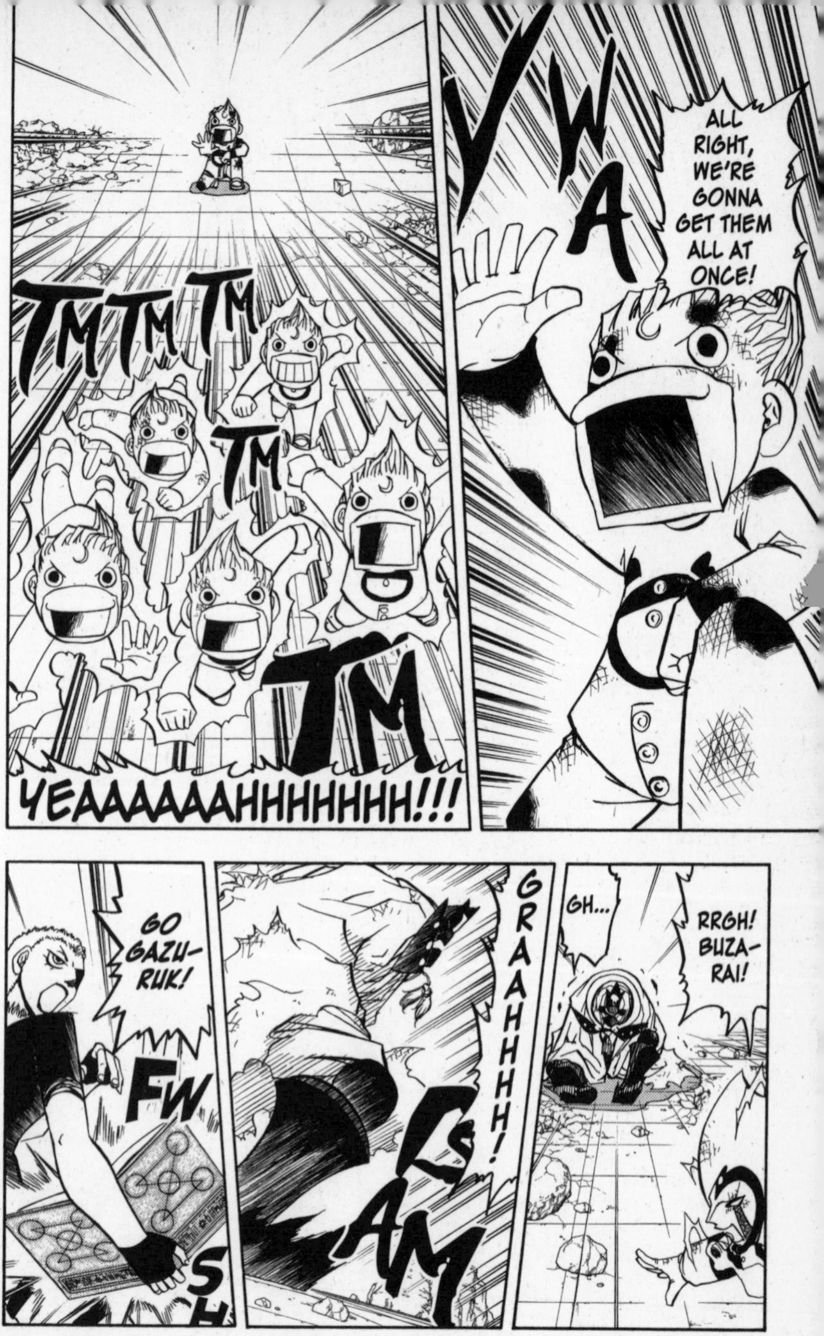
VWA
ALL RIGHT, WE'RE GONNA GET THEM ALL AT ONCE!
TMTMTMTM
TM
TM
YEAAAAAAAHHHHHHH!!!
RRGH! BUZARAI!
GH...
GRAAHHHHH!
SLAM
GO GAZURUK!
FW
SH

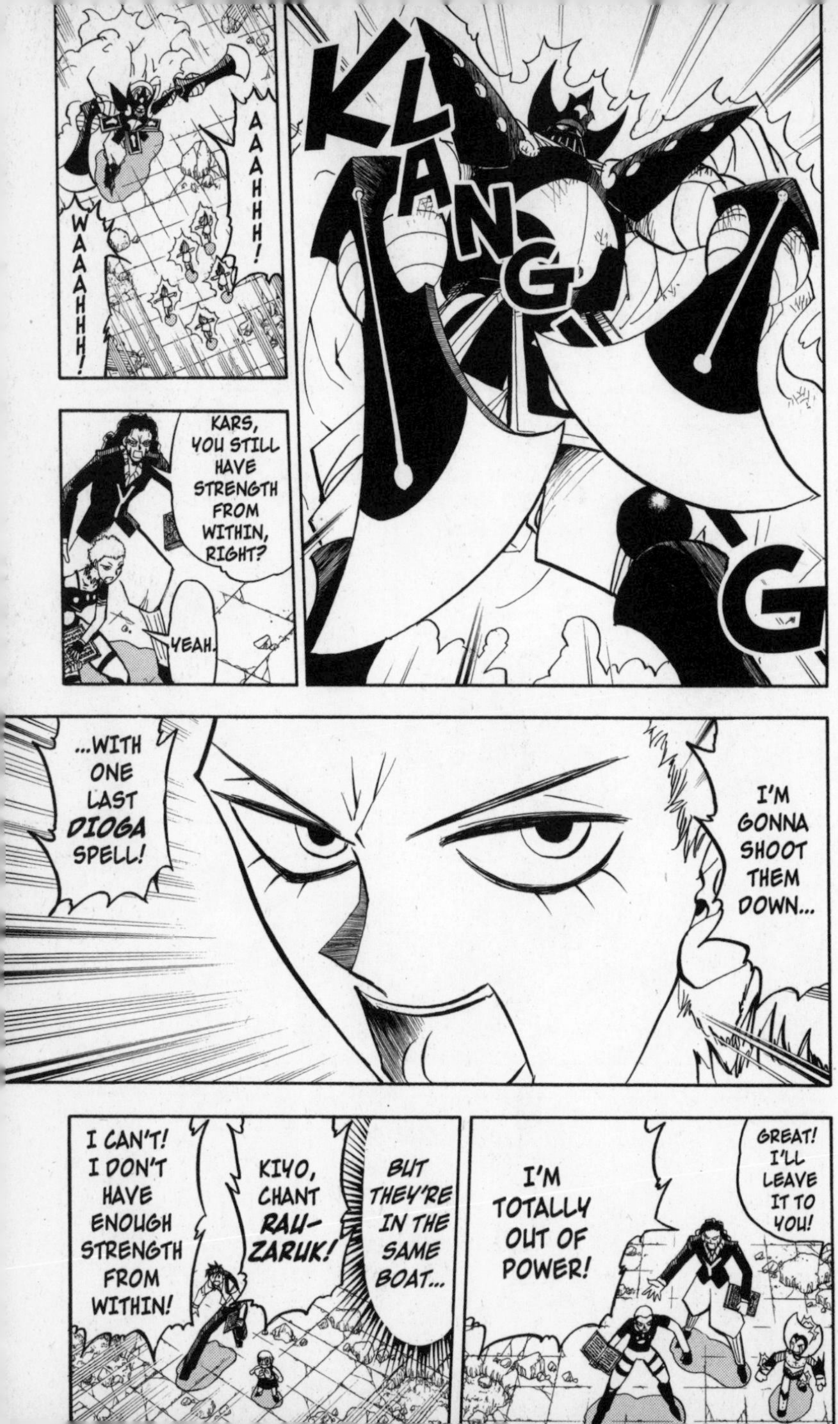
KLANG
G
AAAAHHHH!
WAAAAHHH!
KARS, YOU STILL HAVE STRENGTH FROM WITHIN, RIGHT?
YEAH.
I'M GONNA SHOOT THEM DOWN...
...WITH ONE LAST *DIOGA* SPELL!
GREAT! I'LL LEAVE IT TO YOU!
I'M TOTALLY OUT OF POWER!
BUT THEY'RE IN THE SAME BOAT...
KIYO, CHANT *RAUZARUK!*
I CAN'T! I DON'T HAVE ENOUGH STRENGTH FROM WITHIN!

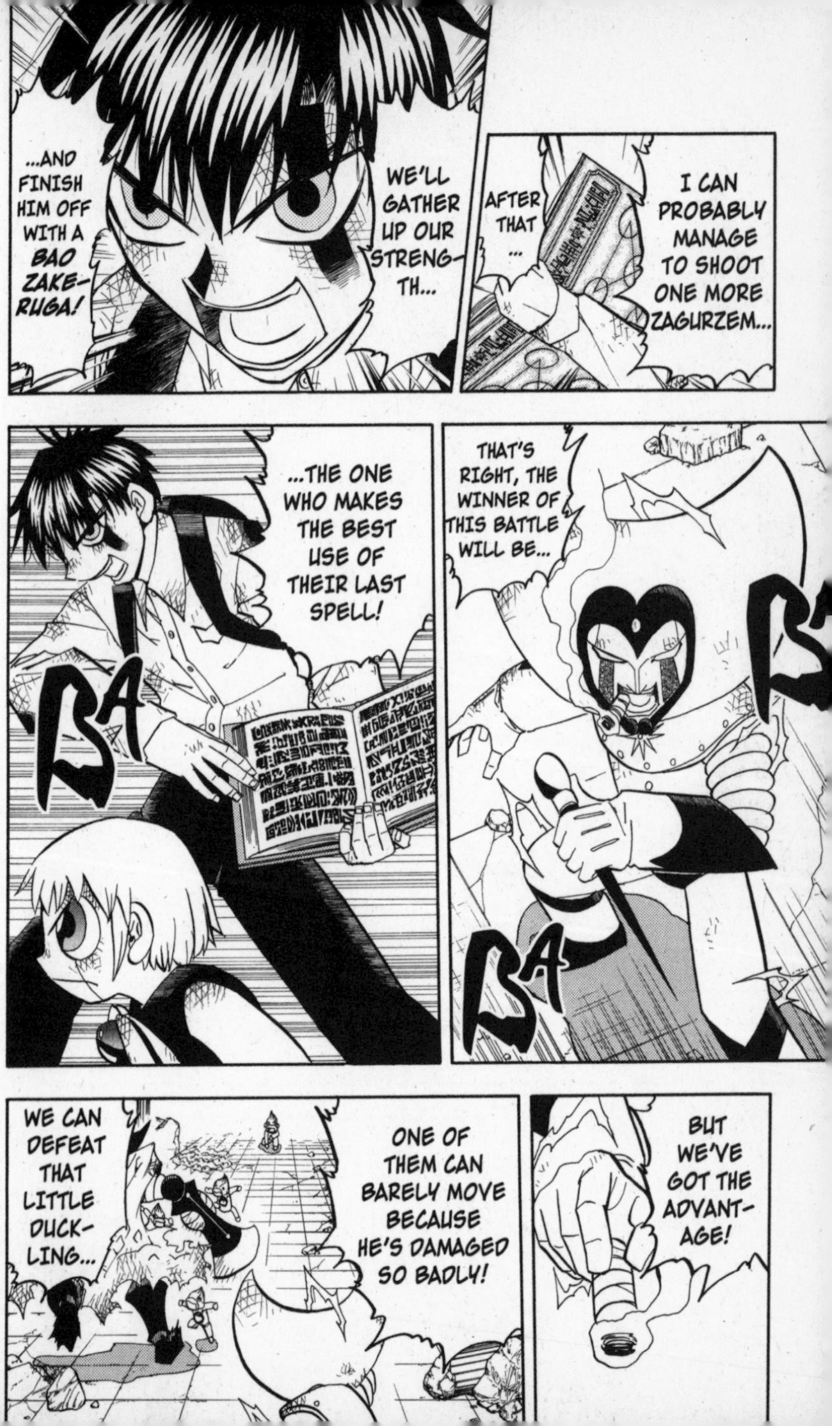
I CAN PROBABLY MANAGE TO SHOOT ONE MORE ZAGURZEM...
AFTER THAT ...
WE'LL GATHER UP OUR STRENG-TH...
...AND FINISH HIM OFF WITH A BAO ZAKE-RUGA!
THAT'S RIGHT, THE WINNER OF THIS BATTLE WILL BE...
BA
BA
...THE ONE WHO MAKES THE BEST USE OF THEIR LAST SPELL!
BA
BUT WE'VE GOT THE ADVANT-AGE!
ONE OF THEM CAN BARELY MOVE BECAUSE HE'S DAMAGED SO BADLY!
WE CAN DEFEAT THAT LITTLE DUCK-LING...

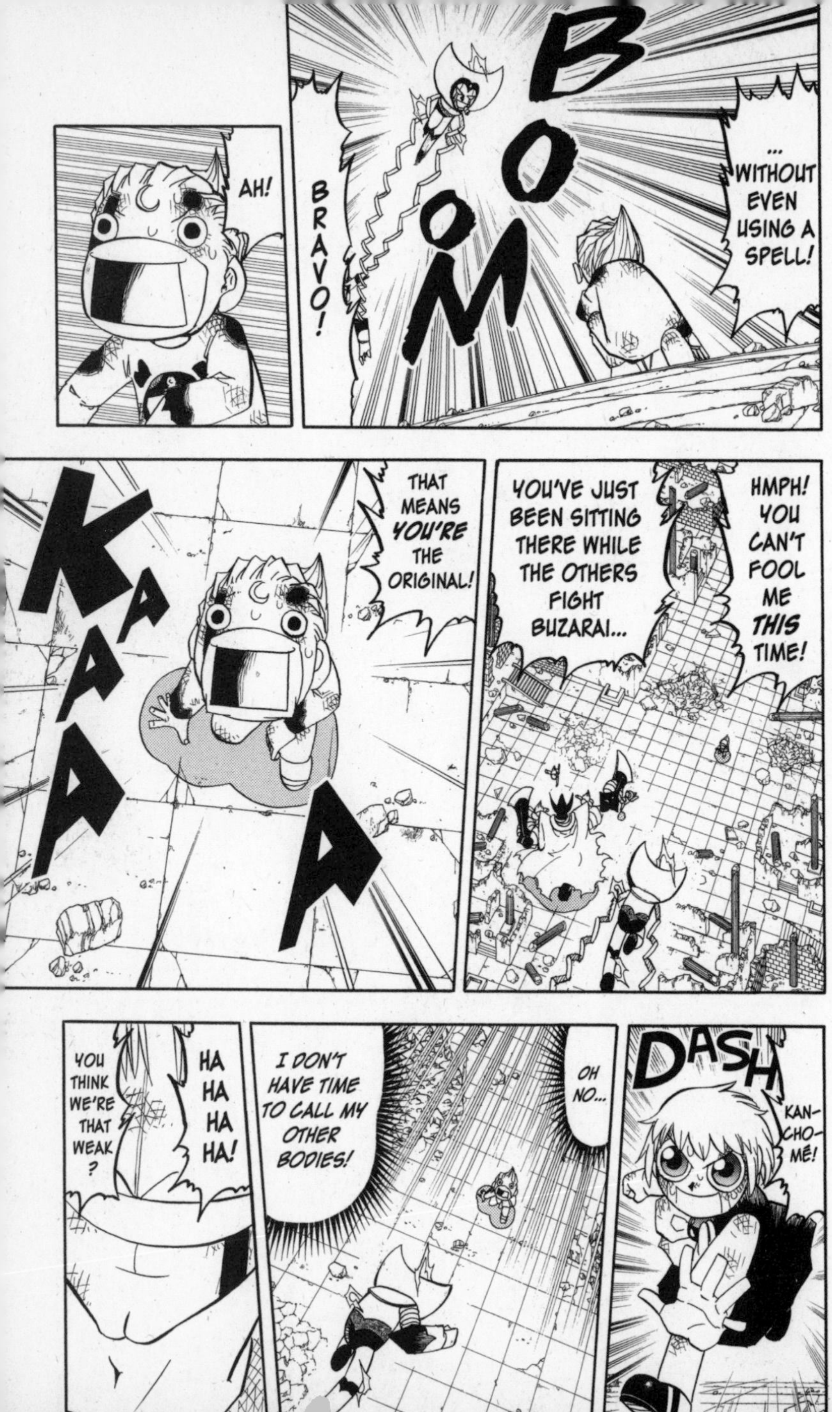
...WITHOUT EVEN USING A SPELL!
BOOM
BRAVO!
AH!
HMPH! YOU CAN'T FOOL ME *THIS* TIME!
YOU'VE JUST BEEN SITTING THERE WHILE THE OTHERS FIGHT BUZARAI...
THAT MEANS *YOU'RE* THE ORIGINAL!
KAPAAPA
DASH
KAN-CHO-MÉ!
OH NO...
*I DON'T HAVE TIME TO CALL MY OTHER BODIES!*
HA HA HA HA!
YOU THINK WE'RE THAT WEAK?

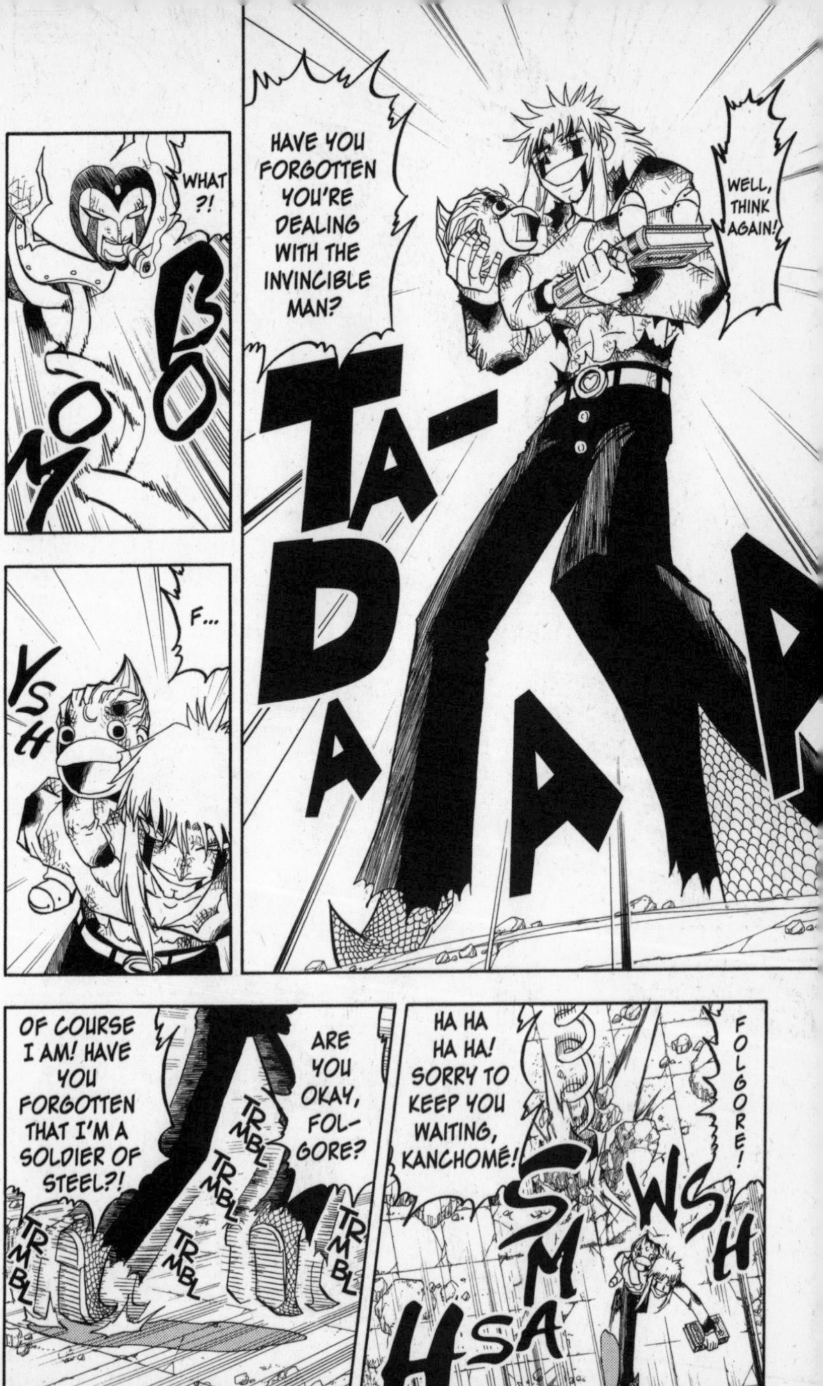

WELL, THINK AGAIN!
HAVE YOU FORGOTTEN YOU'RE DEALING WITH THE INVINCIBLE MAN?
TA-DAAA
WHAT?!
BOOM
F...
YSH
FOLGORE!
HA HA HA HA! SORRY TO KEEP YOU WAITING, KANCHOMÉ!
SWSH
SMASH
ARE YOU OKAY, FOL-GORE?
OF COURSE I AM! HAVE YOU FORGOTTEN THAT I'M A SOLDIER OF STEEL?!
TRMBL
TRMBL
TRMBL
TRMBL

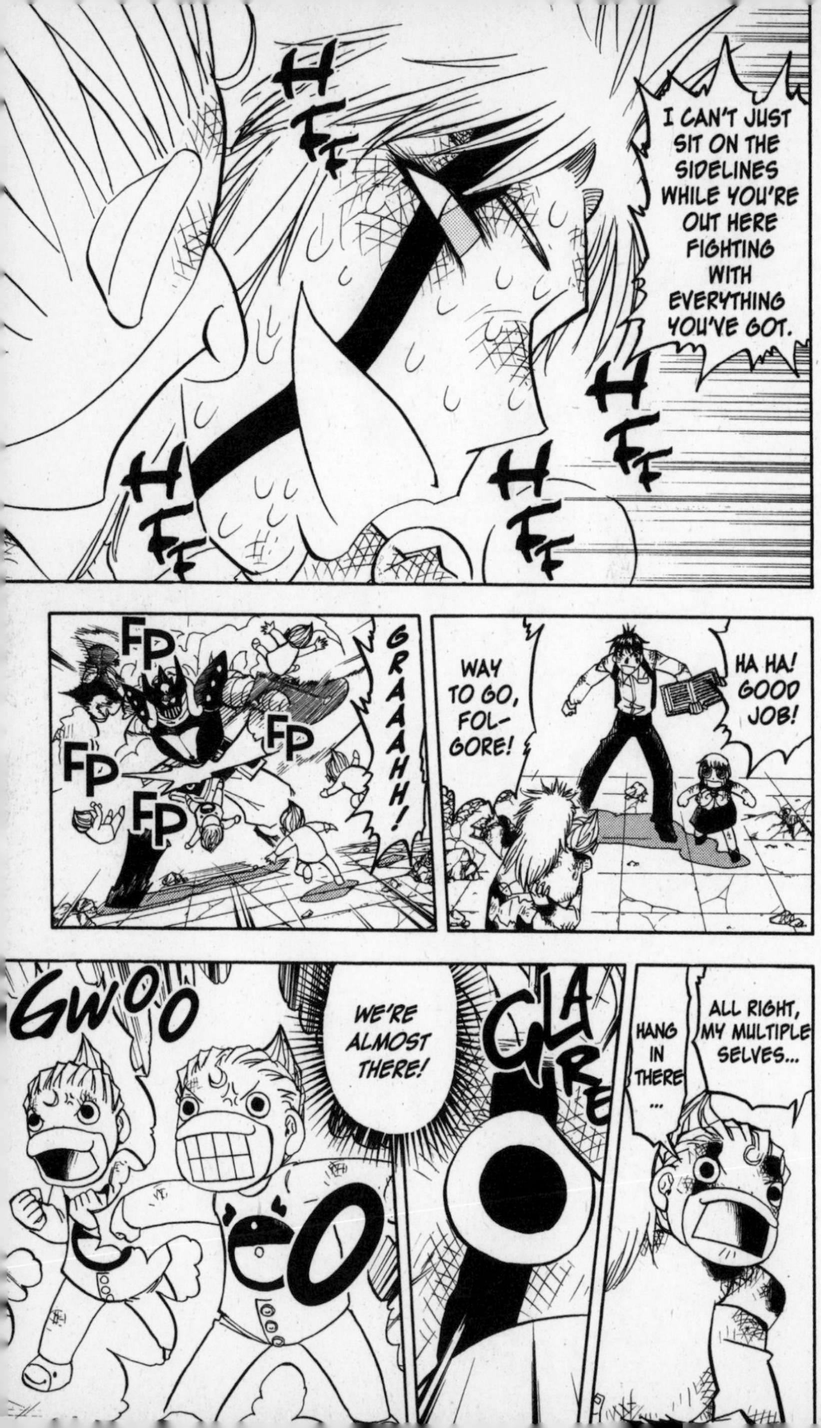
I CAN'T JUST SIT ON THE SIDELINES WHILE YOU'RE OUT HERE FIGHTING WITH EVERYTHING YOU'VE GOT.
HFF
HFF
HFF
HFF
HA HA! GOOD JOB!
WAY TO GO, FOL-GORE!
GRAAAHH!
FP
FP
FP
FP
ALL RIGHT, MY MULTIPLE SELVES...
HANG IN THERE...
GLARE
WE'RE ALMOST THERE!
GWOOO

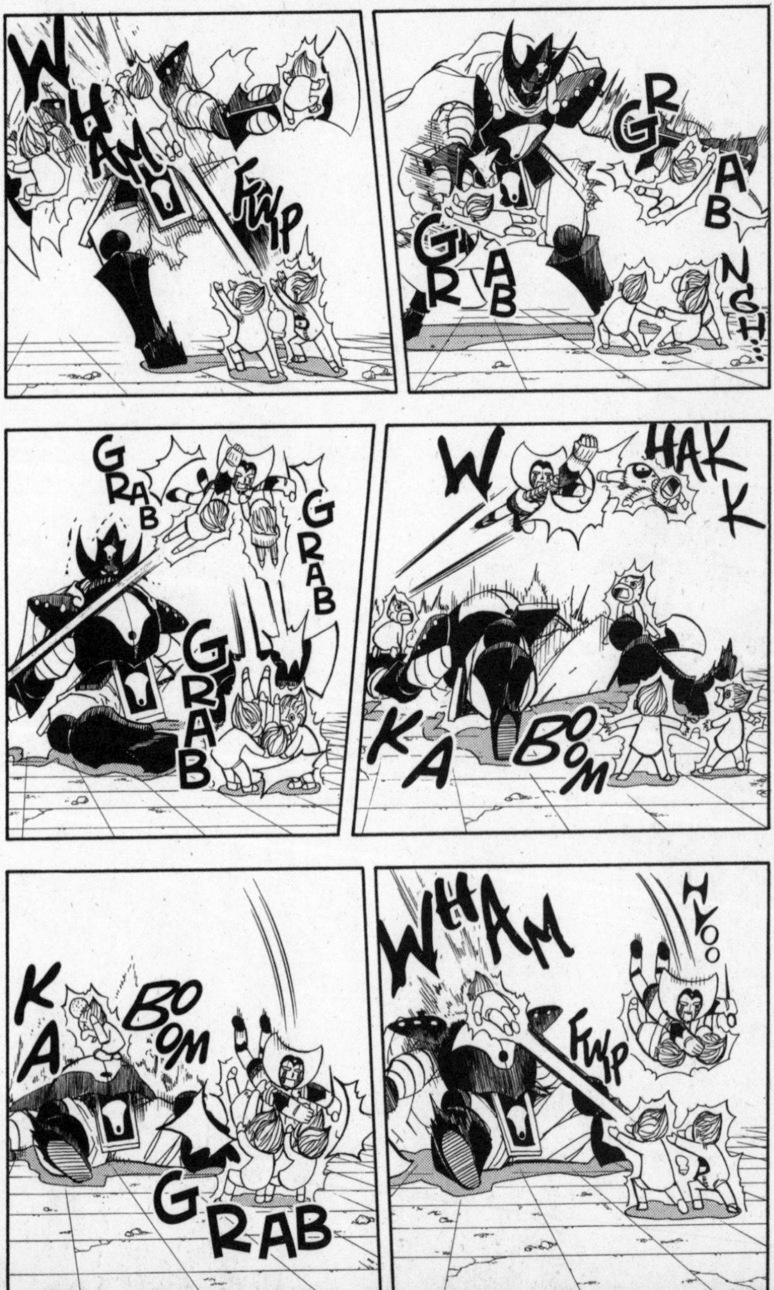
GRAB
GRAB
NGH!!
WHAM
FWIP
HAK
K
W
KA BOOM
GRAB
GRAB
GRAB
WHAM
HYOO
FWIP
KA BOOM
GRAB

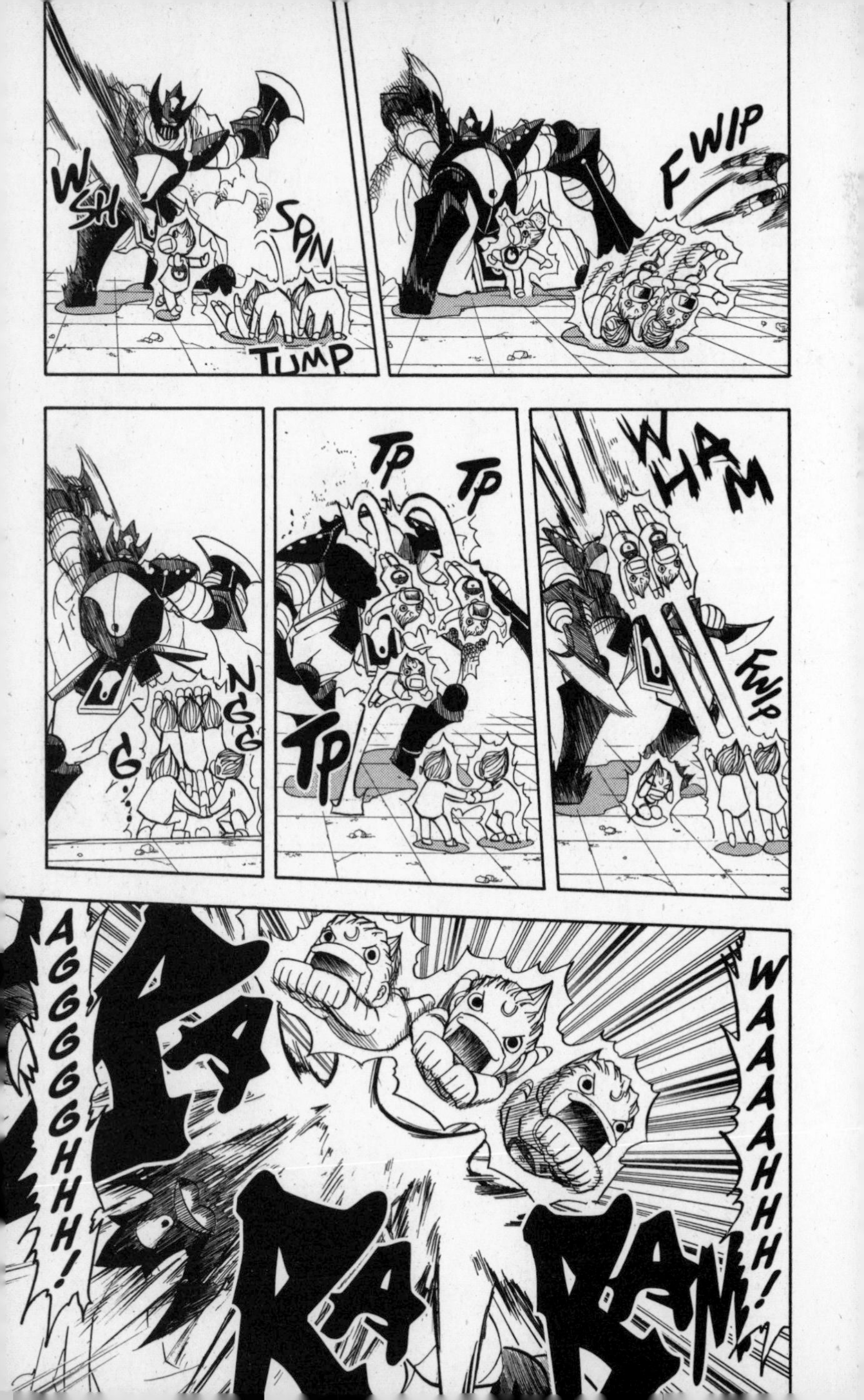
FWIP
WSH
SPIN
TUMP
WHAM
FWIP
TP
TP
TP
NGG
G...
WAAAAAHHHH!
BAM
AGGGGGGHHH!

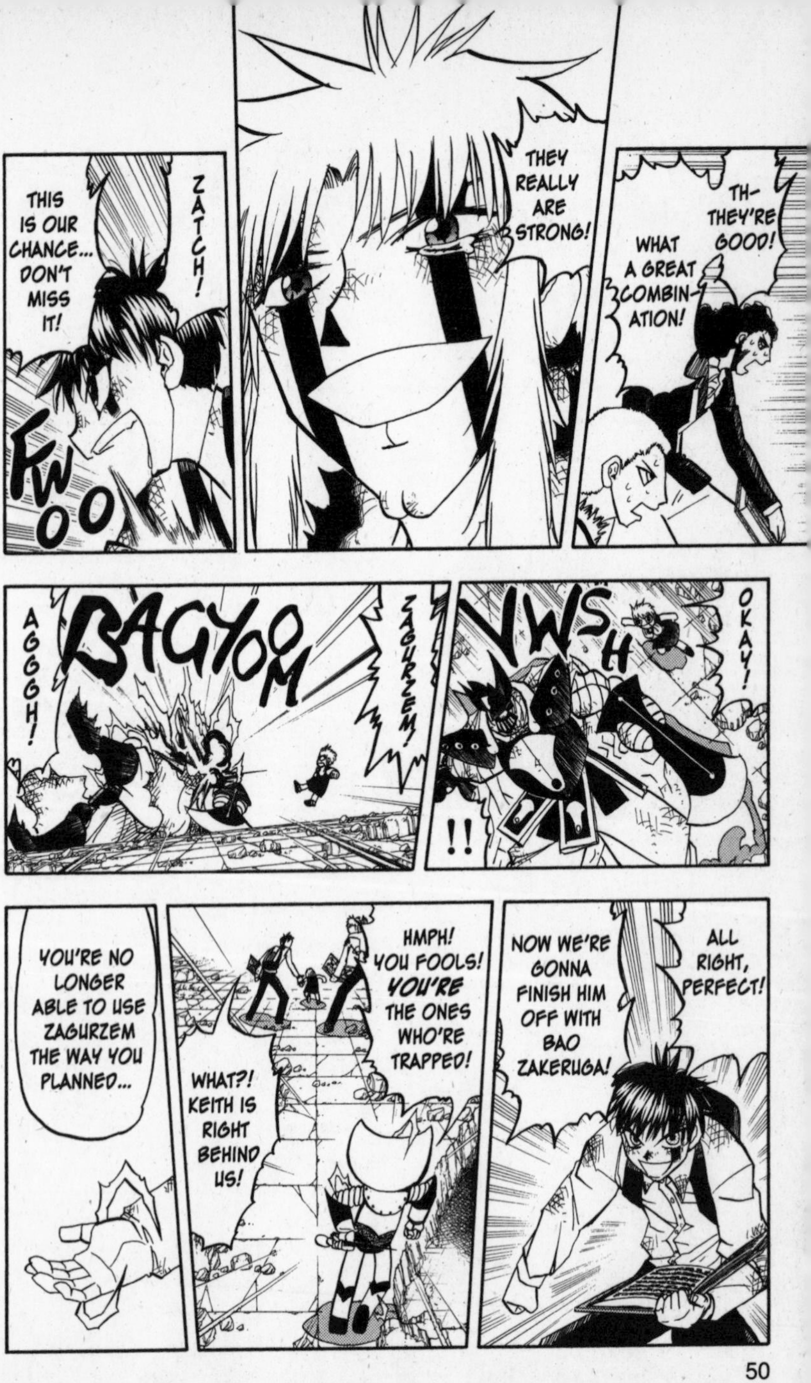

TH- THEY'RE GOOD!
WHAT A GREAT COMBINATION!
THEY REALLY ARE STRONG!
ZATCH!
THIS IS OUR CHANCE... DON'T MISS IT!
FWOOO
OKAY!
VWSH
!!
ZAGURZEM!
BAGYOOM
AGGGH!
ALL RIGHT, PERFECT!
NOW WE'RE GONNA FINISH HIM OFF WITH BAO ZAKERUGA!
HMPH! YOU FOOLS! *YOU'RE* THE ONES WHO'RE TRAPPED!
WHAT?! KEITH IS RIGHT BEHIND US!
YOU'RE NO LONGER ABLE TO USE ZAGURZEM THE WAY YOU PLANNED...

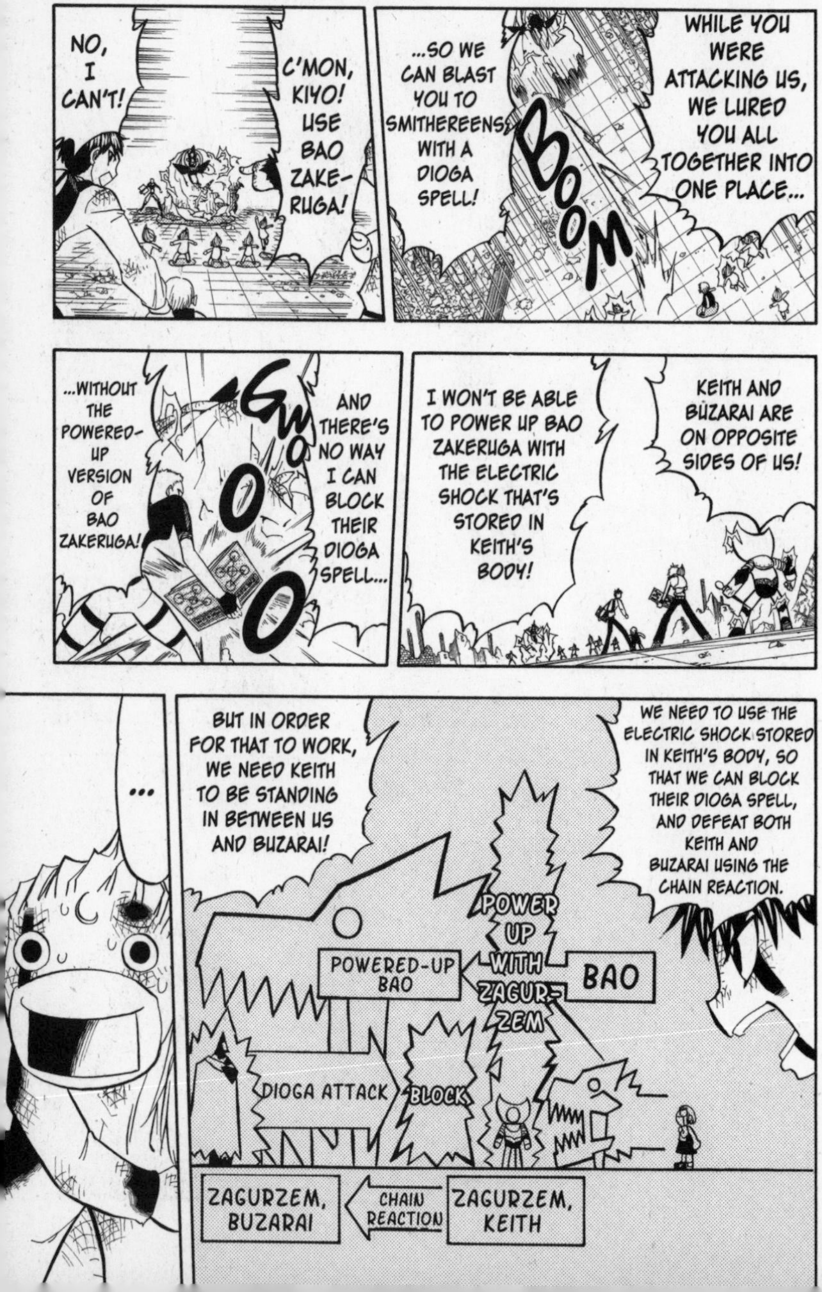
WHILE YOU WERE ATTACKING US, WE LURED YOU ALL TOGETHER INTO ONE PLACE...
...SO WE CAN BLAST YOU TO SMITHEREENS WITH A DIOGA SPELL!
BOOM
C'MON, KIYO! USE BAO ZAKE-RUGA!
NO, I CAN'T!
KEITH AND BÜZARAI ARE ON OPPOSITE SIDES OF US!
I WON'T BE ABLE TO POWER UP BAO ZAKERUGA WITH THE ELECTRIC SHOCK THAT'S STORED IN KEITH'S BODY!
AND THERE'S NO WAY I CAN BLOCK THEIR DIOGA SPELL...
GWOOO
...WITHOUT THE POWERED-UP VERSION OF BAO ZAKERUGA!
WE NEED TO USE THE ELECTRIC SHOCK STORED IN KEITH'S BODY, SO THAT WE CAN BLOCK THEIR DIOGA SPELL, AND DEFEAT BOTH KEITH AND BUZARAI USING THE CHAIN REACTION.
BUT IN ORDER FOR THAT TO WORK, WE NEED KEITH TO BE STANDING IN BETWEEN US AND BUZARAI!
BAO
POWER UP WITH ZAGUR-ZEM
POWERED-UP BAO
BLOCK
DIOGA ATTACK
ZAGURZEM, KEITH
CHAIN REACTION
ZAGURZEM, BUZARAI
...

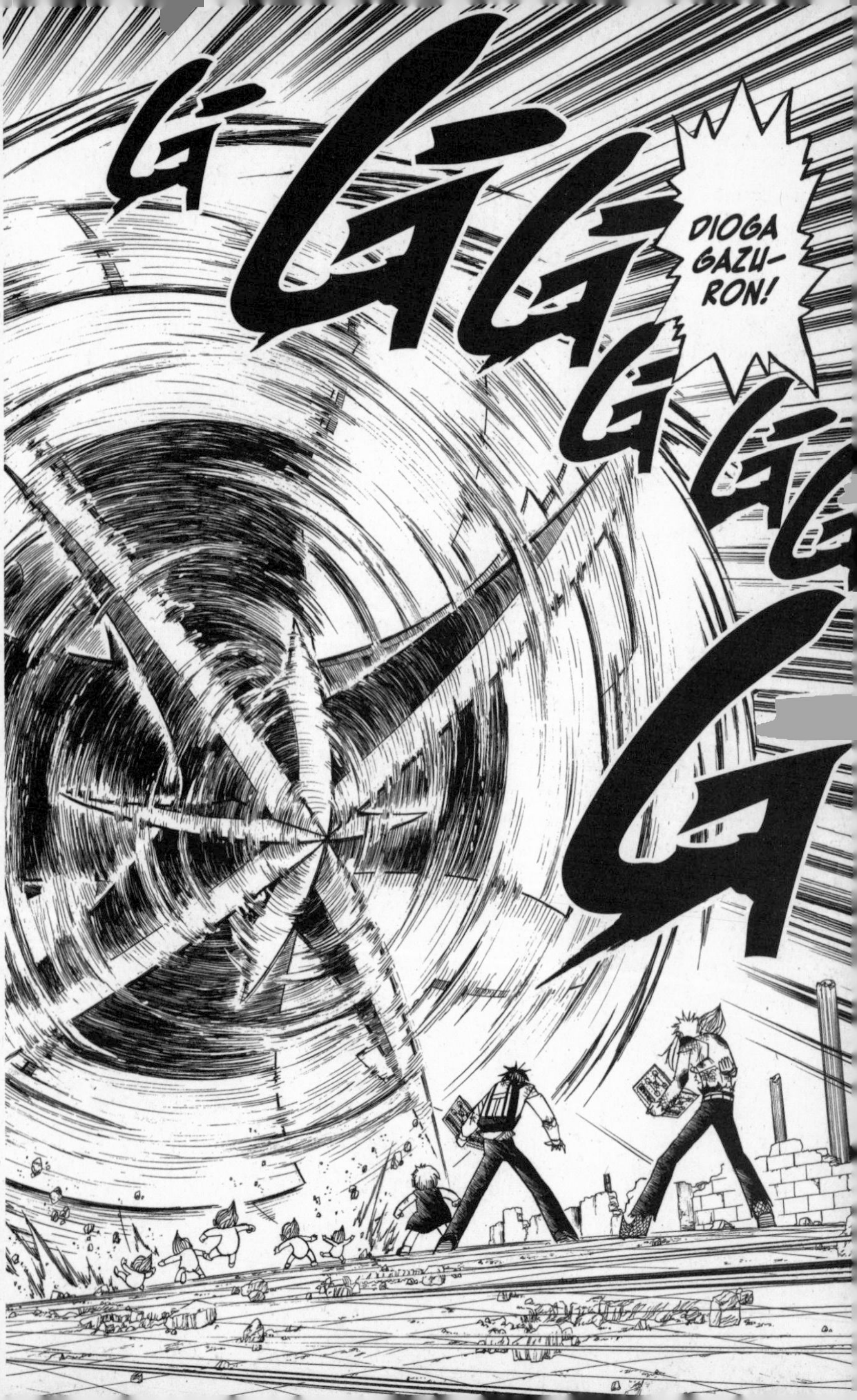
DIOGA GAZURON!
GGGGGG

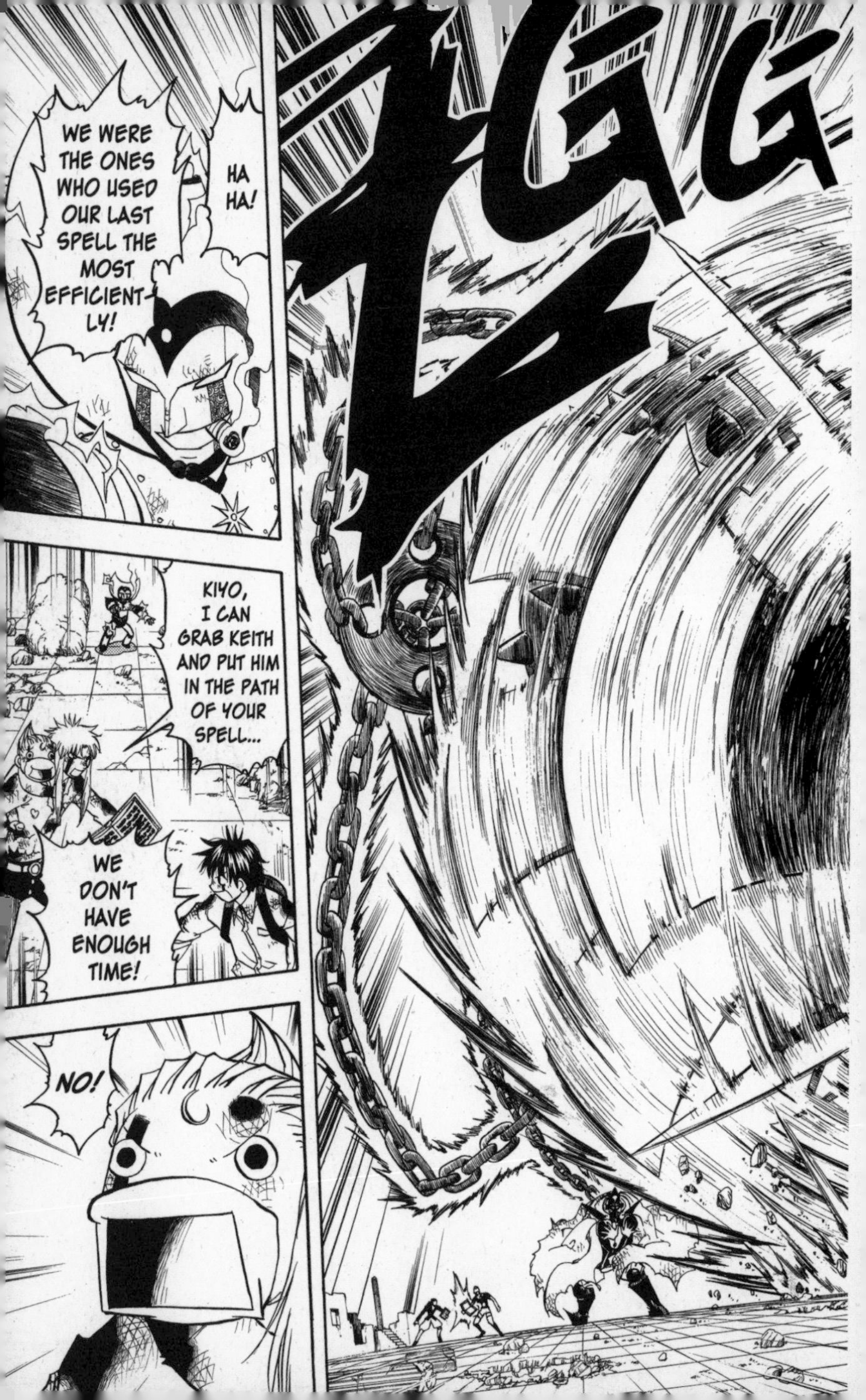
ZGG
HA HA!
WE WERE THE ONES WHO USED OUR LAST SPELL THE MOST EFFICIENT-LY!
KIYO, I CAN GRAB KEITH AND PUT HIM IN THE PATH OF YOUR SPELL...
WE DON'T HAVE ENOUGH TIME!
NO!

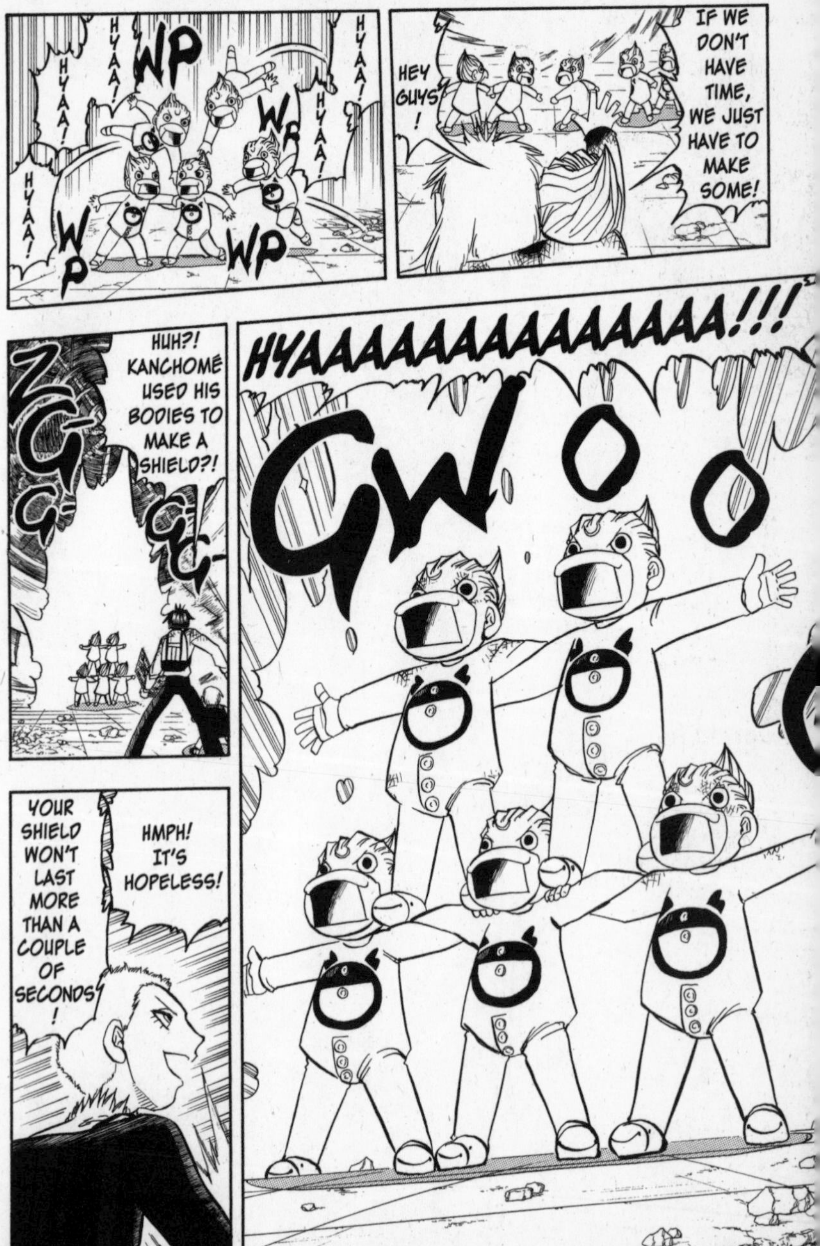
IF WE DON'T HAVE TIME, WE JUST HAVE TO MAKE SOME!
HEY GUYS!
HYAAA!
WP
HYAAA!
HYAAA!
WR
HYAAA!
HYAAA!
HYAAA!
WP
WP
HYAAAAAAAAAAAAA!!!
GWOOO
HUH?! KANCHOMÉ USED HIS BODIES TO MAKE A SHIELD?!
ZGG
HMPH! IT'S HOPELESS!
YOUR SHIELD WON'T LAST MORE THAN A COUPLE OF SECONDS!

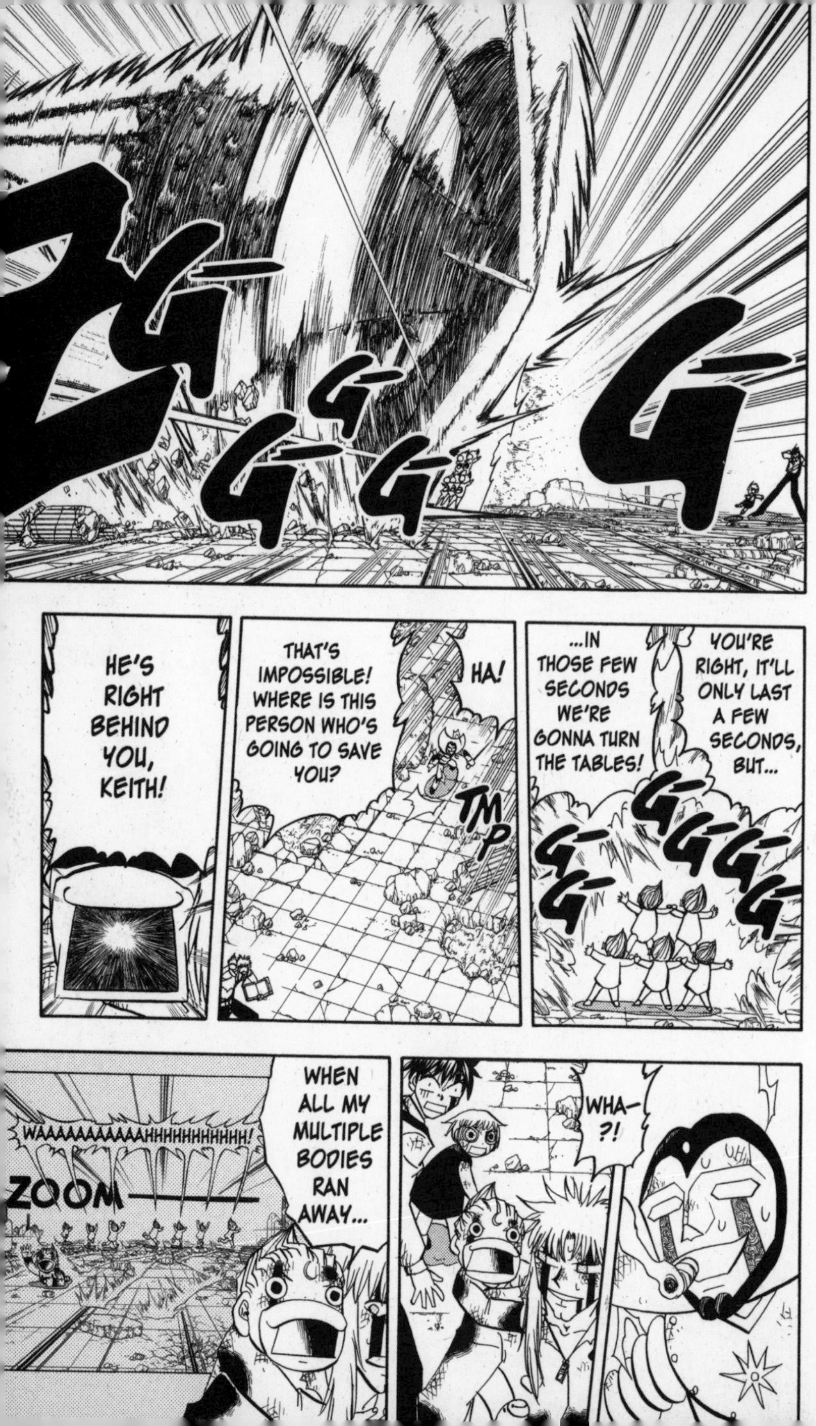

ZGGGGG
YOU'RE RIGHT, IT'LL ONLY LAST A FEW SECONDS, BUT...
...IN THOSE FEW SECONDS WE'RE GONNA TURN THE TABLES!
GGGGGG
HA!
THAT'S IMPOSSIBLE! WHERE IS THIS PERSON WHO'S GOING TO SAVE YOU?
TMP
HE'S RIGHT BEHIND YOU, KEITH!
WHA-?!
WHEN ALL MY MULTIPLE BODIES RAN AWAY...
WAAAAAAAAAAAHHHHHHHHHHH!
ZOOM

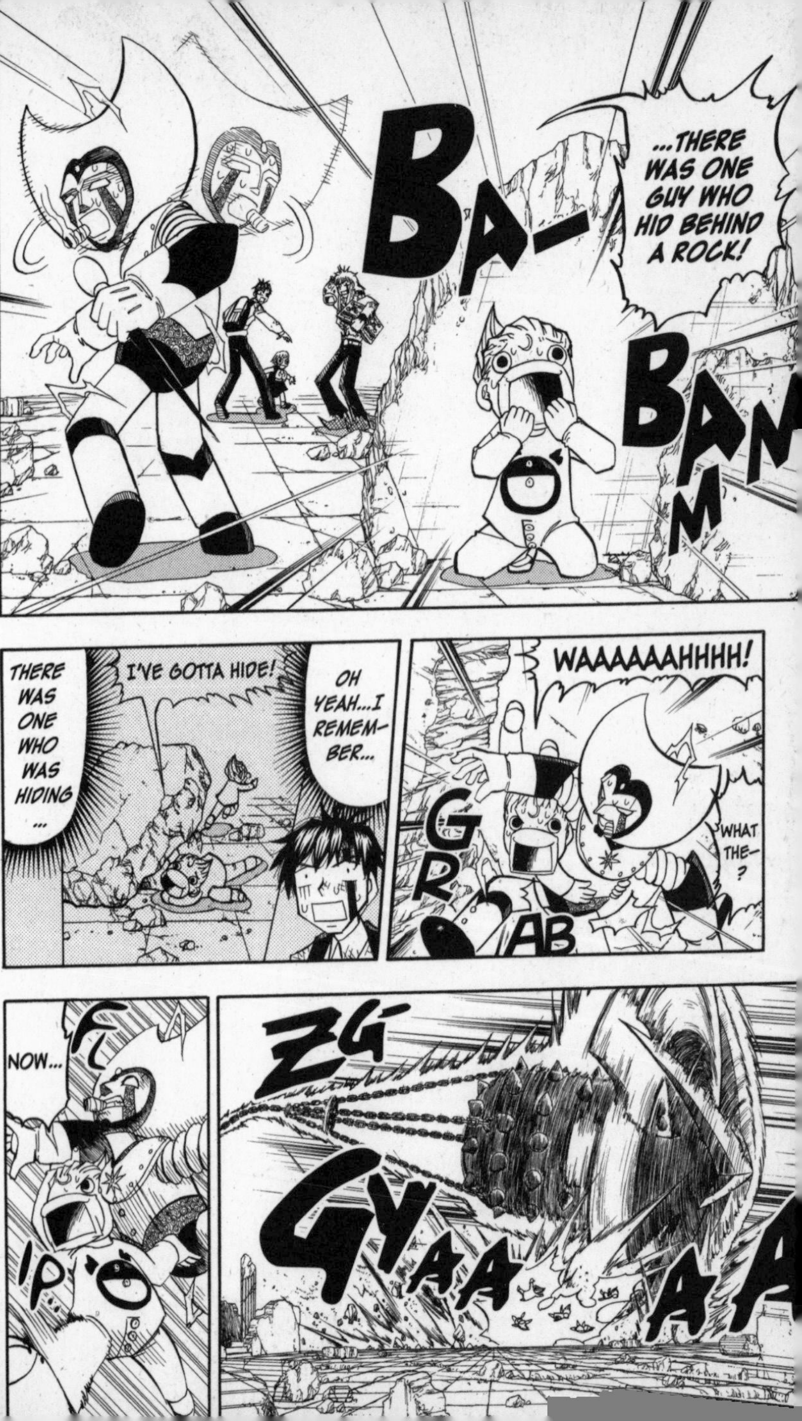
...THERE WAS ONE GUY WHO HID BEHIND A ROCK!
BA-
BAMM
WAAAAAAHHHH!
WHAT THE-?
GRAB
OH YEAH...I REMEMBER...
I'VE GOTTA HIDE!
THERE WAS ONE WHO WAS HIDING...
ZG
GYAAA
NOW...
FLIP

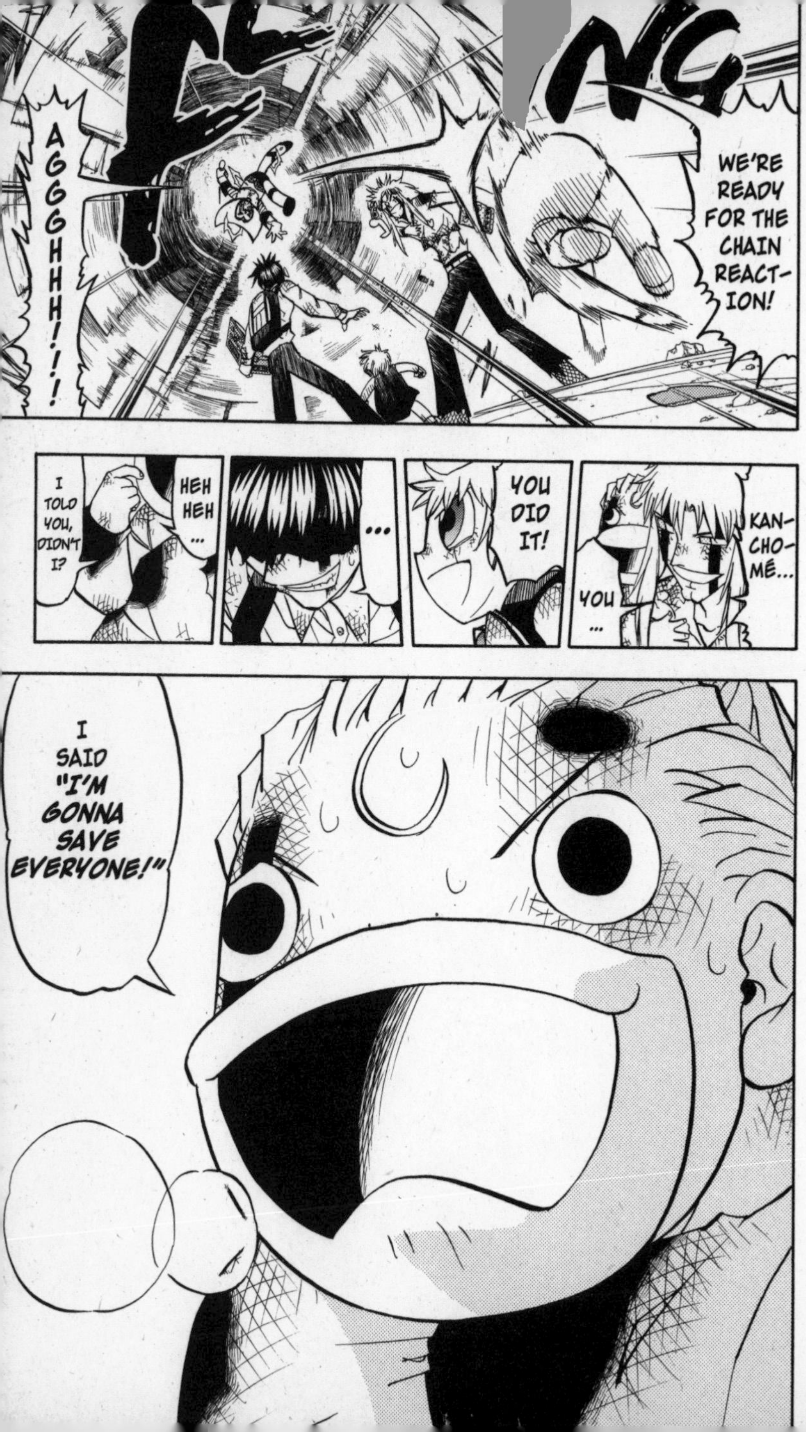
NG
WE'RE READY FOR THE CHAIN REACTION!
AGGGHHHH!!!!
KAN-CHO-MÉ...
YOU...
YOU DID IT!
...
HEH HEH...
I TOLD YOU, DIDN'T I?
I SAID "I'M GONNA SAVE EVERYONE!"

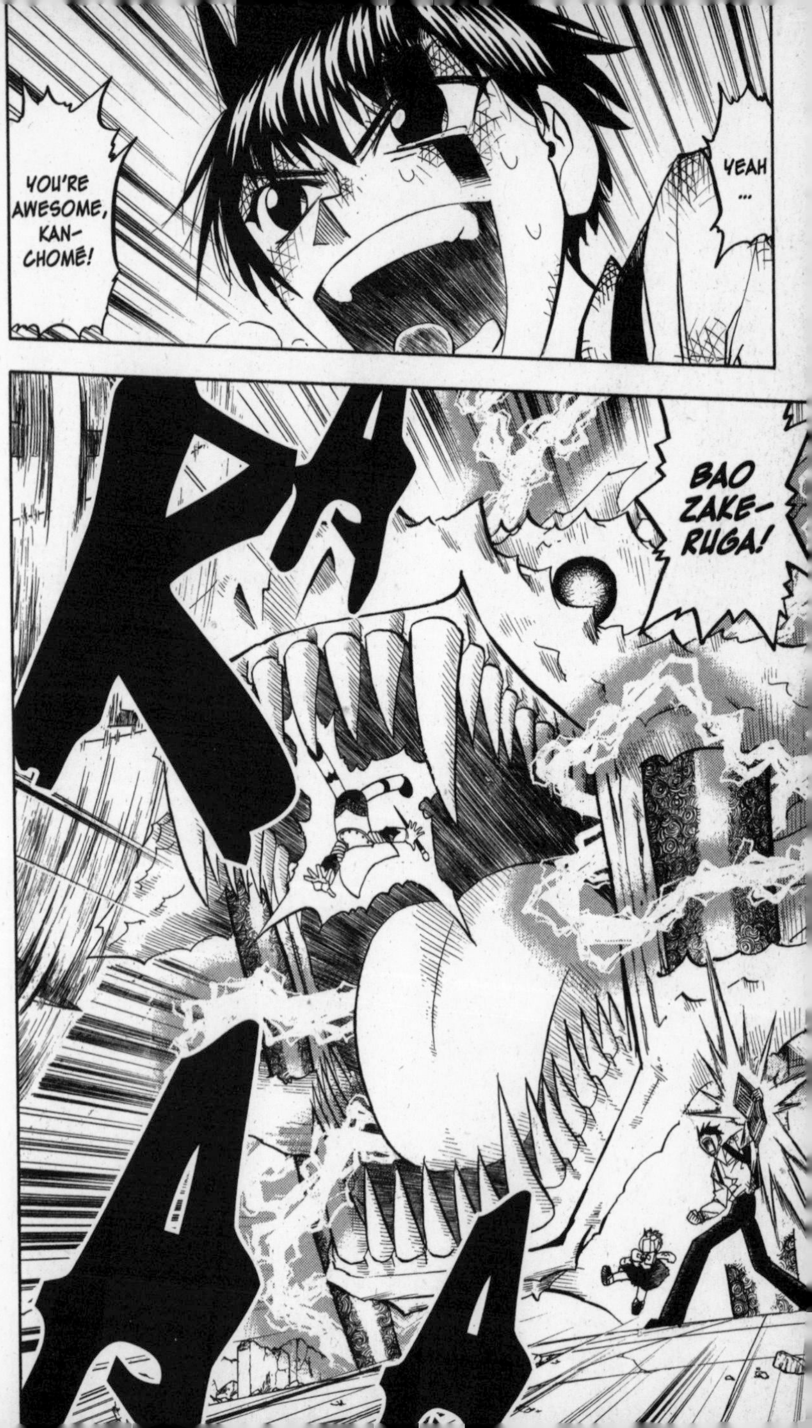
YEAH ...
YOU'RE AWESOME, KAN-CHOMÉ!
BAO ZAKE-RUGA!

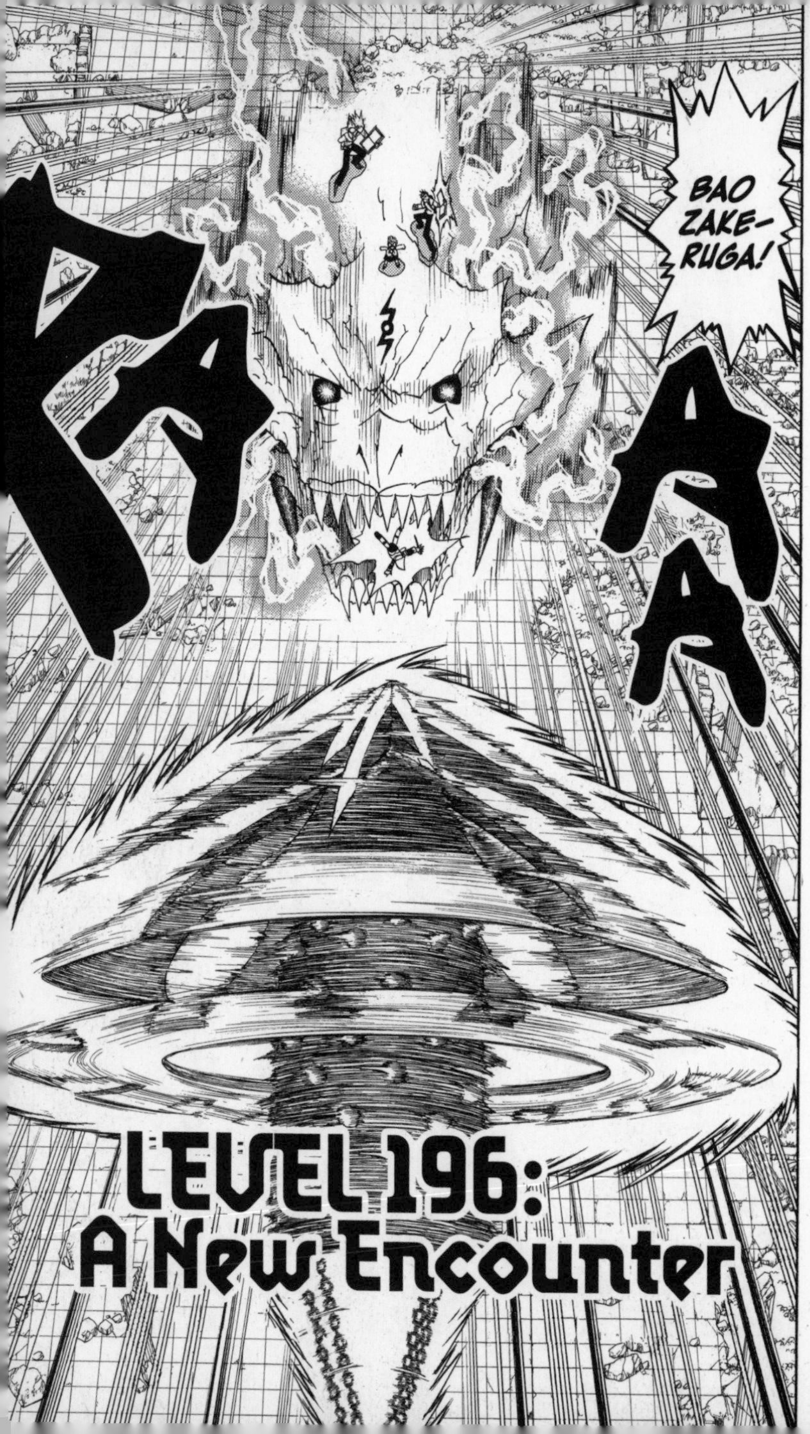
BAO ZAKE-RUGA!
LEVEL 196:
A New Encounter

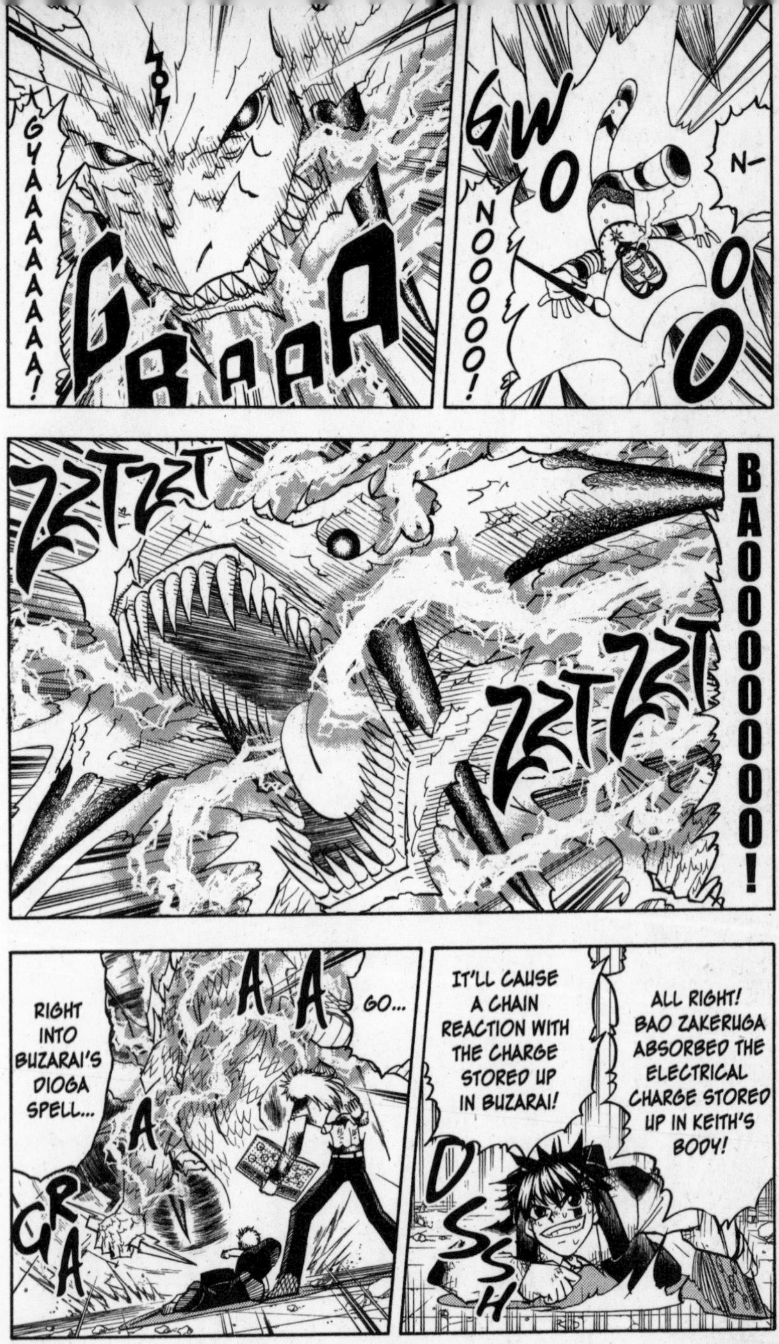
GWOOOO
N-
NOOOOOO!
GYAAAAAAAAAAA!
GRAAAA
BAOOOOOOOO!
ZZTZZT
ZZTZZT
ALL RIGHT! BAO ZAKERUGA ABSORBED THE ELECTRICAL CHARGE STORED UP IN KEITH'S BODY!
IT'LL CAUSE A CHAIN REACTION WITH THE CHARGE STORED UP IN BUZARAI!
DOSSH
GO...
RIGHT INTO BUZARAI'S DIOGA SPELL...
AAA
GRGA

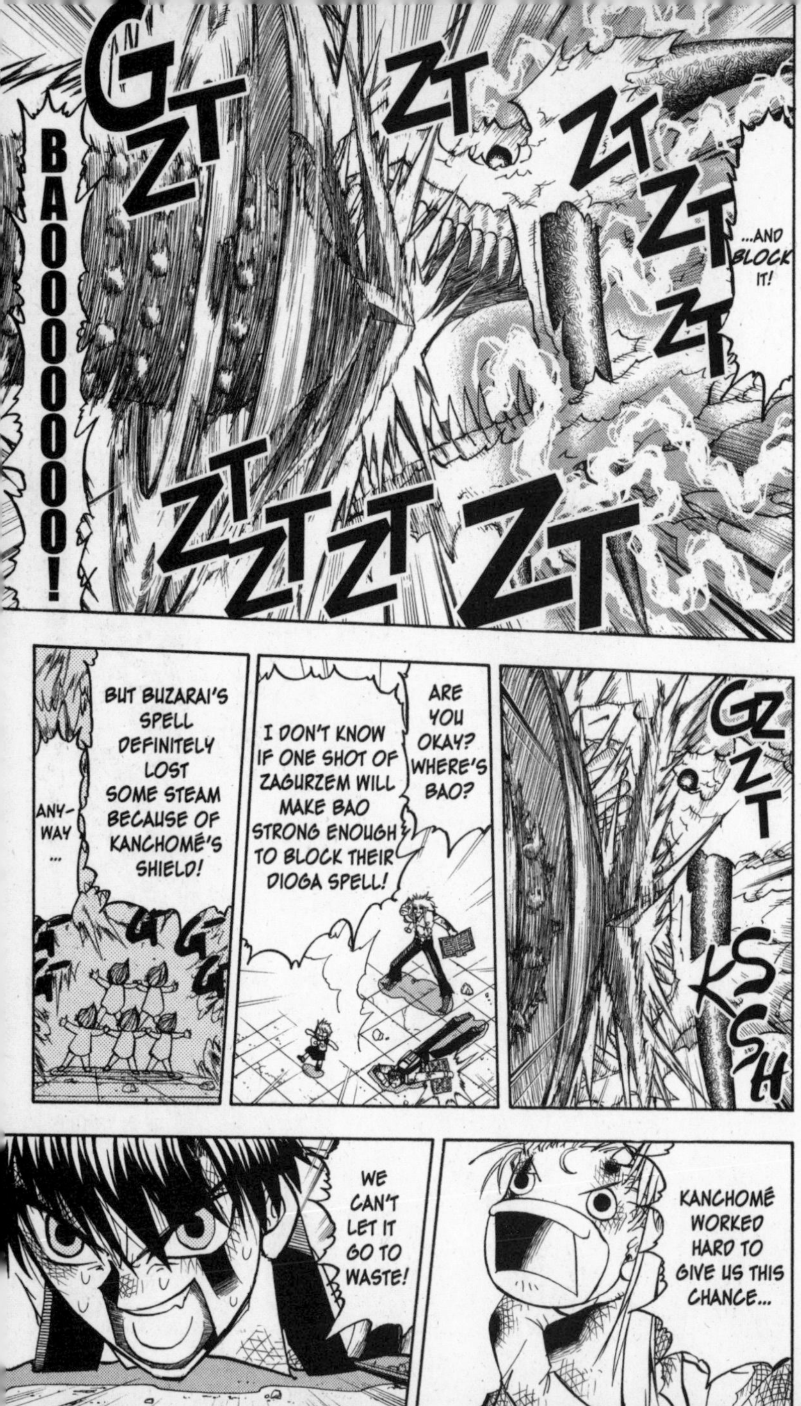
...AND BLOCK IT!
ZT ZZT ZZT ZZT
ZT ZT ZZT ZZT
GZT
BAOOOOOOOO!
GZZT
KSSH
ARE YOU OKAY? WHERE'S BAO?
I DON'T KNOW IF ONE SHOT OF ZAGURZEM WILL MAKE BAO STRONG ENOUGH TO BLOCK THEIR DIOGA SPELL!
BUT BUZARAI'S SPELL DEFINITELY LOST SOME STEAM BECAUSE OF KANCHOMÉ'S SHIELD!
ANYWAY...
KANCHOMÉ WORKED HARD TO GIVE US THIS CHANCE...
WE CAN'T LET IT GO TO WASTE!

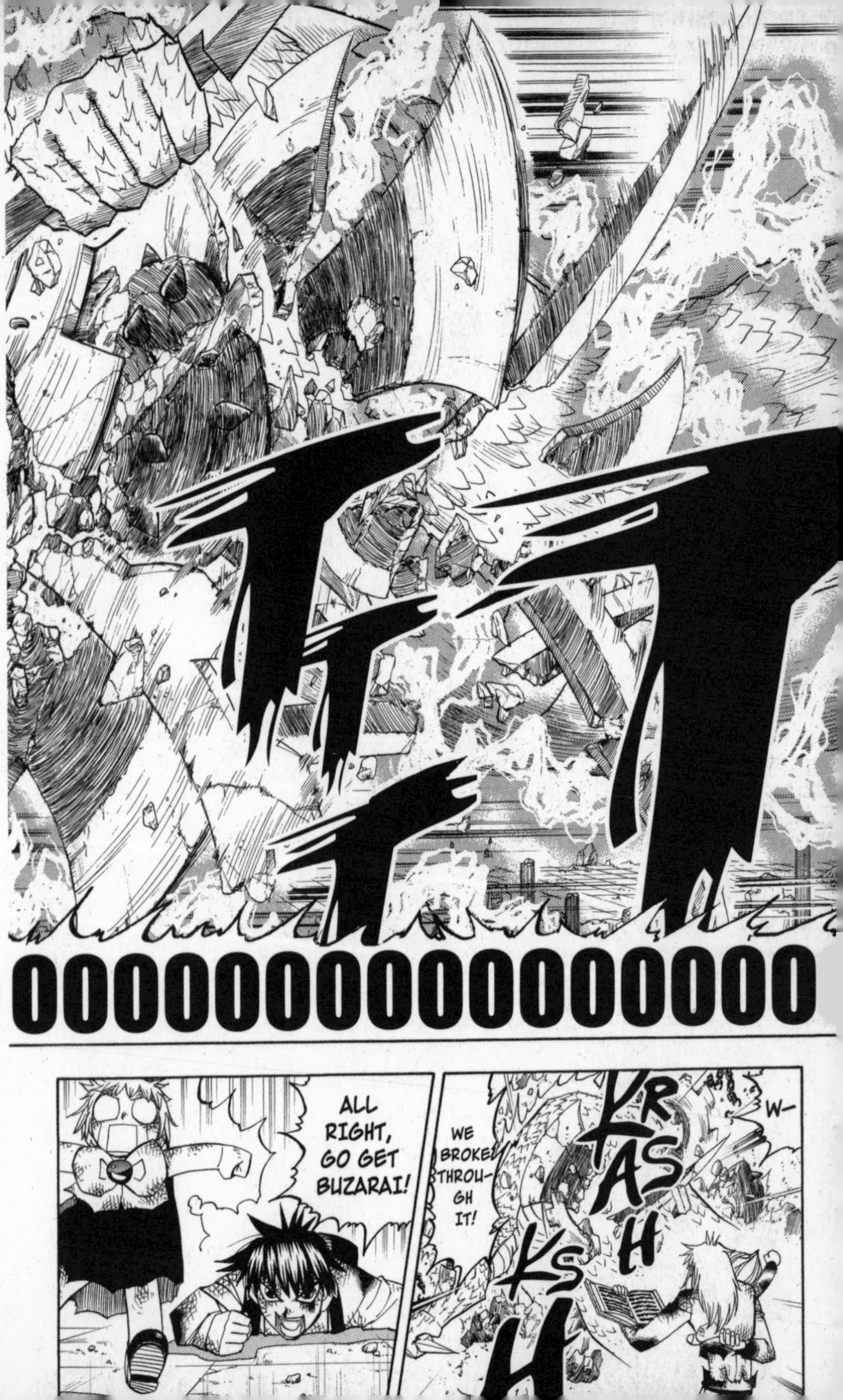
OOOOOOOOOOOOOOOO
W-
KRASH
KSH
WE BROKE THROUGH IT!
ALL RIGHT, GO GET BUZARAI!

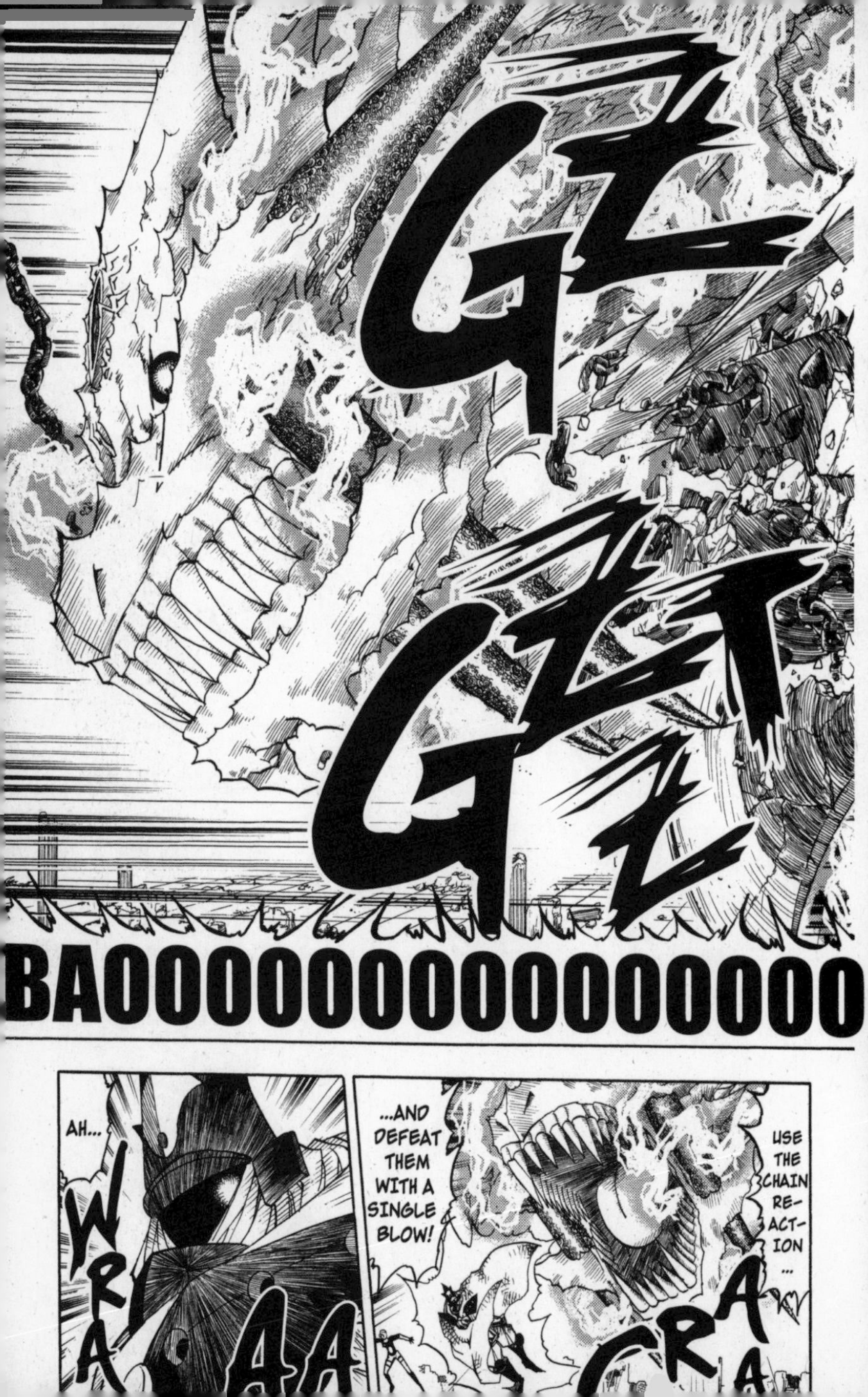
BAOOOOOOOOOOOOOOOO
USE THE CHAIN RE-ACT-ION ...
...AND DEFEAT THEM WITH A SINGLE BLOW!
CRA
CRA
AH...

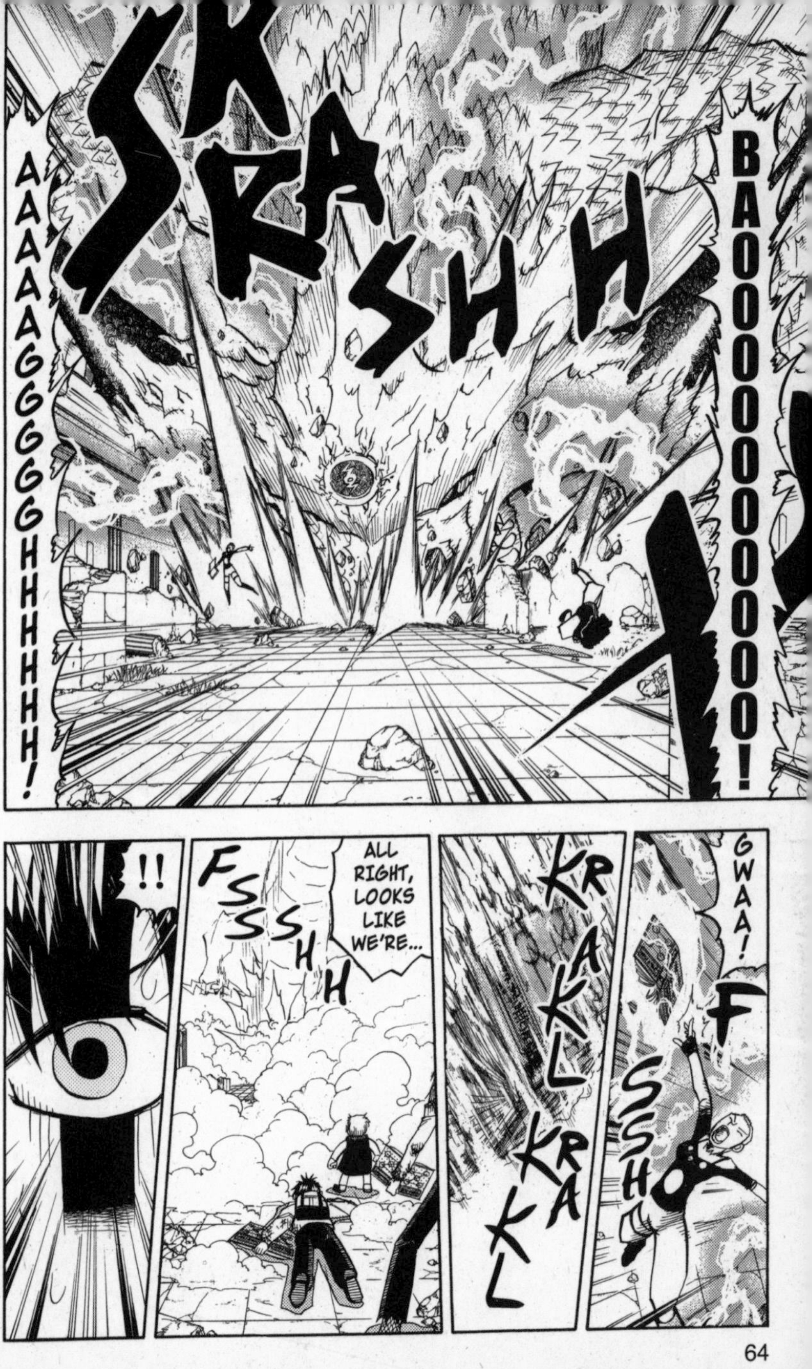
BAOOOOOOOOOOOO!
KRASHH
AAAAAGGGGGHHHHHH!
GWAA!
FSSHO
KRAKL KRAKL
ALL RIGHT, LOOKS LIKE WE'RE...
FSSSHH
!!

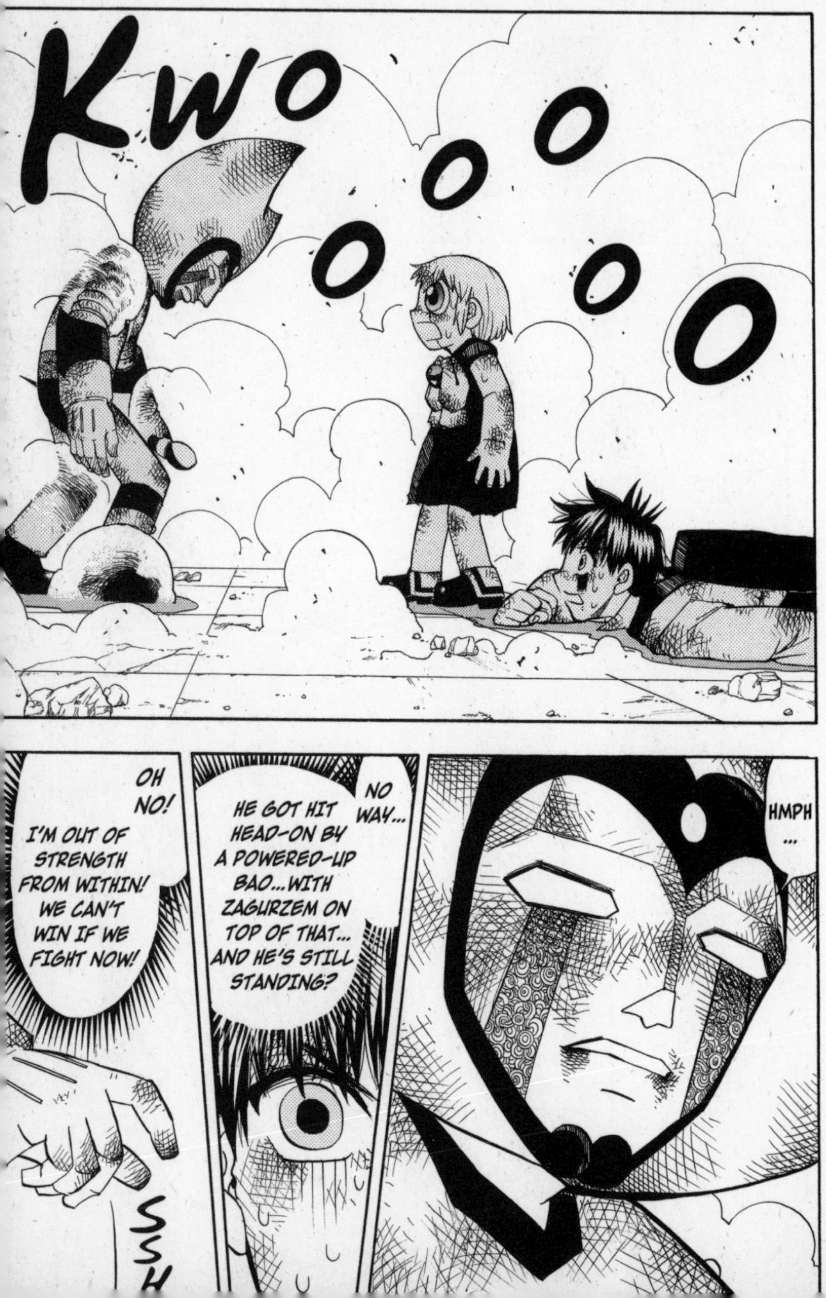
KWOOOOOO
HMPH ...
NO WAY...
HE GOT HIT HEAD-ON BY A POWERED-UP BAO...WITH ZAGURZEM ON TOP OF THAT... AND HE'S STILL STANDING?
OH NO!
I'M OUT OF STRENGTH FROM WITHIN! WE CAN'T WIN IF WE FIGHT NOW!
SSH

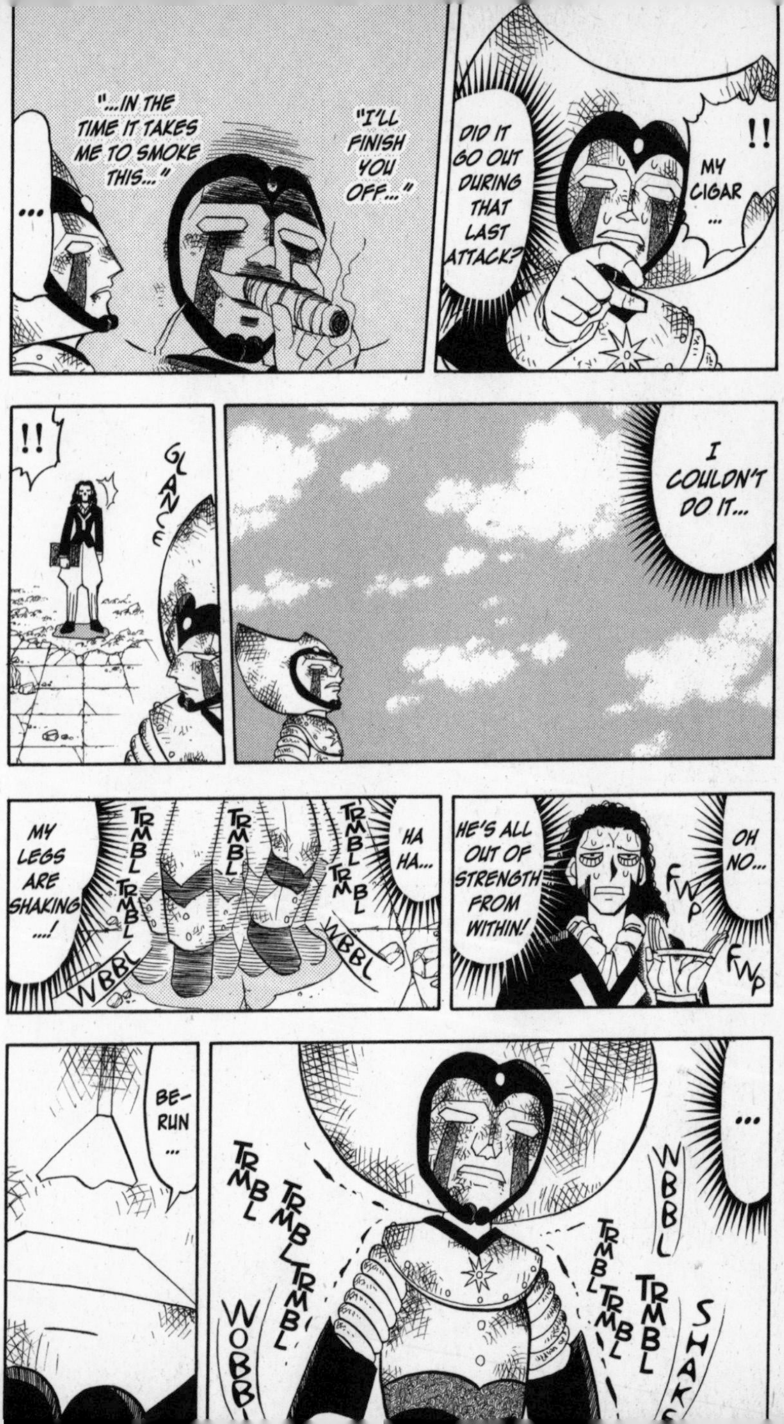
!!
MY CIGAR ...
DID IT GO OUT DURING THAT LAST ATTACK?
"I'LL FINISH YOU OFF..."
"...IN THE TIME IT TAKES ME TO SMOKE THIS..."
...
I COULDN'T DO IT...
GLANCE
!!
OH NO...
FWP
FWP
HE'S ALL OUT OF STRENGTH FROM WITHIN!
HA HA...
TRMBL
TRMBL
WBBL
TRMBL
TRMBL
MY LEGS ARE SHAKING...!
TRMBL
WBBL
...
SHAKE
WBBL
TRMBL
TRMBL
TRMBL
TRMBL
TRMBL
TRMBL
WOBBL
BE-RUN ...

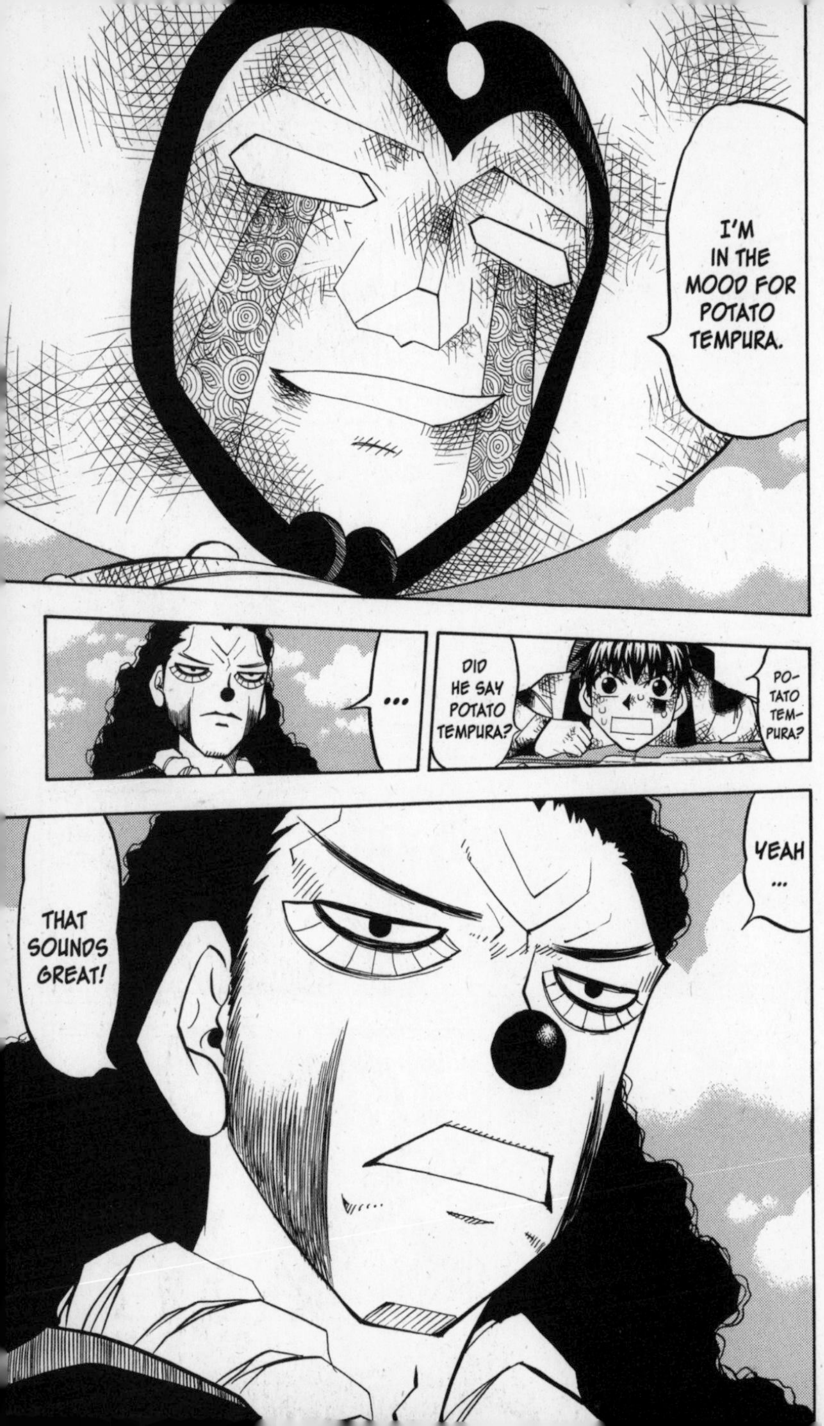
I'M IN THE MOOD FOR POTATO TEMPURA.
PO-TATO TEM-PURA?
DID HE SAY POTATO TEMPURA?
...
YEAH ...
THAT SOUNDS GREAT!

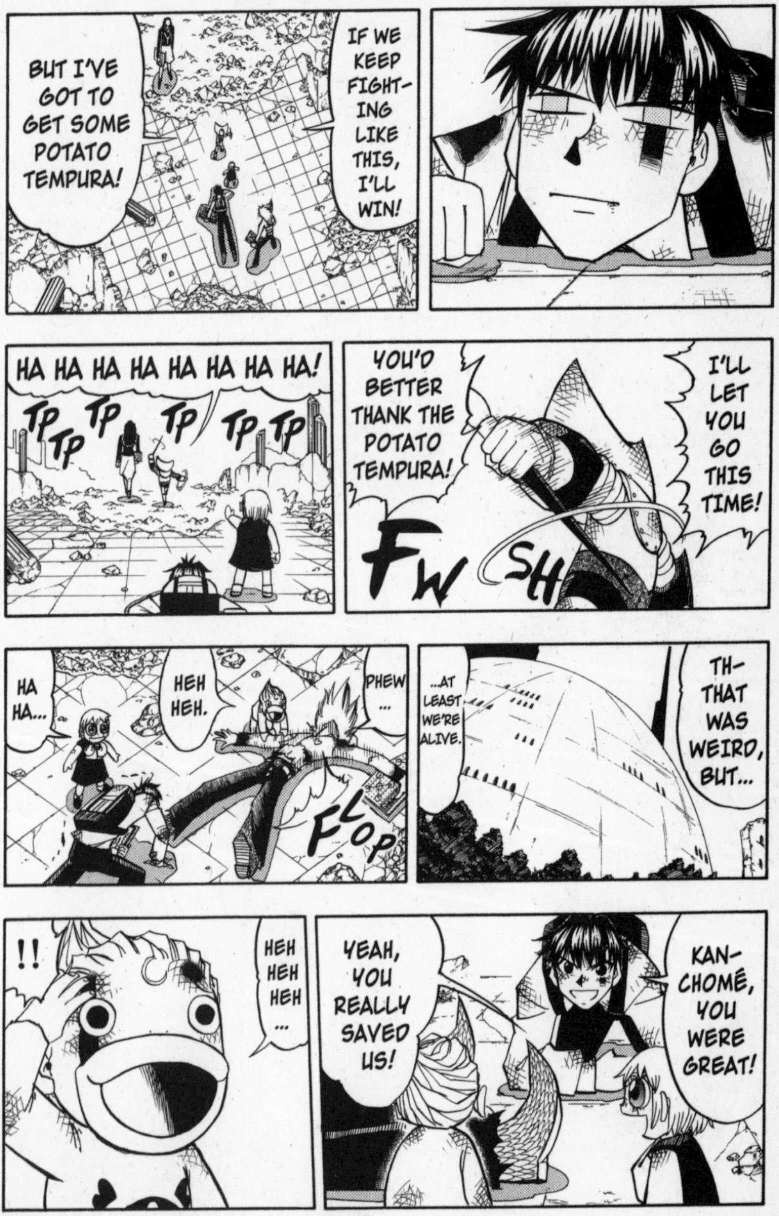
IF WE KEEP FIGHTING LIKE THIS, I'LL WIN!
BUT I'VE GOT TO GET SOME POTATO TEMPURA!
I'LL LET YOU GO THIS TIME!
YOU'D BETTER THANK THE POTATO TEMPURA!
FWSH
HA HA HA HA HA HA HA HA!
TP TP TP TP TP TP
TH-THAT WAS WEIRD, BUT...
...AT LEAST WE'RE ALIVE.
PHEW...
HEH HEH.
HA HA...
FLOP
KAN-CHOMÉ, YOU WERE GREAT!
YEAH, YOU REALLY SAVED US!
HEH HEH HEH...
!!

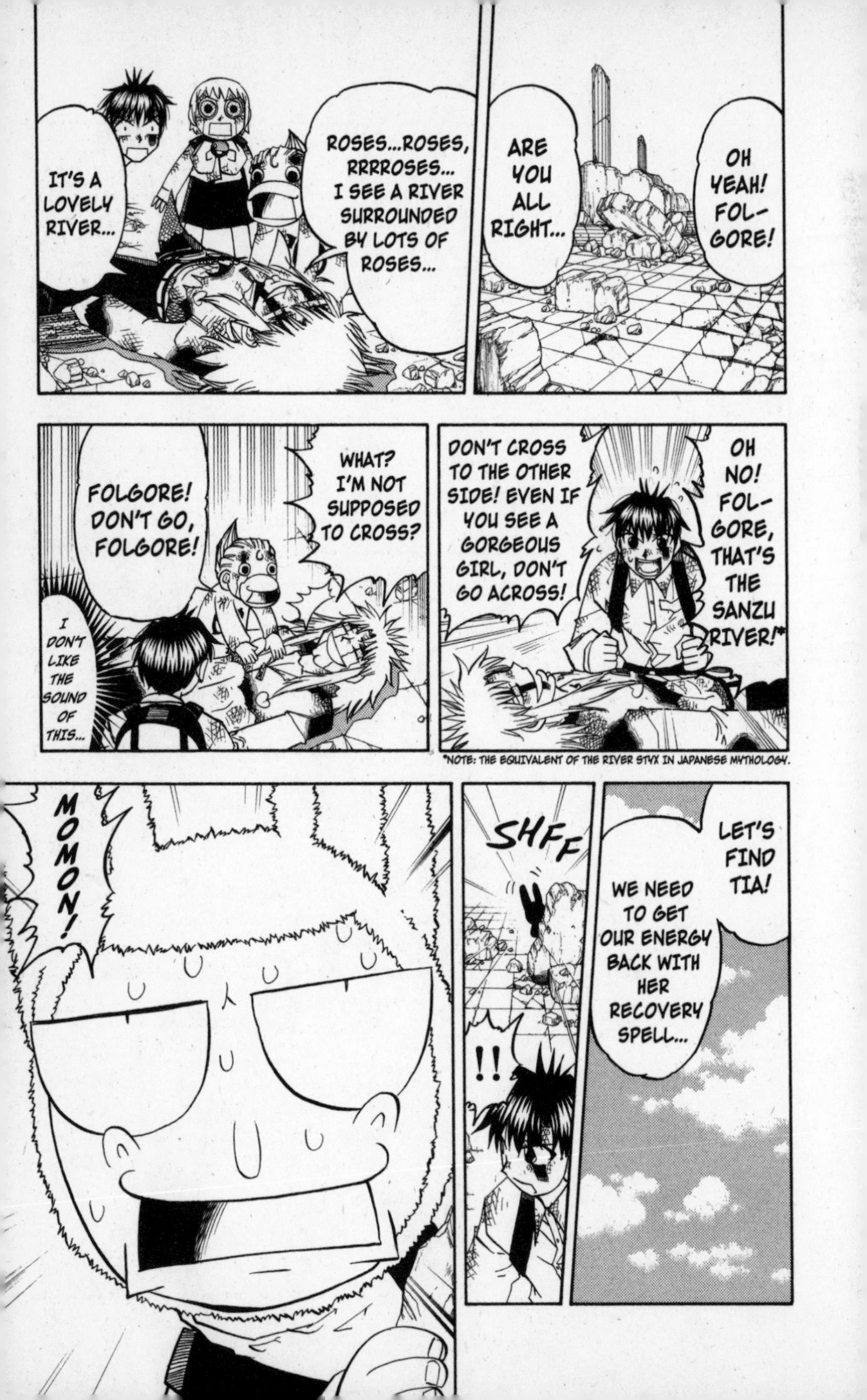
OH YEAH! FOL-GORE!
ARE YOU ALL RIGHT...
ROSES...ROSES, RRRROSES... I SEE A RIVER SURROUNDED BY LOTS OF ROSES...
IT'S A LOVELY RIVER...
OH NO! FOL-GORE, THAT'S THE SANZU RIVER!*
DON'T CROSS TO THE OTHER SIDE! EVEN IF YOU SEE A GORGEOUS GIRL, DON'T GO ACROSS!
WHAT? I'M NOT SUPPOSED TO CROSS?
FOLGORE! DON'T GO, FOLGORE!
I DON'T LIKE THE SOUND OF THIS...
LET'S FIND TIA!
WE NEED TO GET OUR ENERGY BACK WITH HER RECOVERY SPELL...
SHFF
!!
MOMON!

*NOTE: THE EQUIVALENT OF THE RIVER STYX IN JAPANESE MYTHOLOGY.

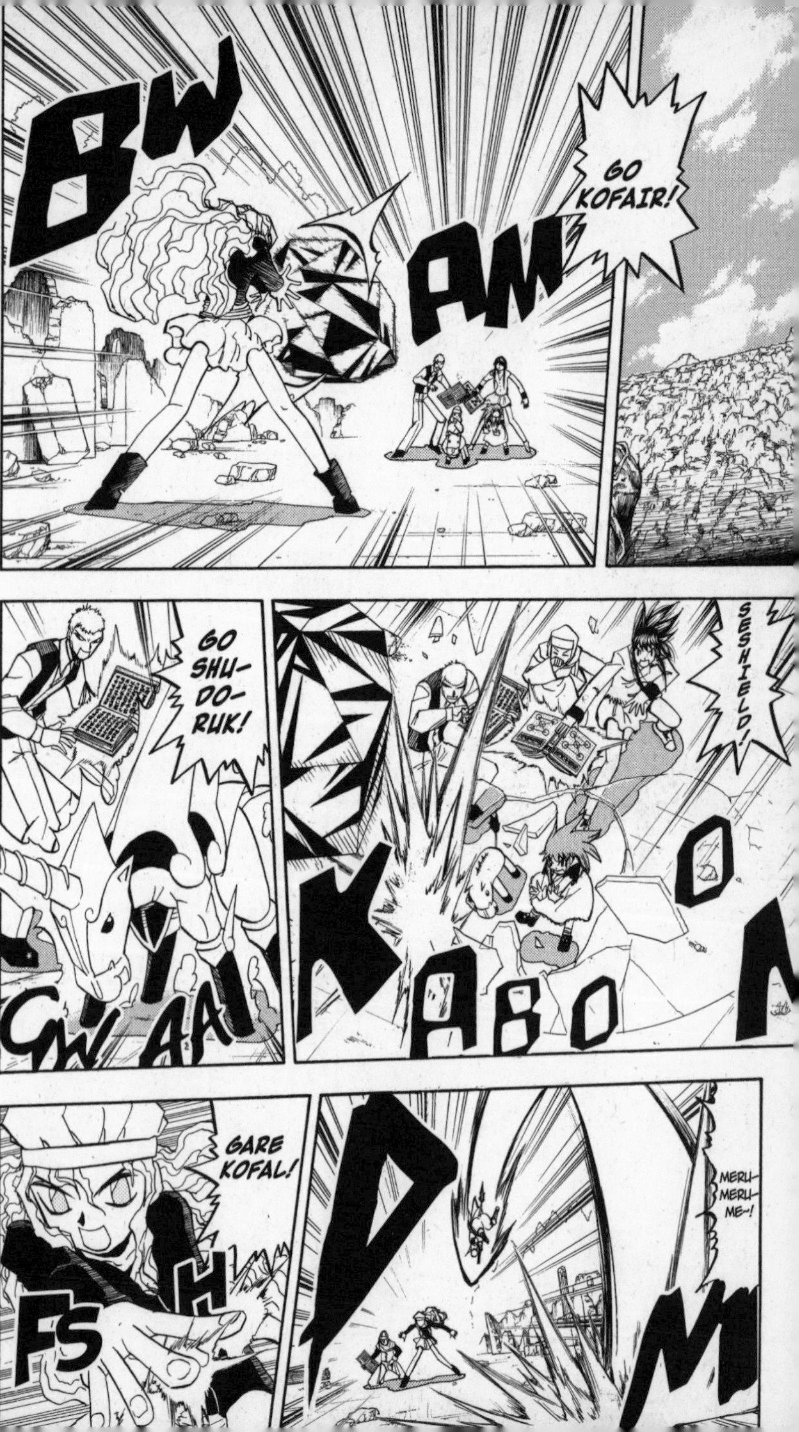
GO KOFAIR!
BWAM
SESHIELD!
KABOOM
GO SHUDO-RUK!
GWAA
MERU MERU ME~!
GARE KOFAL!
FSHH

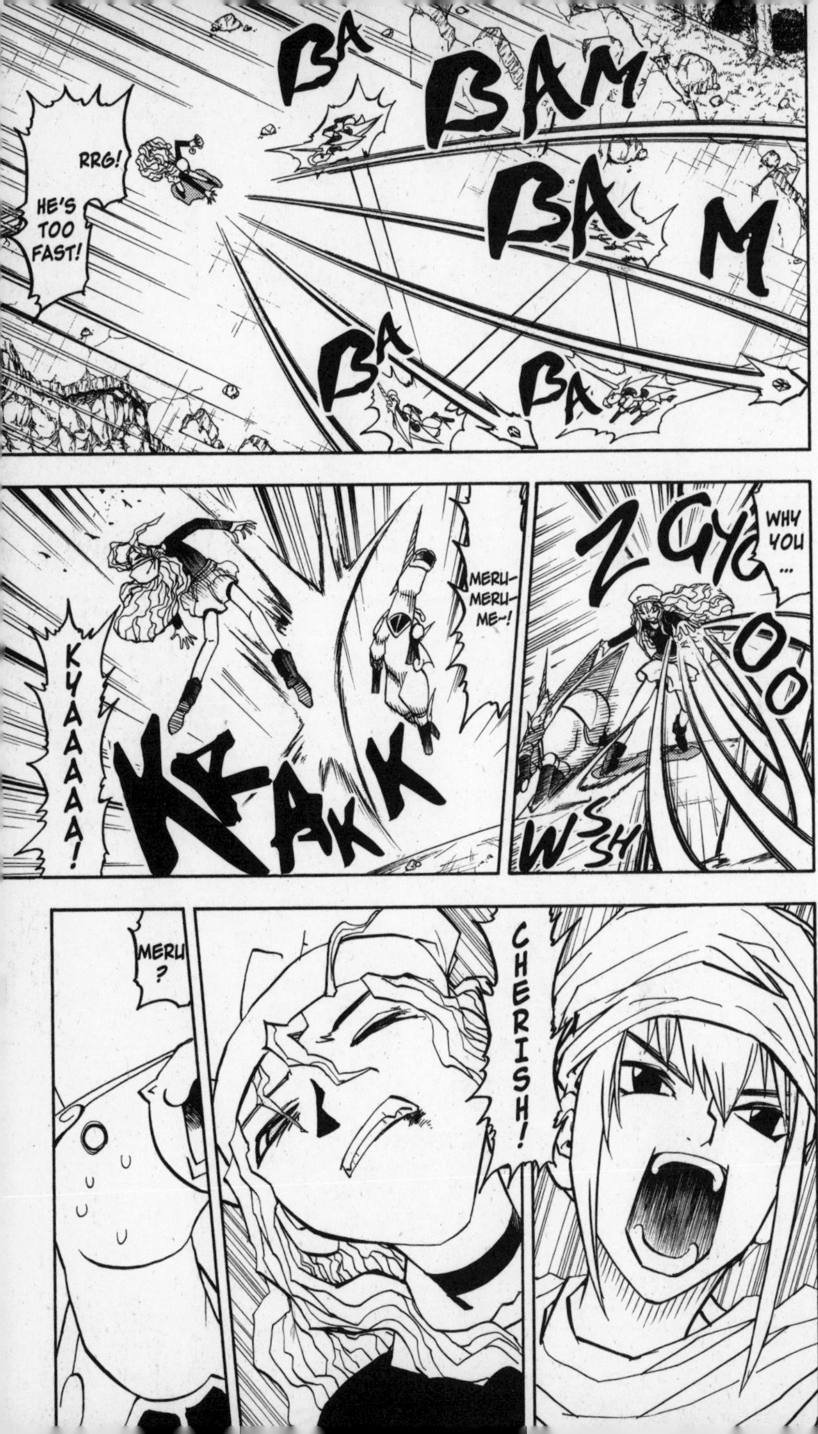
BA BAM
BA BA M
RRG!
HE'S TOO FAST!
BA
BA
WHY YOU...
ZGYOOOO
WSHSH
MERU-MERU-ME~!
KRAKK
KYAAAAAA!
CHERISH!
MERU?

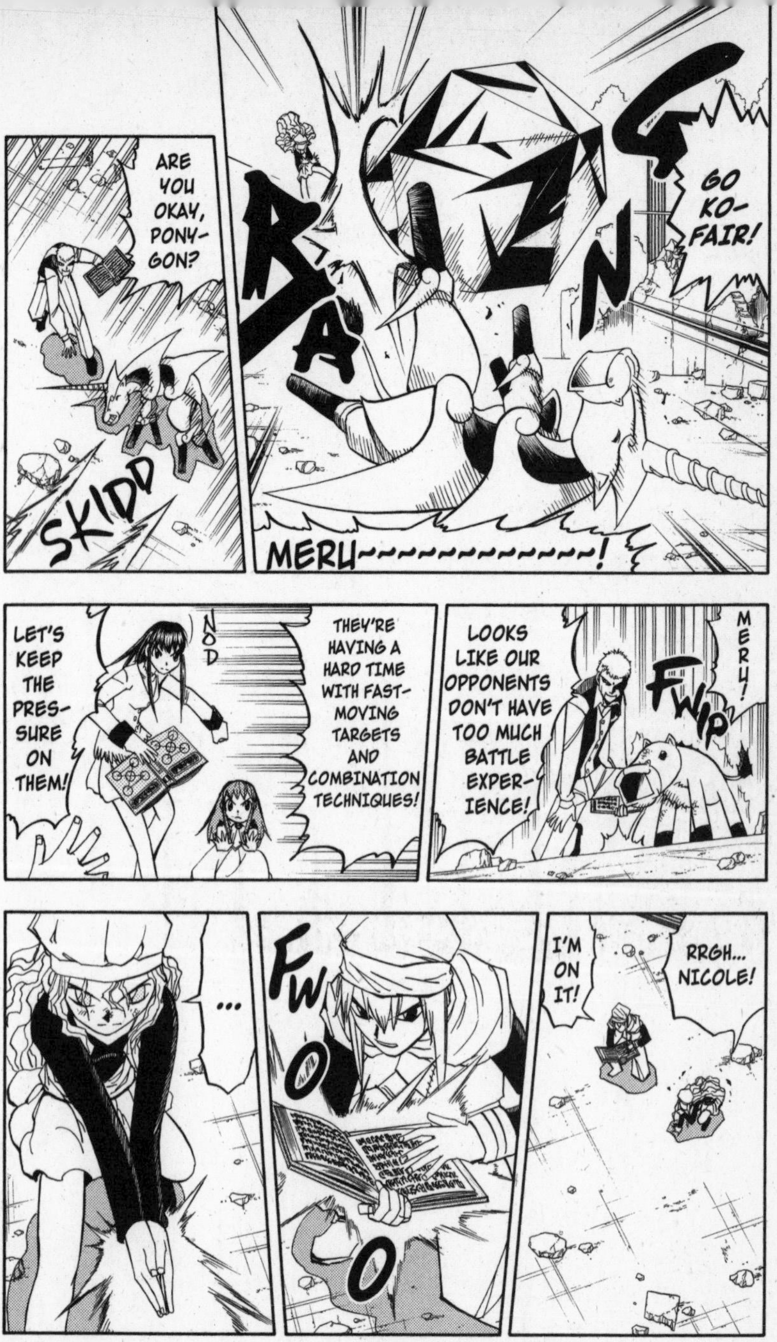
GO KO-FAIR!
MERU~~~~~~~~~~~~~!
ARE YOU OKAY, PONYGON?
SKIDD
MERU!
FWIP
LOOKS LIKE OUR OPPONENTS DON'T HAVE TOO MUCH BATTLE EXPERIENCE!
THEY'RE HAVING A HARD TIME WITH FAST-MOVING TARGETS AND COMBINATION TECHNIQUES!
NOD
LET'S KEEP THE PRESSURE ON THEM!
RRGH... NICOLE!
I'M ON IT!
FWOOO
...

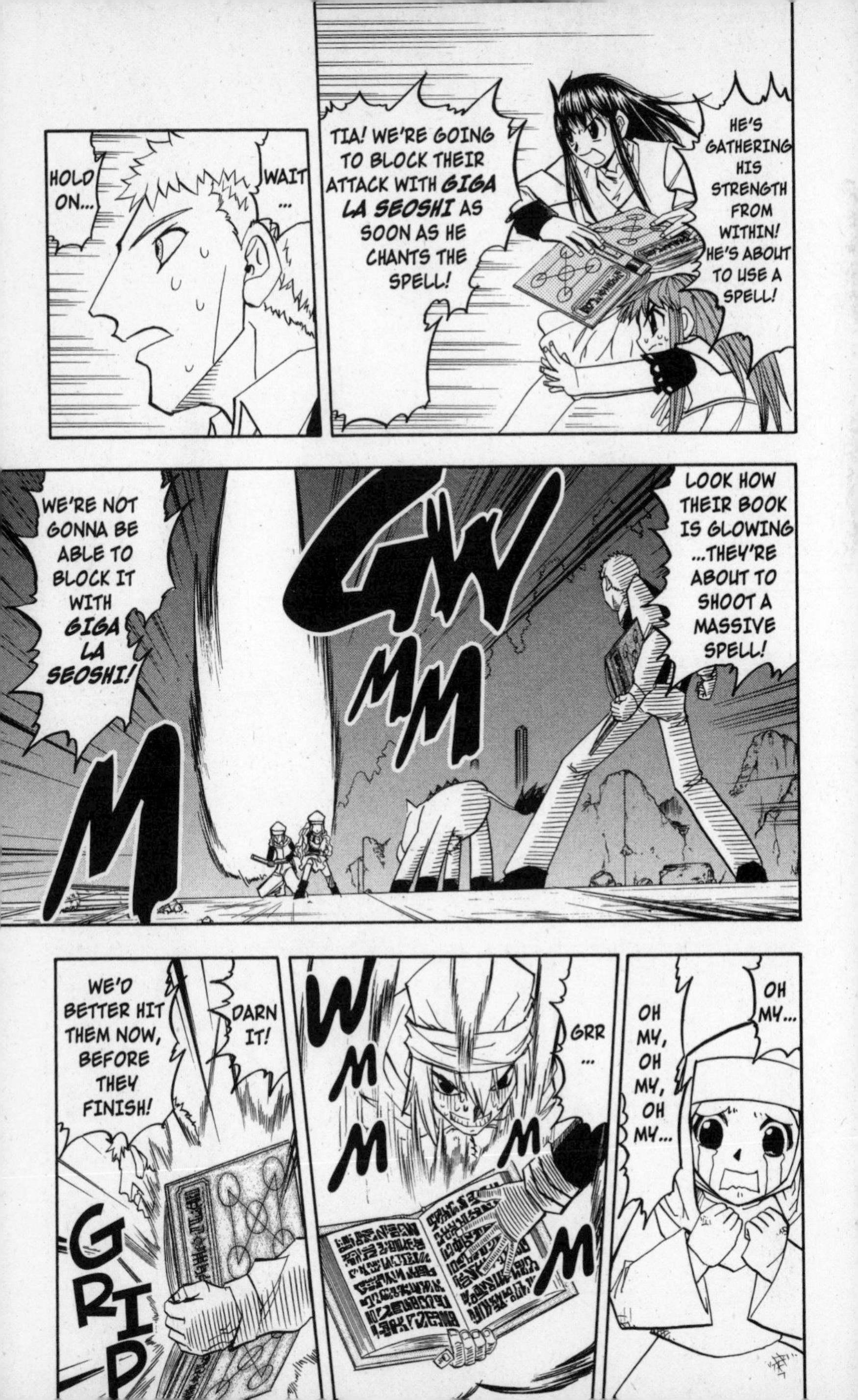

HE'S GATHERING HIS STRENGTH FROM WITHIN! HE'S ABOUT TO USE A SPELL!
TIA! WE'RE GOING TO BLOCK THEIR ATTACK WITH GIGA LA SEOSHI AS SOON AS HE CHANTS THE SPELL!
WAIT...
HOLD ON...
LOOK HOW THEIR BOOK IS GLOWING ...THEY'RE ABOUT TO SHOOT A MASSIVE SPELL!
GWMMM
WE'RE NOT GONNA BE ABLE TO BLOCK IT WITH GIGA LA SEOSHI!
M
OH MY...
OH MY, OH MY, OH MY...
GRR...
WMMMMM
DARN IT!
WE'D BETTER HIT THEM NOW, BEFORE THEY FINISH!
GRIP

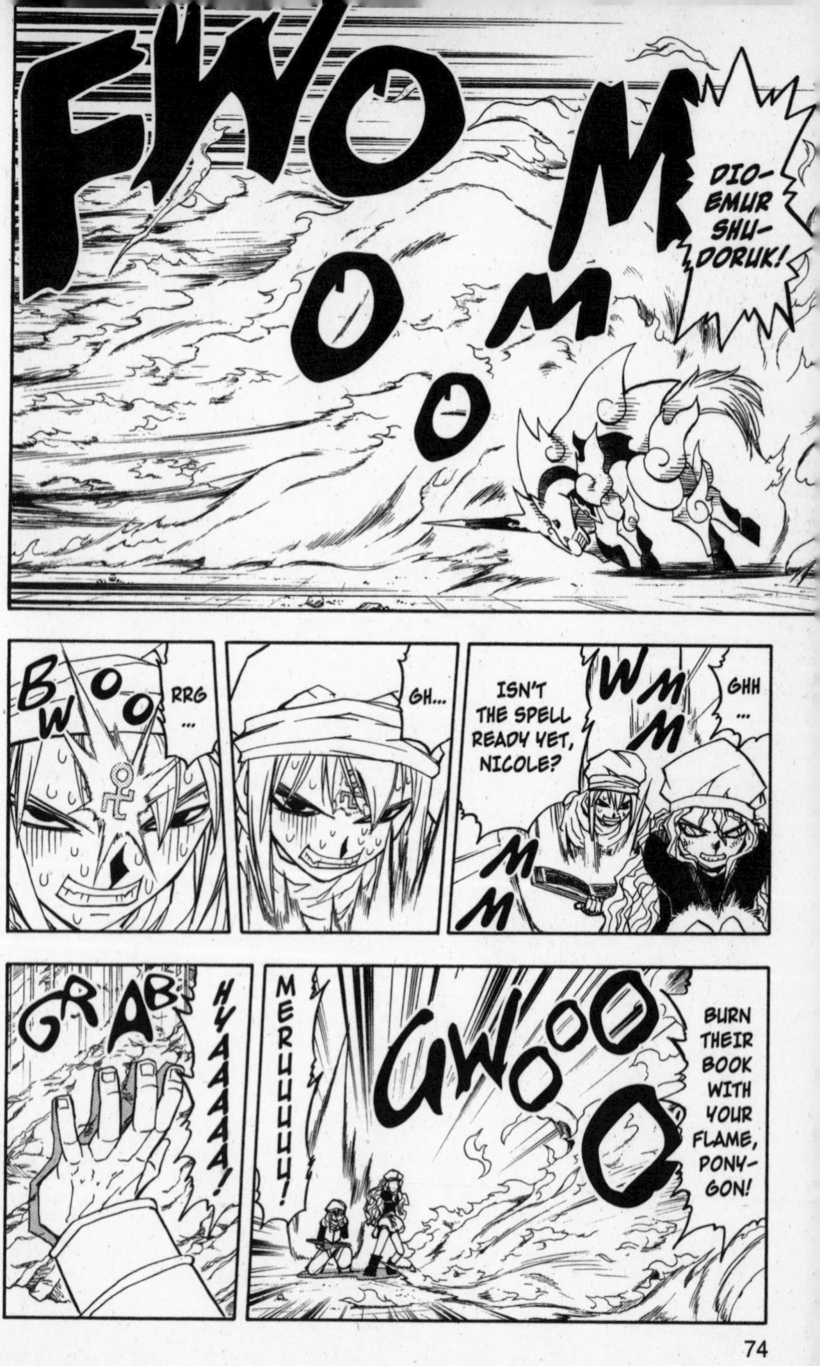

DIO-EMUR SHU-DORUK!
FWOOOOMM
GHH ...
WMMM
ISN'T THE SPELL READY YET, NICOLE?
MMM
GH...
RRG ...
BWOO
BURN THEIR BOOK WITH YOUR FLAME, PONY-GON!
GWOOOO
MERUUUUU!
HYAAAAAA!
GRAB

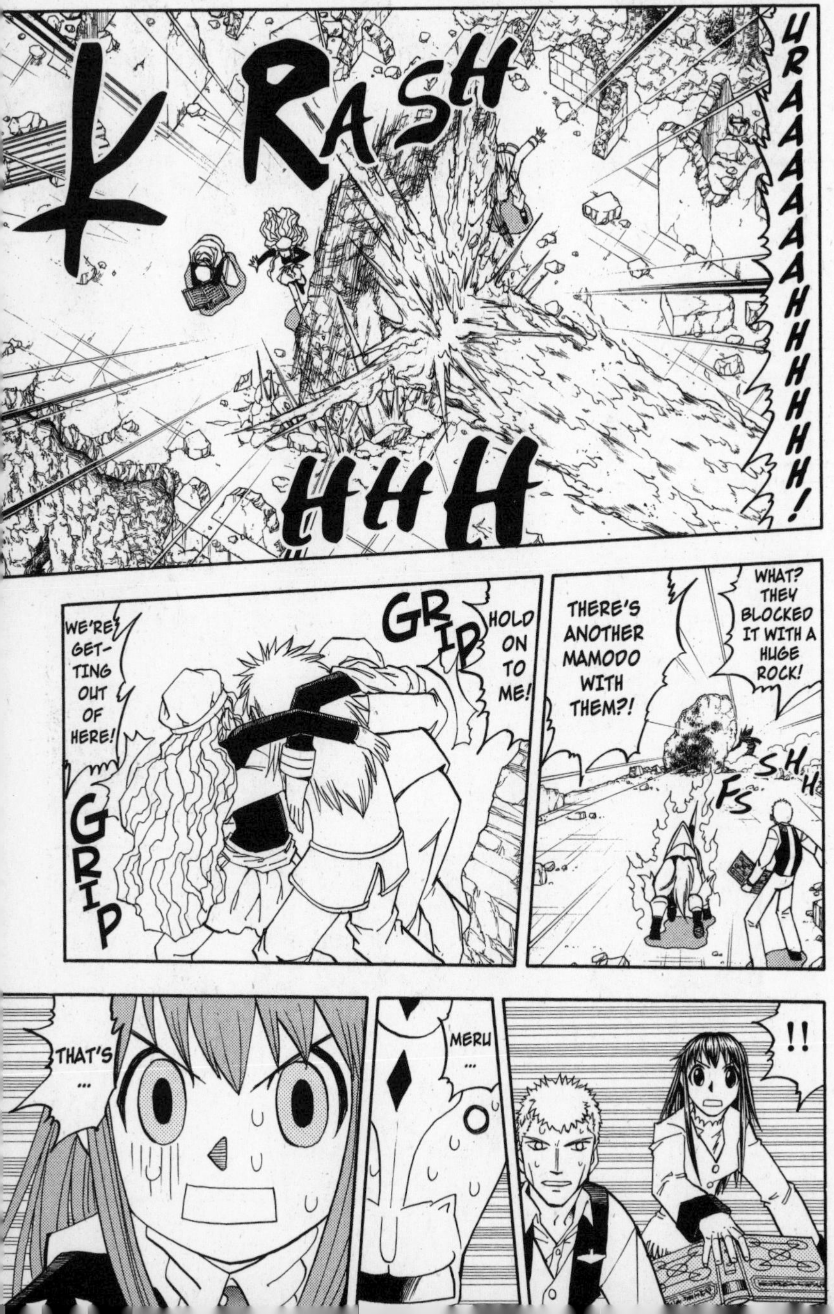
URAAAAAAHHHHHHH!
KRASH
HHH
WHAT? THEY BLOCKED IT WITH A HUGE ROCK!
THERE'S ANOTHER MAMODO WITH THEM?!
SHH
FS
HOLD ON TO ME!
GRIP
WE'RE GET-TING OUT OF HERE!
GRIP
!!
MERU ...
THAT'S ...

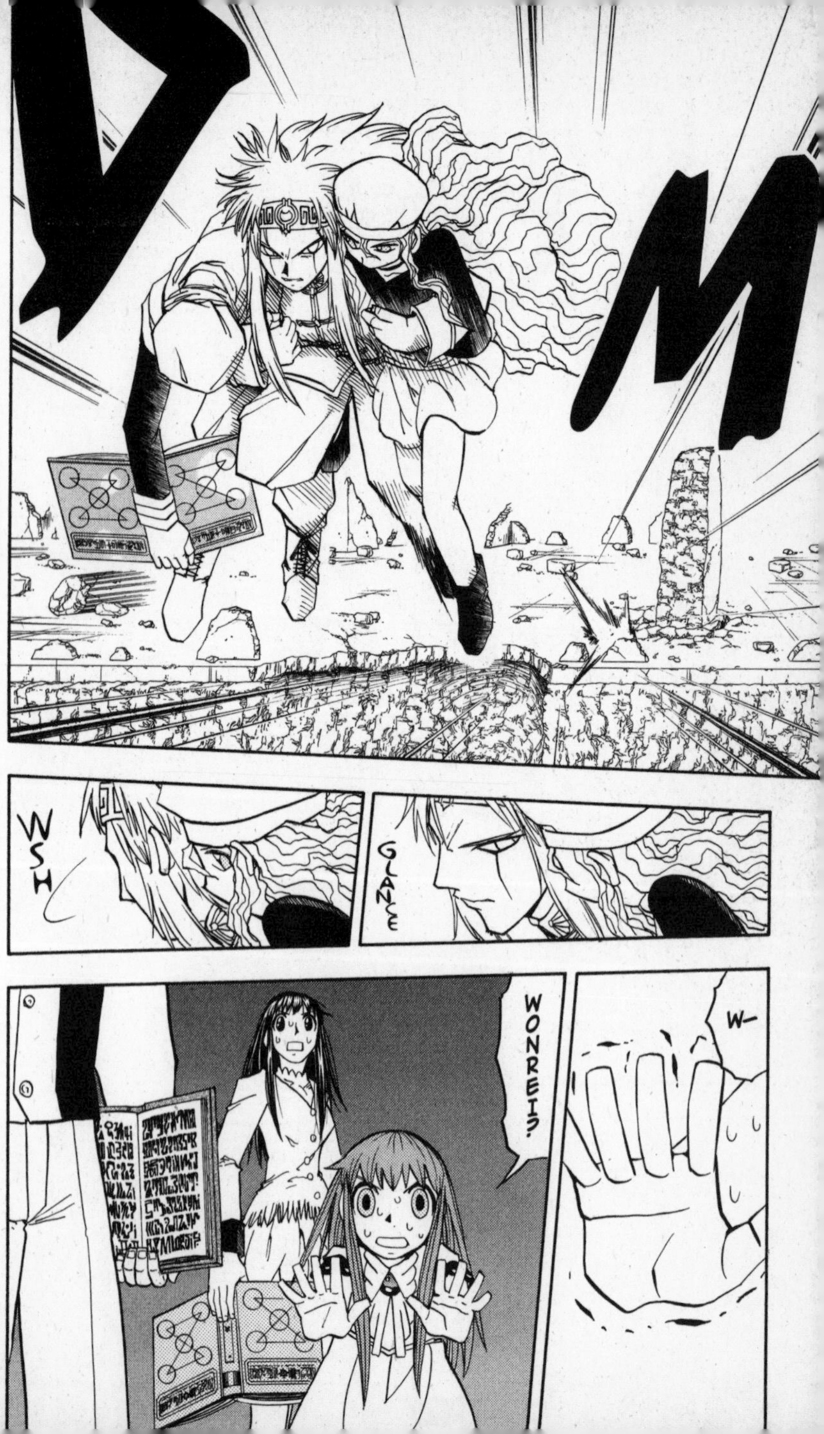
GLANCE
WSH
W-
WONREI?

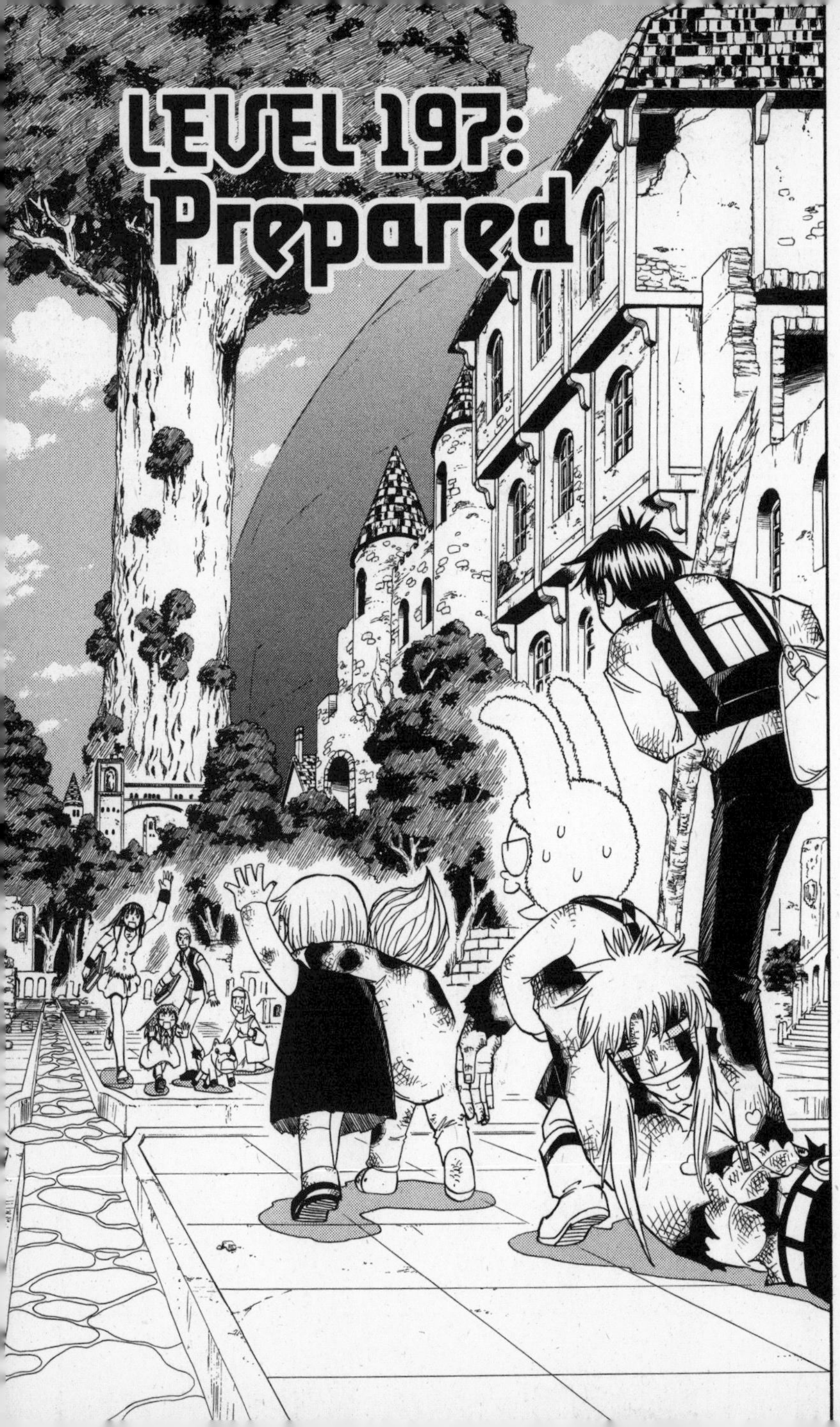
LEVEL 197: Prepared

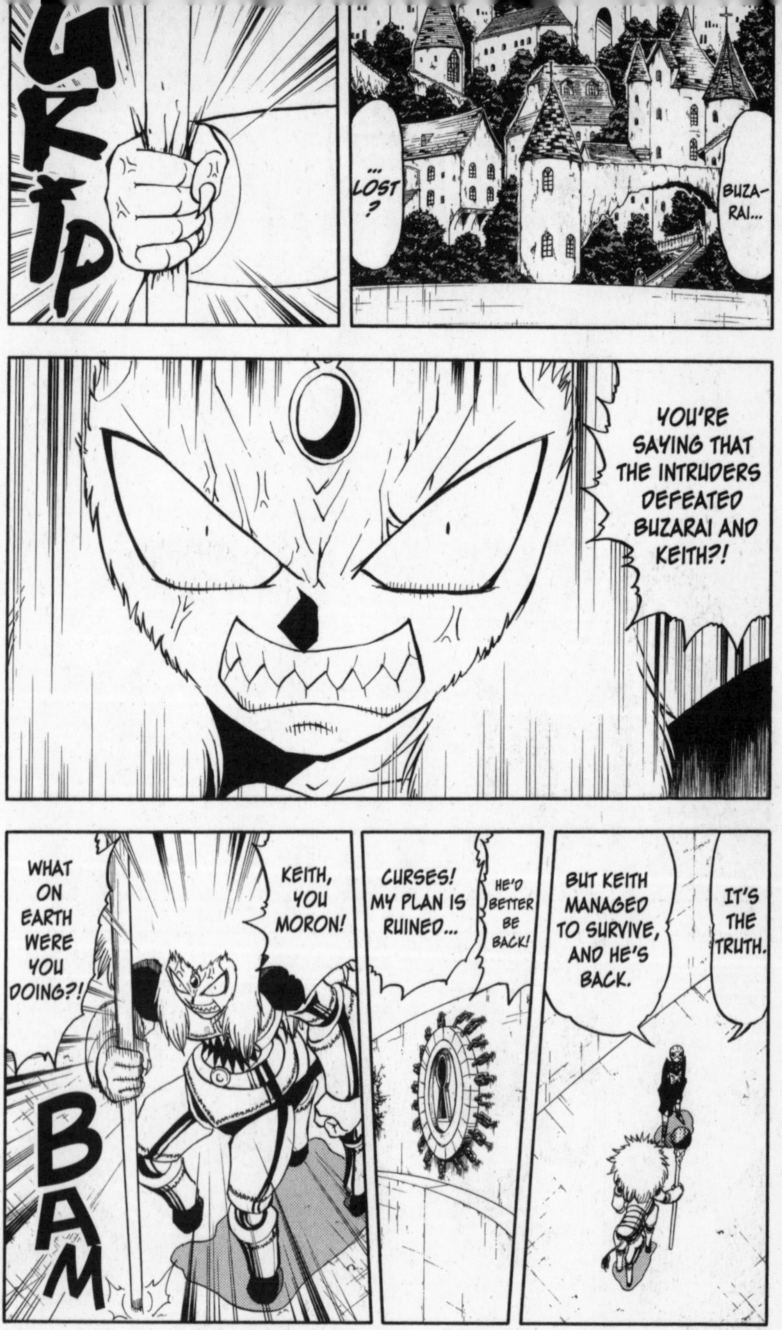
BUZARAI...
...LOST?
GRIP
YOU'RE SAYING THAT THE INTRUDERS DEFEATED BUZARAI AND KEITH?!
IT'S THE TRUTH.
BUT KEITH MANAGED TO SURVIVE, AND HE'S BACK.
HE'D BETTER BE BACK!
CURSES! MY PLAN IS RUINED...
KEITH, YOU MORON!
WHAT ON EARTH WERE YOU DOING?!
BAM

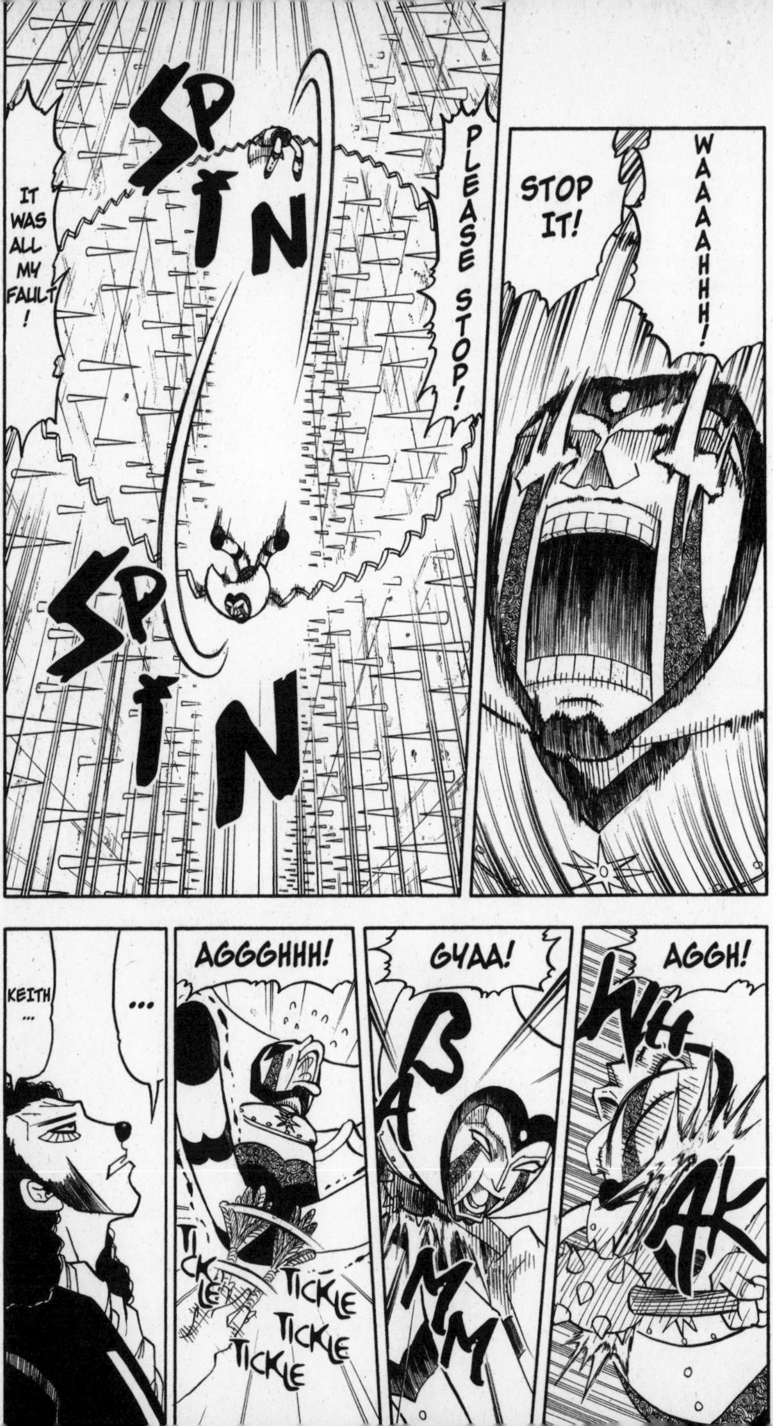
WAAAAAHHH!
STOP IT!
PLEASE STOP!
SPIN
IT WAS ALL MY FAULT!
SPIN
AGGH!
WHAK
GYAA!
BAMM
AGGGHHH!
TICKLE
TICKLE
TICKLE
TICKLE
...
KEITH ...

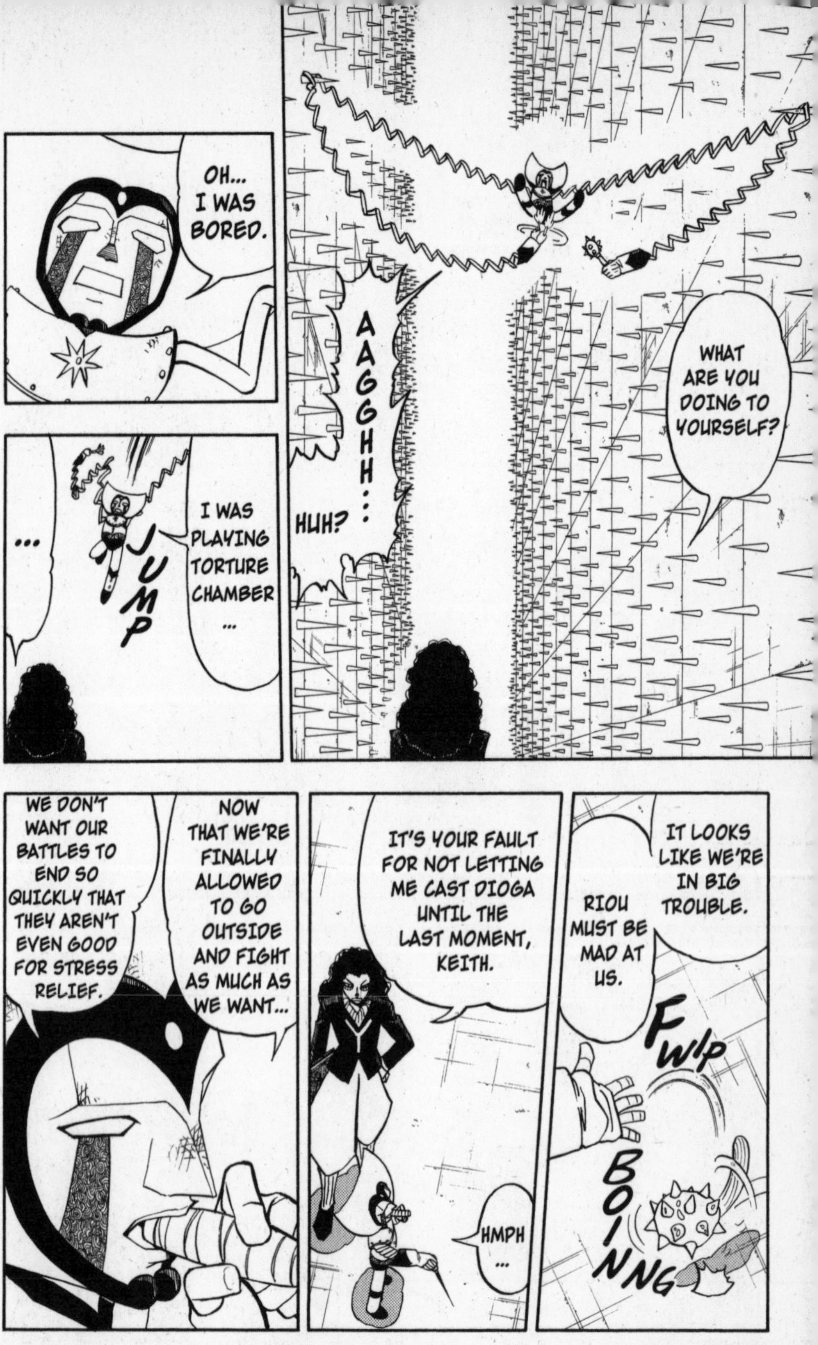
WHAT ARE YOU DOING TO YOURSELF?
AAGGHH...
HUH?
OH... I WAS BORED.
I WAS PLAYING TORTURE CHAMBER...
JUMP
...
IT LOOKS LIKE WE'RE IN BIG TROUBLE.
RIOU MUST BE MAD AT US.
FWIP
BOINNG
IT'S YOUR FAULT FOR NOT LETTING ME CAST DIOGA UNTIL THE LAST MOMENT, KEITH.
HMPH...
NOW THAT WE'RE FINALLY ALLOWED TO GO OUTSIDE AND FIGHT AS MUCH AS WE WANT...
WE DON'T WANT OUR BATTLES TO END SO QUICKLY THAT THEY AREN'T EVEN GOOD FOR STRESS RELIEF.

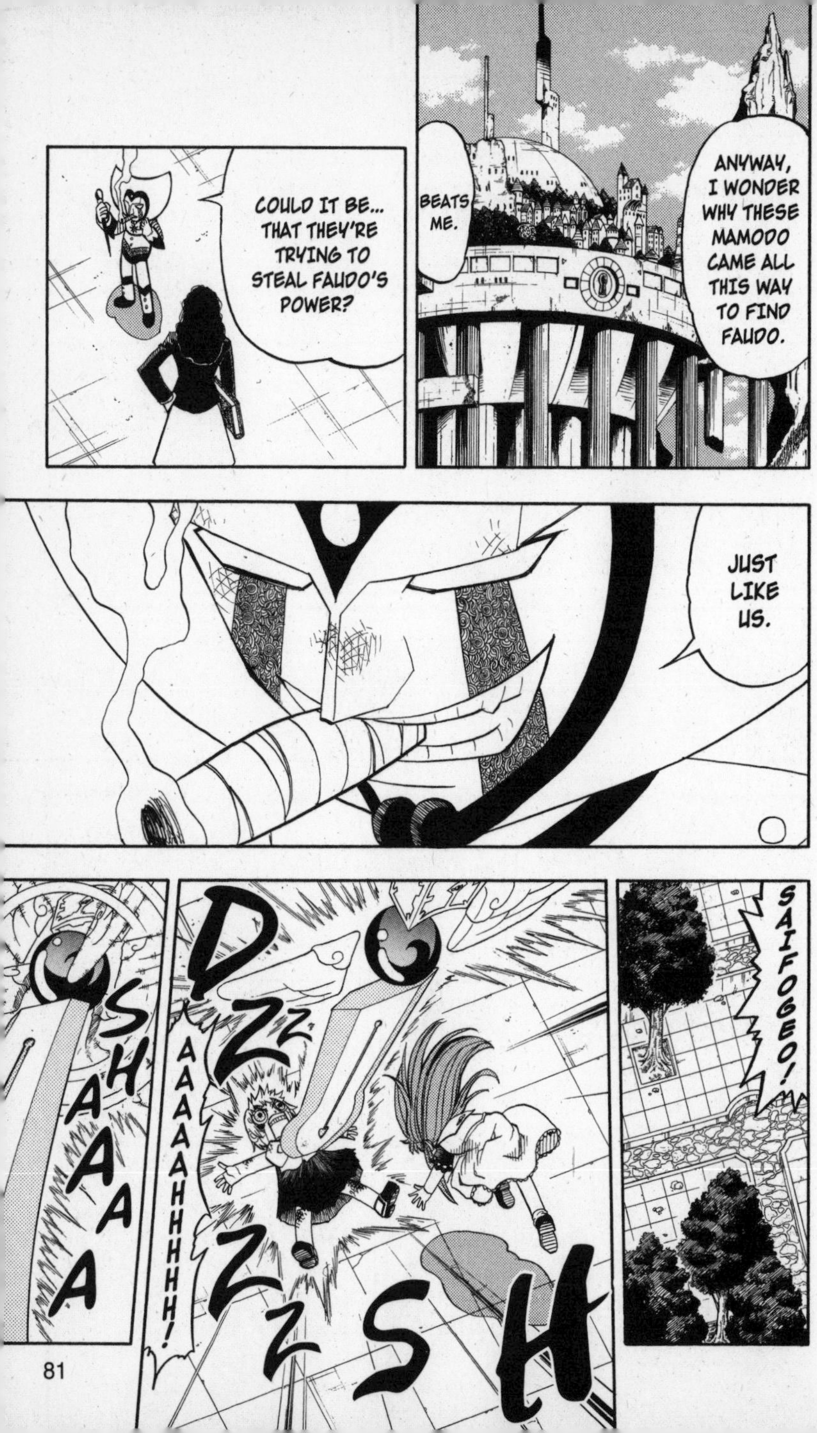
ANYWAY, I WONDER WHY THESE MAMODO CAME ALL THIS WAY TO FIND FAUDO.
BEATS ME.
COULD IT BE... THAT THEY'RE TRYING TO STEAL FAUDO'S POWER?
JUST LIKE US.
SAIFOGEO!
DZZZZSH
AAAAAAHHHHHH!
SHAAAAA

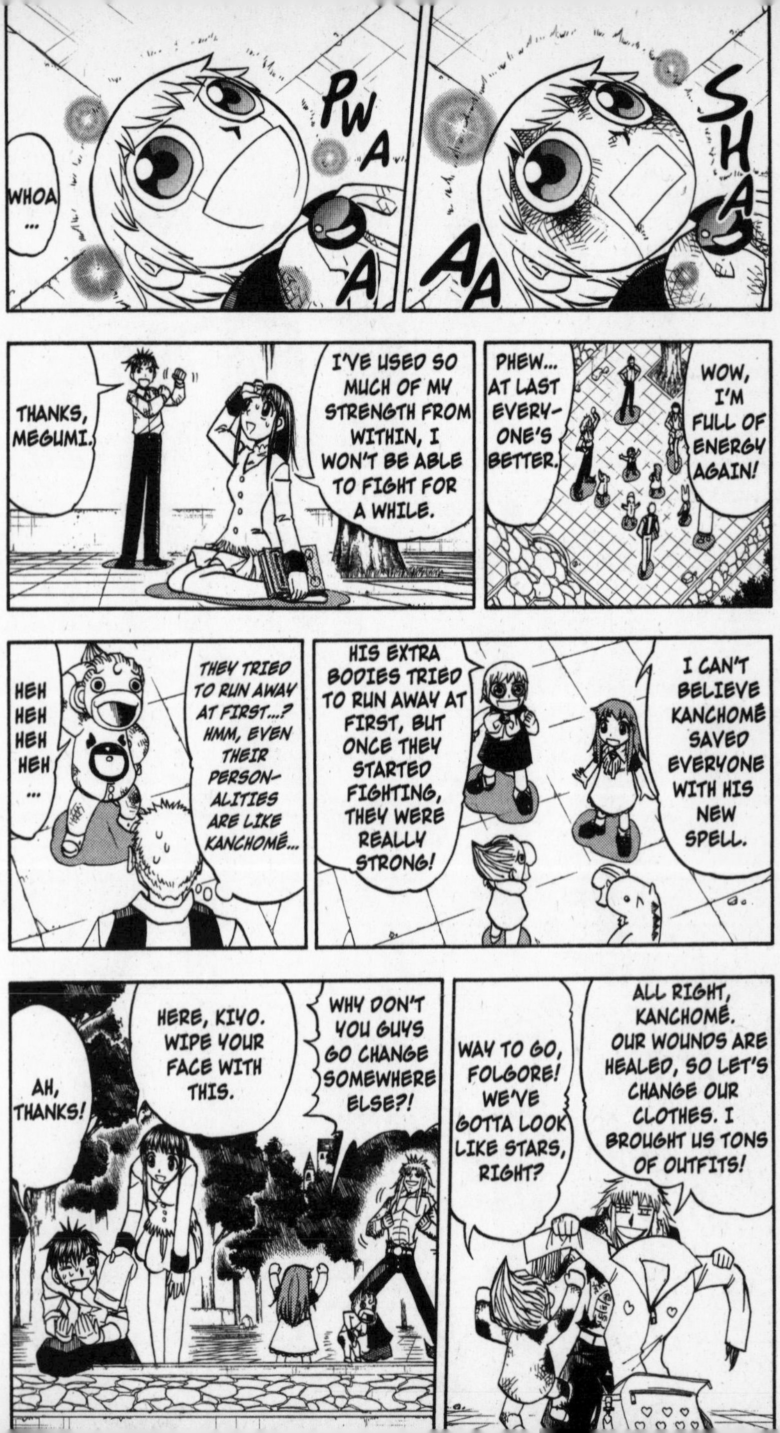
SHA
AA
PWA
A
WHOA ...
WOW, I'M FULL OF ENERGY AGAIN!
PHEW... AT LAST EVERYONE'S BETTER.
I'VE USED SO MUCH OF MY STRENGTH FROM WITHIN, I WON'T BE ABLE TO FIGHT FOR A WHILE.
THANKS, MEGUMI.
I CAN'T BELIEVE KANCHOMÉ SAVED EVERYONE WITH HIS NEW SPELL.
HIS EXTRA BODIES TRIED TO RUN AWAY AT FIRST, BUT ONCE THEY STARTED FIGHTING, THEY WERE REALLY STRONG!
THEY TRIED TO RUN AWAY AT FIRST...? HMM, EVEN THEIR PERSONALITIES ARE LIKE KANCHOMÉ...
HEH HEH HEH HEH ...
ALL RIGHT, KANCHOMÉ. OUR WOUNDS ARE HEALED, SO LET'S CHANGE OUR CLOTHES. I BROUGHT US TONS OF OUTFITS!
WAY TO GO, FOLGORE! WE'VE GOTTA LOOK LIKE STARS, RIGHT?
WHY DON'T YOU GUYS GO CHANGE SOMEWHERE ELSE?!
HERE, KIYO. WIPE YOUR FACE WITH THIS.
AH, THANKS!

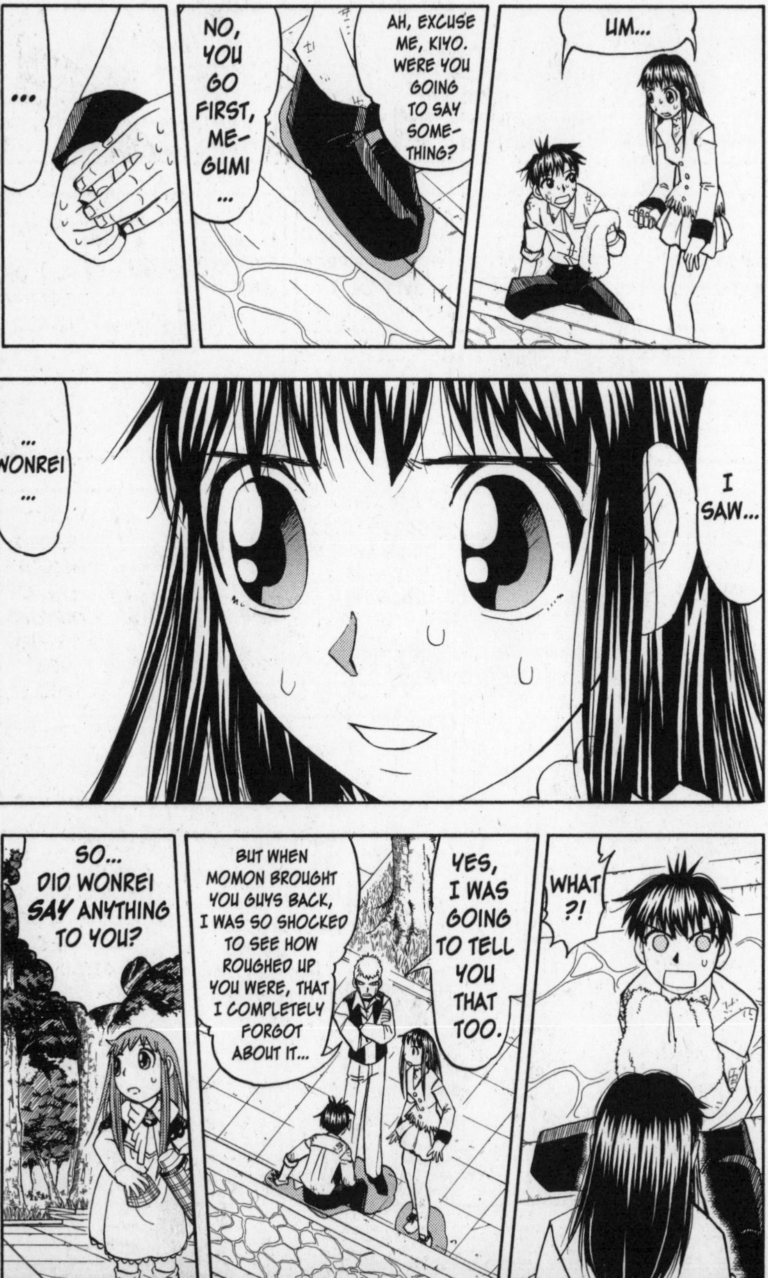

UM...
AH, EXCUSE ME, KIYO. WERE YOU GOING TO SAY SOME-THING?
NO, YOU GO FIRST, ME-GUMI...
...
I SAW...
...WONREI...
WHAT?!
YES, I WAS GOING TO TELL YOU THAT TOO.
BUT WHEN MOMON BROUGHT YOU GUYS BACK, I WAS SO SHOCKED TO SEE HOW ROUGHED UP YOU WERE, THAT I COMPLETELY FORGOT ABOUT IT...
SO... DID WONREI SAY ANYTHING TO YOU?

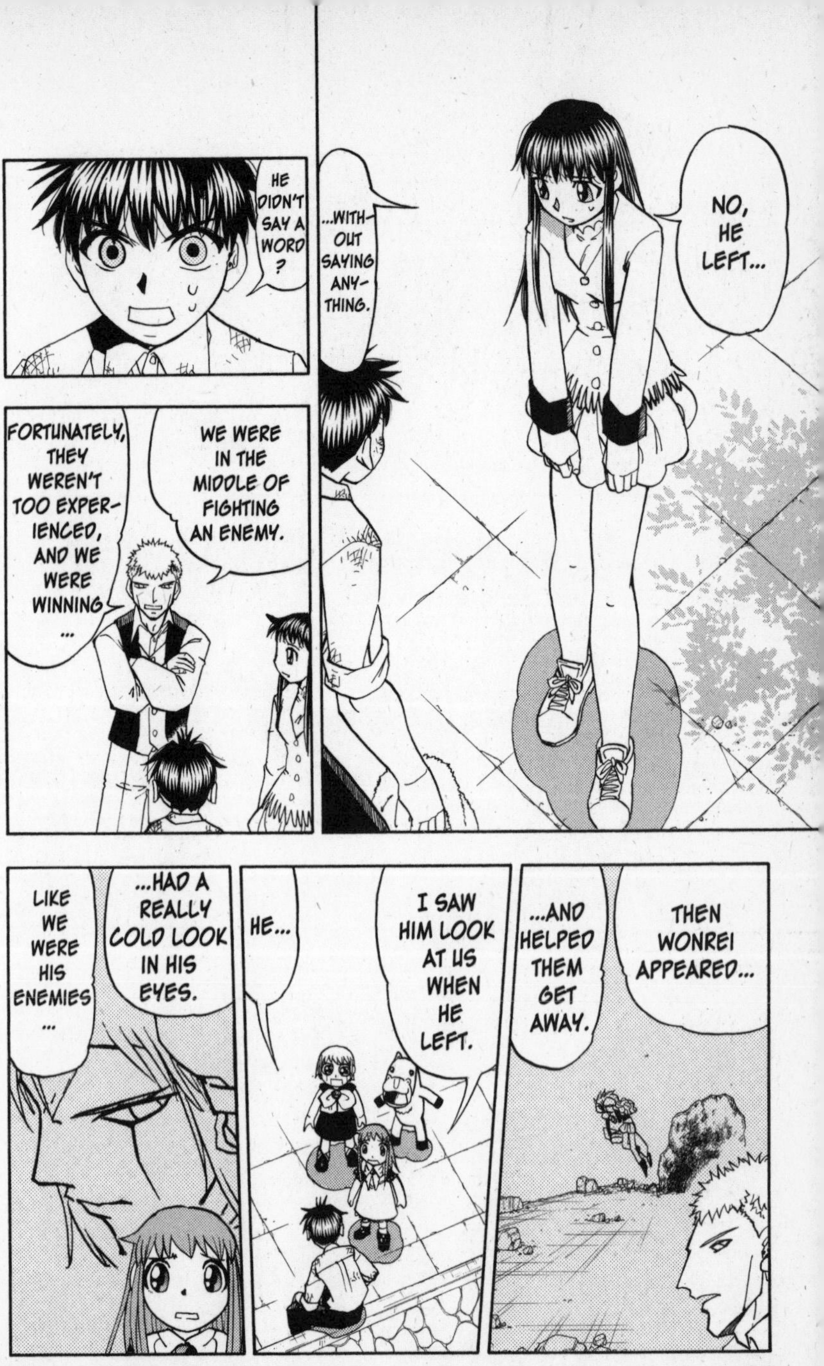
NO, HE LEFT...
...WITHOUT SAYING ANYTHING.
HE DIDN'T SAY A WORD?
WE WERE IN THE MIDDLE OF FIGHTING AN ENEMY.
FORTUNATELY, THEY WEREN'T TOO EXPERIENCED, AND WE WERE WINNING...
THEN WONREI APPEARED...
...AND HELPED THEM GET AWAY.
I SAW HIM LOOK AT US WHEN HE LEFT.
HE...
...HAD A REALLY COLD LOOK IN HIS EYES.
LIKE WE WERE HIS ENEMIES...

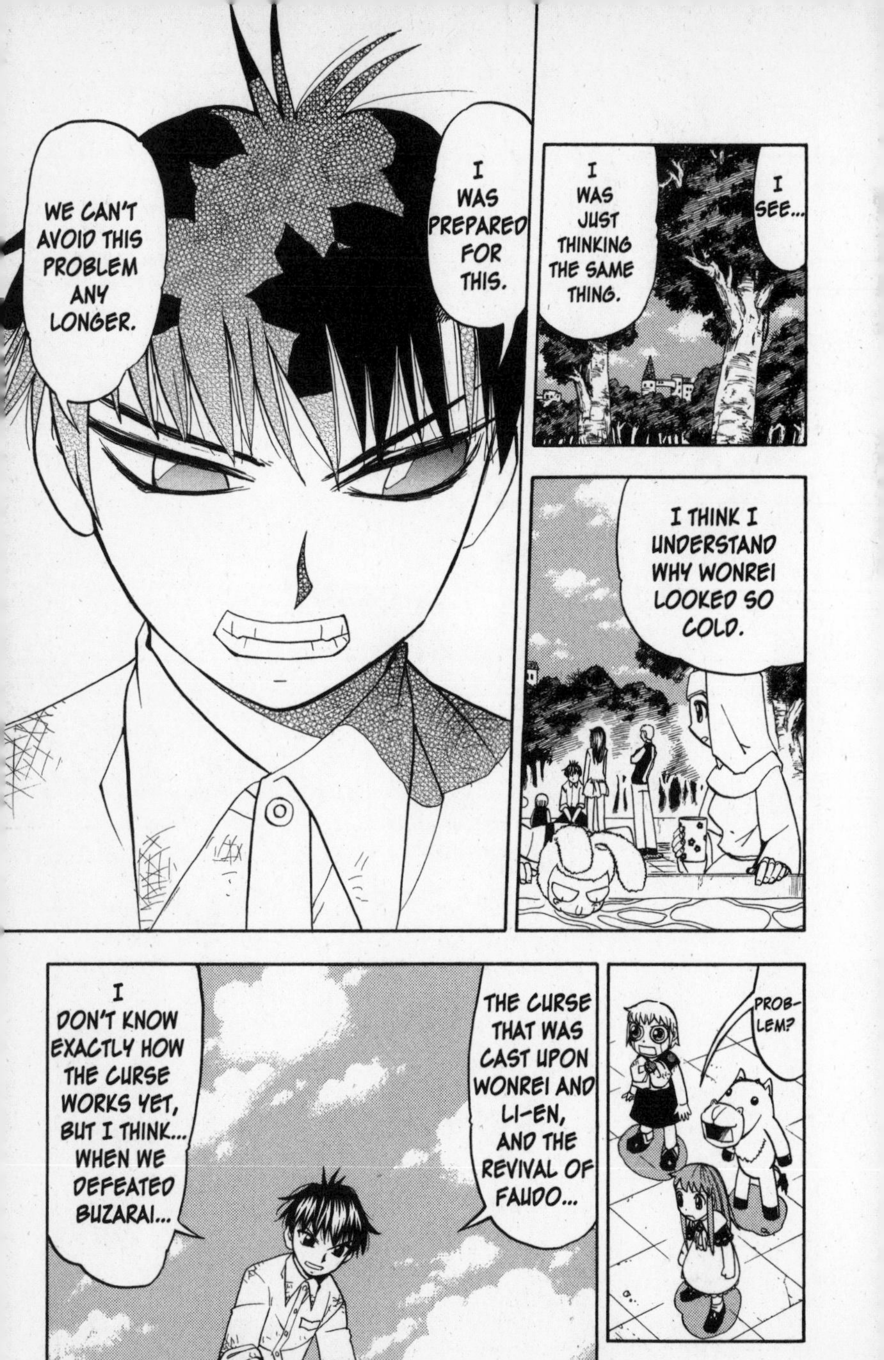
I SEE...
I WAS JUST THINKING THE SAME THING.
I THINK I UNDERSTAND WHY WONREI LOOKED SO COLD.
I WAS PREPARED FOR THIS.
WE CAN'T AVOID THIS PROBLEM ANY LONGER.
PROB-LEM?
THE CURSE THAT WAS CAST UPON WONREI AND LI-EN, AND THE REVIVAL OF FAUDO...
I DON'T KNOW EXACTLY HOW THE CURSE WORKS YET, BUT I THINK... WHEN WE DEFEATED BUZARAI...

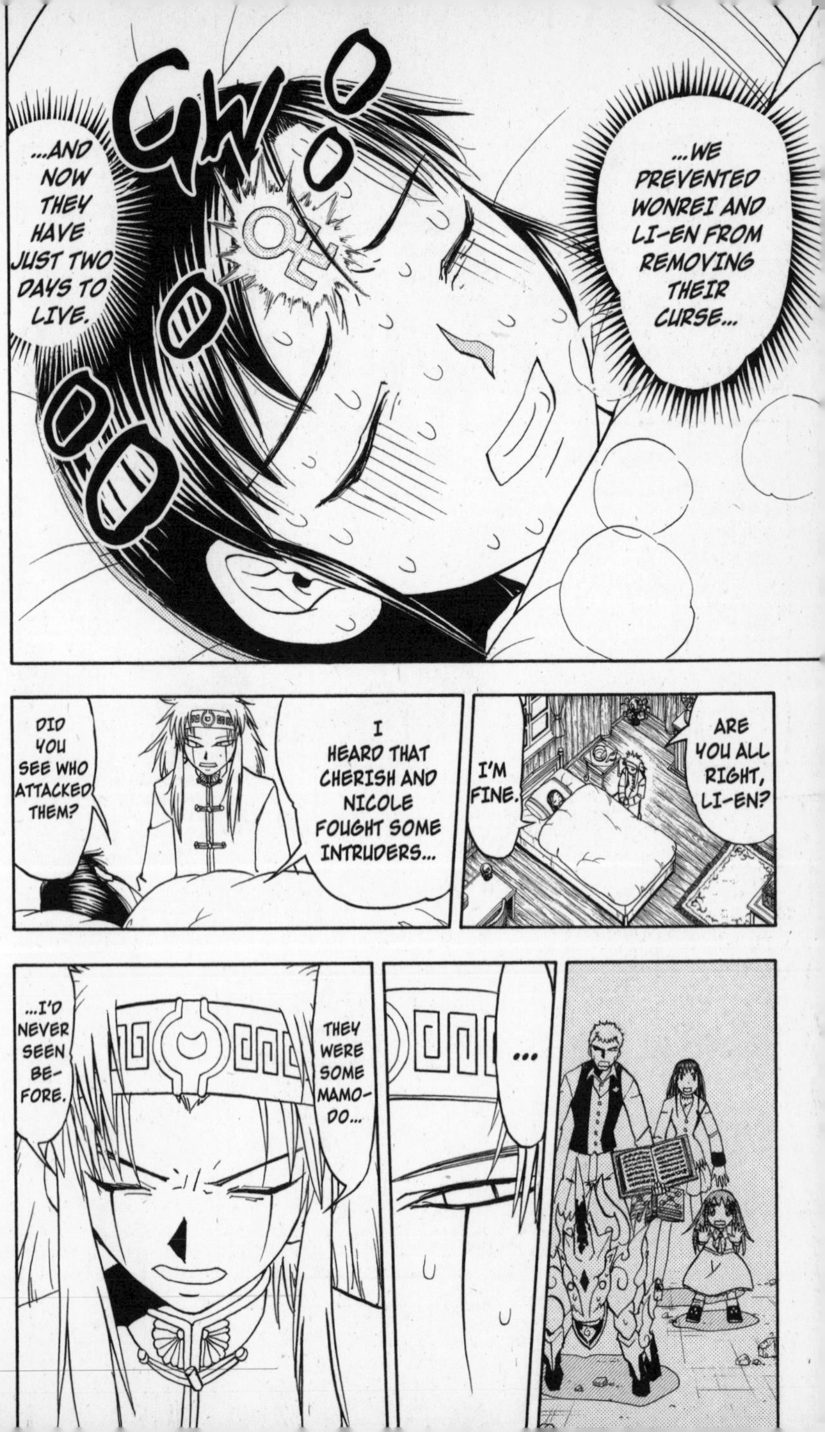
...WE PREVENTED WONREI AND LI-EN FROM REMOVING THEIR CURSE...
GWOOOOOO
...AND NOW THEY HAVE JUST TWO DAYS TO LIVE.
ARE YOU ALL RIGHT, LI-EN?
I'M FINE.
I HEARD THAT CHERISH AND NICOLE FOUGHT SOME INTRUDERS...
DID YOU SEE WHO ATTACKED THEM?
...
THEY WERE SOME MAMO-DO...
...I'D NEVER SEEN BE-FORE.

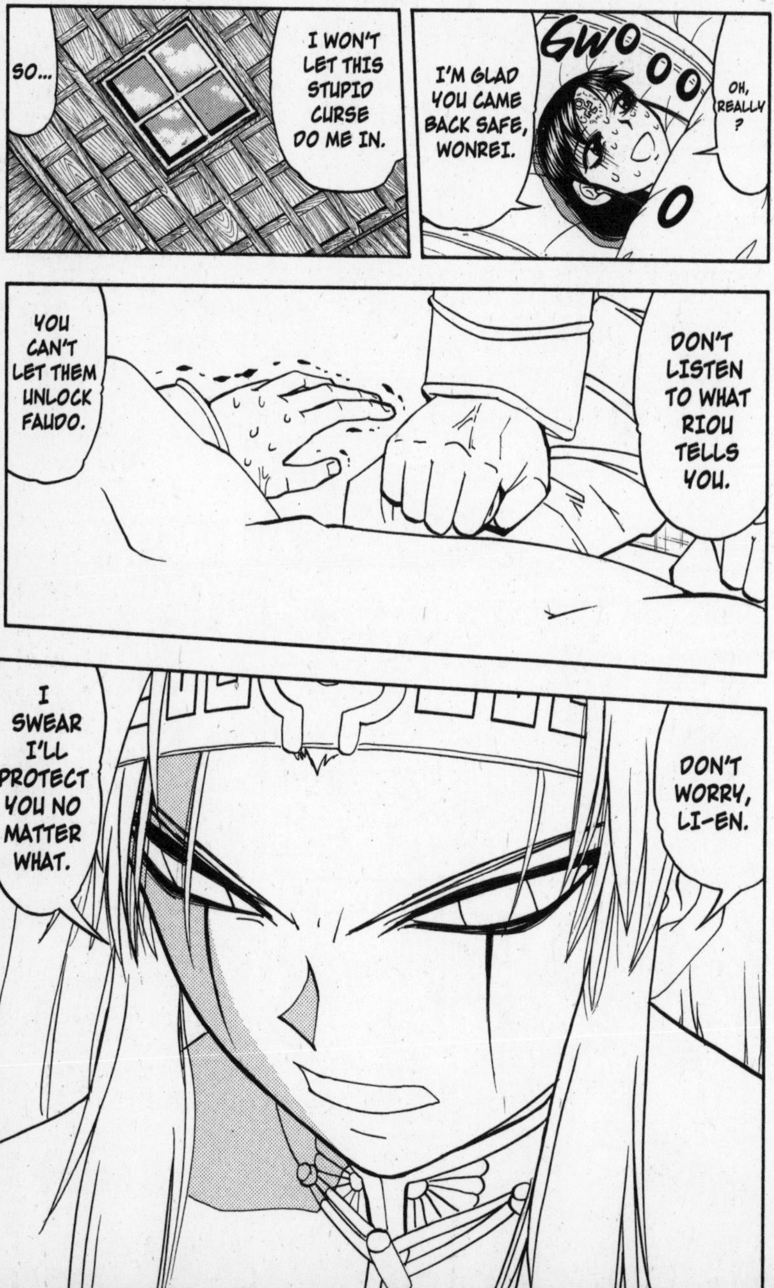
OH, REALLY?
GWOOOOO
I'M GLAD YOU CAME BACK SAFE, WONREI.
I WON'T LET THIS STUPID CURSE DO ME IN.
SO...
DON'T LISTEN TO WHAT RIOU TELLS YOU.
YOU CAN'T LET THEM UNLOCK FAUDO.
DON'T WORRY, LI-EN.
I SWEAR I'LL PROTECT YOU NO MATTER WHAT.

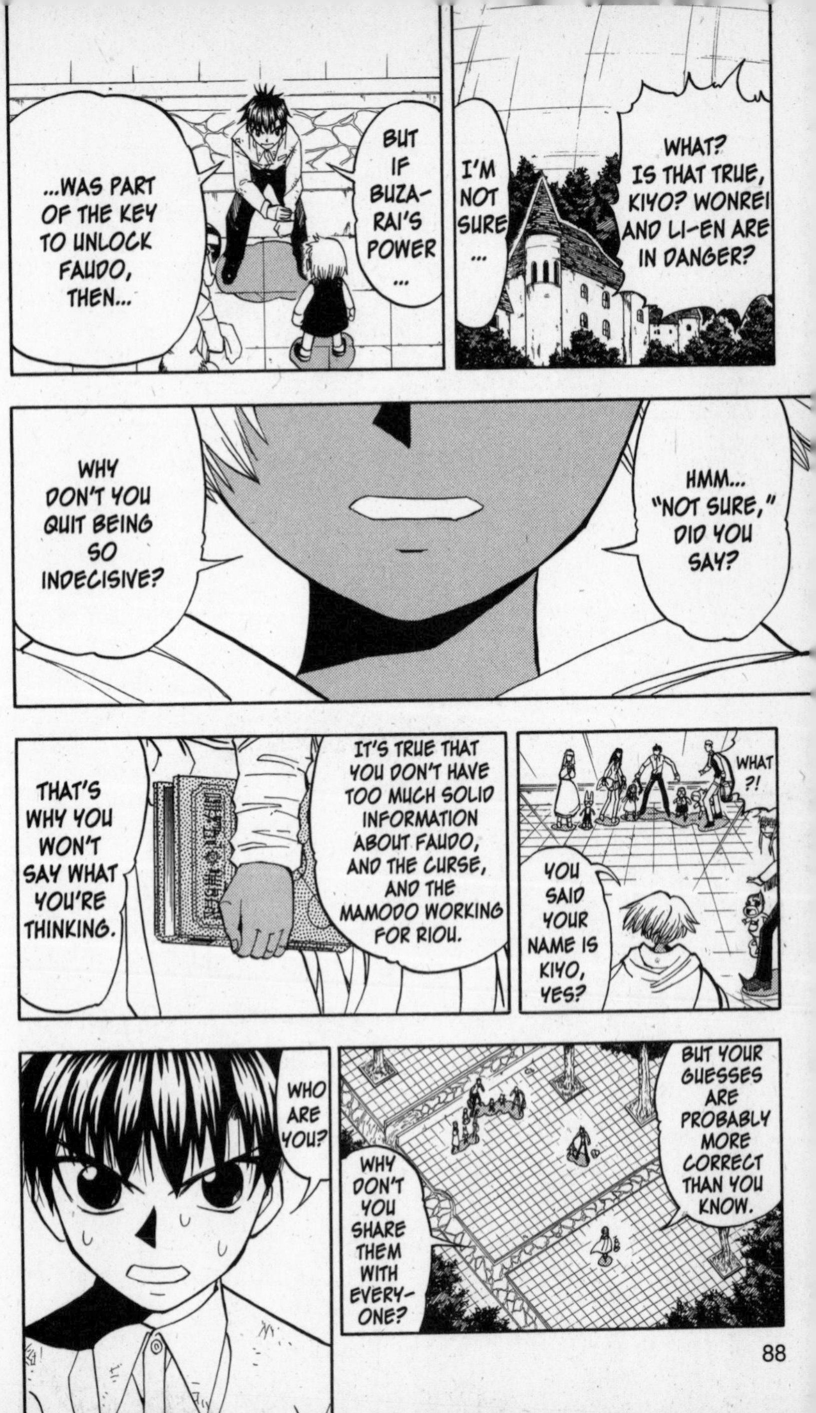
WHAT? IS THAT TRUE, KIYO? WONREI AND LI-EN ARE IN DANGER?
I'M NOT SURE ...
BUT IF BUZARAI'S POWER ...
...WAS PART OF THE KEY TO UNLOCK FAUDO, THEN...
HMM... "NOT SURE," DID YOU SAY?
WHY DON'T YOU QUIT BEING SO INDECISIVE?
WHAT?!
YOU SAID YOUR NAME IS KIYO, YES?
IT'S TRUE THAT YOU DON'T HAVE TOO MUCH SOLID INFORMATION ABOUT FAUDO, AND THE CURSE, AND THE MAMODO WORKING FOR RIOU.
THAT'S WHY YOU WON'T SAY WHAT YOU'RE THINKING.
BUT YOUR GUESSES ARE PROBABLY MORE CORRECT THAN YOU KNOW.
WHY DON'T YOU SHARE THEM WITH EVERY-ONE?
WHO ARE YOU?

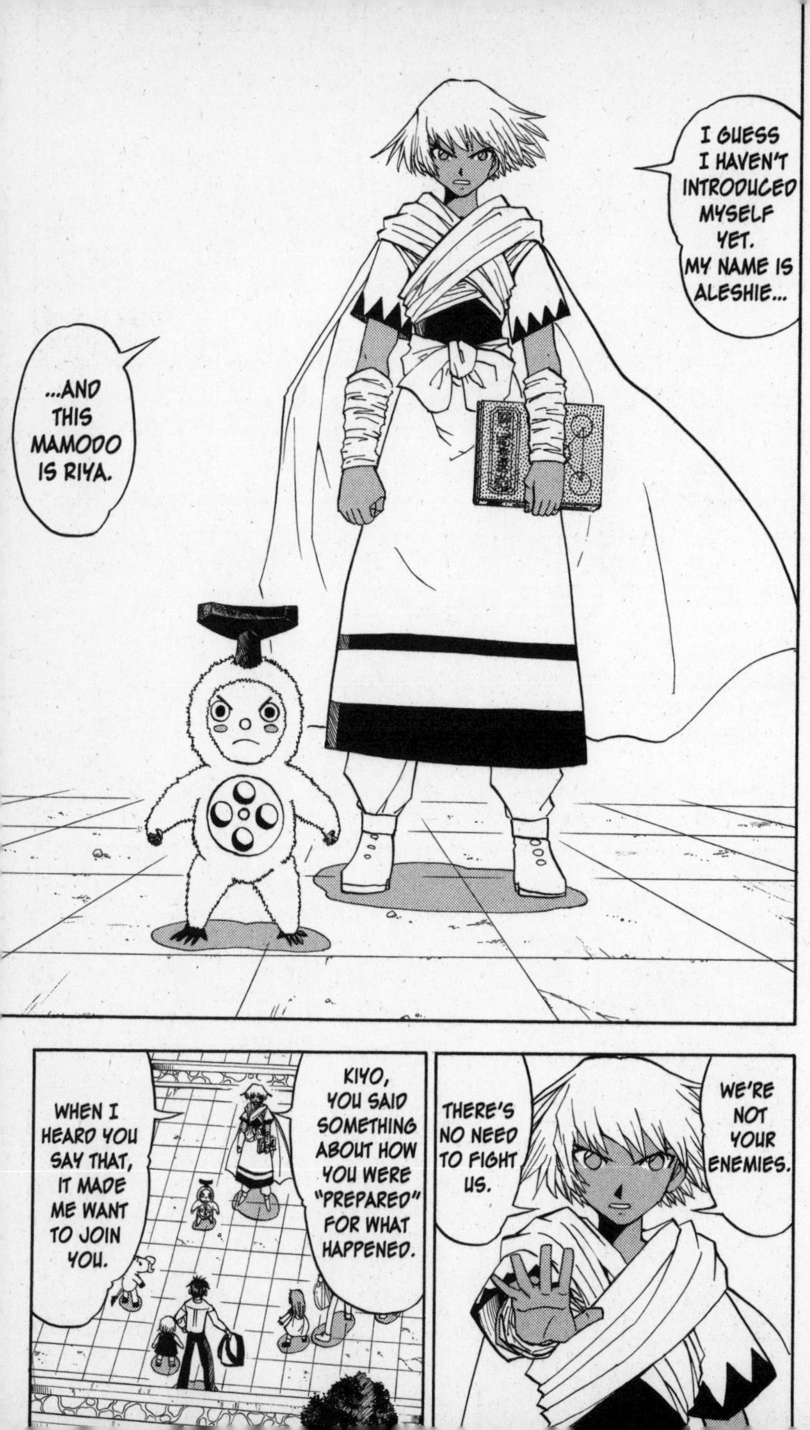
I GUESS I HAVEN'T INTRODUCED MYSELF YET. MY NAME IS ALESHIE...
...AND THIS MAMODO IS RIYA.
WE'RE NOT YOUR ENEMIES.
THERE'S NO NEED TO FIGHT US.
KIYO, YOU SAID SOMETHING ABOUT HOW YOU WERE "PREPARED" FOR WHAT HAPPENED.
WHEN I HEARD YOU SAY THAT, IT MADE ME WANT TO JOIN YOU.

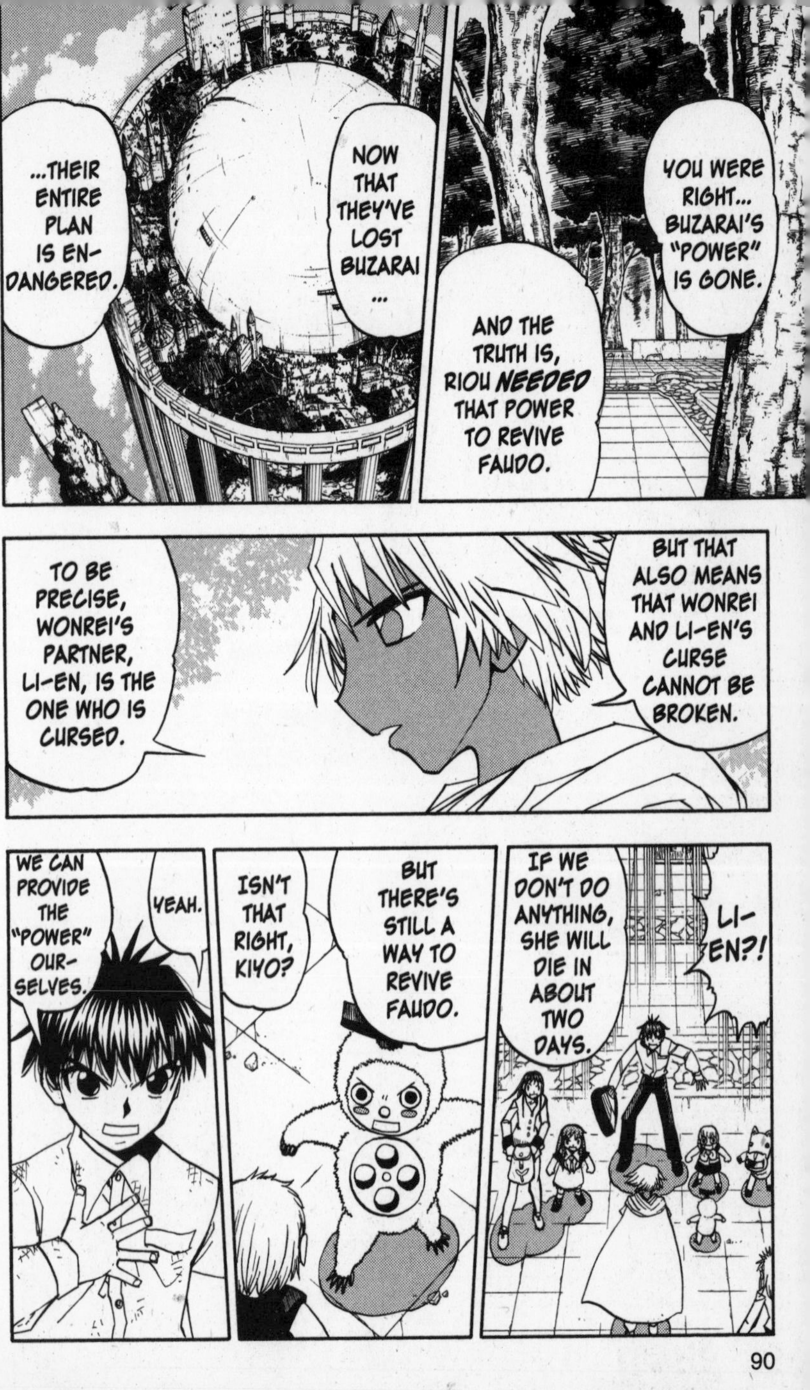
YOU WERE RIGHT... BUZARAI'S "POWER" IS GONE.
AND THE TRUTH IS, RIOU *NEEDED* THAT POWER TO REVIVE FAUDO.
NOW THAT THEY'VE LOST BUZARAI ...
...THEIR ENTIRE PLAN IS EN-DANGERED.
BUT THAT ALSO MEANS THAT WONREI AND LI-EN'S CURSE CANNOT BE BROKEN.
TO BE PRECISE, WONREI'S PARTNER, LI-EN, IS THE ONE WHO IS CURSED.
LI-EN?!
IF WE DON'T DO ANYTHING, SHE WILL DIE IN ABOUT TWO DAYS.
BUT THERE'S STILL A WAY TO REVIVE FAUDO.
ISN'T THAT RIGHT, KIYO?
YEAH.
WE CAN PROVIDE THE "POWER" OUR-SELVES.

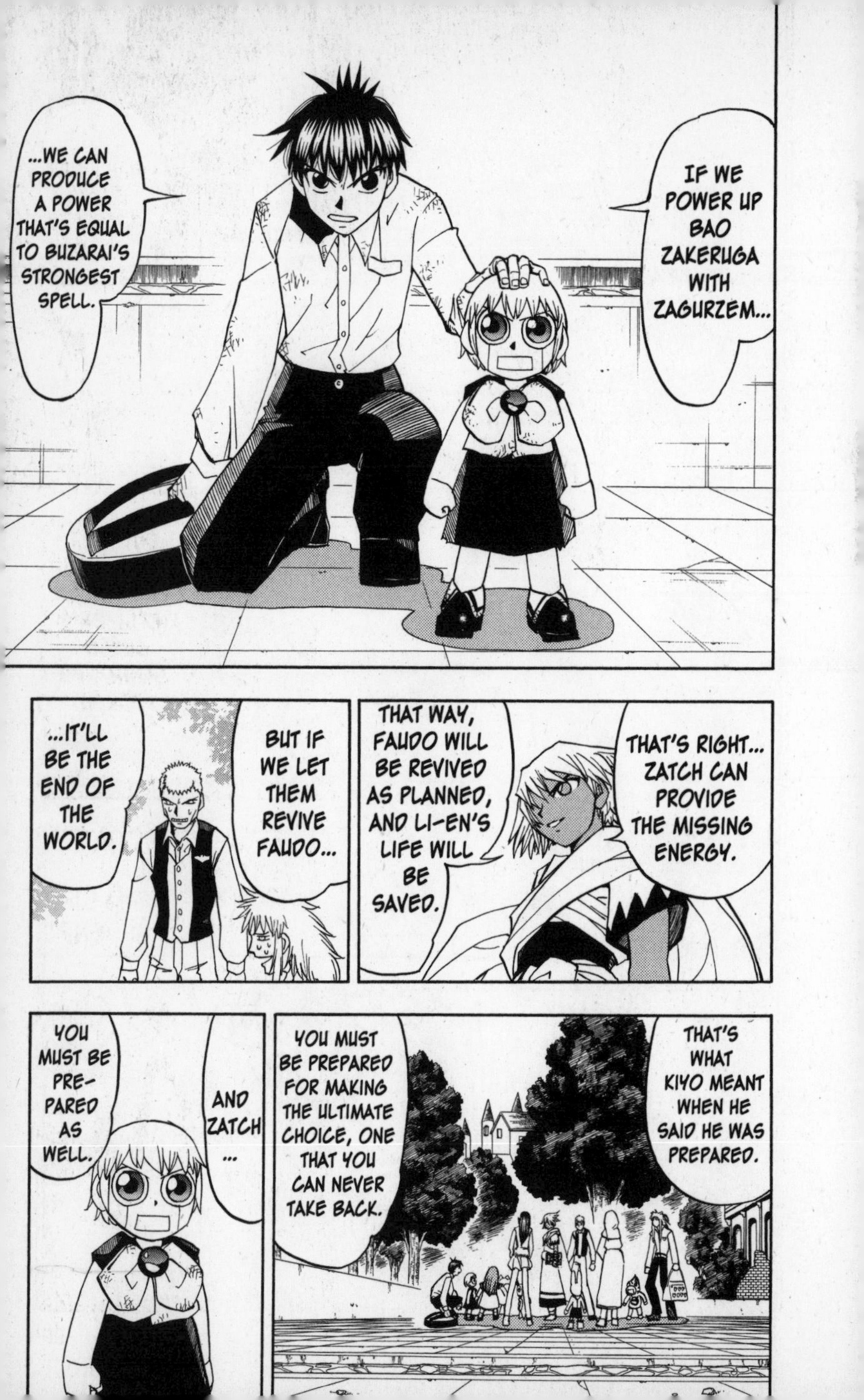
IF WE POWER UP BAO ZAKERUGA WITH ZAGURZEM...
...WE CAN PRODUCE A POWER THAT'S EQUAL TO BUZARAI'S STRONGEST SPELL.
THAT'S RIGHT... ZATCH CAN PROVIDE THE MISSING ENERGY.
THAT WAY, FAUDO WILL BE REVIVED AS PLANNED, AND LI-EN'S LIFE WILL BE SAVED.
BUT IF WE LET THEM REVIVE FAUDO...
...IT'LL BE THE END OF THE WORLD.
THAT'S WHAT KIYO MEANT WHEN HE SAID HE WAS PREPARED.
YOU MUST BE PREPARED FOR MAKING THE ULTIMATE CHOICE, ONE THAT YOU CAN NEVER TAKE BACK.
AND ZATCH ...
YOU MUST BE PRE-PARED AS WELL.

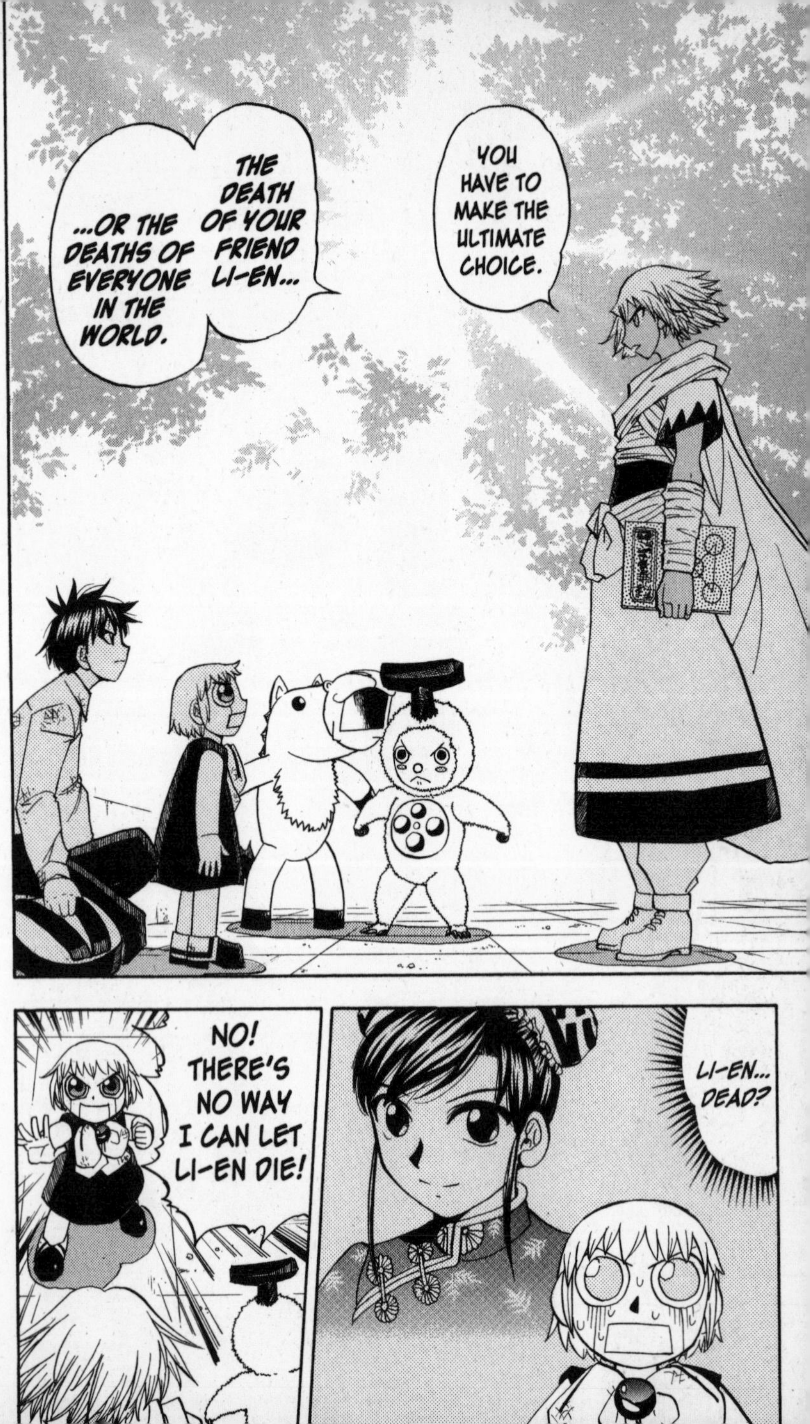
YOU HAVE TO MAKE THE ULTIMATE CHOICE.
THE DEATH OF YOUR FRIEND LI-EN...
...OR THE DEATHS OF EVERYONE IN THE WORLD.
LI-EN... DEAD?
NO! THERE'S NO WAY I CAN LET LI-EN DIE!

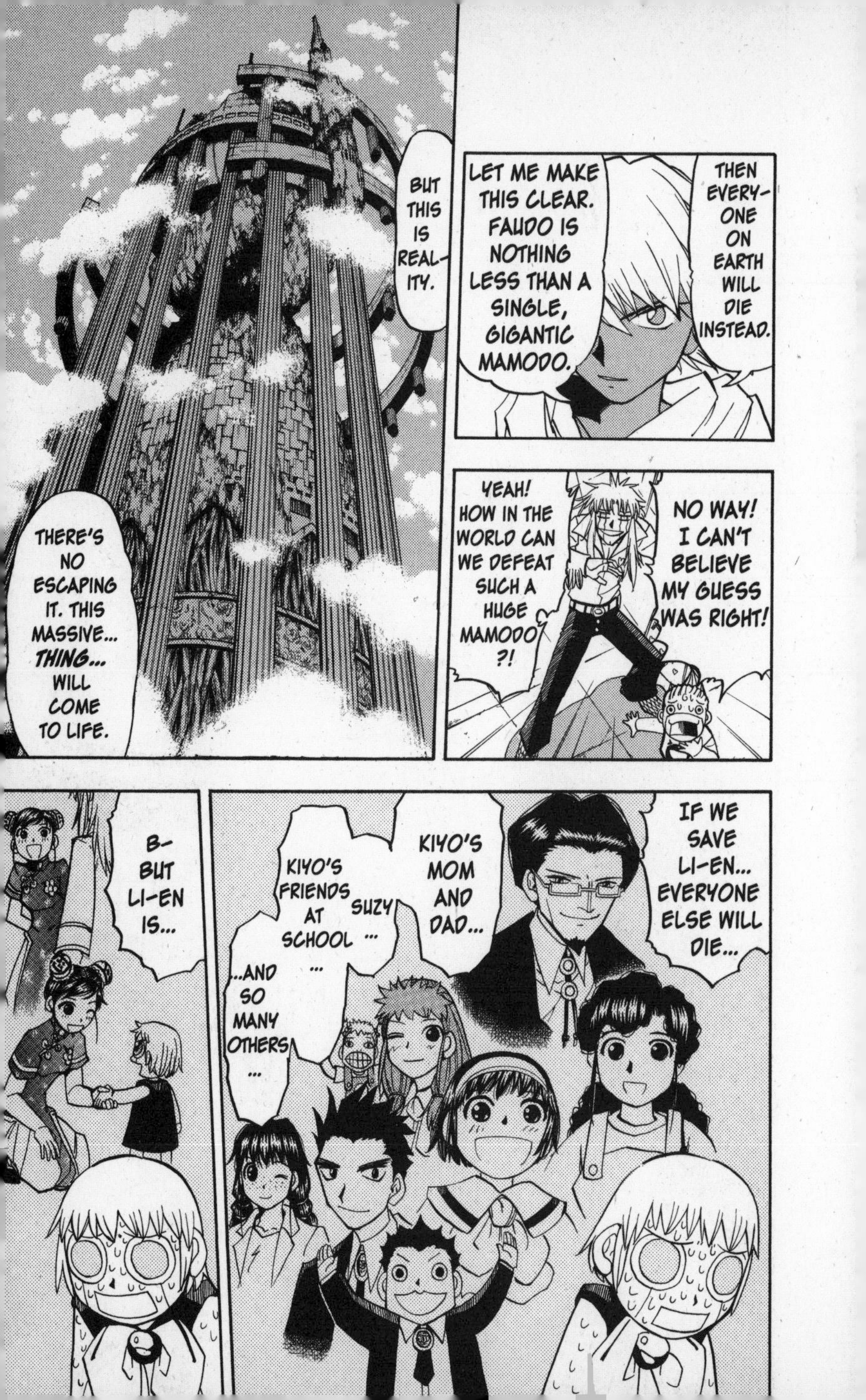
THEN EVERY-ONE ON EARTH WILL DIE INSTEAD.
LET ME MAKE THIS CLEAR. FAUDO IS NOTHING LESS THAN A SINGLE, GIGANTIC MAMODO.
NO WAY! I CAN'T BELIEVE MY GUESS WAS RIGHT!
YEAH! HOW IN THE WORLD CAN WE DEFEAT SUCH A HUGE MAMODO ?!
BUT THIS IS REAL-ITY.
THERE'S NO ESCAPING IT. THIS MASSIVE... *THING...* WILL COME TO LIFE.
IF WE SAVE LI-EN... EVERYONE ELSE WILL DIE...
KIYO'S MOM AND DAD...
SUZY ...
KIYO'S FRIENDS AT SCHOOL ...
...AND SO MANY OTHERS ...
B-BUT LI-EN IS...

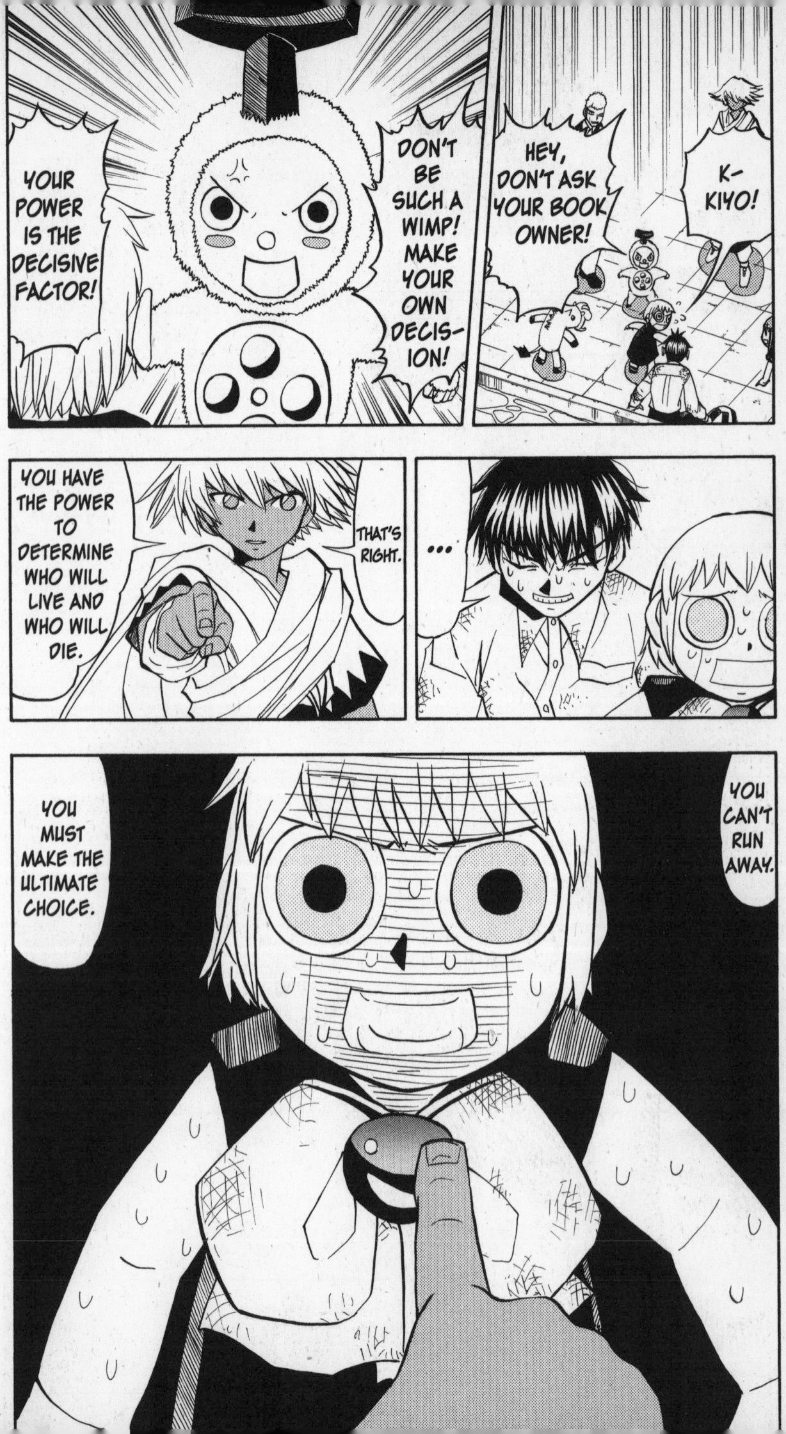
K-KIYO!
HEY, DON'T ASK YOUR BOOK OWNER!
DON'T BE SUCH A WIMP! MAKE YOUR OWN DECISION!
YOUR POWER IS THE DECISIVE FACTOR!
...
THAT'S RIGHT.
YOU HAVE THE POWER TO DETERMINE WHO WILL LIVE AND WHO WILL DIE.
YOU CAN'T RUN AWAY.
YOU MUST MAKE THE ULTIMATE CHOICE.

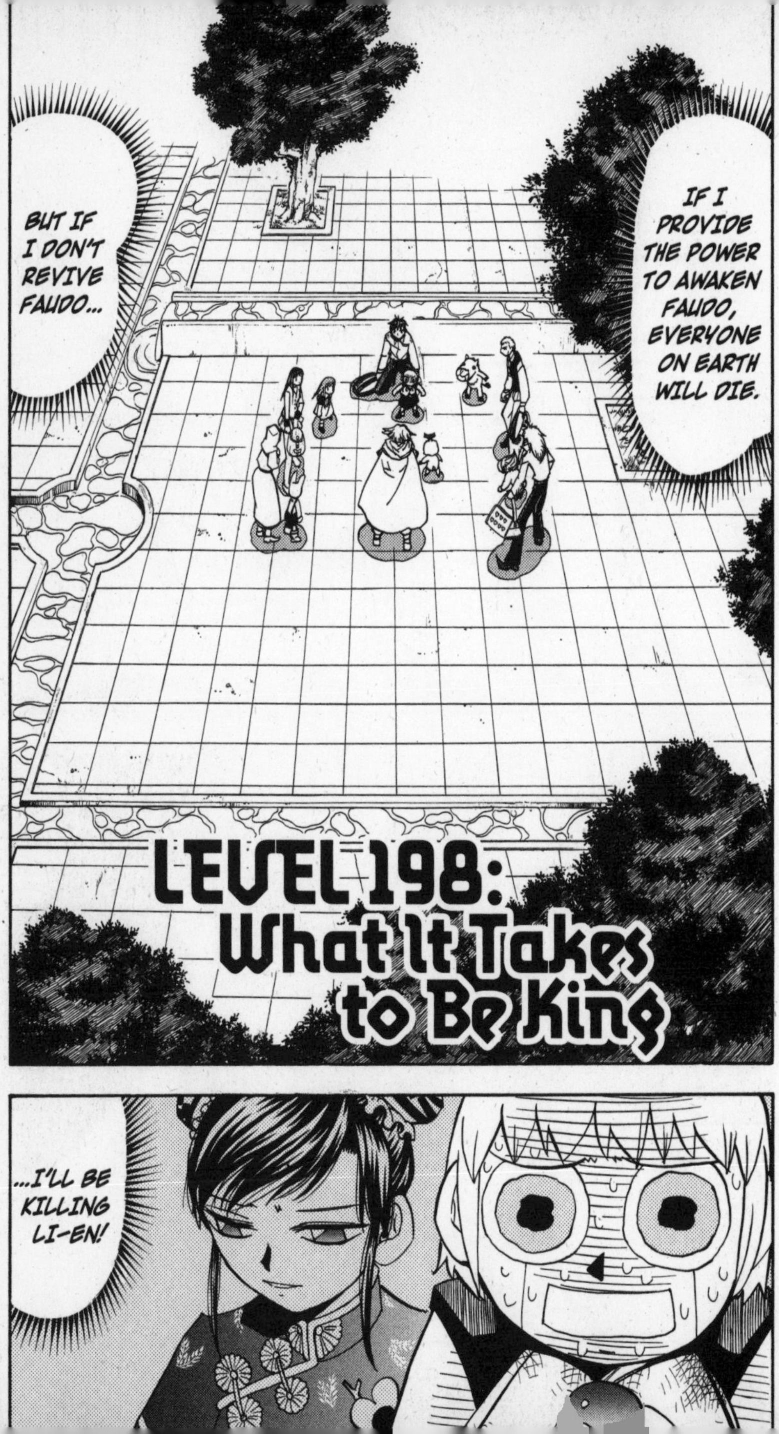
IF I PROVIDE THE POWER TO AWAKEN FAUDO, EVERYONE ON EARTH WILL DIE.
BUT IF I DON'T REVIVE FAUDO...
LEVEL 198: What It Takes to Be King
...I'LL BE KILLING LI-EN!

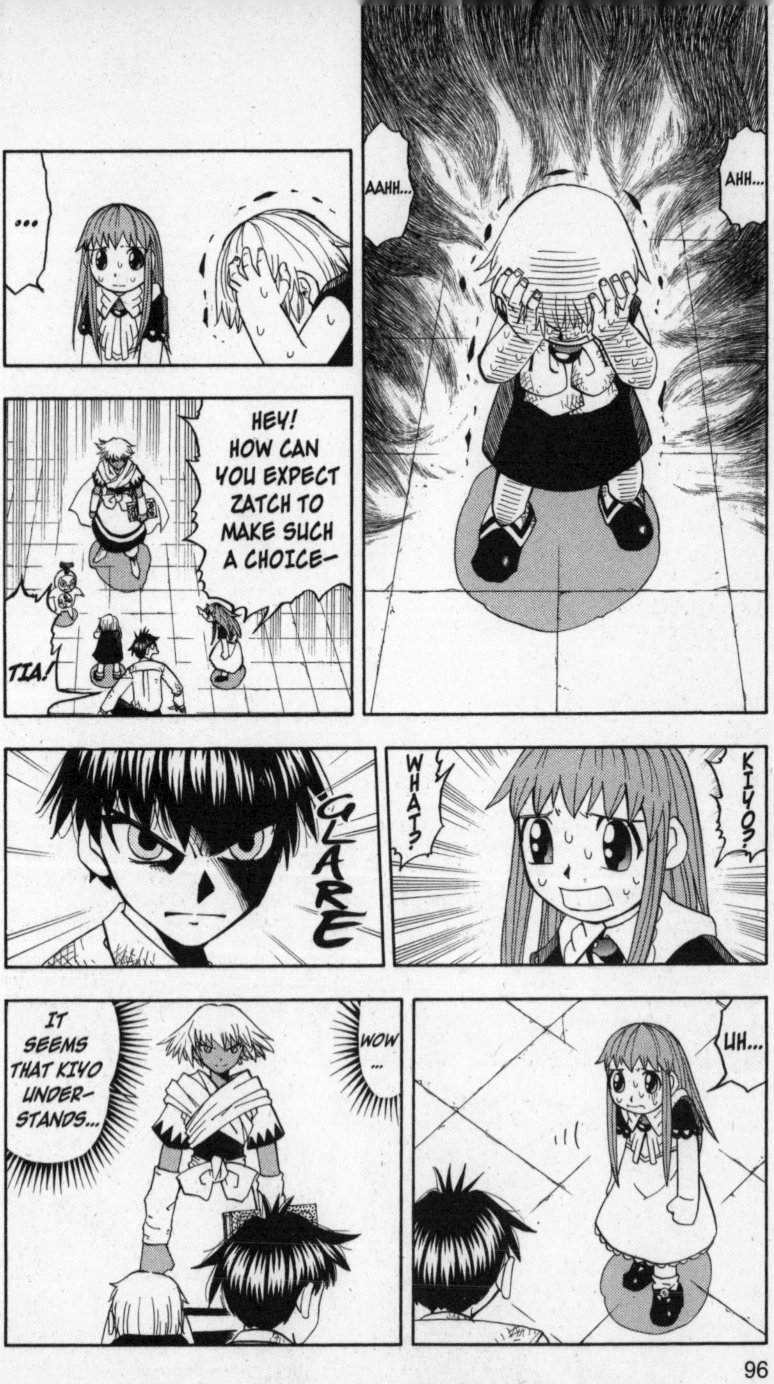
AHH...
AAHH...
...
HEY! HOW CAN YOU EXPECT ZATCH TO MAKE SUCH A CHOICE—
TIA!
KIYO?!
WHAT?
GLARE
UH...
WOW ...
IT SEEMS THAT KIYO UNDER-STANDS...

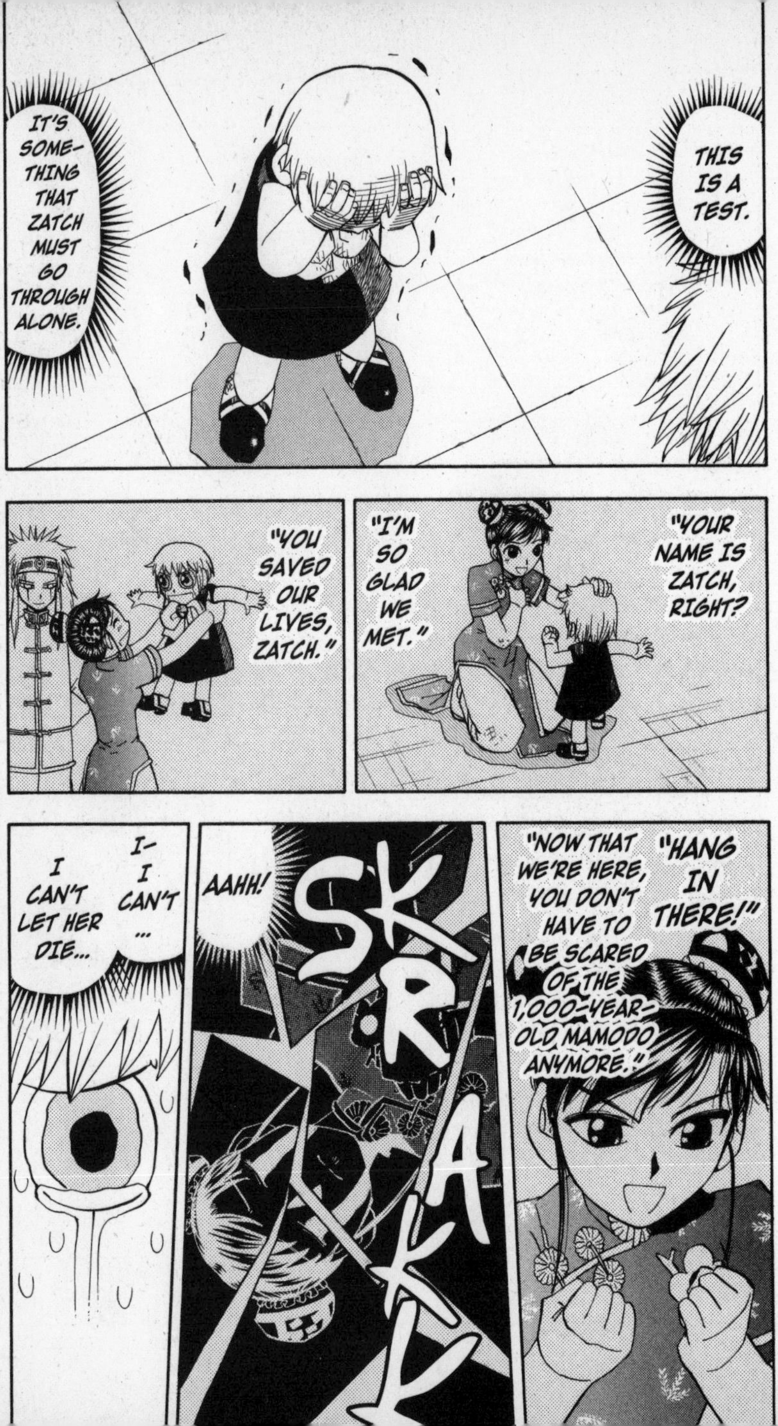
THIS IS A TEST.
IT'S SOMETHING THAT ZATCH MUST GO THROUGH ALONE.
"YOUR NAME IS ZATCH, RIGHT?
"I'M SO GLAD WE MET."
"YOU SAVED OUR LIVES, ZATCH."
"HANG IN THERE!"
"NOW THAT WE'RE HERE, YOU DON'T HAVE TO BE SCARED OF THE 1,000-YEAR-OLD MAMODO ANYMORE."
AAHH!
SKRAKK
I- I CAN'T ...
I CAN'T LET HER DIE...

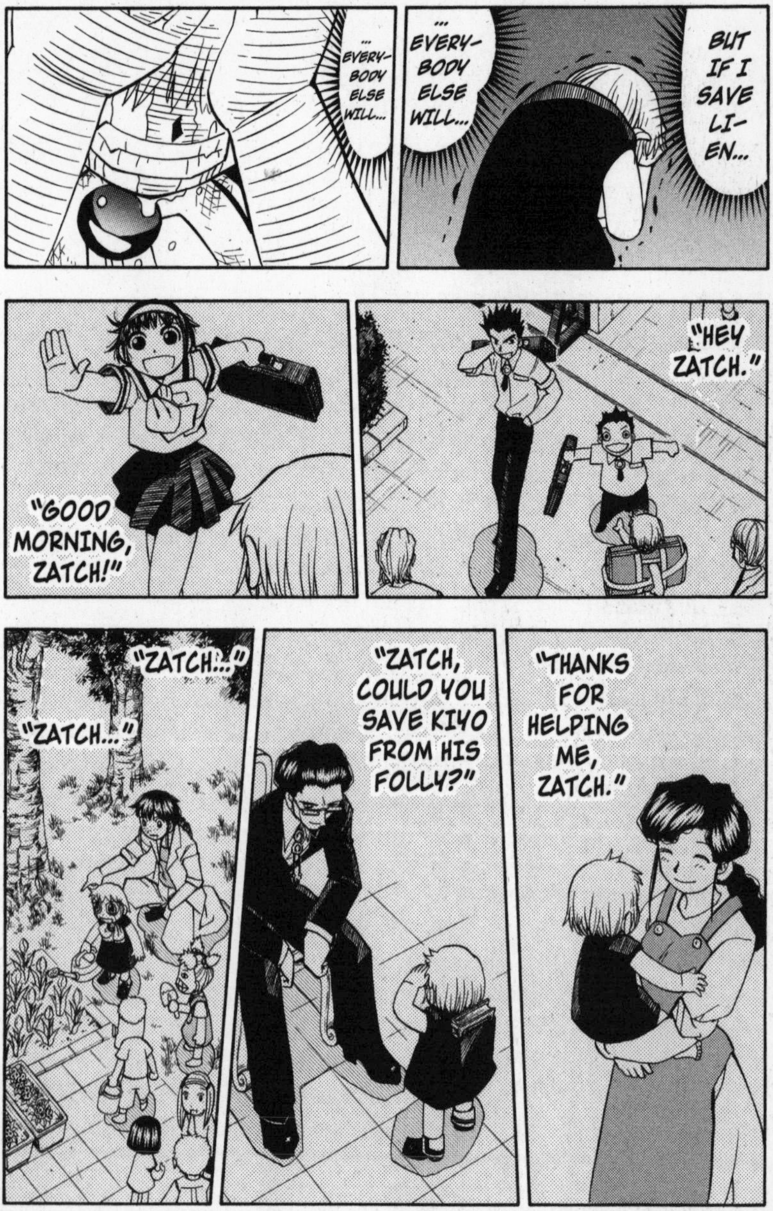
BUT IF I SAVE LI-EN...
... EVERY-BODY ELSE WILL...
... EVERY-BODY ELSE WILL...
"HEY ZATCH."
"GOOD MORNING, ZATCH!"
"THANKS FOR HELPING ME, ZATCH."
"ZATCH, COULD YOU SAVE KIYO FROM HIS FOLLY?"
"ZATCH..."
"ZATCH..."

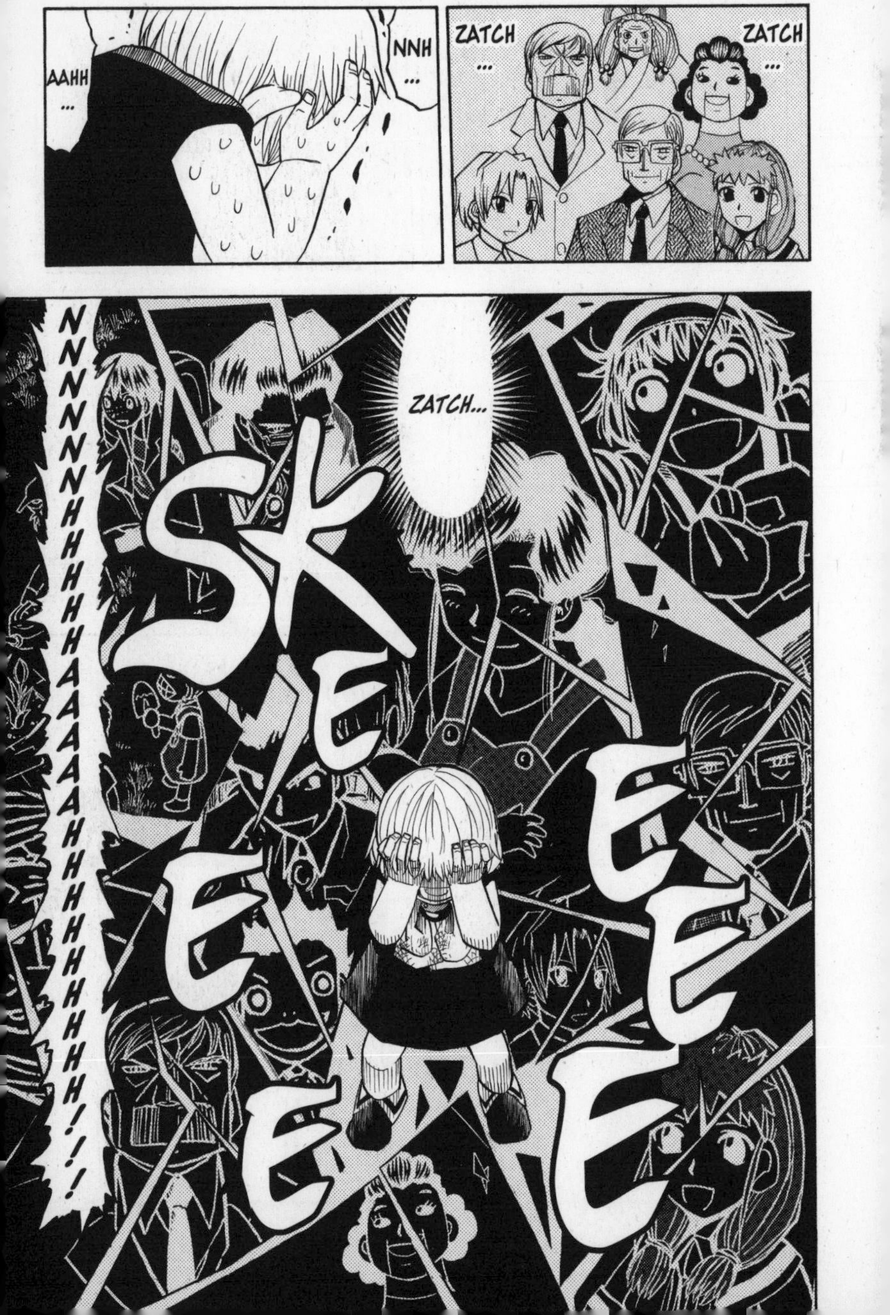

ZATCH ...
ZATCH ...
NNH ...
AAHH ...
ZATCH...
SEEEEEEE
NNNNNNHHHHHAAAAAAHHHHHHHHHHHH!!!

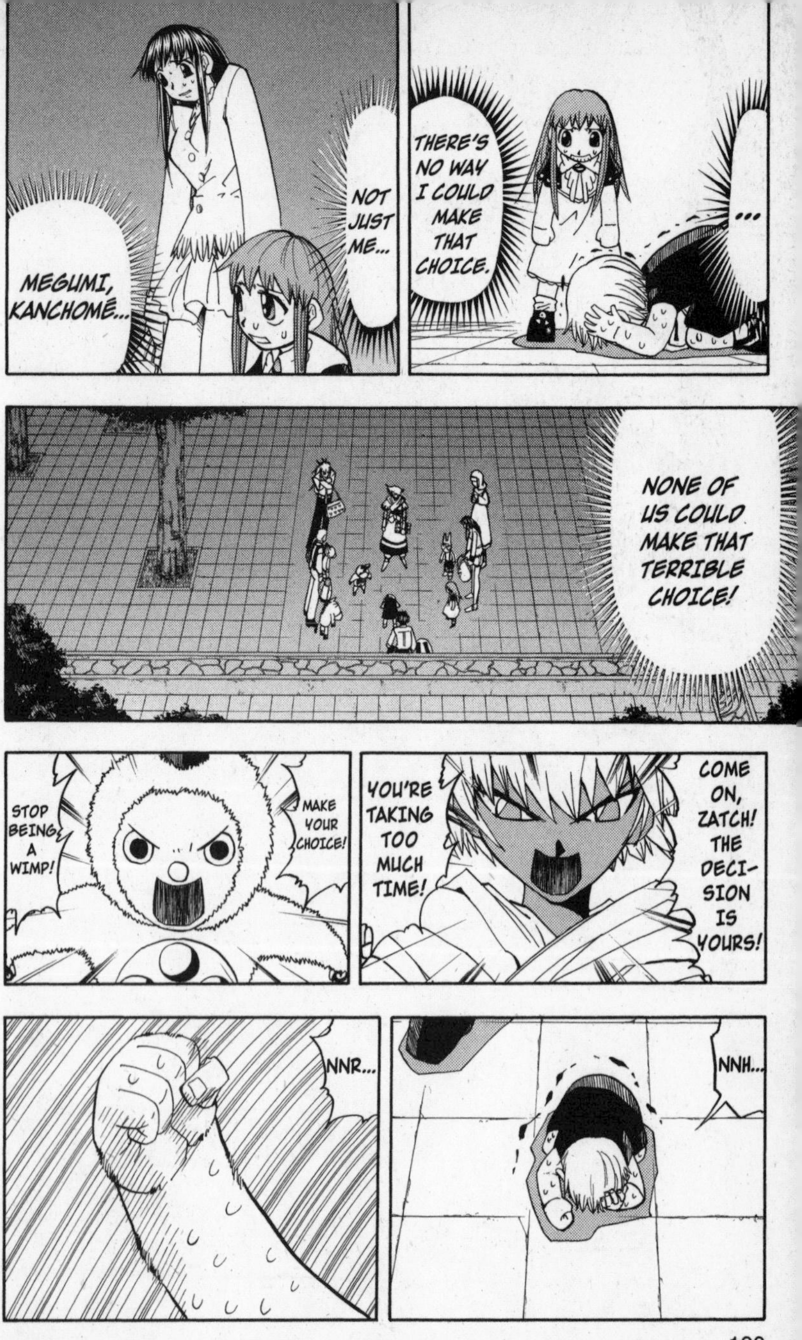
...
THERE'S NO WAY I COULD MAKE THAT CHOICE.
NOT JUST ME...
MEGUMI, KANCHOME...
NONE OF US COULD MAKE THAT TERRIBLE CHOICE!
COME ON, ZATCH! THE DECI-SION IS YOURS!
YOU'RE TAKING TOO MUCH TIME!
MAKE YOUR CHOICE!
STOP BEING A WIMP!
NNH...
NNR...

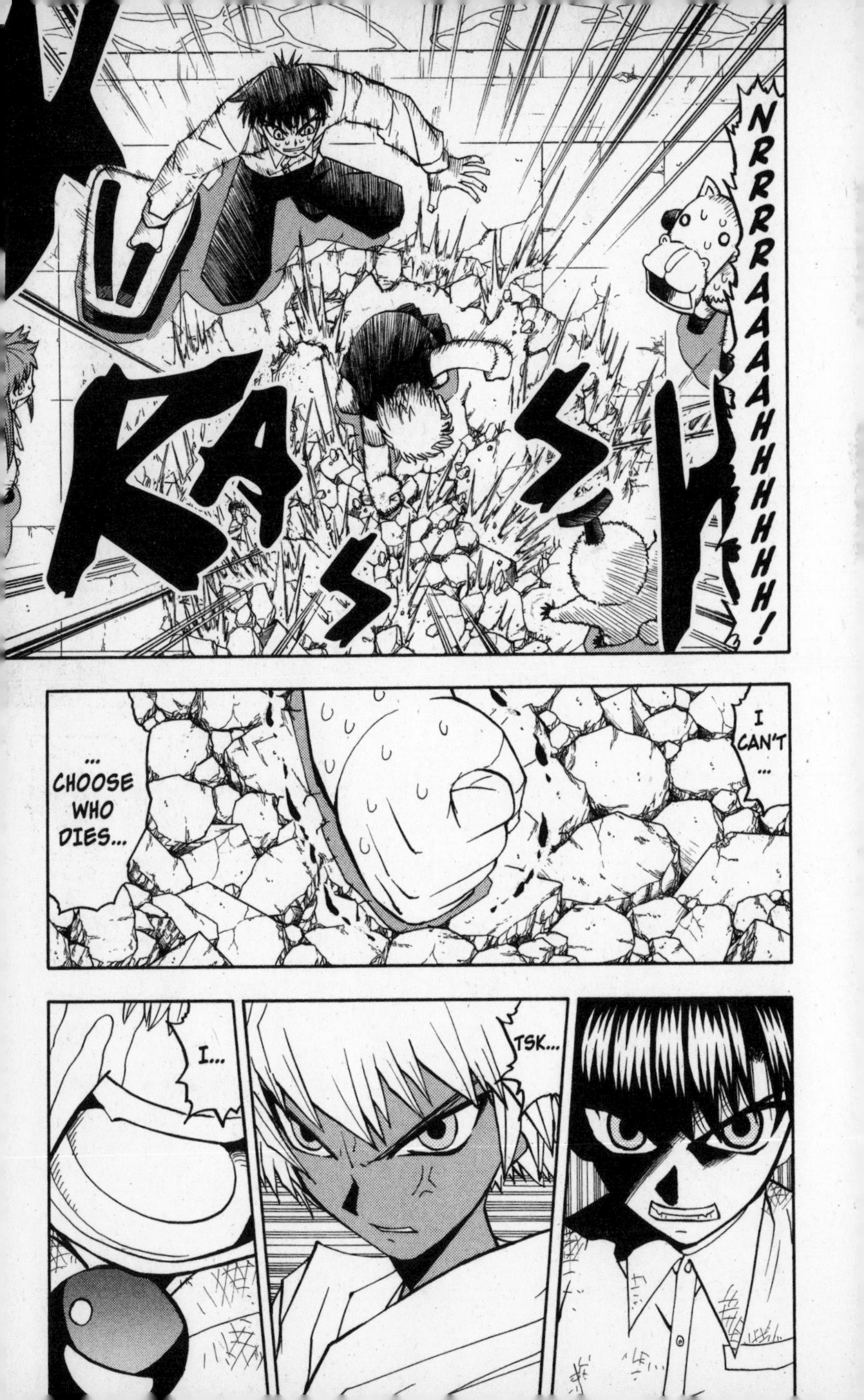
NRRRRAAAAHHHHHH!
KASSK
I CAN'T...
...CHOOSE WHO DIES...
TSK...
I...

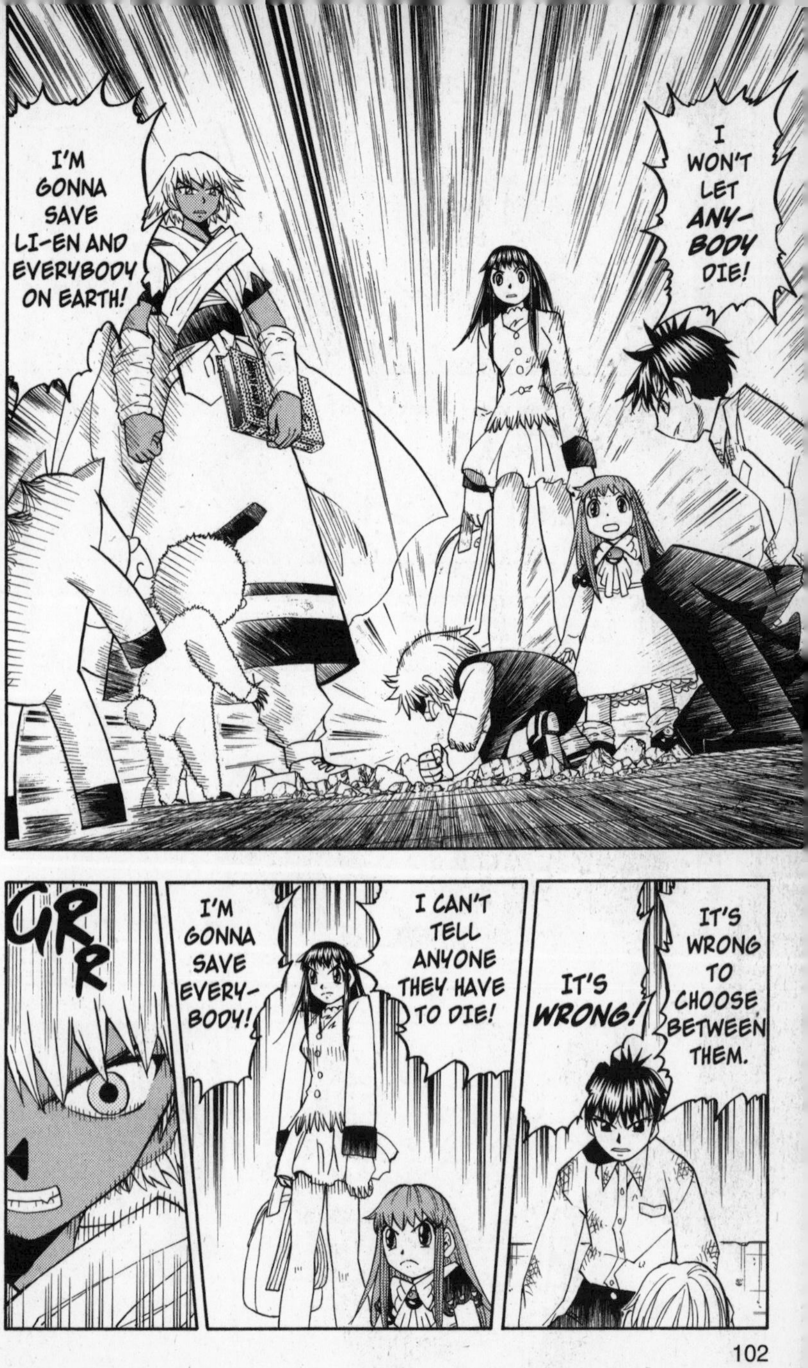
I WON'T LET ANY-BODY DIE!
I'M GONNA SAVE LI-EN AND EVERYBODY ON EARTH!
IT'S WRONG TO CHOOSE BETWEEN THEM.
IT'S WRONG!
I CAN'T TELL ANYONE THEY HAVE TO DIE!
I'M GONNA SAVE EVERY-BODY!
GRR

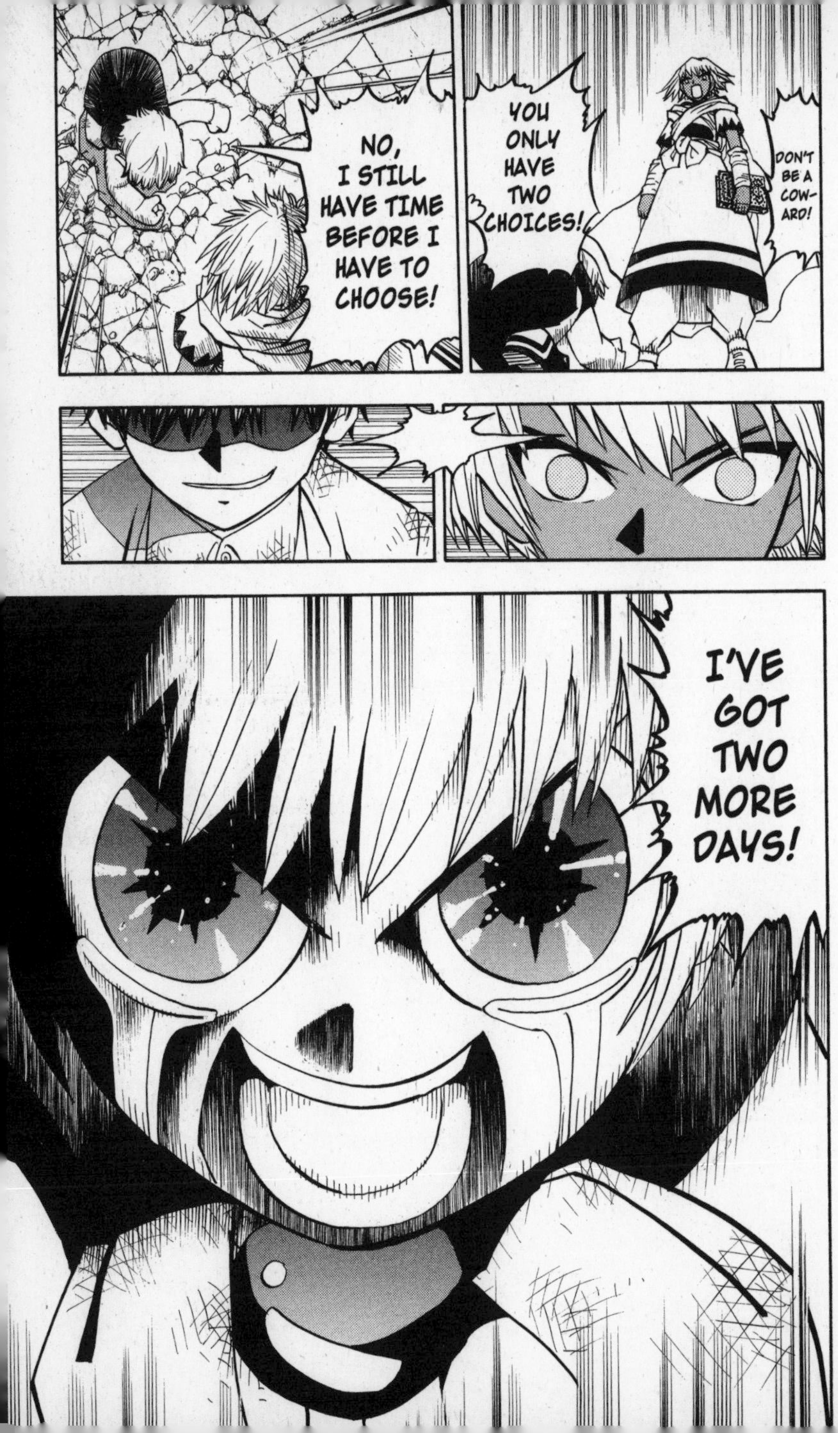
YOU ONLY HAVE TWO CHOICES!
DON'T BE A COW-ARD!
NO, I STILL HAVE TIME BEFORE I HAVE TO CHOOSE!
I'VE GOT TWO MORE DAYS!

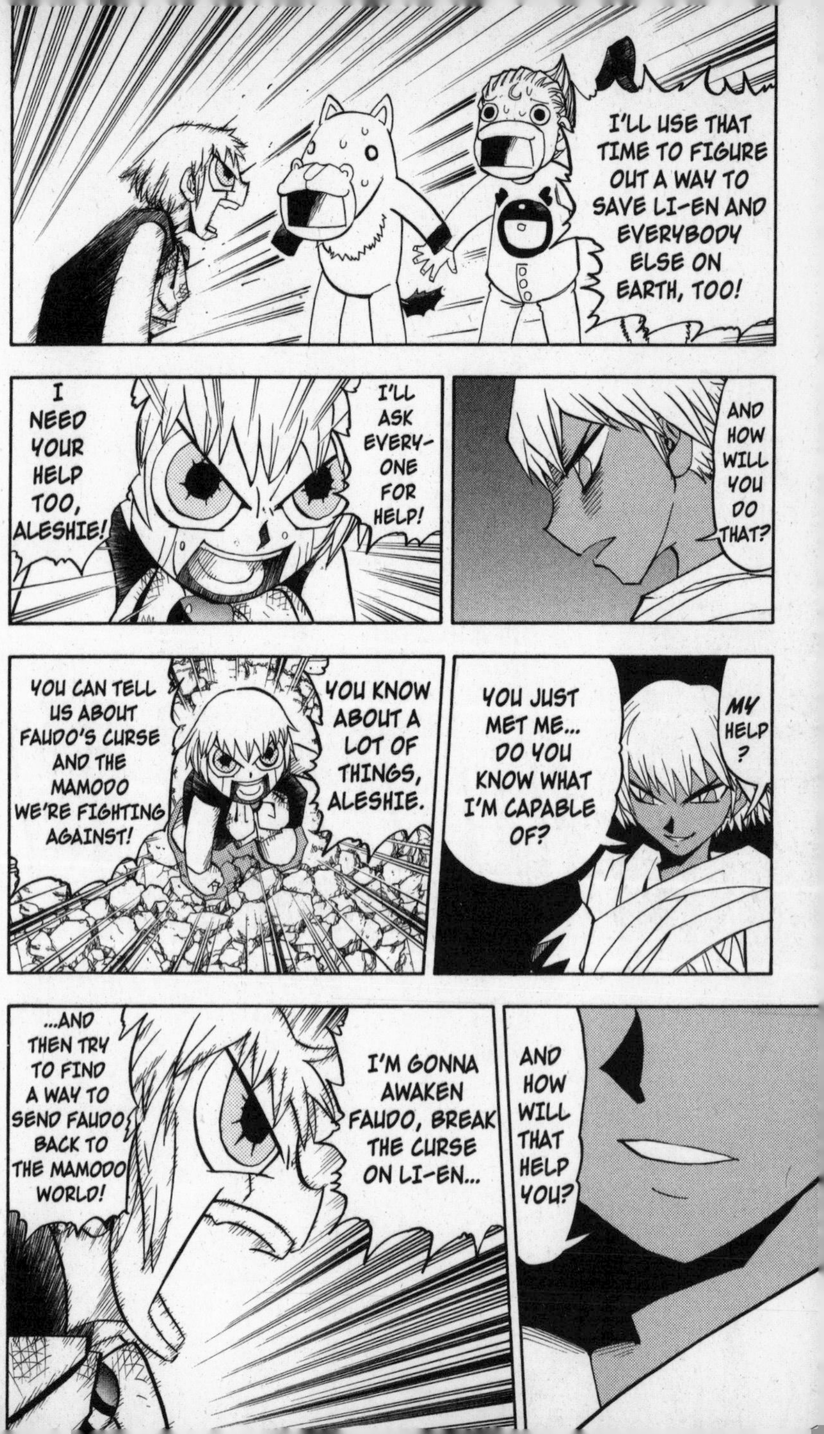
I'LL USE THAT TIME TO FIGURE OUT A WAY TO SAVE LI-EN AND EVERYBODY ELSE ON EARTH, TOO!
AND HOW WILL YOU DO THAT?
I'LL ASK EVERYONE FOR HELP!
I NEED YOUR HELP TOO, ALESHIE!
MY HELP?
YOU JUST MET ME... DO YOU KNOW WHAT I'M CAPABLE OF?
YOU KNOW ABOUT A LOT OF THINGS, ALESHIE.
YOU CAN TELL US ABOUT FAUDO'S CURSE AND THE MAMODO WE'RE FIGHTING AGAINST!
AND HOW WILL THAT HELP YOU?
I'M GONNA AWAKEN FAUDO, BREAK THE CURSE ON LI-EN...
...AND THEN TRY TO FIND A WAY TO SEND FAUDO BACK TO THE MAMODO WORLD!

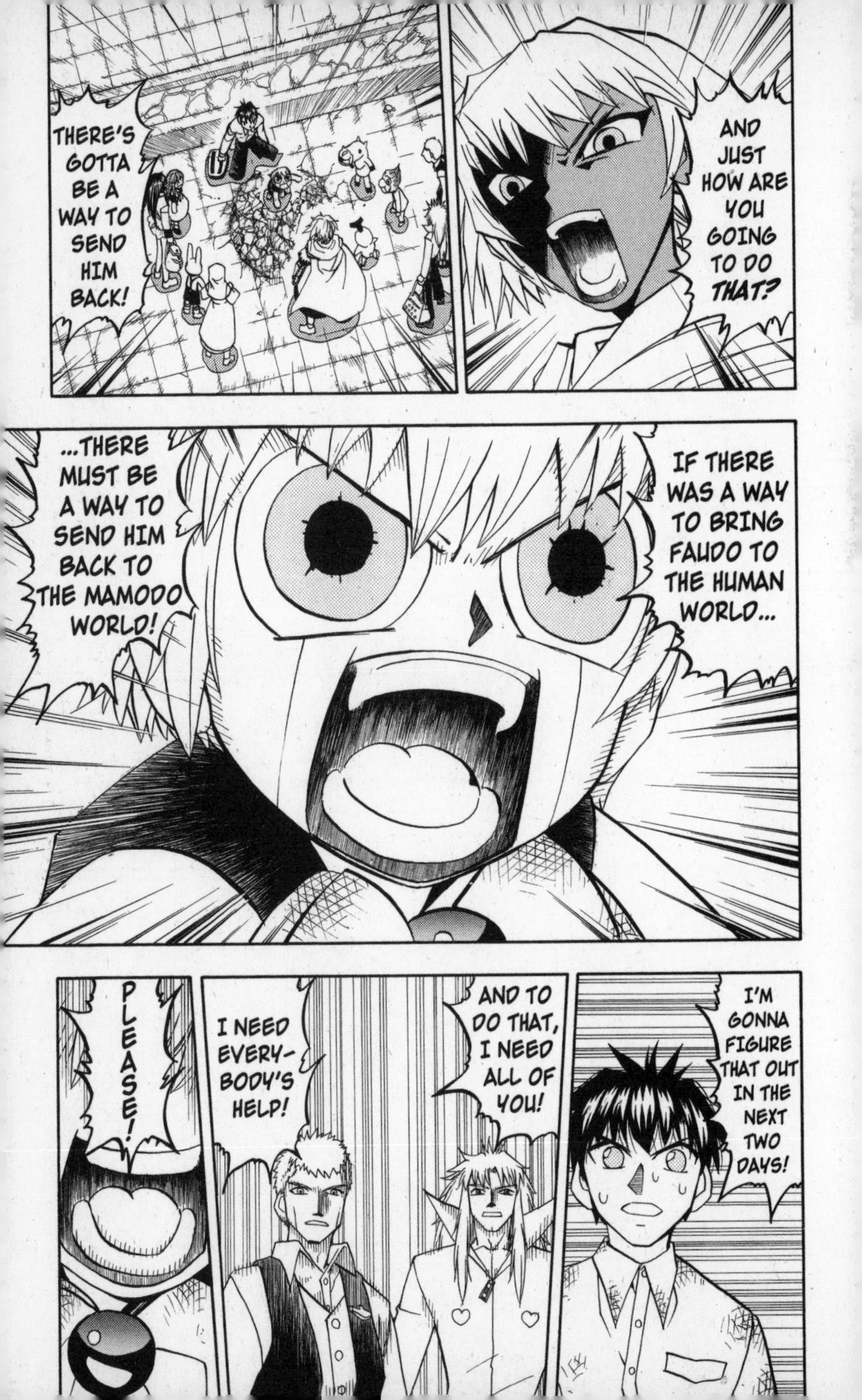
AND JUST HOW ARE YOU GOING TO DO THAT?
THERE'S GOTTA BE A WAY TO SEND HIM BACK!
IF THERE WAS A WAY TO BRING FAUDO TO THE HUMAN WORLD...
...THERE MUST BE A WAY TO SEND HIM BACK TO THE MAMODO WORLD!
I'M GONNA FIGURE THAT OUT IN THE NEXT TWO DAYS!
AND TO DO THAT, I NEED ALL OF YOU!
I NEED EVERYBODY'S HELP!
PLEASE!

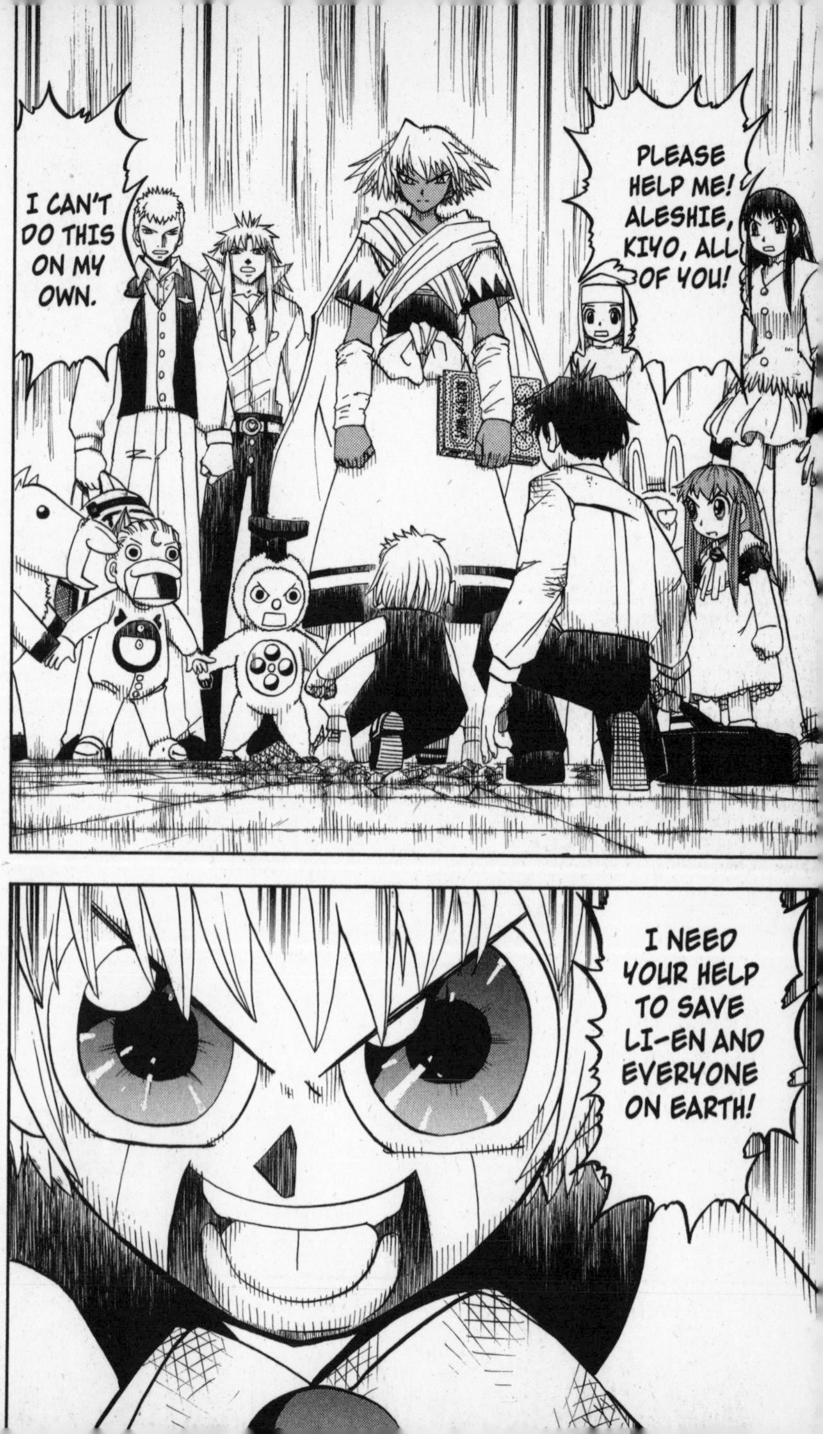
PLEASE HELP ME! ALESHIE, KIYO, ALL OF YOU!
I CAN'T DO THIS ON MY OWN.
I NEED YOUR HELP TO SAVE LI-EN AND EVERYONE ON EARTH!

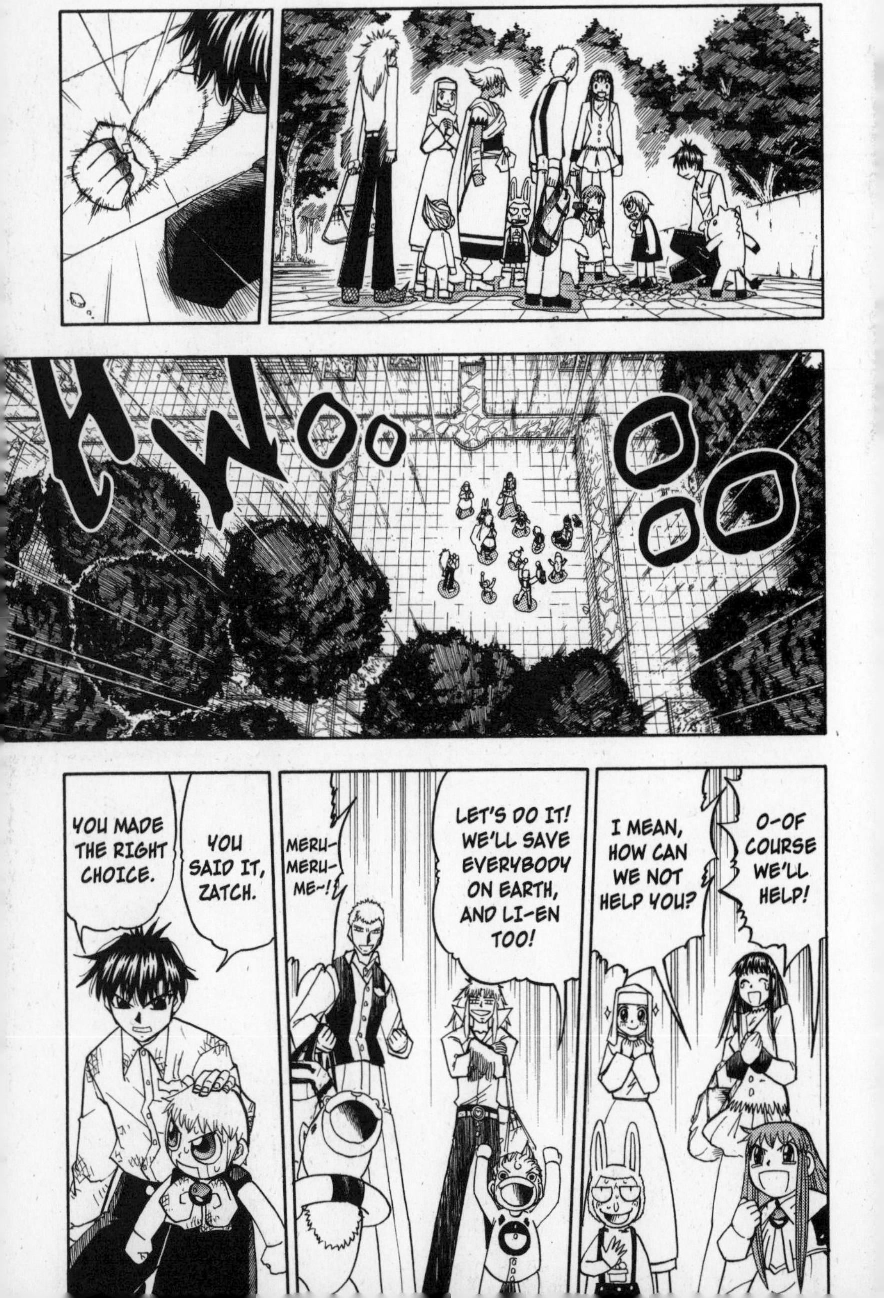
HWOOOOO
O-OF COURSE WE'LL HELP!
I MEAN, HOW CAN WE NOT HELP YOU?
LET'S DO IT! WE'LL SAVE EVERYBODY ON EARTH, AND LI-EN TOO!
MERU-MERU-ME~!
YOU SAID IT, ZATCH.
YOU MADE THE RIGHT CHOICE.

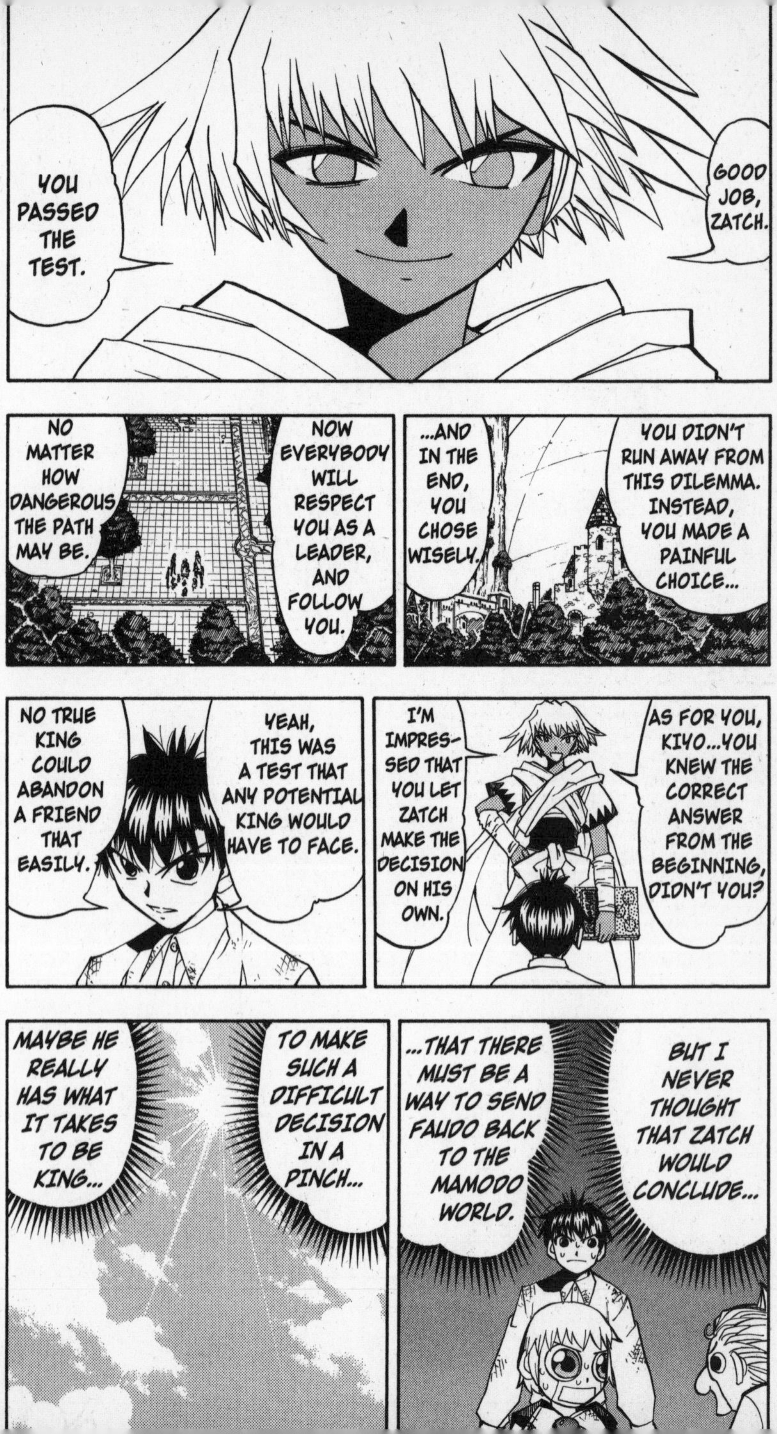
GOOD JOB, ZATCH.
YOU PASSED THE TEST.
YOU DIDN'T RUN AWAY FROM THIS DILEMMA. INSTEAD, YOU MADE A PAINFUL CHOICE...
...AND IN THE END, YOU CHOSE WISELY.
NOW EVERYBODY WILL RESPECT YOU AS A LEADER, AND FOLLOW YOU.
NO MATTER HOW DANGEROUS THE PATH MAY BE.
AS FOR YOU, KIYO...YOU KNEW THE CORRECT ANSWER FROM THE BEGINNING, DIDN'T YOU?
I'M IMPRES-SED THAT YOU LET ZATCH MAKE THE DECISION ON HIS OWN.
YEAH, THIS WAS A TEST THAT ANY POTENTIAL KING WOULD HAVE TO FACE.
NO TRUE KING COULD ABANDON A FRIEND THAT EASILY.
BUT I NEVER THOUGHT THAT ZATCH WOULD CONCLUDE...
...THAT THERE MUST BE A WAY TO SEND FAUDO BACK TO THE MAMODO WORLD.
TO MAKE SUCH A DIFFICULT DECISION IN A PINCH...
MAYBE HE REALLY HAS WHAT IT TAKES TO BE KING...

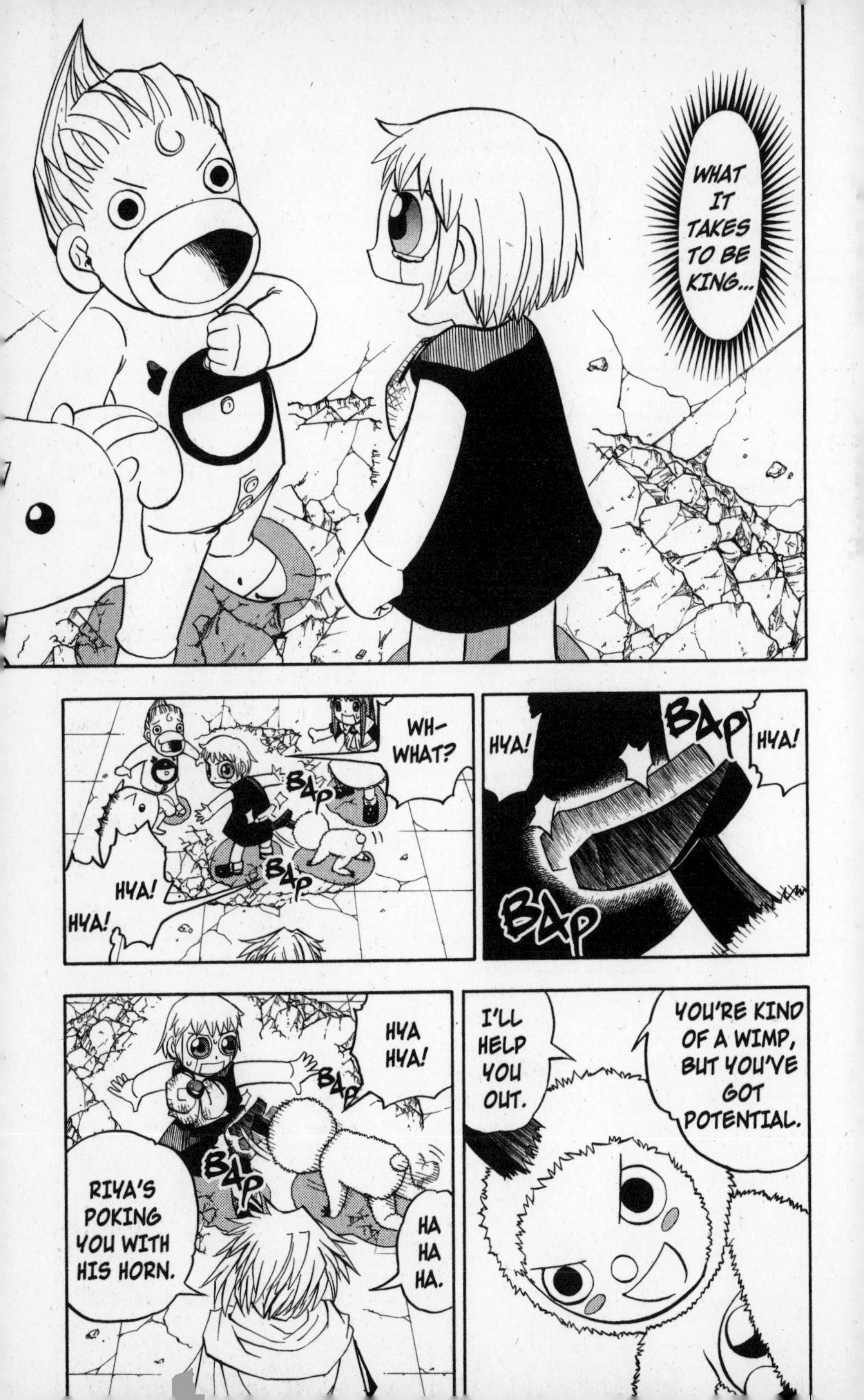
WHAT IT TAKES TO BE KING...
HYA!
BAP
HYA!
BAP
WH- WHAT?
BAP
BAP
HYA!
HYA!
YOU'RE KIND OF A WIMP, BUT YOU'VE GOT POTENTIAL.
I'LL HELP YOU OUT.
HYA HYA!
BAP
BAP
HA HA HA.
RIYA'S POKING YOU WITH HIS HORN.

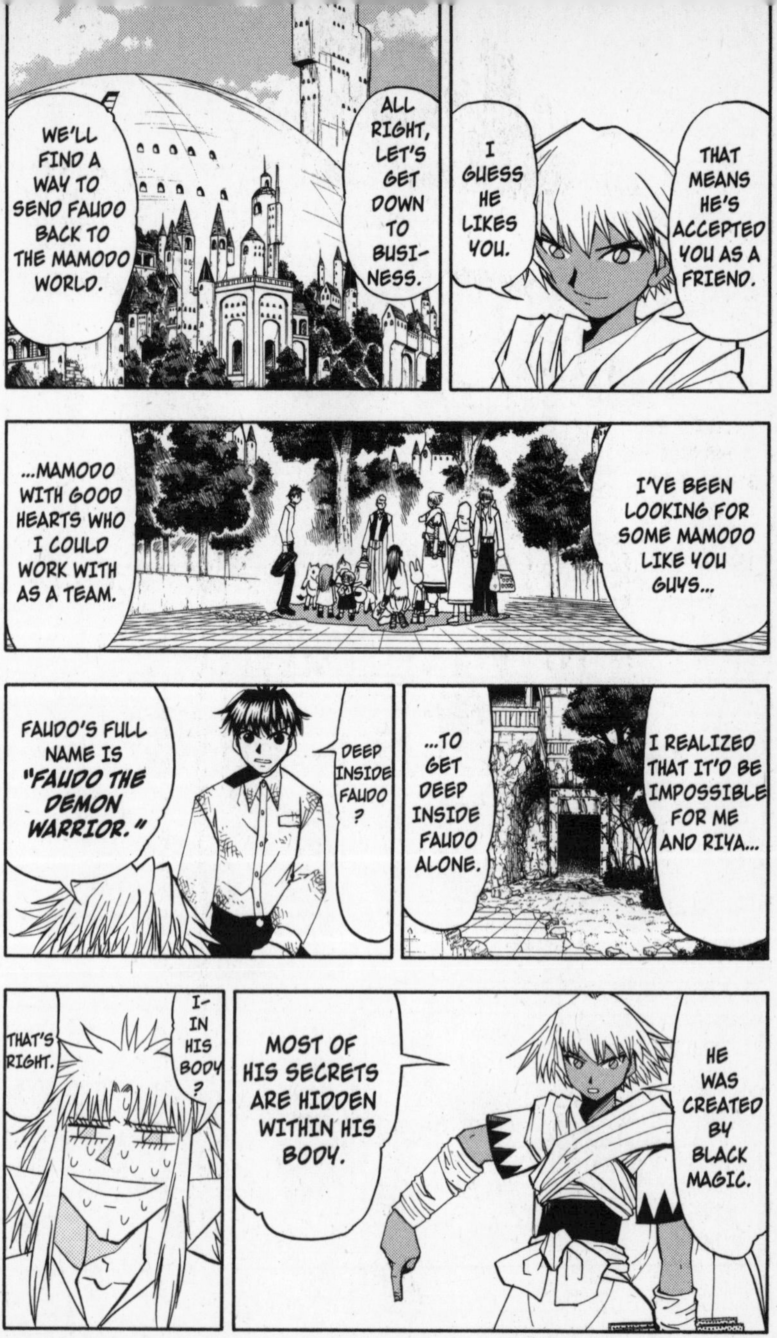
THAT MEANS HE'S ACCEPTED YOU AS A FRIEND.
I GUESS HE LIKES YOU.
ALL RIGHT, LET'S GET DOWN TO BUSI-NESS.
WE'LL FIND A WAY TO SEND FAUDO BACK TO THE MAMODO WORLD.
I'VE BEEN LOOKING FOR SOME MAMODO LIKE YOU GUYS...
...MAMODO WITH GOOD HEARTS WHO I COULD WORK WITH AS A TEAM.
I REALIZED THAT IT'D BE IMPOSSIBLE FOR ME AND RIYA...
...TO GET DEEP INSIDE FAUDO ALONE.
DEEP INSIDE FAUDO?
FAUDO'S FULL NAME IS "FAUDO THE DEMON WARRIOR."
HE WAS CREATED BY BLACK MAGIC.
MOST OF HIS SECRETS ARE HIDDEN WITHIN HIS BODY.
I-IN HIS BODY?
THAT'S RIGHT.

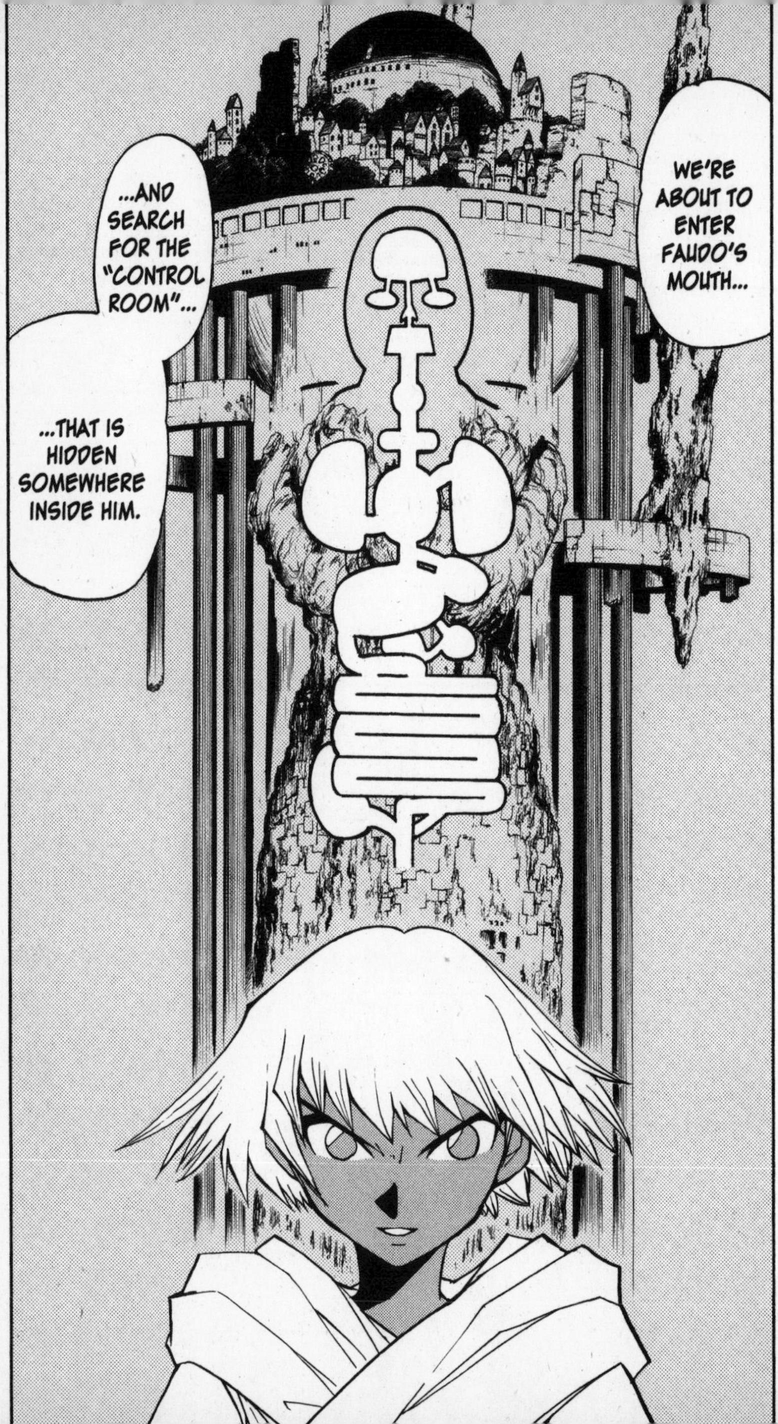
WE'RE ABOUT TO ENTER FAUDO'S MOUTH...
...AND SEARCH FOR THE "CONTROL ROOM"...
...THAT IS HIDDEN SOMEWHERE INSIDE HIM.

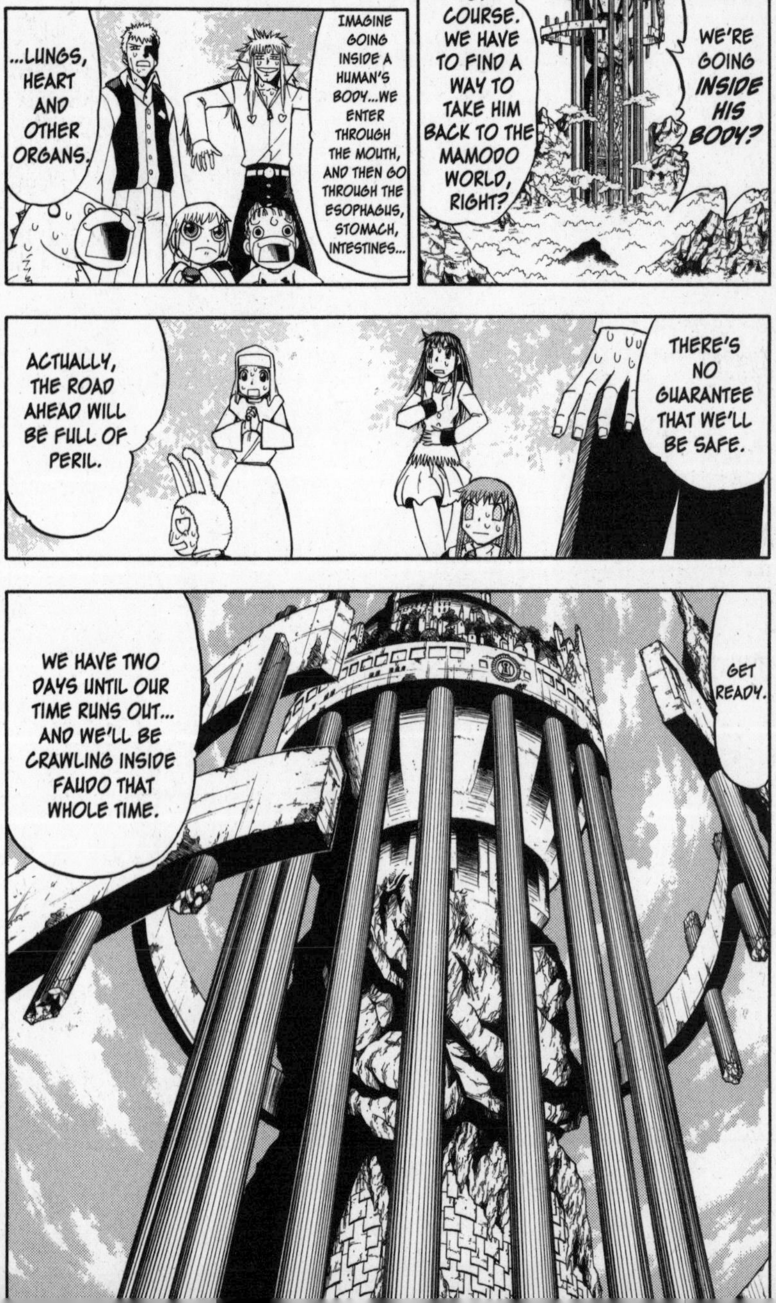
WE'RE GOING INSIDE HIS BODY?
OF COURSE. WE HAVE TO FIND A WAY TO TAKE HIM BACK TO THE MAMODO WORLD, RIGHT?
IMAGINE GOING INSIDE A HUMAN'S BODY...WE ENTER THROUGH THE MOUTH, AND THEN GO THROUGH THE ESOPHAGUS, STOMACH, INTESTINES...
...LUNGS, HEART AND OTHER ORGANS.
THERE'S NO GUARANTEE THAT WE'LL BE SAFE.
ACTUALLY, THE ROAD AHEAD WILL BE FULL OF PERIL.
GET READY.
WE HAVE TWO DAYS UNTIL OUR TIME RUNS OUT... AND WE'LL BE CRAWLING INSIDE FAUDO THAT WHOLE TIME.

# LEVEL 199: The First Test

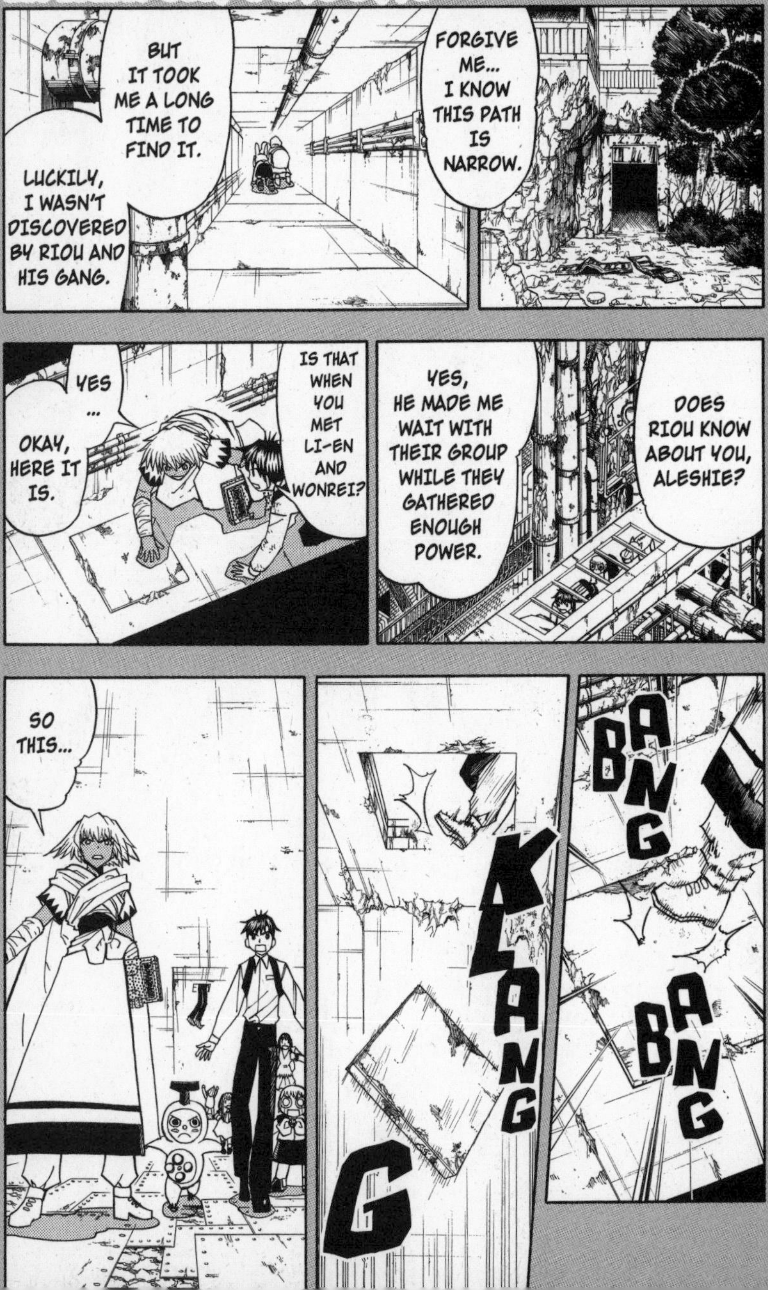
FORGIVE ME... I KNOW THIS PATH IS NARROW.
BUT IT TOOK ME A LONG TIME TO FIND IT.
LUCKILY, I WASN'T DISCOVERED BY RIOU AND HIS GANG.
DOES RIOU KNOW ABOUT YOU, ALESHIE?
YES, HE MADE ME WAIT WITH THEIR GROUP WHILE THEY GATHERED ENOUGH POWER.
IS THAT WHEN YOU MET LI-EN AND WONREI?
YES ...
OKAY, HERE IT IS.
BANG
BANG
KLANG
G
SO THIS...

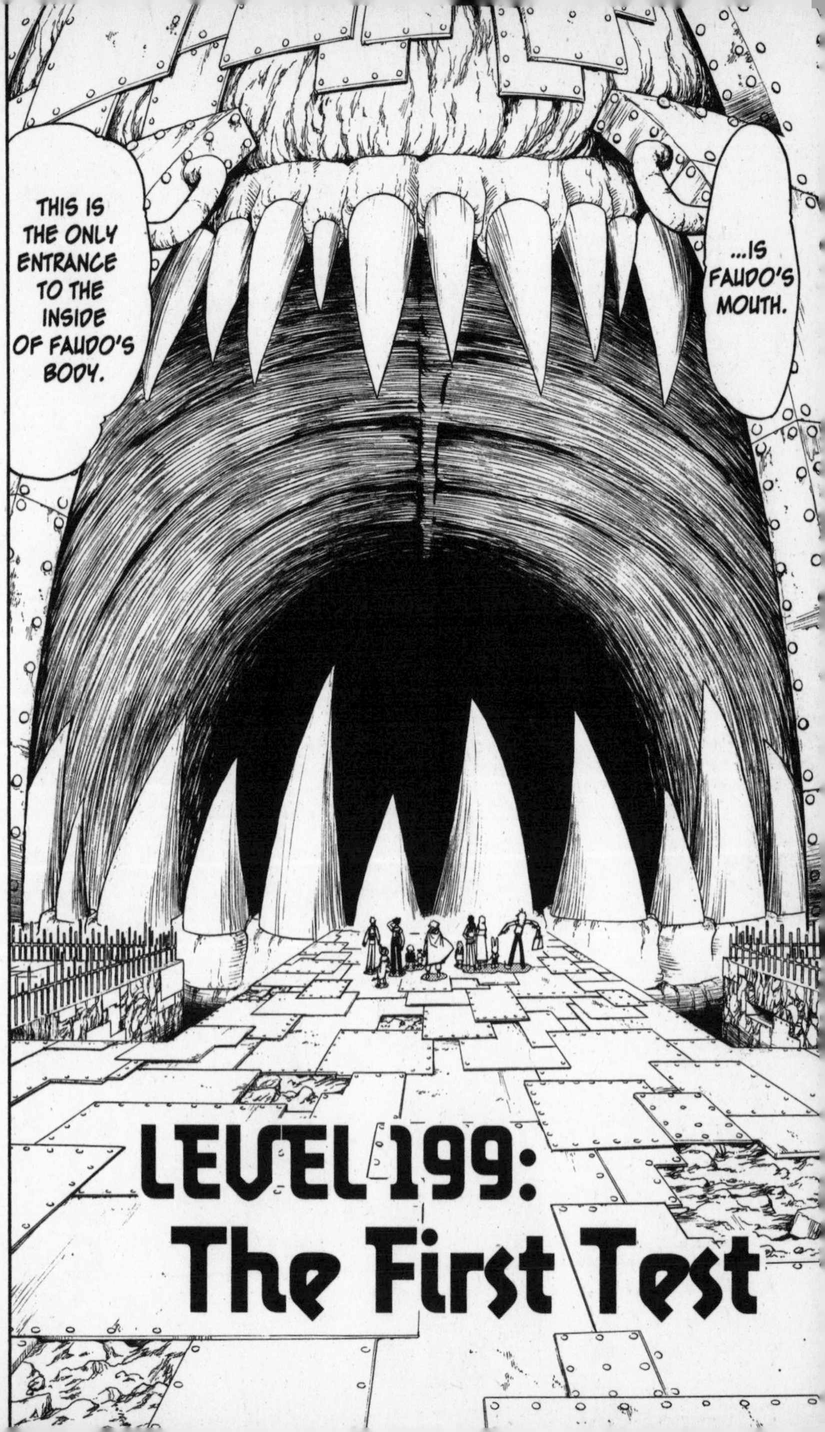
THIS IS THE ONLY ENTRANCE TO THE INSIDE OF FAUDO'S BODY.
...IS FAUDO'S MOUTH.

# LEVEL 199: The First Test

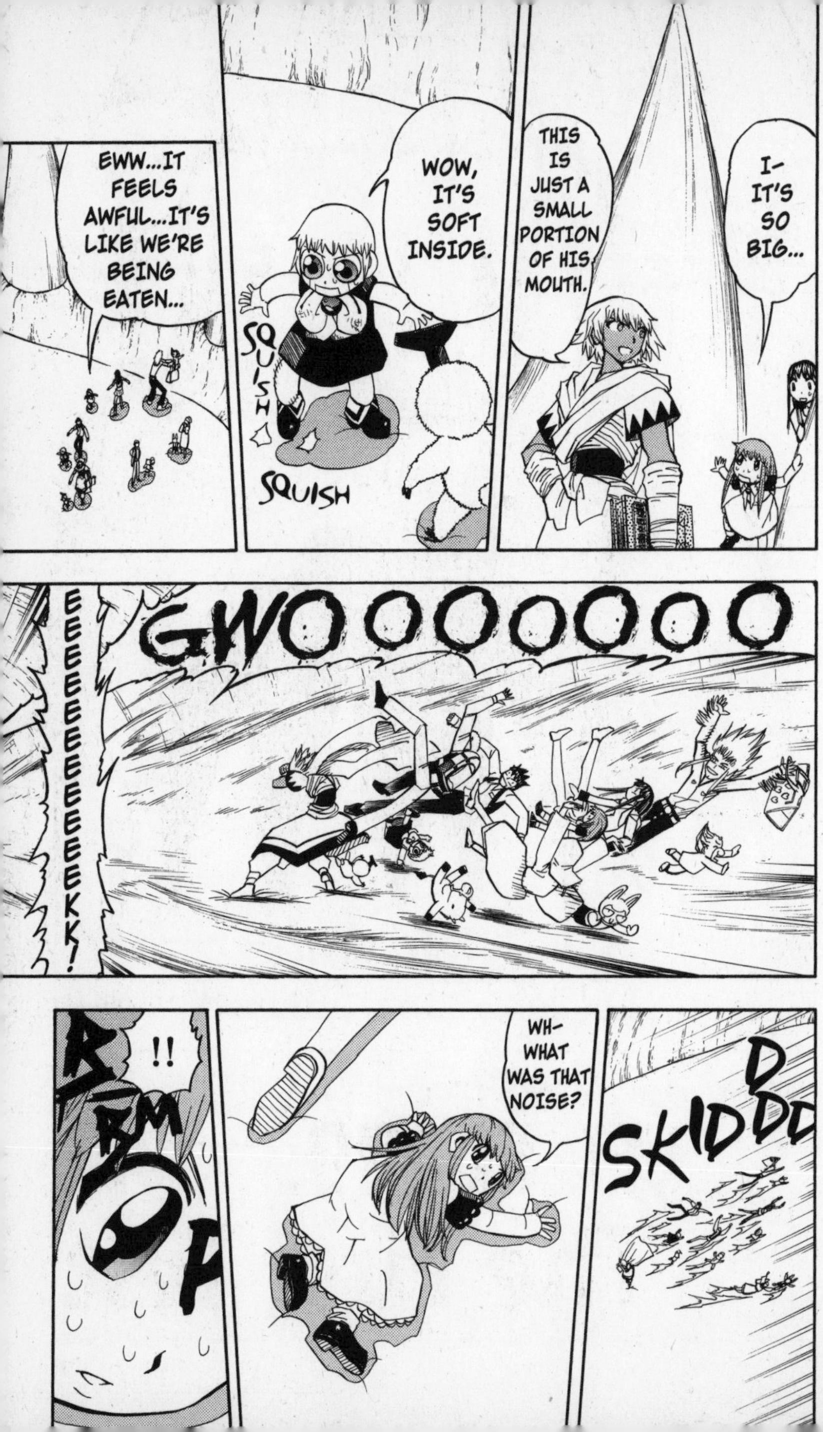
I- IT'S SO BIG...
THIS IS JUST A SMALL PORTION OF HIS MOUTH.
WOW, IT'S SOFT INSIDE.
SQUISH
SQUISH
EWW...IT FEELS AWFUL...IT'S LIKE WE'RE BEING EATEN...
GWOOOOOOOO
EEEEEEEEEEEEEEEEKK!
SKIDDDD
WH- WHAT WAS THAT NOISE?
!!

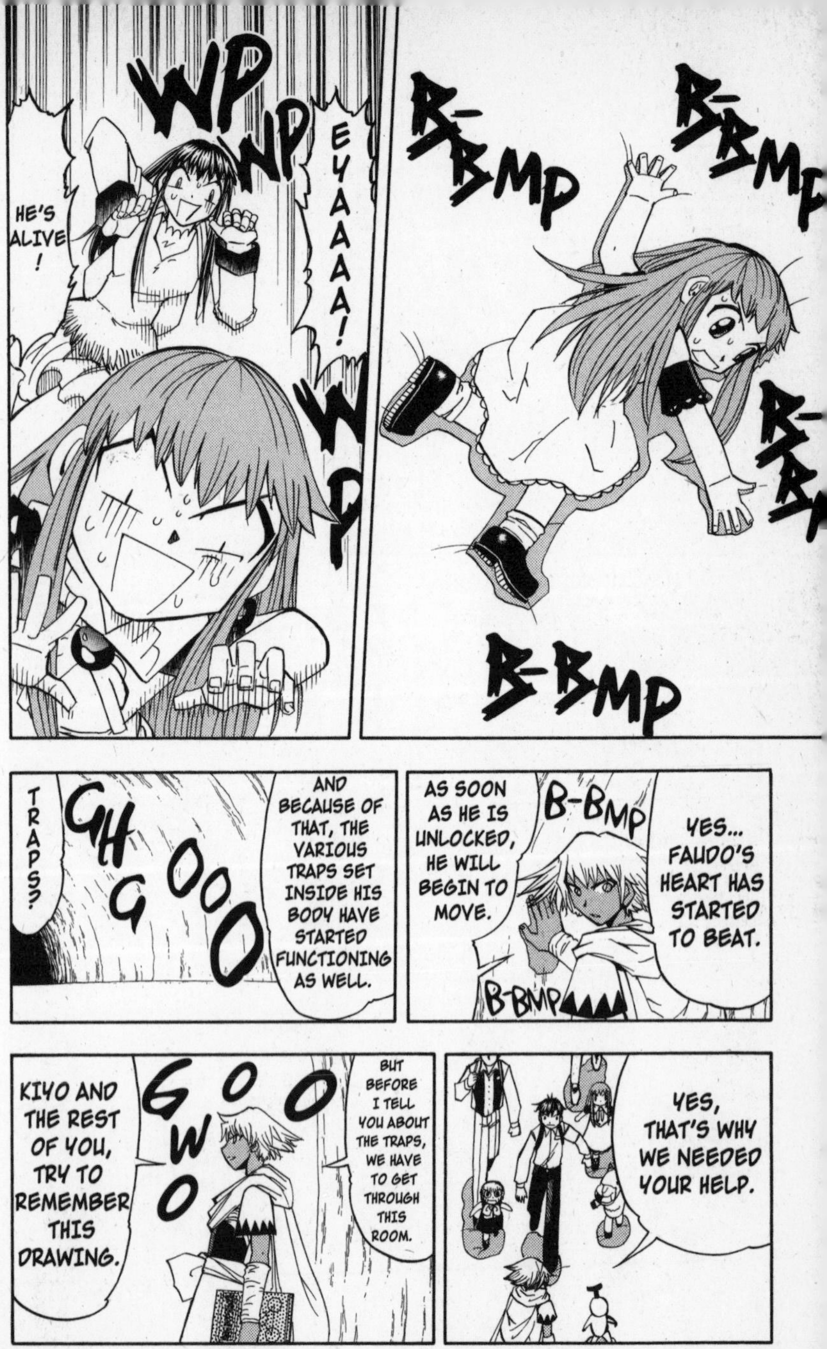
R-BMP
R-BMP
B-BMP
WP WP
EYAAAAA!
HE'S ALIVE!
WP
YES... FAUDO'S HEART HAS STARTED TO BEAT.
B-BMP
AS SOON AS HE IS UNLOCKED, HE WILL BEGIN TO MOVE.
B-BMP
AND BECAUSE OF THAT, THE VARIOUS TRAPS SET INSIDE HIS BODY HAVE STARTED FUNCTIONING AS WELL.
GHGOOO
TRAPS?
YES, THAT'S WHY WE NEEDED YOUR HELP.
BUT BEFORE I TELL YOU ABOUT THE TRAPS, WE HAVE TO GET THROUGH THIS ROOM.
GOOWOO
KIYO AND THE REST OF YOU, TRY TO REMEMBER THIS DRAWING.

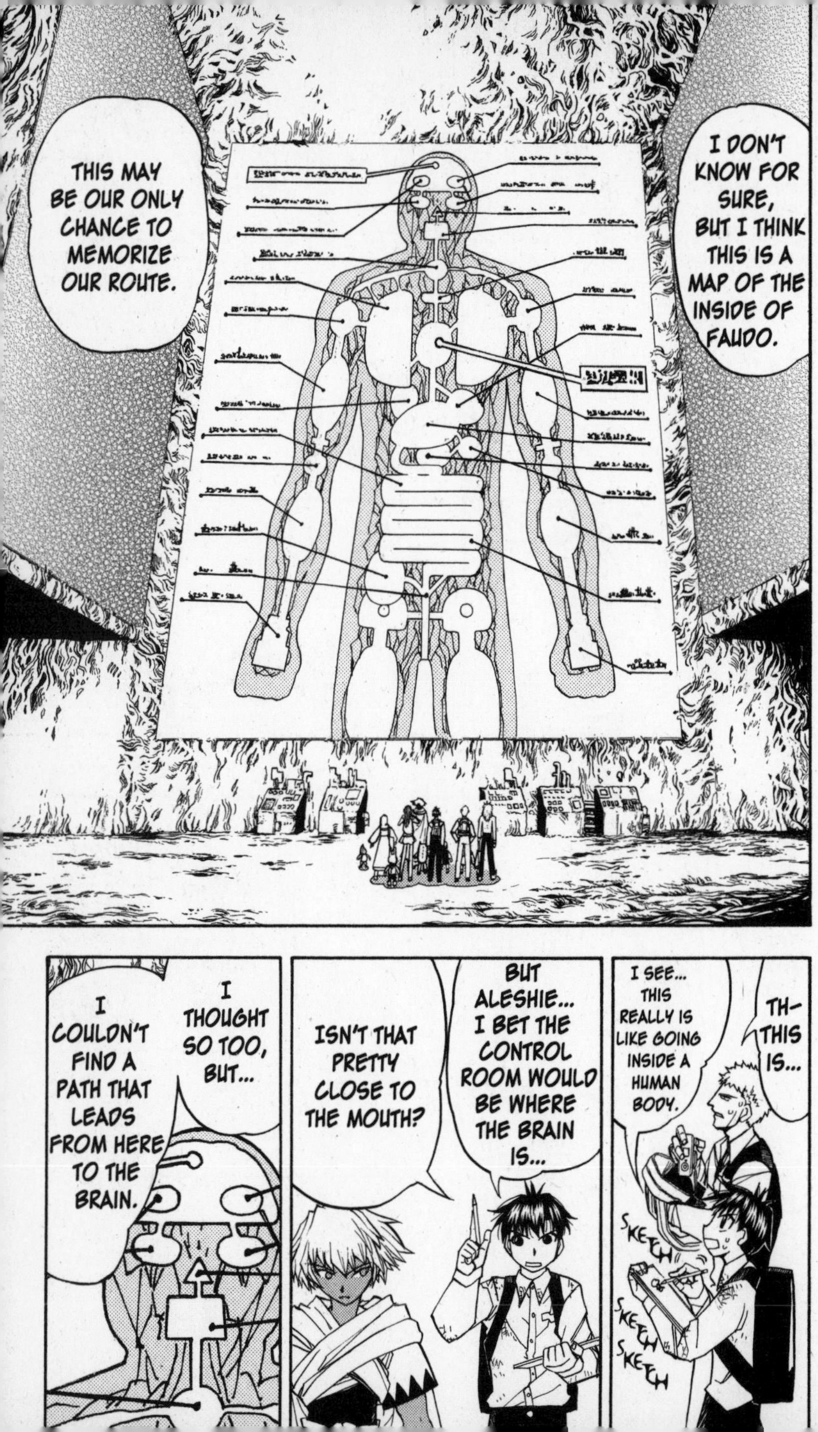
I DON'T KNOW FOR SURE, BUT I THINK THIS IS A MAP OF THE INSIDE OF FAUDO.
THIS MAY BE OUR ONLY CHANCE TO MEMORIZE OUR ROUTE.
TH- THIS IS...
I SEE... THIS REALLY IS LIKE GOING INSIDE A HUMAN BODY.
SKETCH
SKETCH
SKETCH
BUT ALESHIE... I BET THE CONTROL ROOM WOULD BE WHERE THE BRAIN IS...
ISN'T THAT PRETTY CLOSE TO THE MOUTH?
I THOUGHT SO TOO, BUT...
I COULDN'T FIND A PATH THAT LEADS FROM HERE TO THE BRAIN.

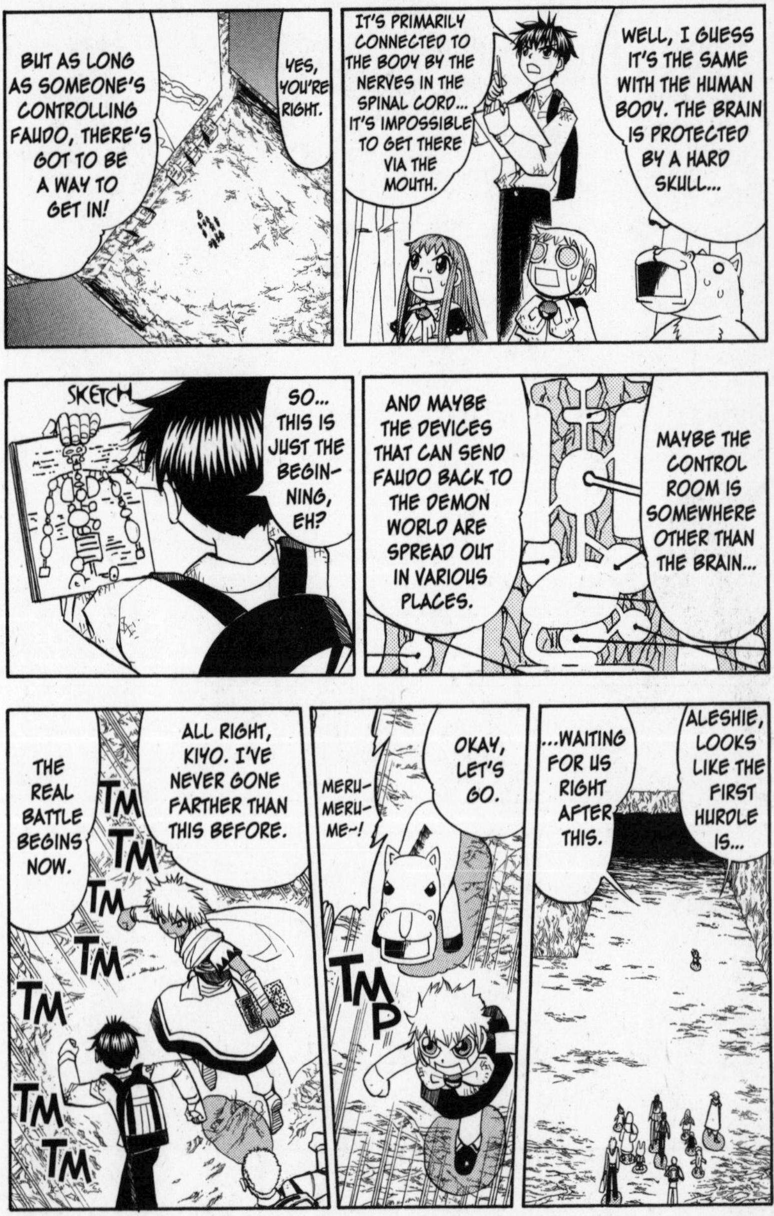
WELL, I GUESS IT'S THE SAME WITH THE HUMAN BODY. THE BRAIN IS PROTECTED BY A HARD SKULL...
IT'S PRIMARILY CONNECTED TO THE BODY BY THE NERVES IN THE SPINAL CORD... IT'S IMPOSSIBLE TO GET THERE VIA THE MOUTH.
YES, YOU'RE RIGHT.
BUT AS LONG AS SOMEONE'S CONTROLLING FAUDO, THERE'S GOT TO BE A WAY TO GET IN!
MAYBE THE CONTROL ROOM IS SOMEWHERE OTHER THAN THE BRAIN...
AND MAYBE THE DEVICES THAT CAN SEND FAUDO BACK TO THE DEMON WORLD ARE SPREAD OUT IN VARIOUS PLACES.
SO... THIS IS JUST THE BEGIN-NING, EH?
SKETCH
ALESHIE, LOOKS LIKE THE FIRST HURDLE IS...
...WAITING FOR US RIGHT AFTER THIS.
OKAY, LET'S GO.
MERU-MERU-ME~!
TMP
ALL RIGHT, KIYO. I'VE NEVER GONE FARTHER THAN THIS BEFORE.
THE REAL BATTLE BEGINS NOW.
TM TM TM TM TM TM TM

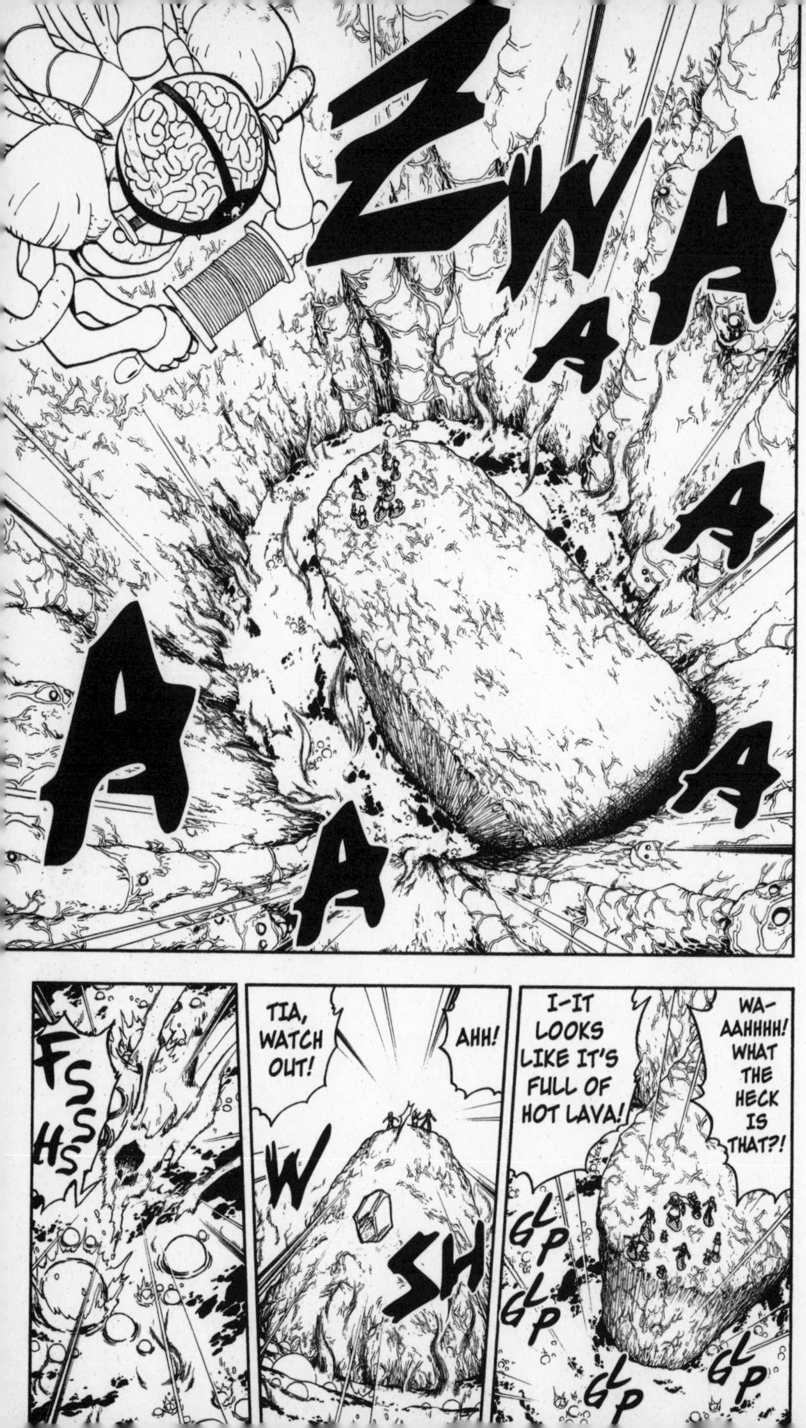
ZWAAAAAA
WA-AAHHHH! WHAT THE HECK IS THAT?!
I-IT LOOKS LIKE IT'S FULL OF HOT LAVA!
GLP GLP
GLP GLP
AHH!
TIA, WATCH OUT!
WSH
FSSHS

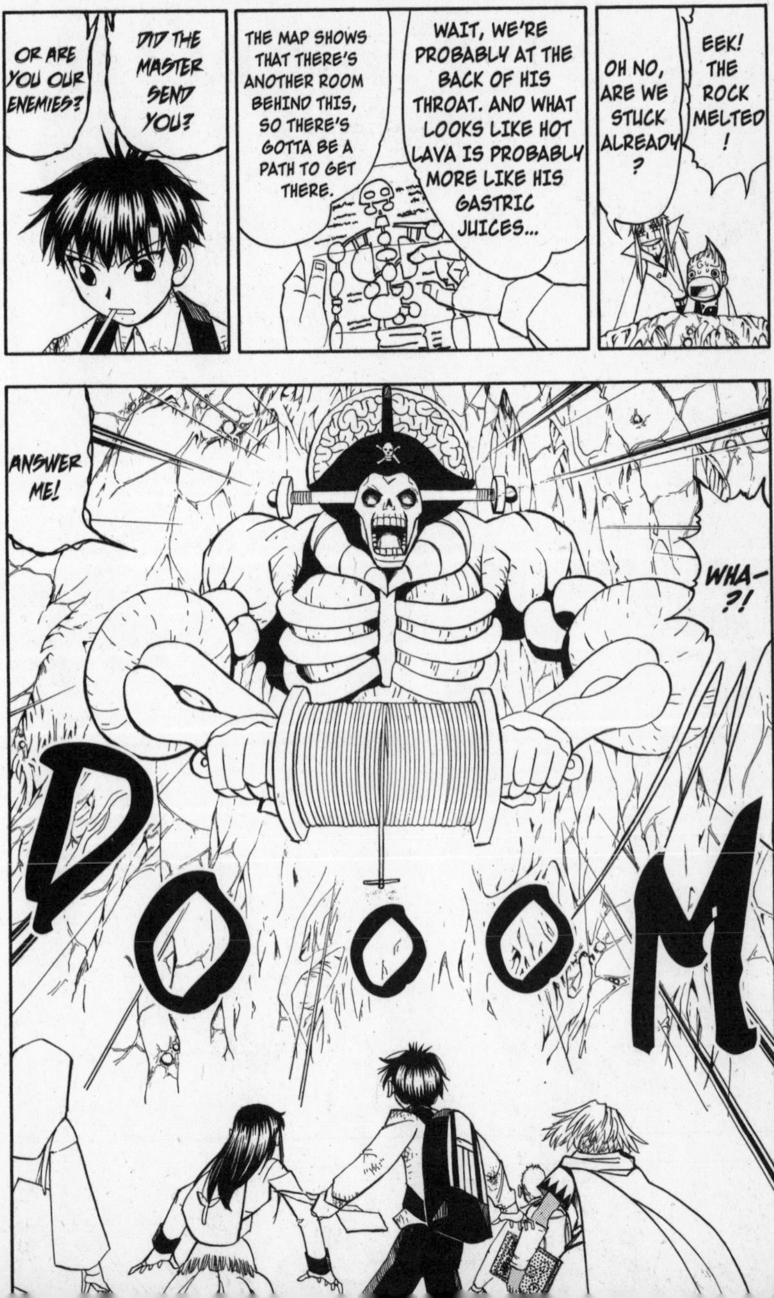
EEK! THE ROCK MELTED!
OH NO, ARE WE STUCK ALREADY?
WAIT, WE'RE PROBABLY AT THE BACK OF HIS THROAT. AND WHAT LOOKS LIKE HOT LAVA IS PROBABLY MORE LIKE HIS GASTRIC JUICES...
THE MAP SHOWS THAT THERE'S ANOTHER ROOM BEHIND THIS, SO THERE'S GOTTA BE A PATH TO GET THERE.
DID THE MASTER SEND YOU?
OR ARE YOU OUR ENEMIES?
ANSWER ME!
WHA-?!
DOOOM

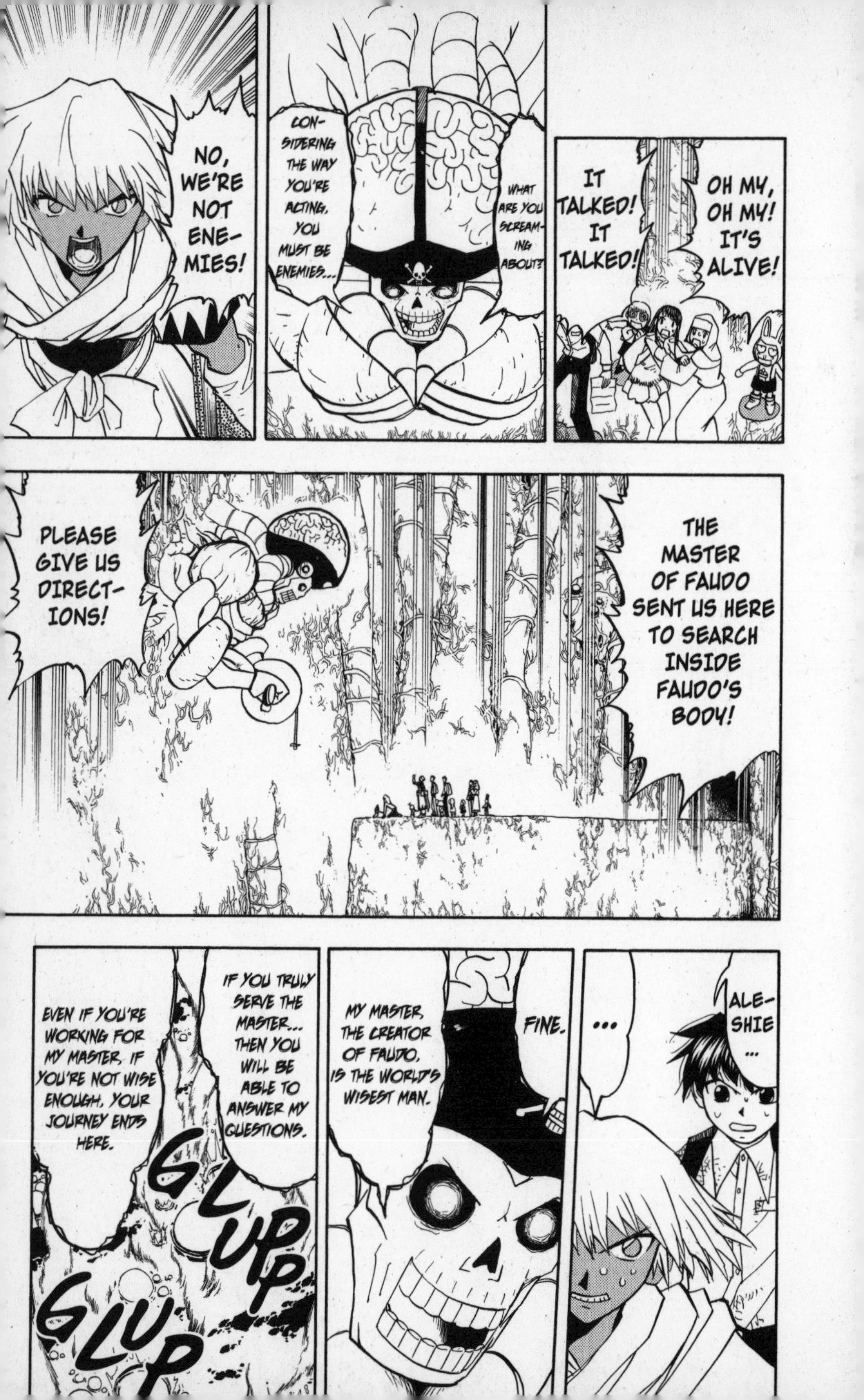
OH MY, OH MY! IT'S ALIVE!
IT TALKED! IT TALKED!
WHAT ARE YOU SCREAMING ABOUT?
CONSIDERING THE WAY YOU'RE ACTING, YOU MUST BE ENEMIES...
NO, WE'RE NOT ENEMIES!
THE MASTER OF FAUDO SENT US HERE TO SEARCH INSIDE FAUDO'S BODY!
PLEASE GIVE US DIRECTIONS!
ALESHIE...
...
FINE.
MY MASTER, THE CREATOR OF FAUDO, IS THE WORLD'S WISEST MAN.
IF YOU TRULY SERVE THE MASTER... THEN YOU WILL BE ABLE TO ANSWER MY QUESTIONS.
EVEN IF YOU'RE WORKING FOR MY MASTER, IF YOU'RE NOT WISE ENOUGH, YOUR JOURNEY ENDS HERE.
GLUP
GLUP

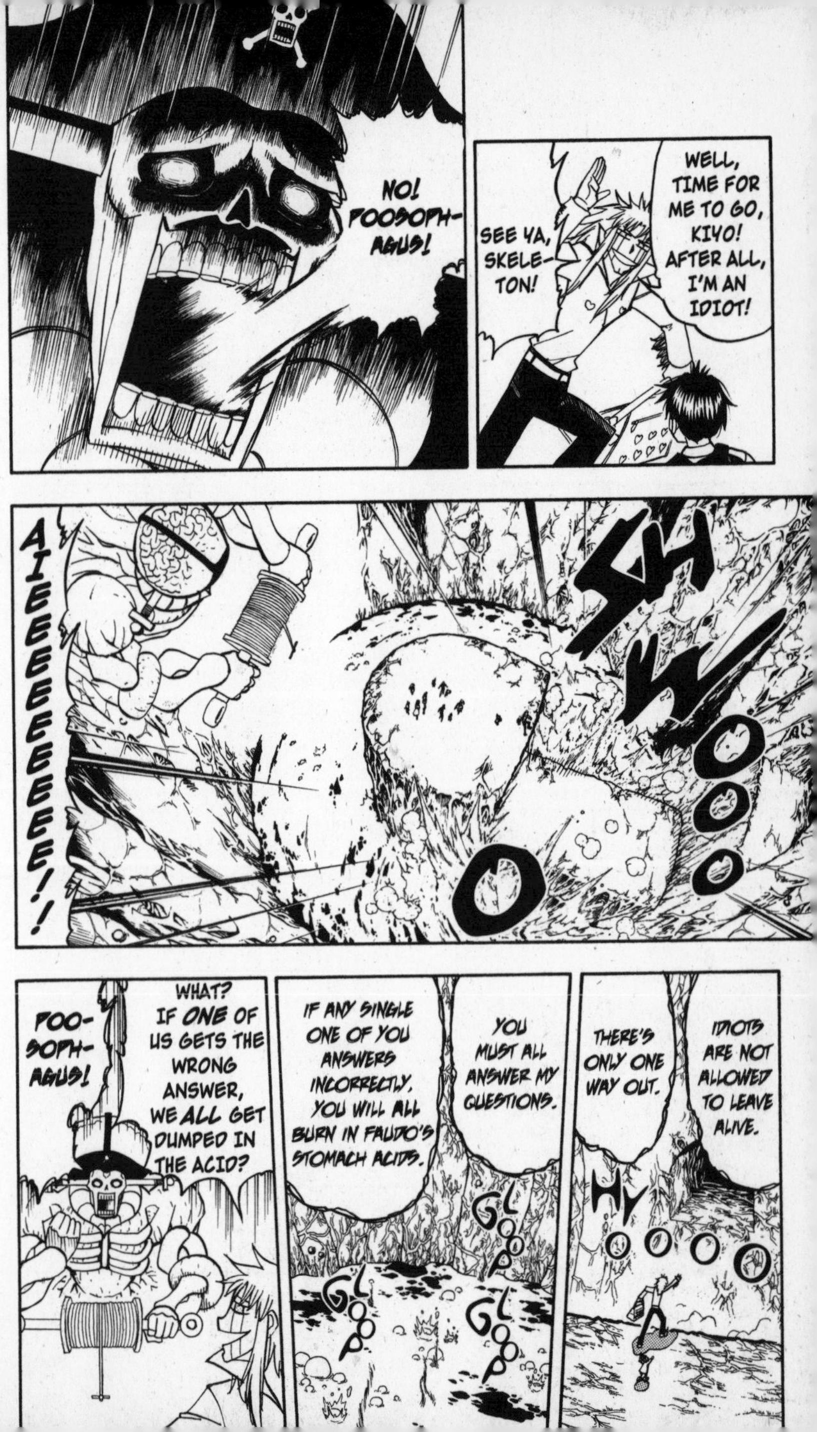
WELL, TIME FOR ME TO GO, KIYO! AFTER ALL, I'M AN IDIOT!
SEE YA, SKELETON!
NO! POOSOPHAGUS!
SHWOOOOOO
AIEEEEEEEEEE!!
IDIOTS ARE NOT ALLOWED TO LEAVE ALIVE.
THERE'S ONLY ONE WAY OUT.
HYOOOOO
YOU MUST ALL ANSWER MY QUESTIONS.
IF ANY SINGLE ONE OF YOU ANSWERS INCORRECTLY, YOU WILL ALL BURN IN FAUDO'S STOMACH ACIDS.
GLOOP
GLOOP
GLOOP
WHAT? IF ONE OF US GETS THE WRONG ANSWER, WE ALL GET DUMPED IN THE ACID?
POOSOPHAGUS!

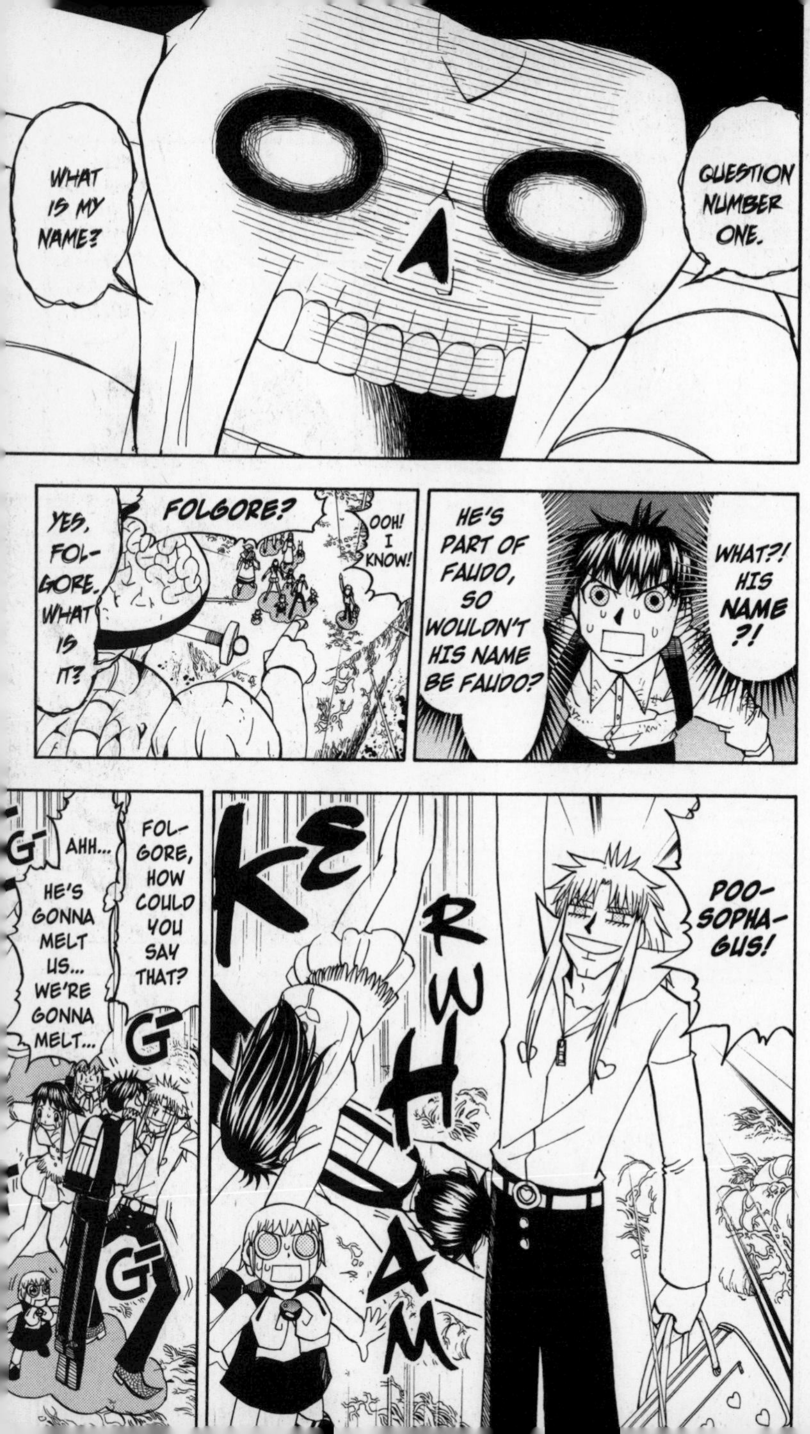
QUESTION NUMBER ONE.
WHAT IS MY NAME?
WHAT?! HIS NAME?!
HE'S PART OF FAUDO, SO WOULDN'T HIS NAME BE FAUDO?
OOH! I KNOW!
FOLGORE?
YES, FOLGORE. WHAT IS IT?
POOSOPHAGUS!
KERWHUAM
FOLGORE, HOW COULD YOU SAY THAT?
AHH... HE'S GONNA MELT US... WE'RE GONNA MELT...
G- G- G-

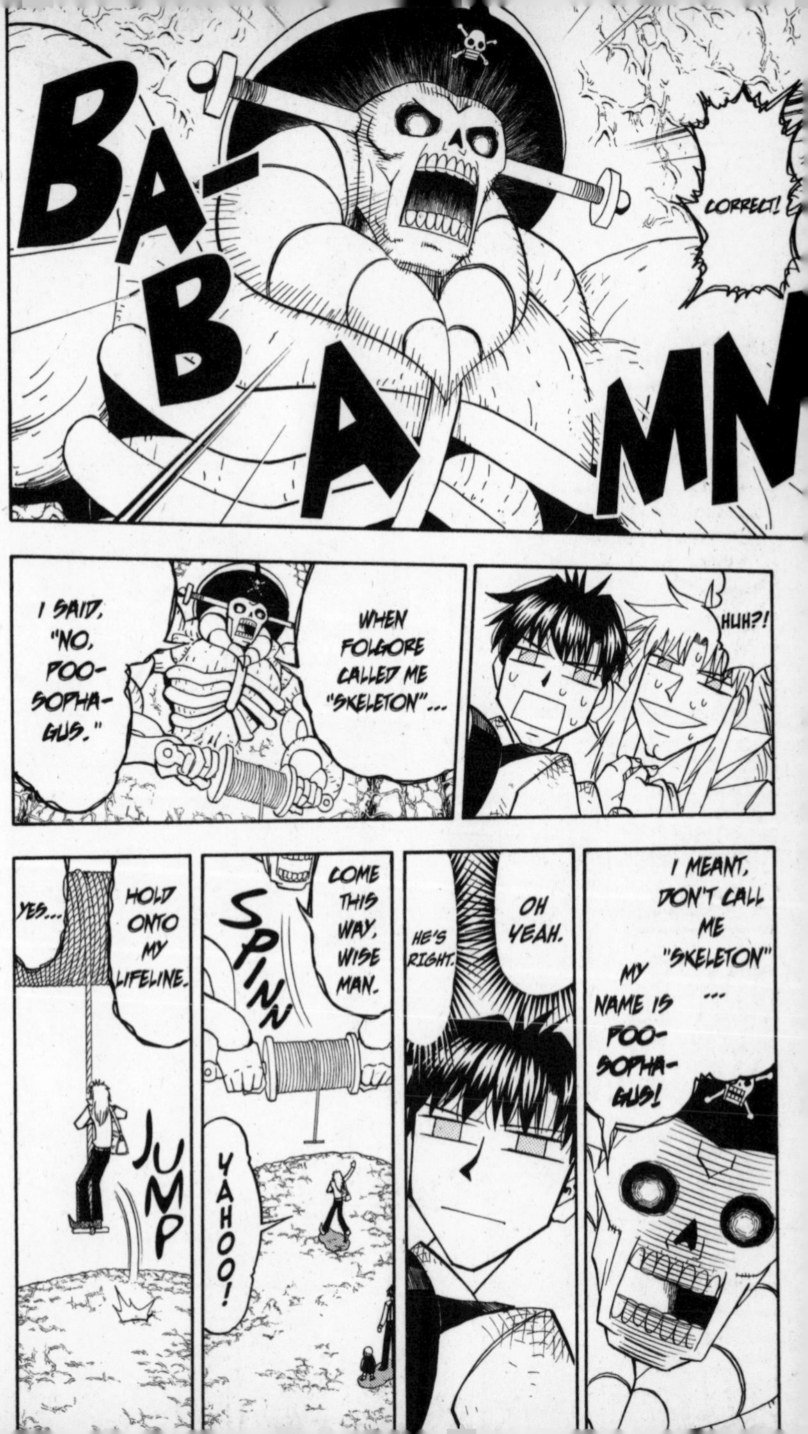
CORRECT!
BA-BAMMN
HUH?!
WHEN FOLGORE CALLED ME "SKELETON"...
I SAID, "NO, POO-SOPHAGUS."
I MEANT, DON'T CALL ME "SKELETON"...
MY NAME IS POO-SOPHAGUS!
OH YEAH.
HE'S RIGHT.
COME THIS WAY, WISE MAN.
SPINN
YAHOO!
HOLD ONTO MY LIFELINE.
YES...
JUMP

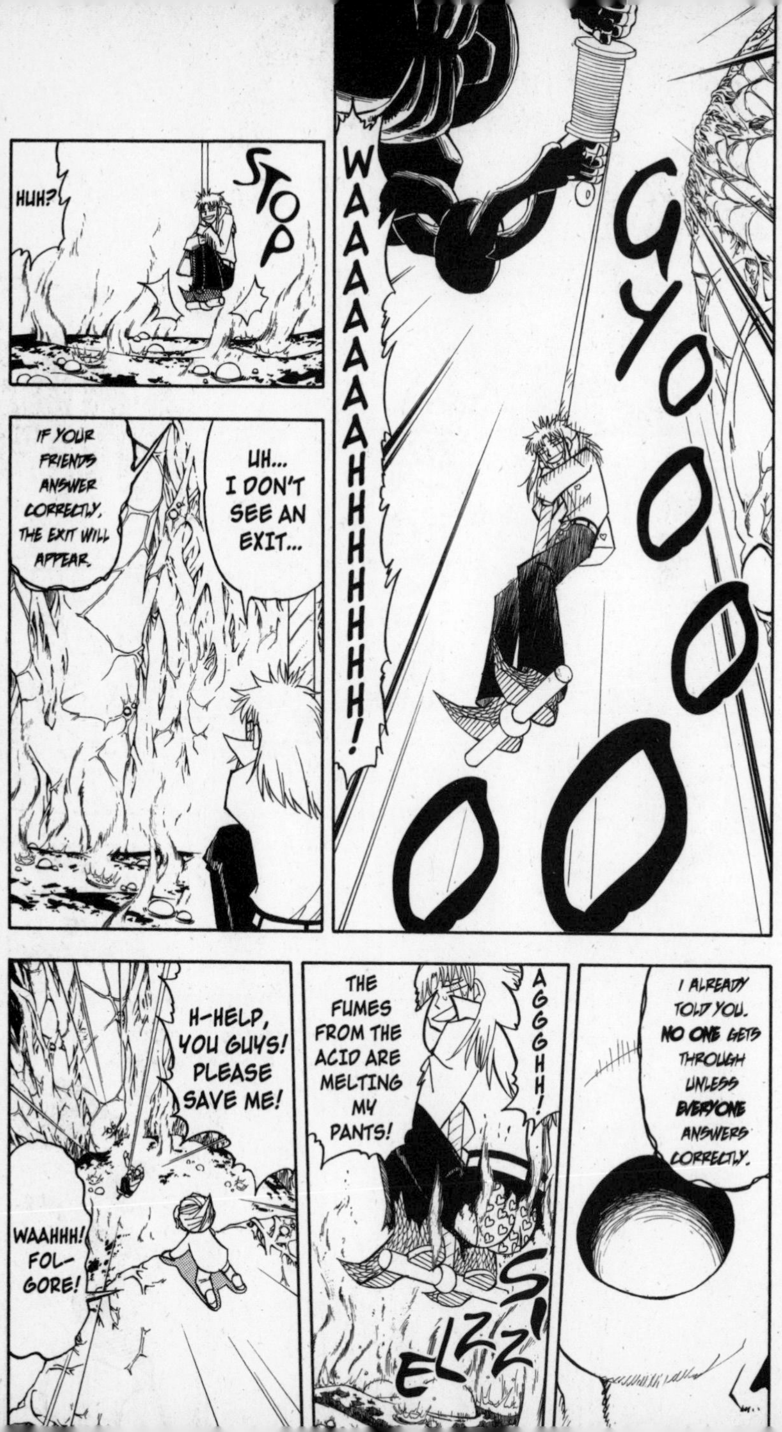

GYOOOOOOOO
WAAAAAAAAAAAHHHHHHHHH!
STOP
HUH?
UH... I DON'T SEE AN EXIT...
IF YOUR FRIENDS ANSWER CORRECTLY, THE EXIT WILL APPEAR.
I ALREADY TOLD YOU. NO ONE GETS THROUGH UNLESS EVERYONE ANSWERS CORRECTLY.
AGGGHH!
THE FUMES FROM THE ACID ARE MELTING MY PANTS!
SIZZLE
H-HELP, YOU GUYS! PLEASE SAVE ME!
WAAHHH! FOL-GORE!

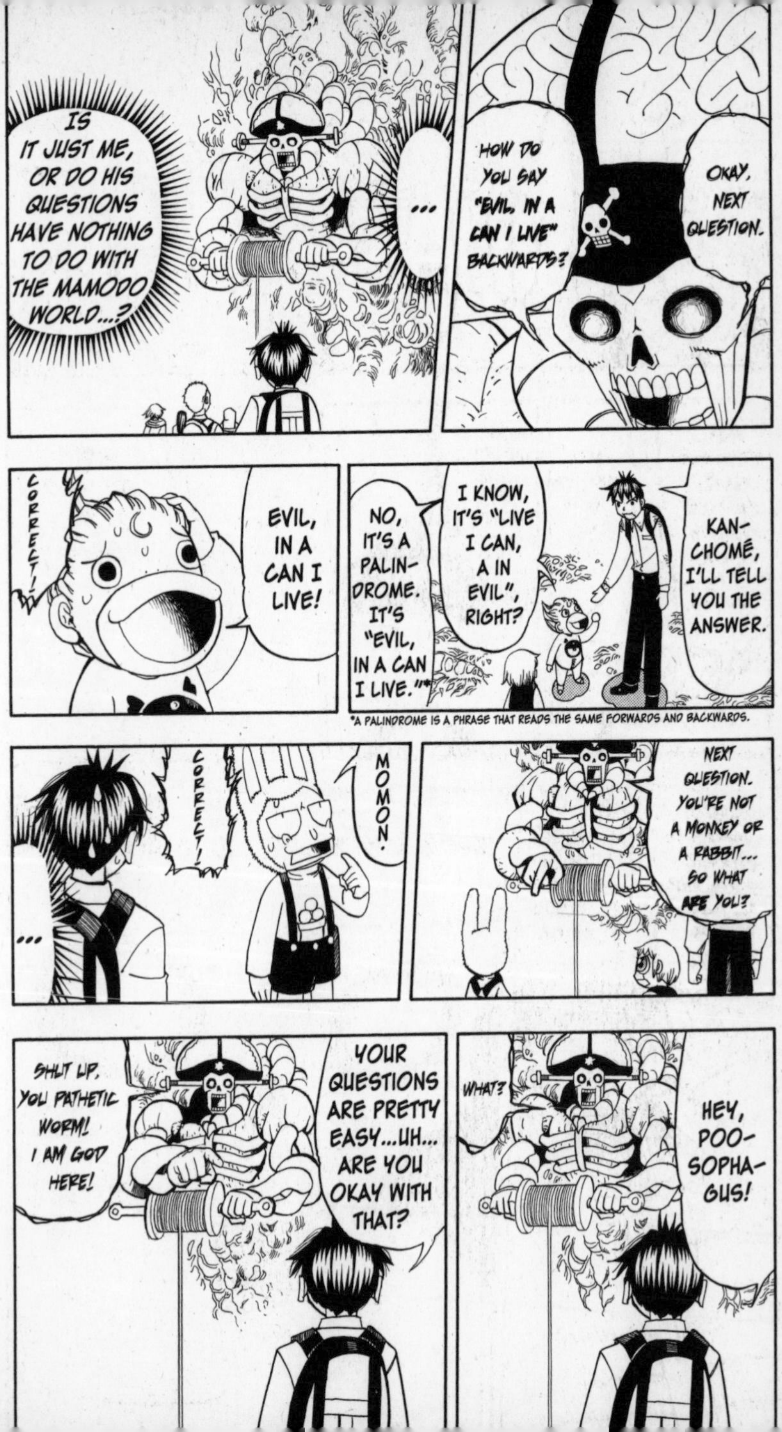
OKAY, NEXT QUESTION.
HOW DO YOU SAY "EVIL, IN A CAN I LIVE" BACKWARDS?
...
IS IT JUST ME, OR DO HIS QUESTIONS HAVE NOTHING TO DO WITH THE MAMODO WORLD...?
KANCHOME, I'LL TELL YOU THE ANSWER.
I KNOW, IT'S "LIVE I CAN, A IN EVIL", RIGHT?
NO, IT'S A PALINDROME. IT'S "EVIL, IN A CAN I LIVE."*
EVIL, IN A CAN I LIVE!
CORRECT!
NEXT QUESTION. YOU'RE NOT A MONKEY OR A RABBIT... SO WHAT ARE YOU?
MOMON.
CORRECT!
...
HEY, POOSOPHAGUS!
WHAT?
YOUR QUESTIONS ARE PRETTY EASY...UH... ARE YOU OKAY WITH THAT?
SHUT UP, YOU PATHETIC WORM! I AM GOD HERE!

*A PALINDROME IS A PHRASE THAT READS THE SAME FORWARDS AND BACKWARDS.

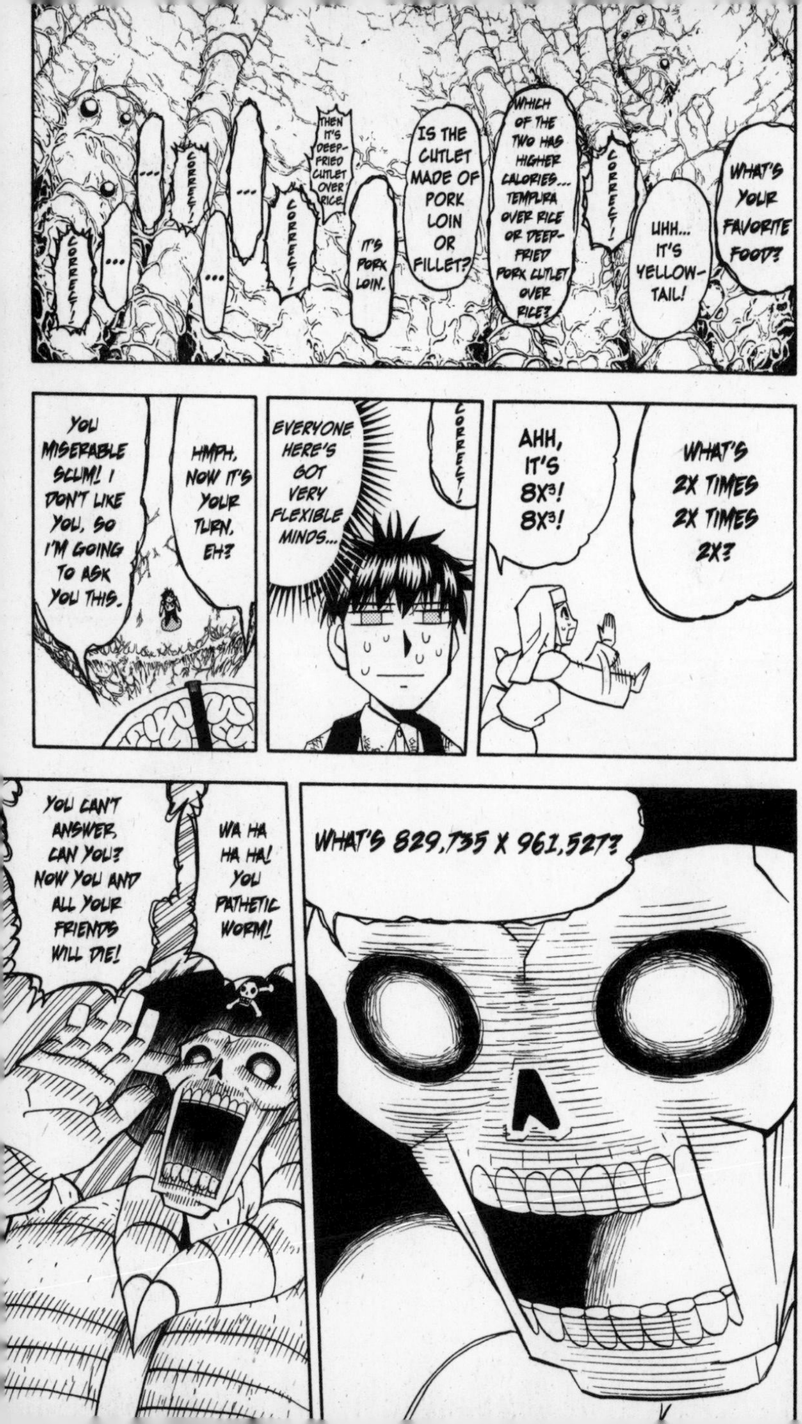
WHAT'S YOUR FAVORITE FOOD?
UHH... IT'S YELLOW-TAIL!
CORRECT!
WHICH OF THE TWO HAS HIGHER CALORIES... TEMPURA OVER RICE OR DEEP-FRIED PORK CUTLET OVER RICE?
THEN IT'S DEEP-FRIED CUTLET OVER RICE.
IS THE CUTLET MADE OF PORK LOIN OR FILLET?
IT'S PORK LOIN.
CORRECT!
...
CORRECT!
...
CORRECT!
...
CORRECT!
WHAT'S 2X TIMES 2X TIMES 2X?
AHH, IT'S $8X^3$! $8X^3$!
CORRECT!
EVERYONE HERE'S GOT VERY FLEXIBLE MINDS...
HMPH, NOW IT'S YOUR TURN, EH?
YOU MISERABLE SCUM! I DON'T LIKE YOU, SO I'M GOING TO ASK YOU THIS.
WHAT'S 829,735 X 961,527?
WA HA HA HA! YOU PATHETIC WORM!
YOU CAN'T ANSWER, CAN YOU? NOW YOU AND ALL YOUR FRIENDS WILL DIE!

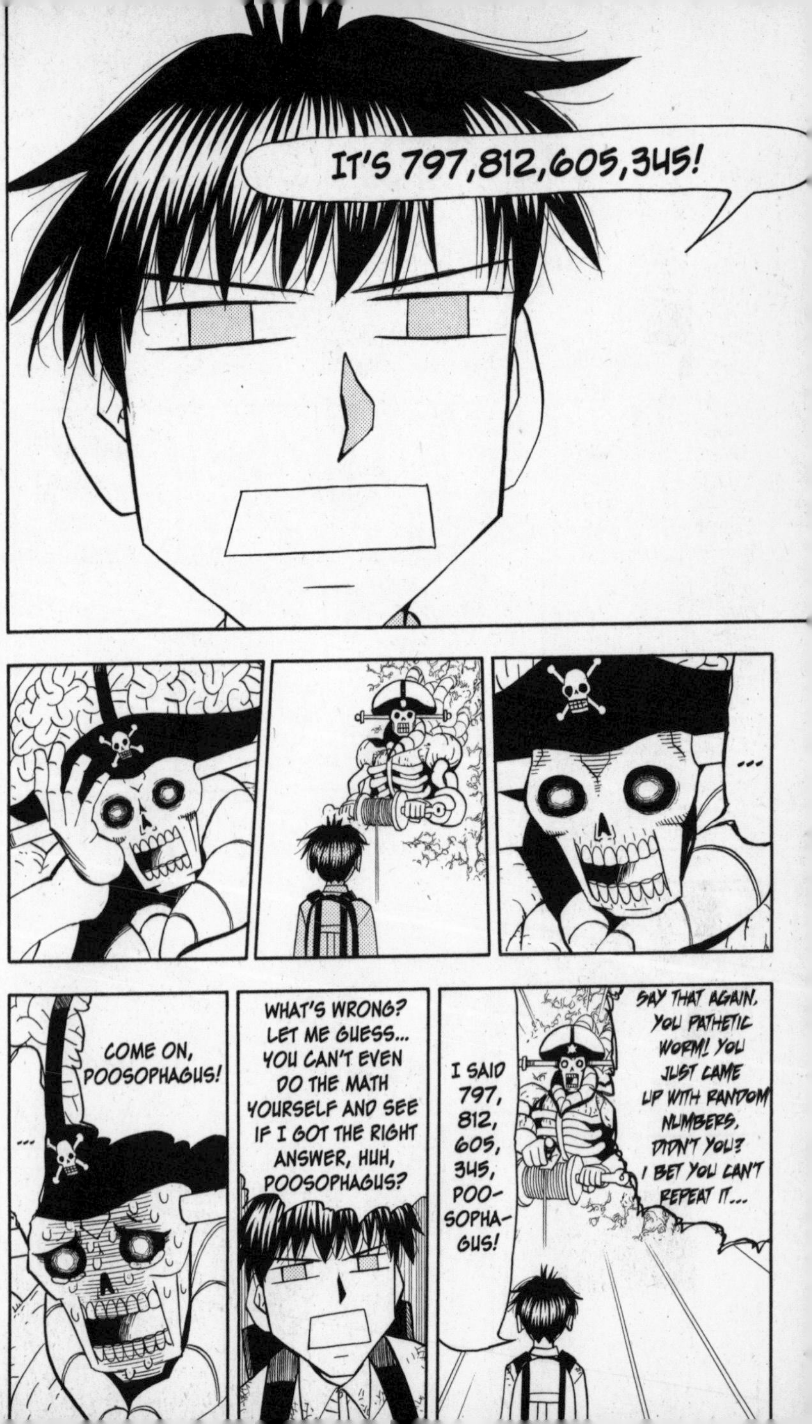
IT'S 797,812,605,345!
...
SAY THAT AGAIN, YOU PATHETIC WORM! YOU JUST CAME UP WITH RANDOM NUMBERS, DIDN'T YOU? I BET YOU CAN'T REPEAT IT...
I SAID 797, 812, 605, 345, POOSOPHAGUS!
WHAT'S WRONG? LET ME GUESS... YOU CAN'T EVEN DO THE MATH YOURSELF AND SEE IF I GOT THE RIGHT ANSWER, HUH, POOSOPHAGUS?
COME ON, POOSOPHAGUS!
...

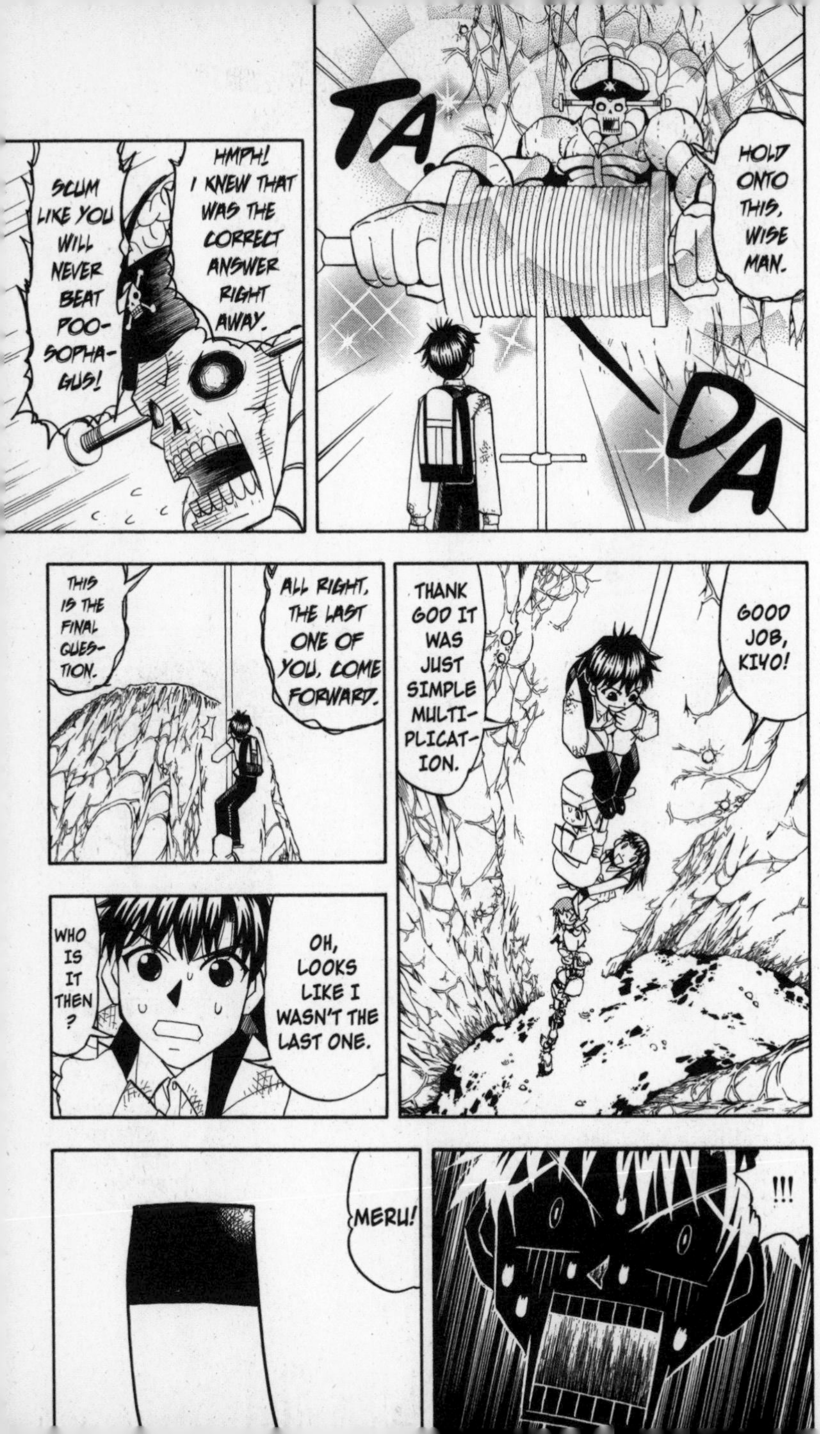
TA
DA
HOLD ONTO THIS, WISE MAN.
HMPH! I KNEW THAT WAS THE CORRECT ANSWER RIGHT AWAY.
SCUM LIKE YOU WILL NEVER BEAT POO-SOPHAGUS!
GOOD JOB, KIYO!
THANK GOD IT WAS JUST SIMPLE MULTI-PLICAT-ION.
ALL RIGHT, THE LAST ONE OF YOU, COME FORWARD.
THIS IS THE FINAL QUES-TION.
OH, LOOKS LIKE I WASN'T THE LAST ONE.
WHO IS IT THEN?
!!!
MERU!

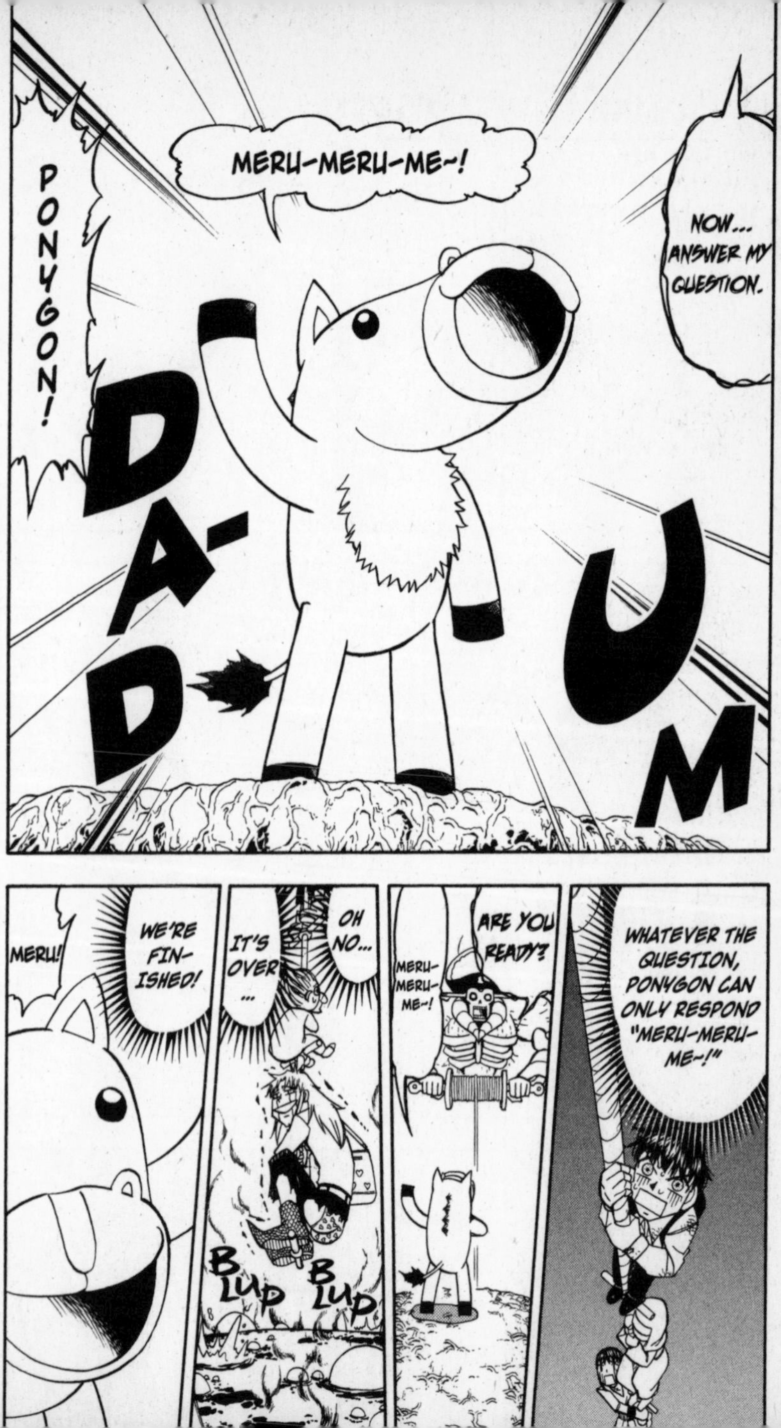
NOW... ANSWER MY QUESTION.
MERU-MERU-ME~!
PONYGON!
DA-DUM
WHATEVER THE QUESTION, PONYGON CAN ONLY RESPOND "MERU-MERU-ME~!"
ARE YOU READY?
MERU-MERU-ME~!
OH NO...
IT'S OVER...
BLUP
BLUP
WE'RE FIN-ISHED!
MERU!

# LEVEL 200: Meru-meru-me~!

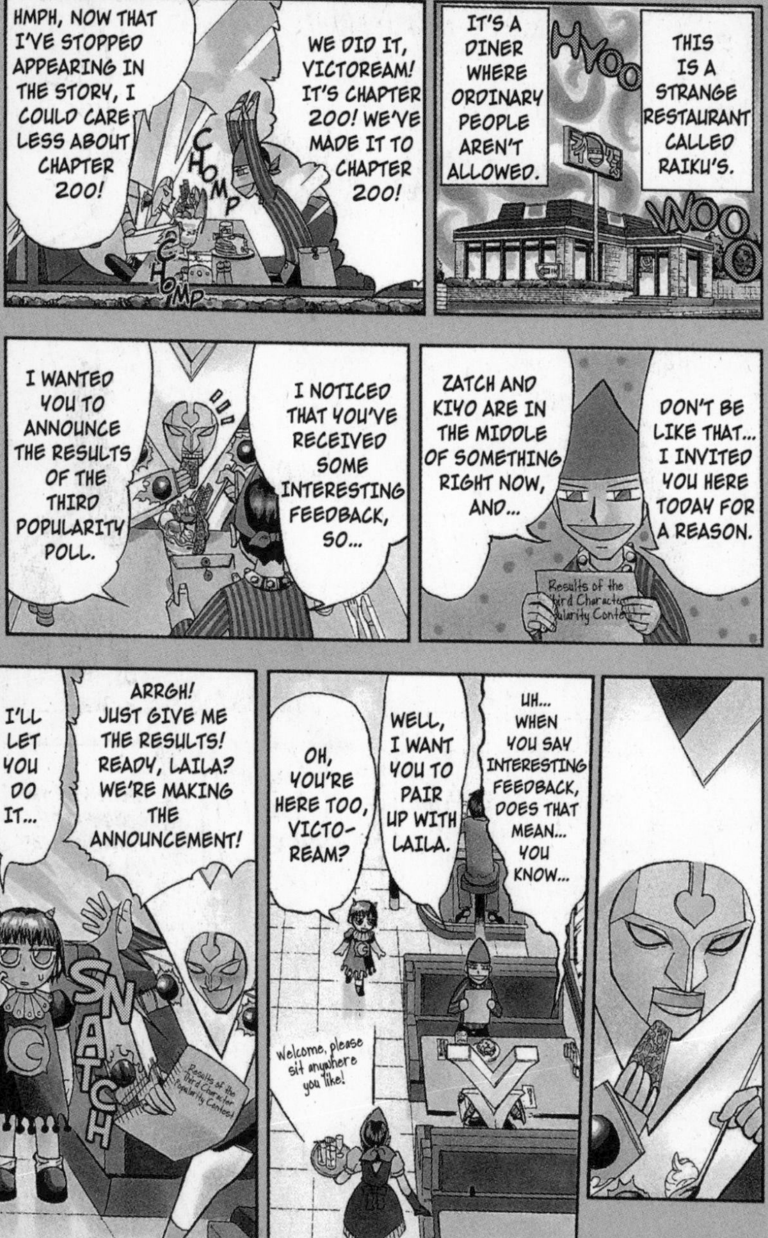
THIS IS A STRANGE RESTAURANT CALLED RAIKU'S.
HYOO
WOO
IT'S A DINER WHERE ORDINARY PEOPLE AREN'T ALLOWED.
WE DID IT, VICTOREAM! IT'S CHAPTER 200! WE'VE MADE IT TO CHAPTER 200!
HMPH, NOW THAT I'VE STOPPED APPEARING IN THE STORY, I COULD CARE LESS ABOUT CHAPTER 200!
CHOMP
CHOMP
DON'T BE LIKE THAT... I INVITED YOU HERE TODAY FOR A REASON.
ZATCH AND KIYO ARE IN THE MIDDLE OF SOMETHING RIGHT NOW, AND...
I NOTICED THAT YOU'VE RECEIVED SOME INTERESTING FEEDBACK, SO...
I WANTED YOU TO ANNOUNCE THE RESULTS OF THE THIRD POPULARITY POLL.
UH... WHEN YOU SAY INTERESTING FEEDBACK, DOES THAT MEAN... YOU KNOW...
WELL, I WANT YOU TO PAIR UP WITH LAILA.
OH, YOU'RE HERE TOO, VICTOREAM?
Welcome, please sit anywhere you like!
ARRGH! JUST GIVE ME THE RESULTS! READY, LAILA? WE'RE MAKING THE ANNOUNCEMENT!
I'LL LET YOU DO IT...
SNATCH
Results of the Third Character Popularity Contest!

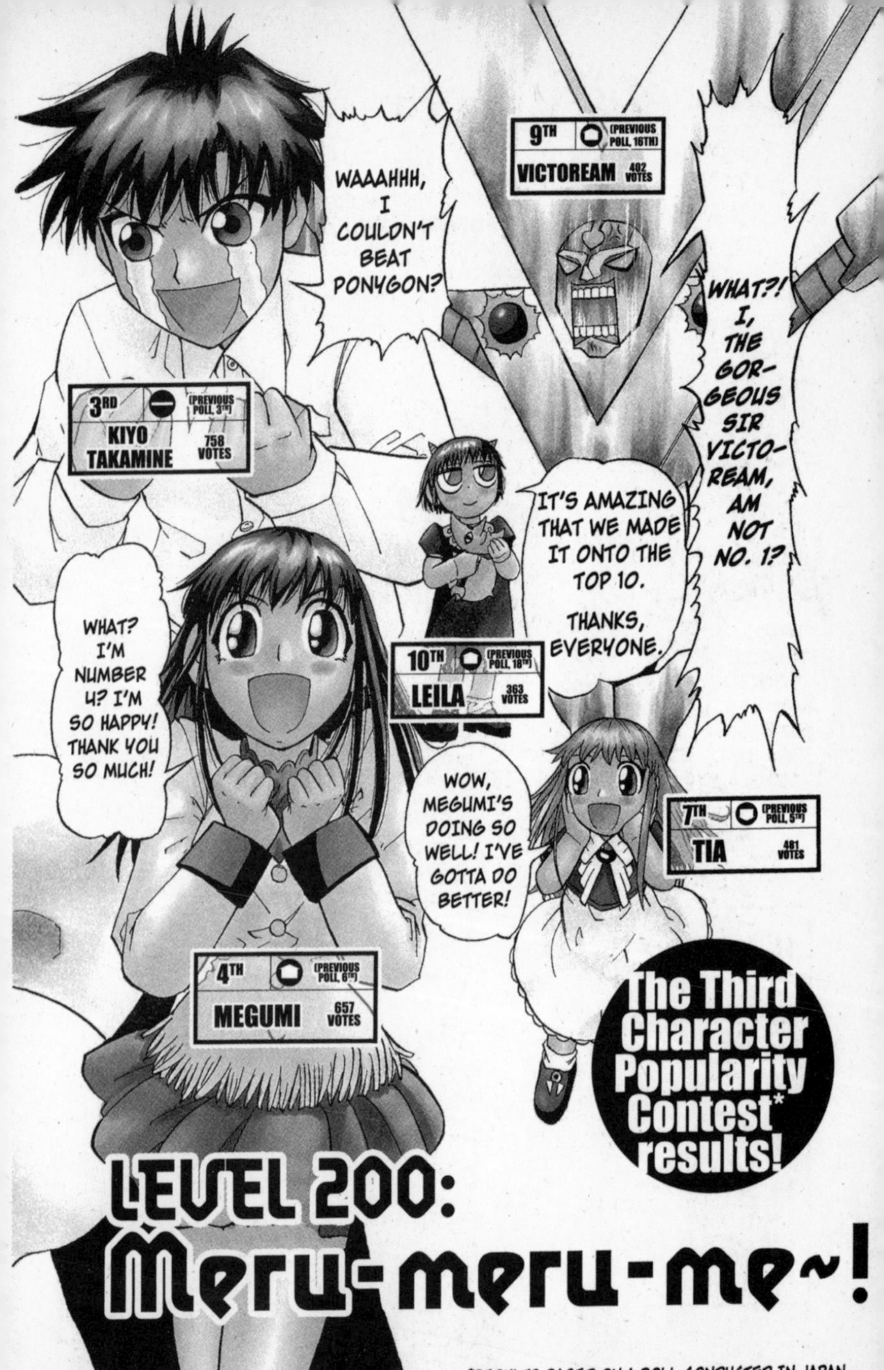
9TH (PREVIOUS POLL, 16TH) VICTOREAM 402 VOTES
WHAT?! I, THE GORGEOUS SIR VICTOREAM, AM NOT NO. 1?
WAAAHHH, I COULDN'T BEAT PONYGON?
3RD (PREVIOUS POLL, 3RD) KIYO TAKAMINE 758 VOTES
IT'S AMAZING THAT WE MADE IT ONTO THE TOP 10.
THANKS, EVERYONE.
10TH (PREVIOUS POLL, 18TH) LEILA 363 VOTES
WHAT? I'M NUMBER 4? I'M SO HAPPY! THANK YOU SO MUCH!
7TH (PREVIOUS POLL, 5TH) TIA 481 VOTES
WOW, MEGUMI'S DOING SO WELL! I'VE GOTTA DO BETTER!
4TH (PREVIOUS POLL, 6TH) MEGUMI 657 VOTES
The Third Character Popularity Contest* results!
LEVEL 200: Meru-meru-me~!

*RESULTS BASED ON A POLL CONDUCTED IN JAPAN.

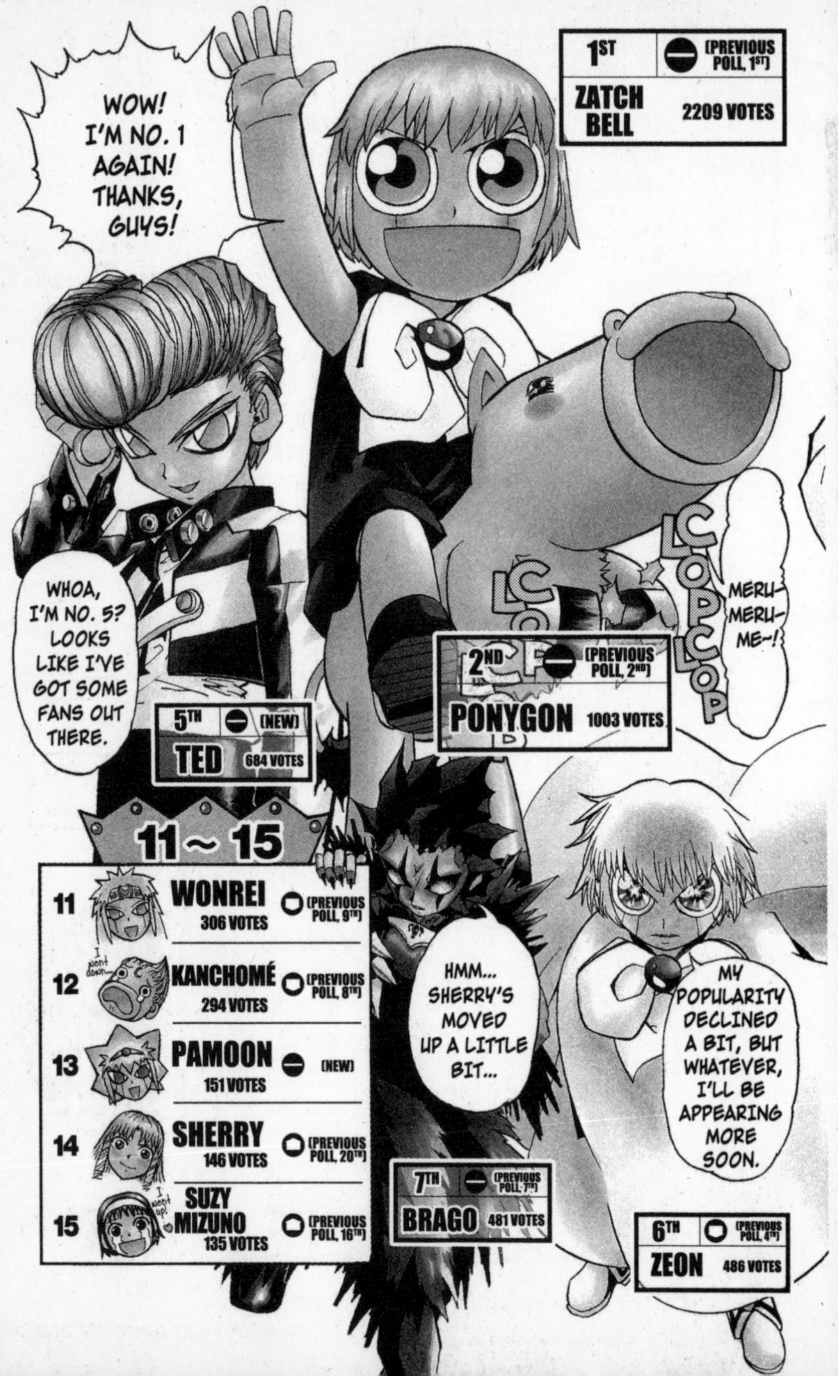
1ST (PREVIOUS POLL, 1ST)
ZATCH BELL 2209 VOTES
WOW! I'M NO. 1 AGAIN! THANKS, GUYS!
MERU-MERU-ME~!
CLOP CLOP
2ND (PREVIOUS POLL, 2ND)
PONYGON 1003 VOTES
WHOA, I'M NO. 5? LOOKS LIKE I'VE GOT SOME FANS OUT THERE.
5TH (NEW)
TED 684 VOTES
MY POPULARITY DECLINED A BIT, BUT WHATEVER, I'LL BE APPEARING MORE SOON.
6TH (PREVIOUS POLL, 4TH)
ZEON 486 VOTES
HMM... SHERRY'S MOVED UP A LITTLE BIT...
7TH (PREVIOUS POLL, 7TH)
BRAGO 481 VOTES
11 ~ 15
11 WONREI 306 VOTES (PREVIOUS POLL, 9TH)
I went down...
12 KANCHOMÉ 294 VOTES (PREVIOUS POLL, 8TH)
13 PAMOON 151 VOTES (NEW)
14 SHERRY 146 VOTES (PREVIOUS POLL, 20TH)
I went up!
15 SUZY MIZUNO 135 VOTES (PREVIOUS POLL, 16TH)

# THE 3RD CHARACTER POPULARITY CONTEST RESULTS!

## 16~46

| | CHARACTER | VOTES | PREVIOUS POLL |
|---|---|---|---|
| 16 | VOLCAN 300 | 126 VOTES | ↓ |
| 17 | DANNY | 107 VOTES | ↓ |
| 18 | KEDO | 102 VOTES | ↓ |
| 19 | PARCO FOLGORE | 93 VOTES | ↓ |
| | ARTH | 93 VOTES | NEW |
| | MOMON | 93 VOTES | NEW |
| 22 | NAOMI | 86 VOTES | ↓ |
| 23 | DUFORT | 71 VOTES | ↑ |
| | KAFK SUNBEAM | 71 VOTES | ↑ |
| | PENNY | 71 VOTES | ↑ |
| | DEMOLT | 71 VOTES | NEW |
| 27 | MISS SUSAN | 62 VOTES | − |
| | ELLIE | 62 VOTES | NEW |
| 29 | REIN | 57 VOTES | NEW |
| 30 | KOKO | 54 VOTES | ↑ |
| | ALBERT | 54 VOTES | NEW |
| 32 | ELLE CHIVAS | 49 VOTES | NEW |
| 33 | MARIKO NAKAMURA | 44 VOTES | ↑ |
| | KORAL Q | 44 VOTES | NEW |
| 35 | DR. RIDDLES | 43 VOTES | ↓ |
| 36 | KOLULU | 36 VOTES | ↓ |
| | LI-EN | 36 VOTES | ↑ |
| | RIOU | 36 VOTES | NEW |
| 39 | TSAO-LON | 35 VOTES | ↓ |
| 40 | ZOFIS | 33 VOTES | ↓ |
| | APOLLO | 33 VOTES | ↓ |
| | BELGIM E.O. | 33 VOTES | ↓ |
| 43 | REYCOM | 18 VOTES | ↑ |
| | PRAYING MANTIS JOE | 18 VOTES | ↓ |
| | BYONKO | 18 VOTES | NEW |
| 46 | NURSE | 13 VOTES | ↓ |
| | WIFE | 13 VOTES | ↑ |
| | ROPS | 13 VOTES | ↓ |
| | JIDO | 13 VOTES | NEW |
| | KARUDIO | 13 VOTES | NEW |
| | WISEMAN | 13 VOTES | NEW |

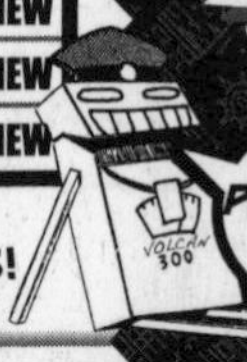
VOLCAN 300

PREVIOUS POLL

THANK YOU SO MUCH FOR SENDING IN YOUR VOTES!

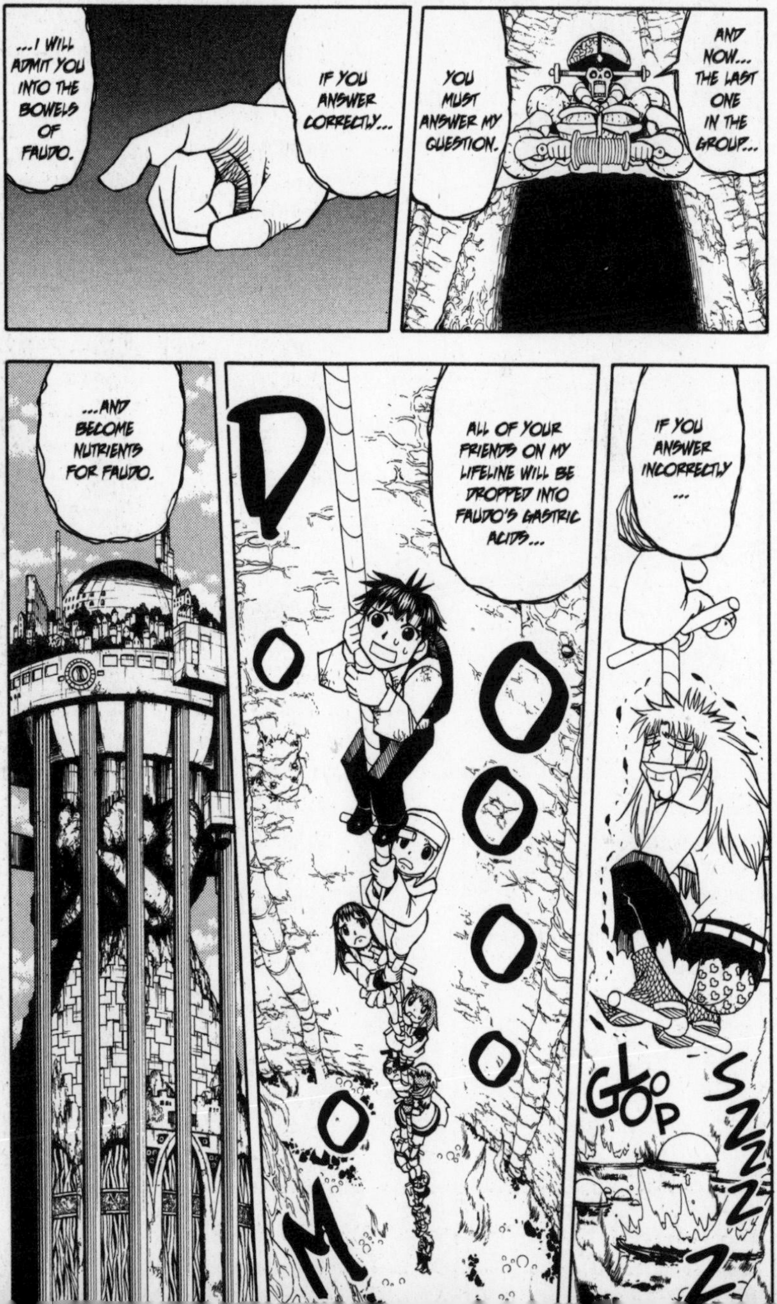
AND NOW... THE LAST ONE IN THE GROUP...
YOU MUST ANSWER MY QUESTION.
IF YOU ANSWER CORRECTLY...
...I WILL ADMIT YOU INTO THE BOWELS OF FAUDO.
IF YOU ANSWER INCORRECTLY ...
GLOOP
SZZZZ
ALL OF YOUR FRIENDS ON MY LIFELINE WILL BE DROPPED INTO FAUDO'S GASTRIC ACIDS...
DOOOOOOM
...AND BECOME NUTRIENTS FOR FAUDO.

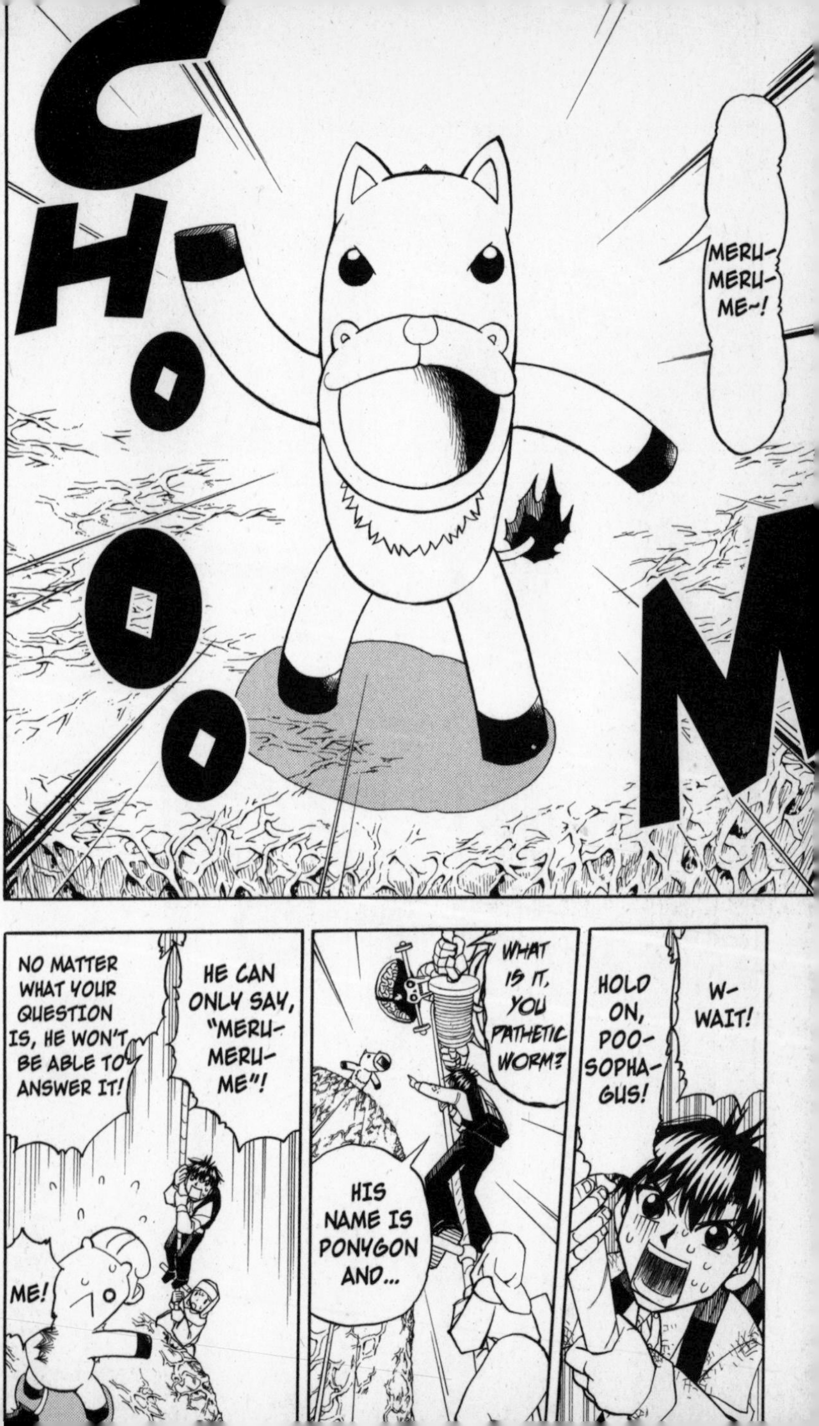
MERU-MERU-ME~!
CHOOOM
W-WAIT!
HOLD ON, POO-SOPHAGUS!
WHAT IS IT, YOU PATHETIC WORM?
HIS NAME IS PONYGON AND...
HE CAN ONLY SAY, "MERU-MERU-ME"!
NO MATTER WHAT YOUR QUESTION IS, HE WON'T BE ABLE TO ANSWER IT!
ME!

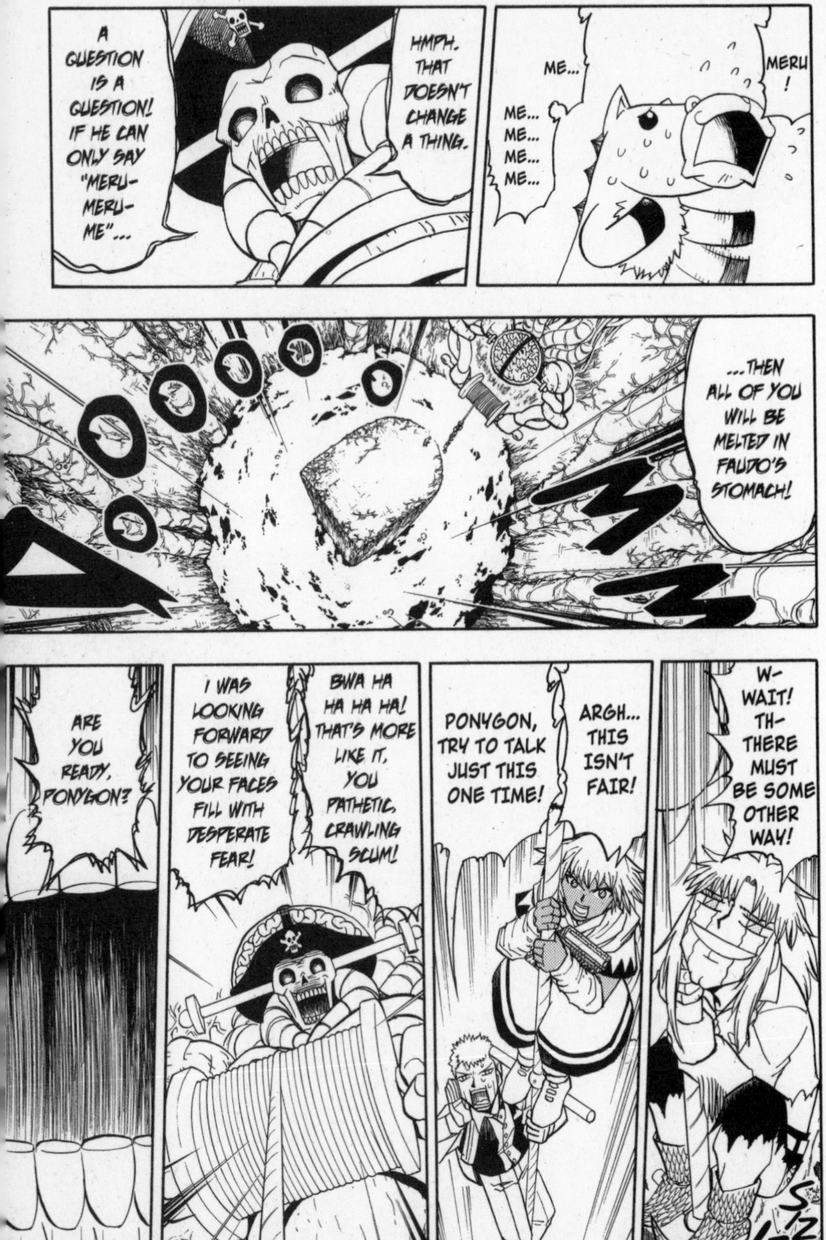
MERU!
ME...
ME... ME... ME... ME...
HMPH. THAT DOESN'T CHANGE A THING.
A QUESTION IS A QUESTION! IF HE CAN ONLY SAY "MERU-MERU-ME"...
...THEN ALL OF YOU WILL BE MELTED IN FAUDO'S STOMACH!
W- WAIT! TH- THERE MUST BE SOME OTHER WAY!
ARGH... THIS ISN'T FAIR!
PONYGON, TRY TO TALK JUST THIS ONE TIME!
BWA HA HA HA HA! THAT'S MORE LIKE IT, YOU PATHETIC, CRAWLING SCUM!
I WAS LOOKING FORWARD TO SEEING YOUR FACES FILL WITH DESPERATE FEAR!
ARE YOU READY, PONYGON?

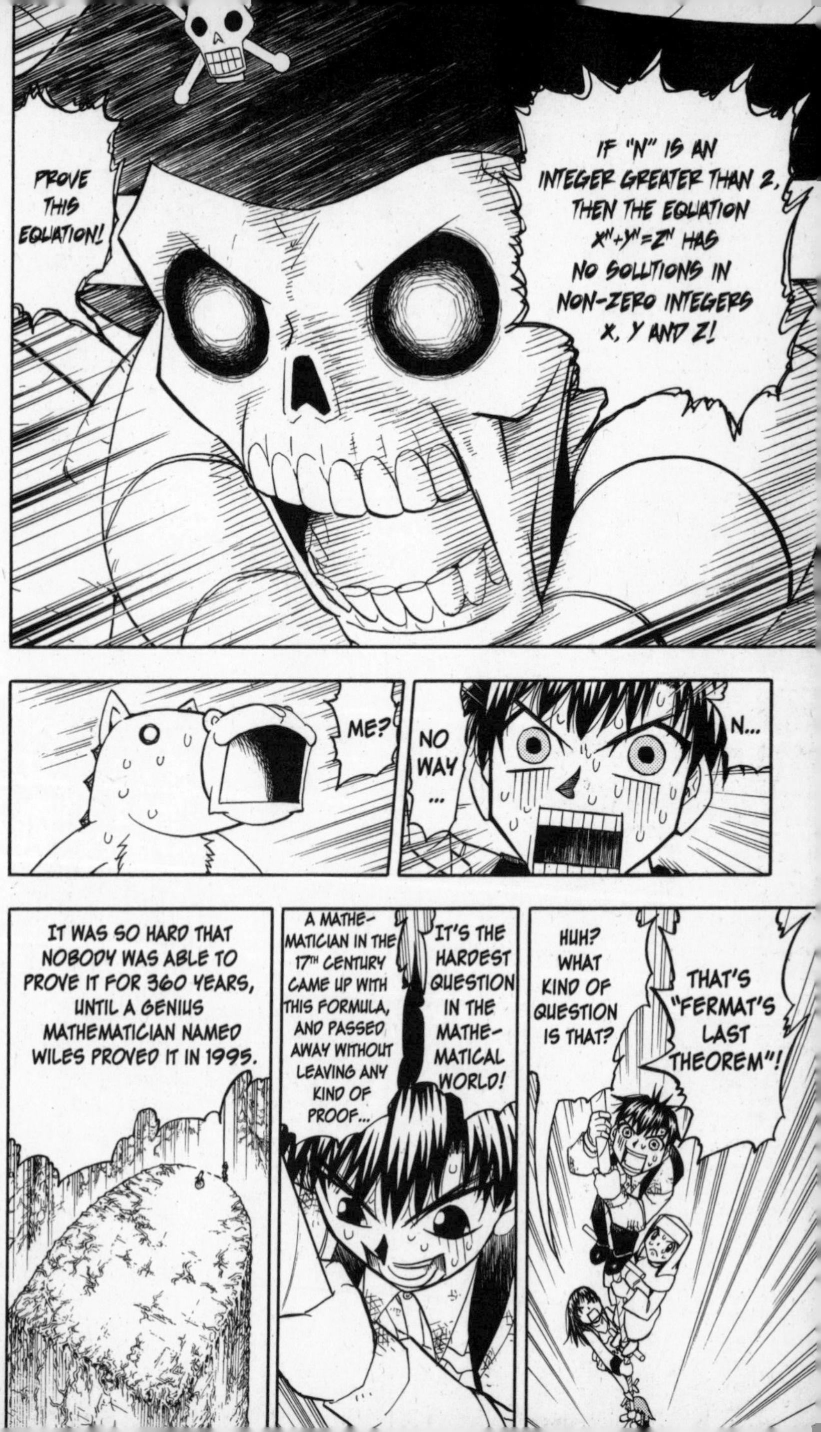
IF "N" IS AN INTEGER GREATER THAN 2, THEN THE EQUATION $X^N+Y^N=Z^N$ HAS NO SOLUTIONS IN NON-ZERO INTEGERS X, Y AND Z!
PROVE THIS EQUATION!
N...
NO WAY ...
ME?
HUH? WHAT KIND OF QUESTION IS THAT?
THAT'S "FERMAT'S LAST THEOREM"!
IT'S THE HARDEST QUESTION IN THE MATHEMATICAL WORLD!
A MATHEMATICIAN IN THE 17TH CENTURY CAME UP WITH THIS FORMULA, AND PASSED AWAY WITHOUT LEAVING ANY KIND OF PROOF...
IT WAS SO HARD THAT NOBODY WAS ABLE TO PROVE IT FOR 360 YEARS, UNTIL A GENIUS MATHEMATICIAN NAMED WILES PROVED IT IN 1995.

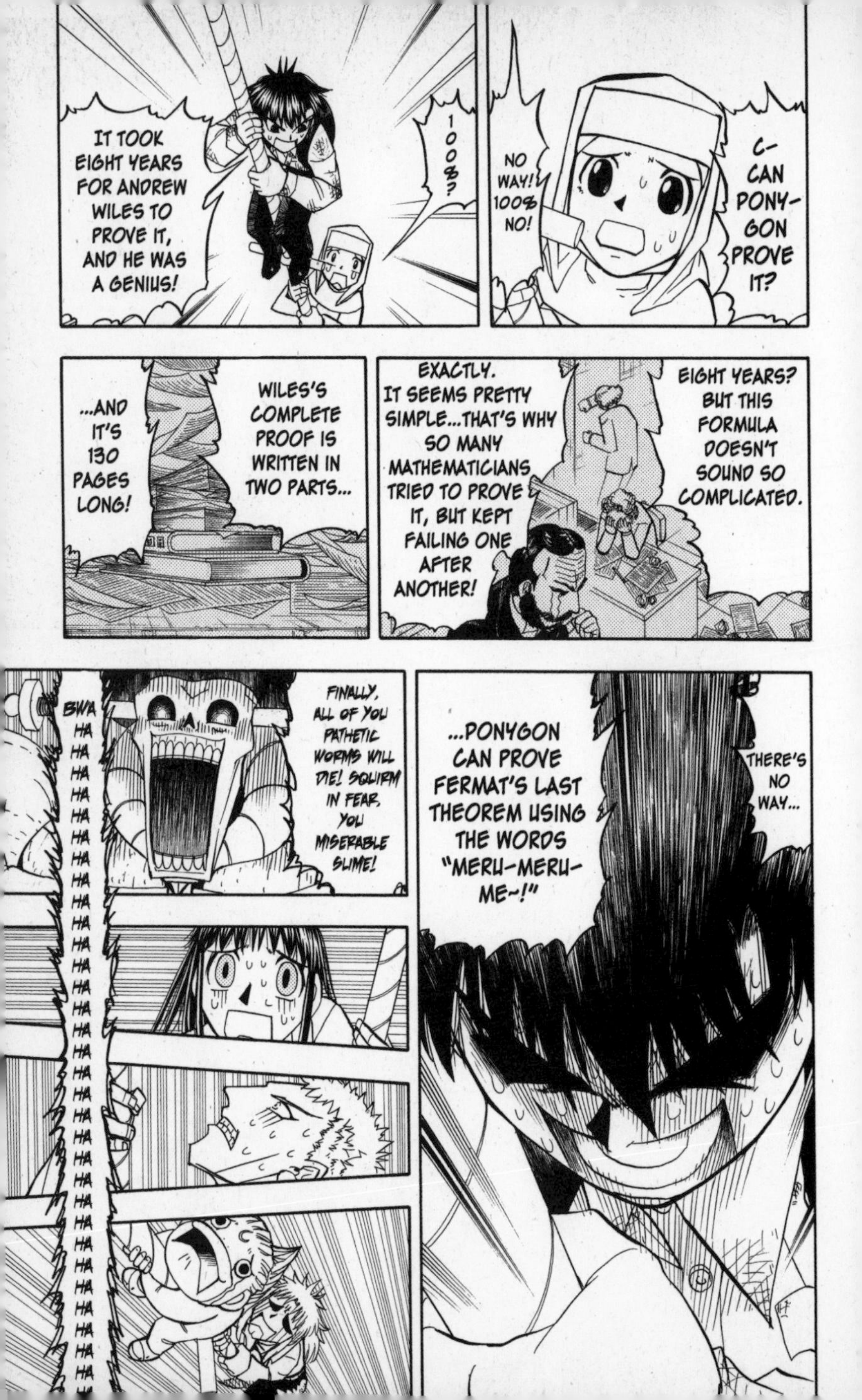
C-CAN PONYGON PROVE IT?
NO WAY! 100% NO!
100%?
IT TOOK EIGHT YEARS FOR ANDREW WILES TO PROVE IT, AND HE WAS A GENIUS!
EIGHT YEARS? BUT THIS FORMULA DOESN'T SOUND SO COMPLICATED.
EXACTLY. IT SEEMS PRETTY SIMPLE...THAT'S WHY SO MANY MATHEMATICIANS TRIED TO PROVE IT, BUT KEPT FAILING ONE AFTER ANOTHER!
WILES'S COMPLETE PROOF IS WRITTEN IN TWO PARTS...
...AND IT'S 130 PAGES LONG!
THERE'S NO WAY...
...PONYGON CAN PROVE FERMAT'S LAST THEOREM USING THE WORDS "MERU-MERU-ME~!"
FINALLY, ALL OF YOU PATHETIC WORMS WILL DIE! SQUIRM IN FEAR, YOU MISERABLE SLIME!
BWA HA HA HA HA HA HA HA HA HA HA HA HA HA HA HA HA HA HA HA HA HA HA HA HA HA HA HA HA HA HA HA HA

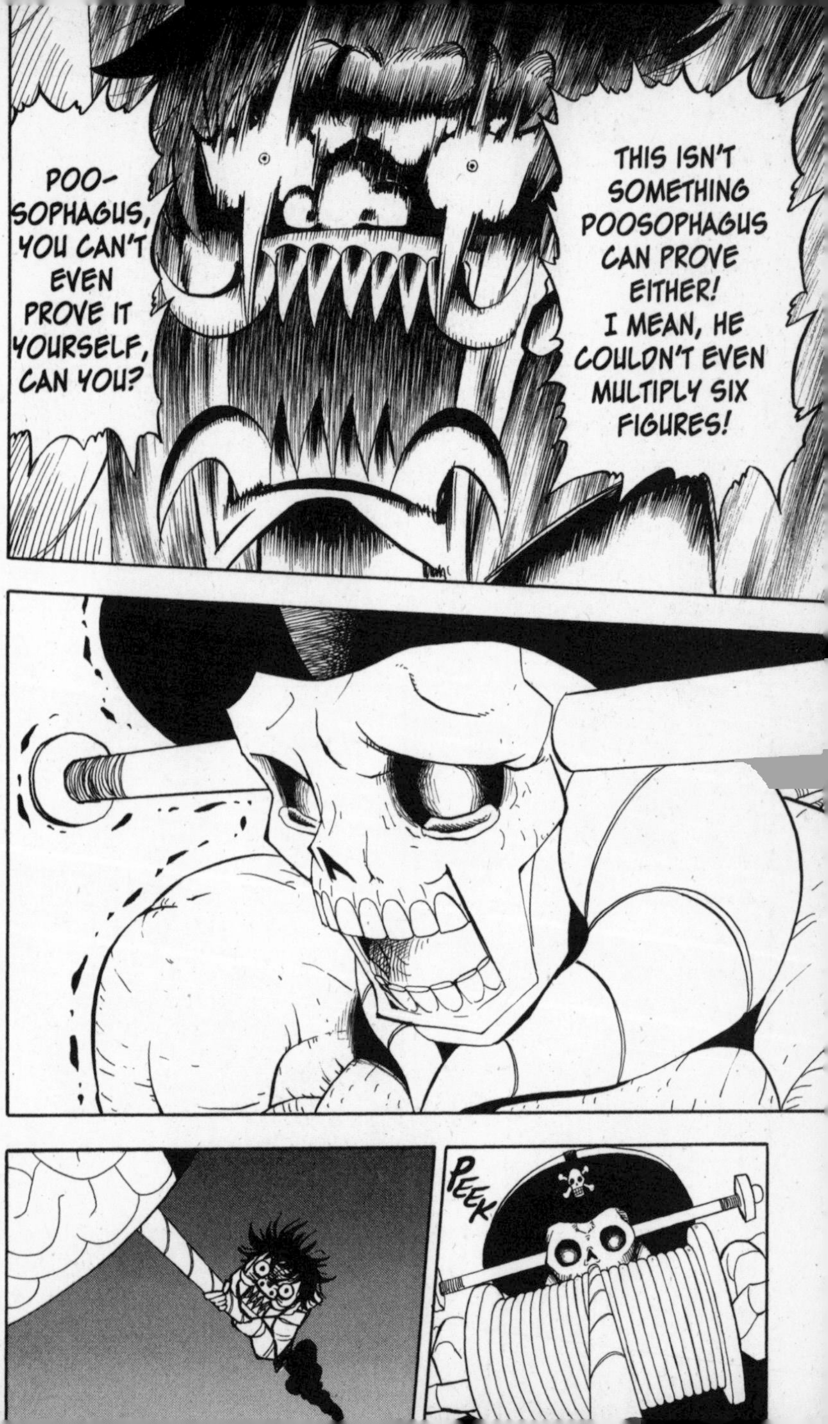
THIS ISN'T SOMETHING POOSOPHAGUS CAN PROVE EITHER! I MEAN, HE COULDN'T EVEN MULTIPLY SIX FIGURES!
POO-SOPHAGUS, YOU CAN'T EVEN PROVE IT YOURSELF, CAN YOU?
PEEK

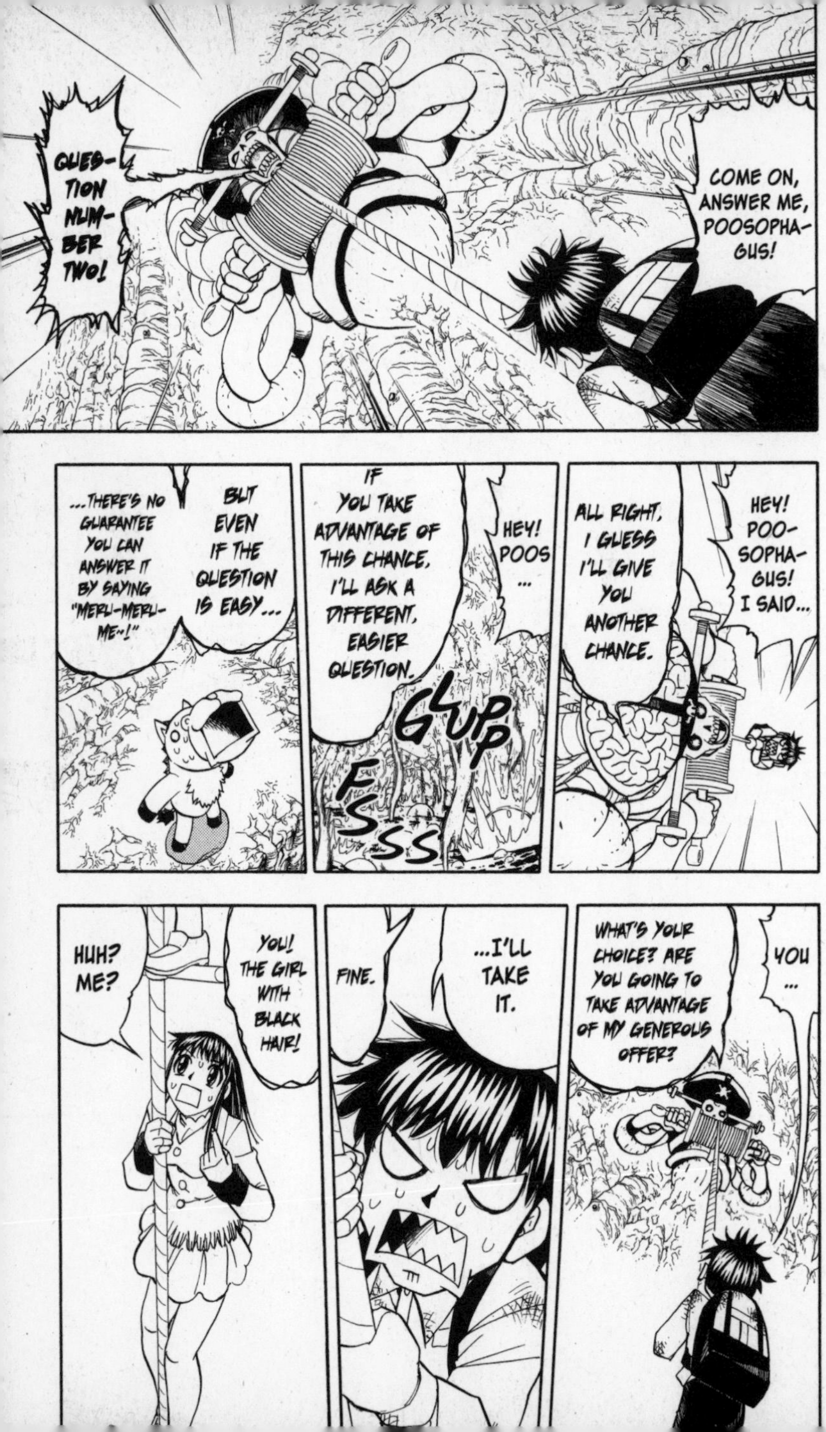
COME ON, ANSWER ME, POOSOPHAGUS!
QUESTION NUMBER TWO!
HEY! POOSOPHAGUS! I SAID...
ALL RIGHT, I GUESS I'LL GIVE YOU ANOTHER CHANCE.
HEY! POOS...
IF YOU TAKE ADVANTAGE OF THIS CHANCE, I'LL ASK A DIFFERENT, EASIER QUESTION.
GLUP
FSSS
BUT EVEN IF THE QUESTION IS EASY...
...THERE'S NO GUARANTEE YOU CAN ANSWER IT BY SAYING "MERU-MERU-ME~!"
YOU...
WHAT'S YOUR CHOICE? ARE YOU GOING TO TAKE ADVANTAGE OF MY GENEROUS OFFER?
...I'LL TAKE IT.
FINE.
YOU! THE GIRL WITH BLACK HAIR!
HUH? ME?

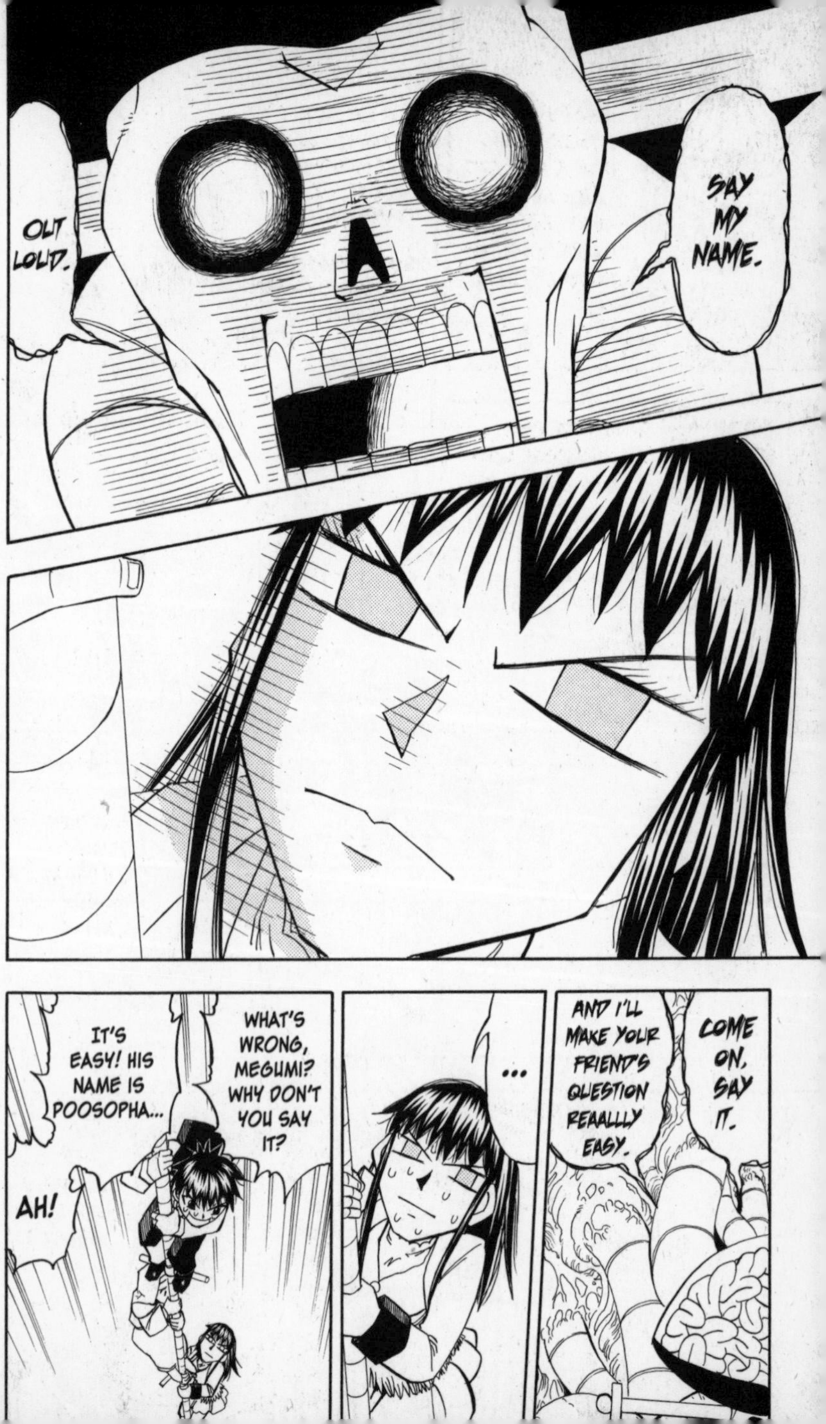
SAY MY NAME.
OUT LOUD.
COME ON, SAY IT.
AND I'LL MAKE YOUR FRIEND'S QUESTION REAALLLY EASY.
...
WHAT'S WRONG, MEGUMI? WHY DON'T YOU SAY IT?
IT'S EASY! HIS NAME IS POOSOPHA...
AH!

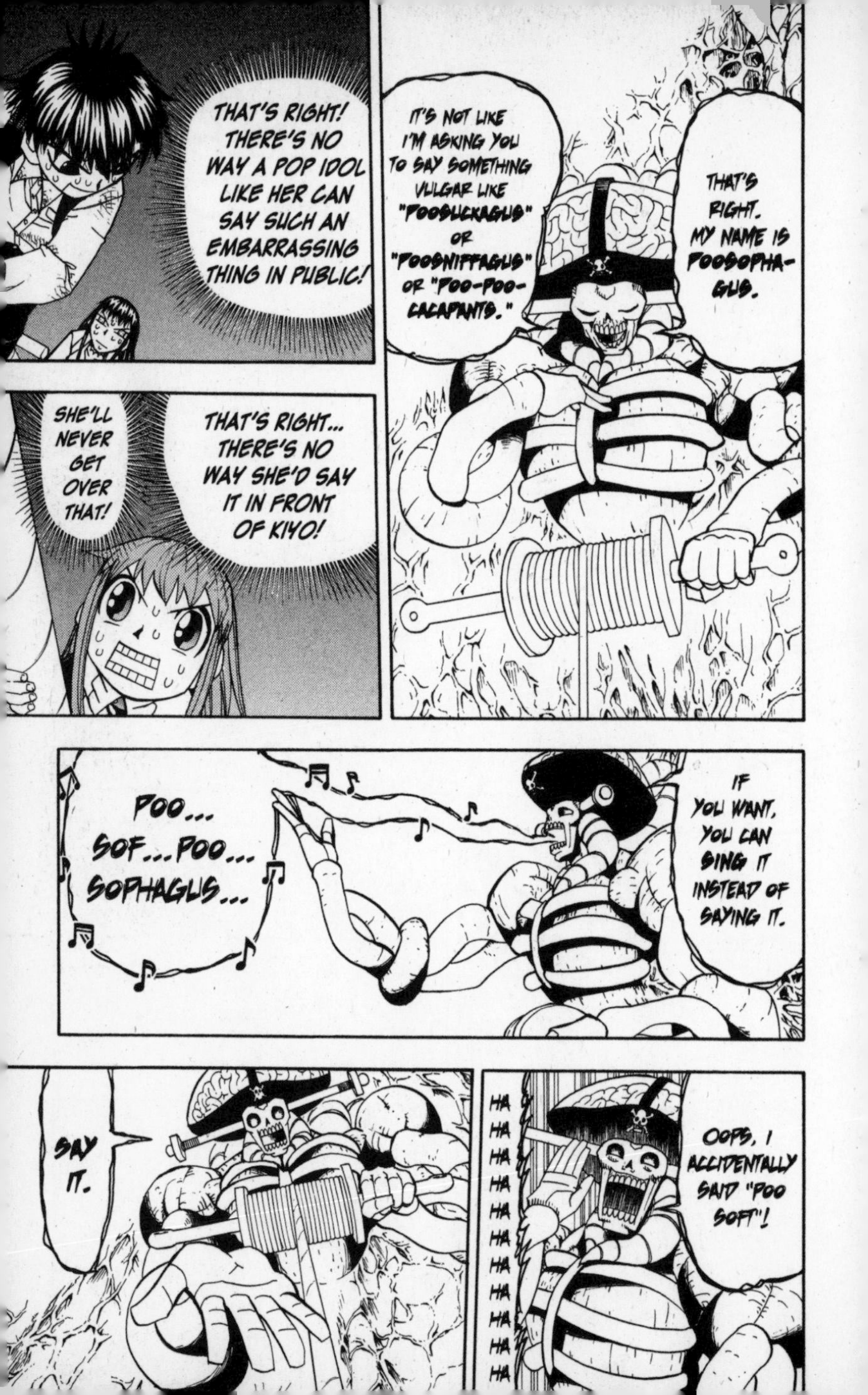
THAT'S RIGHT. MY NAME IS POOSOPHAGUS.
IT'S NOT LIKE I'M ASKING YOU TO SAY SOMETHING VULGAR LIKE "POOSUCKAGUS" OR "POOSNIFFAGUS" OR "POO-POO-CACAPANTS."
THAT'S RIGHT! THERE'S NO WAY A POP IDOL LIKE HER CAN SAY SUCH AN EMBARRASSING THING IN PUBLIC!
THAT'S RIGHT... THERE'S NO WAY SHE'D SAY IT IN FRONT OF KIYO!
SHE'LL NEVER GET OVER THAT!
IF YOU WANT, YOU CAN SING IT INSTEAD OF SAYING IT.
POO... SOF... POO... SOPHAGUS...
OOPS, I ACCIDENTALLY SAID "POO SOFT"!
HA HA HA HA HA HA HA HA HA HA HA HA HA HA
SAY IT.

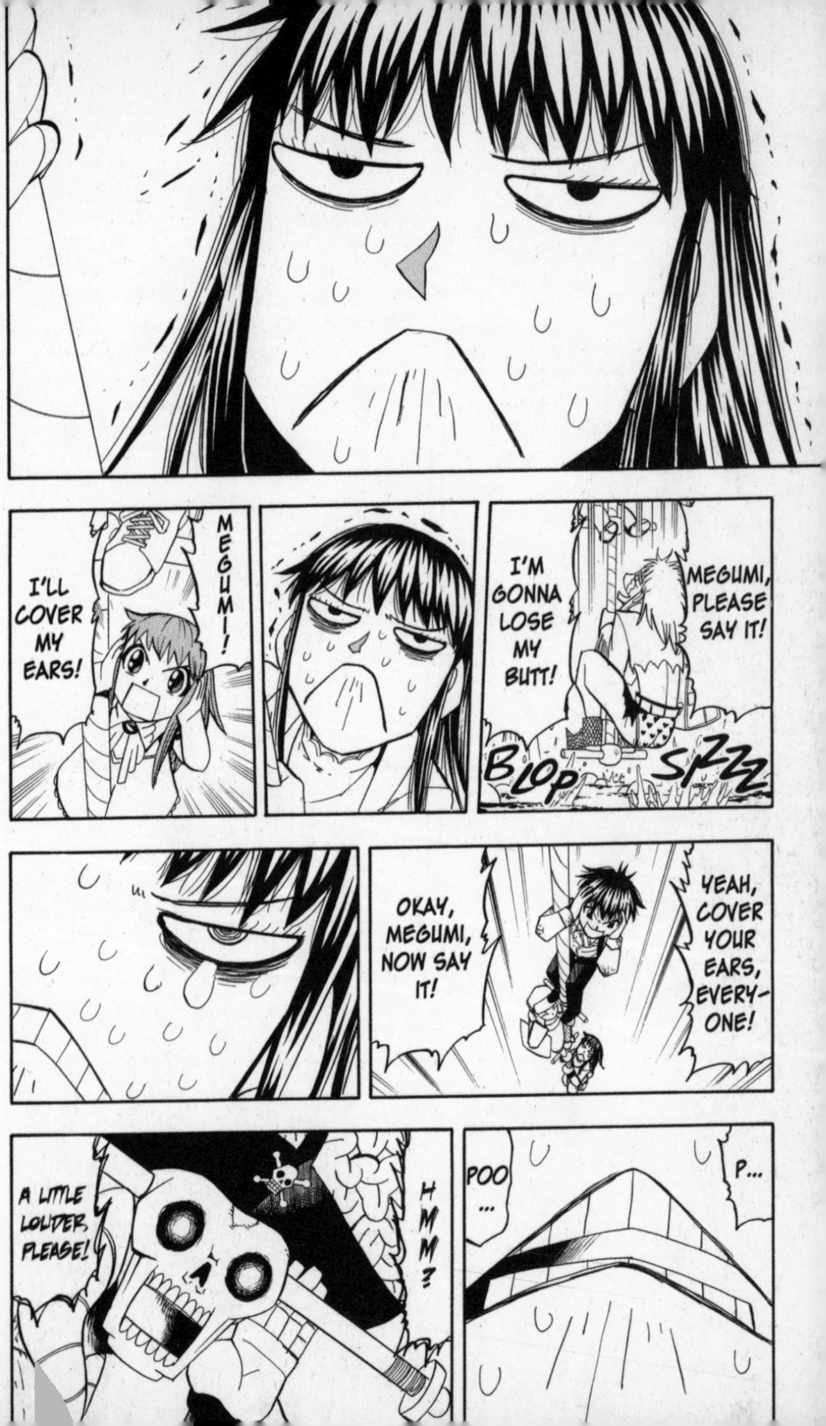
MEGUMI, PLEASE SAY IT!
I'M GONNA LOSE MY BUTT!
SIZZZ
BLOP
MEGUMI!
I'LL COVER MY EARS!
YEAH, COVER YOUR EARS, EVERY-ONE!
OKAY, MEGUMI, NOW SAY IT!
P...
POO ...
HMM?
A LITTLE LOUDER, PLEASE!

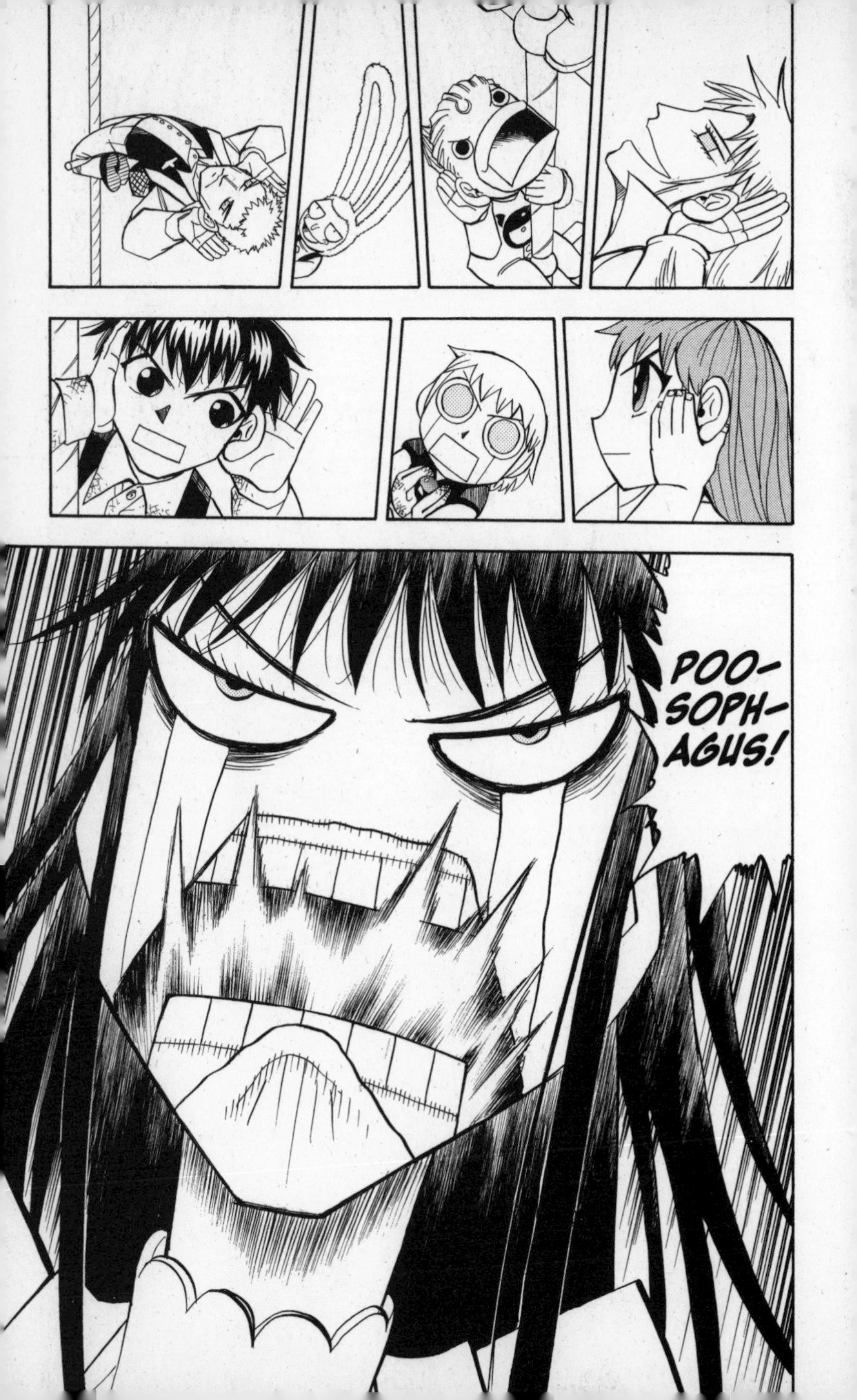
POO-
SOPH-
AGUS!

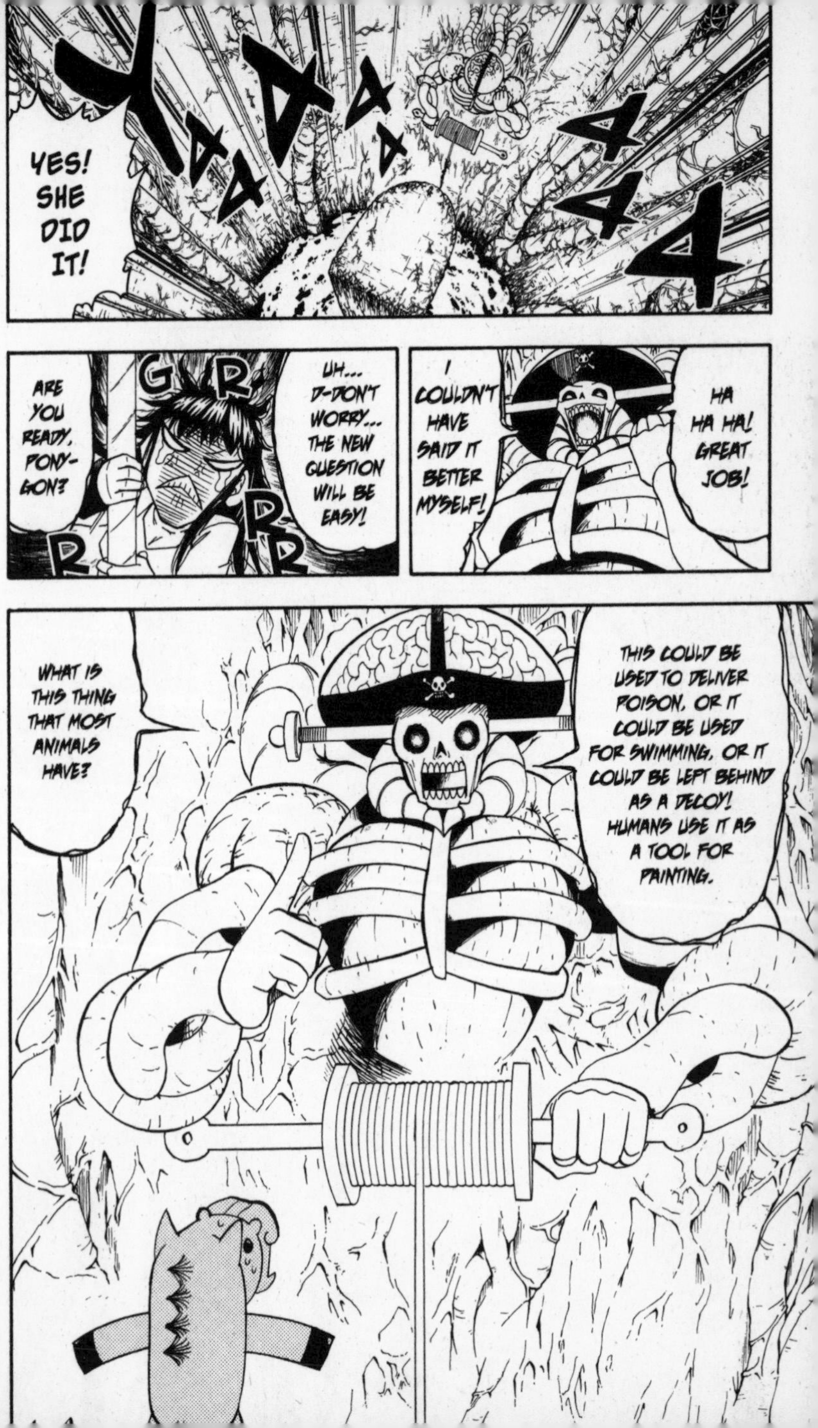
YES! SHE DID IT!
HA HA HA! GREAT JOB!
I COULDN'T HAVE SAID IT BETTER MYSELF!
UH... D-DON'T WORRY... THE NEW QUESTION WILL BE EASY!
ARE YOU READY, PONY-GON?
GRRRR
THIS COULD BE USED TO DELIVER POISON, OR IT COULD BE USED FOR SWIMMING, OR IT COULD BE LEFT BEHIND AS A DECOY! HUMANS USE IT AS A TOOL FOR PAINTING.
WHAT IS THIS THING THAT MOST ANIMALS HAVE?

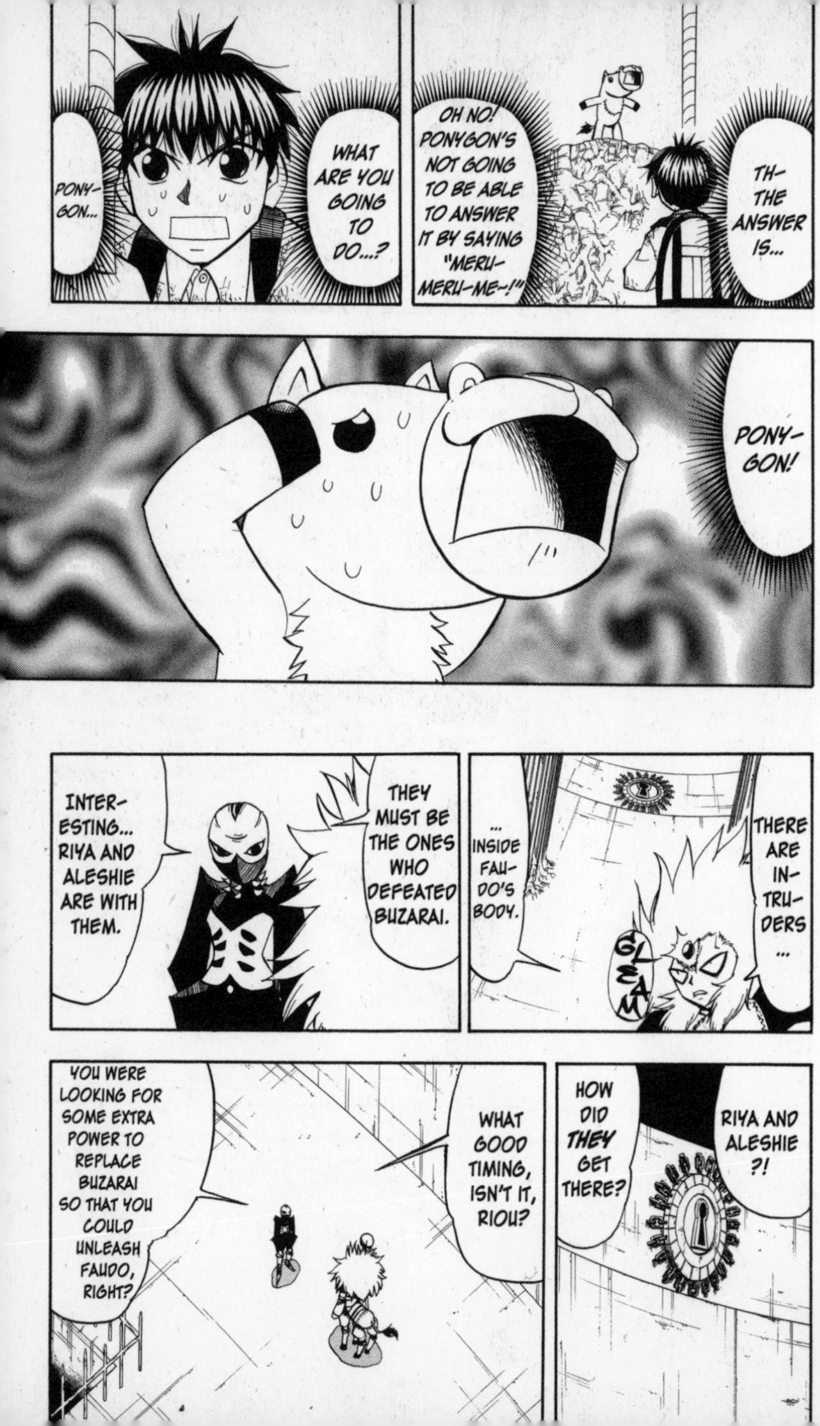
TH- THE ANSWER IS...
OH NO! PONYGON'S NOT GOING TO BE ABLE TO ANSWER IT BY SAYING "MERU-MERU-ME~!"
WHAT ARE YOU GOING TO DO...?
PONY-GON...
PONY-GON!
THERE ARE IN-TRU-DERS...
GLEAM
...INSIDE FAU-DO'S BODY.
THEY MUST BE THE ONES WHO DEFEATED BUZARAI.
INTER-ESTING... RIYA AND ALESHIE ARE WITH THEM.
RIYA AND ALESHIE?!
HOW DID *THEY* GET THERE?
WHAT GOOD TIMING, ISN'T IT, RIOU?
YOU WERE LOOKING FOR SOME EXTRA POWER TO REPLACE BUZARAI SO THAT YOU COULD UNLEASH FAUDO, RIGHT?

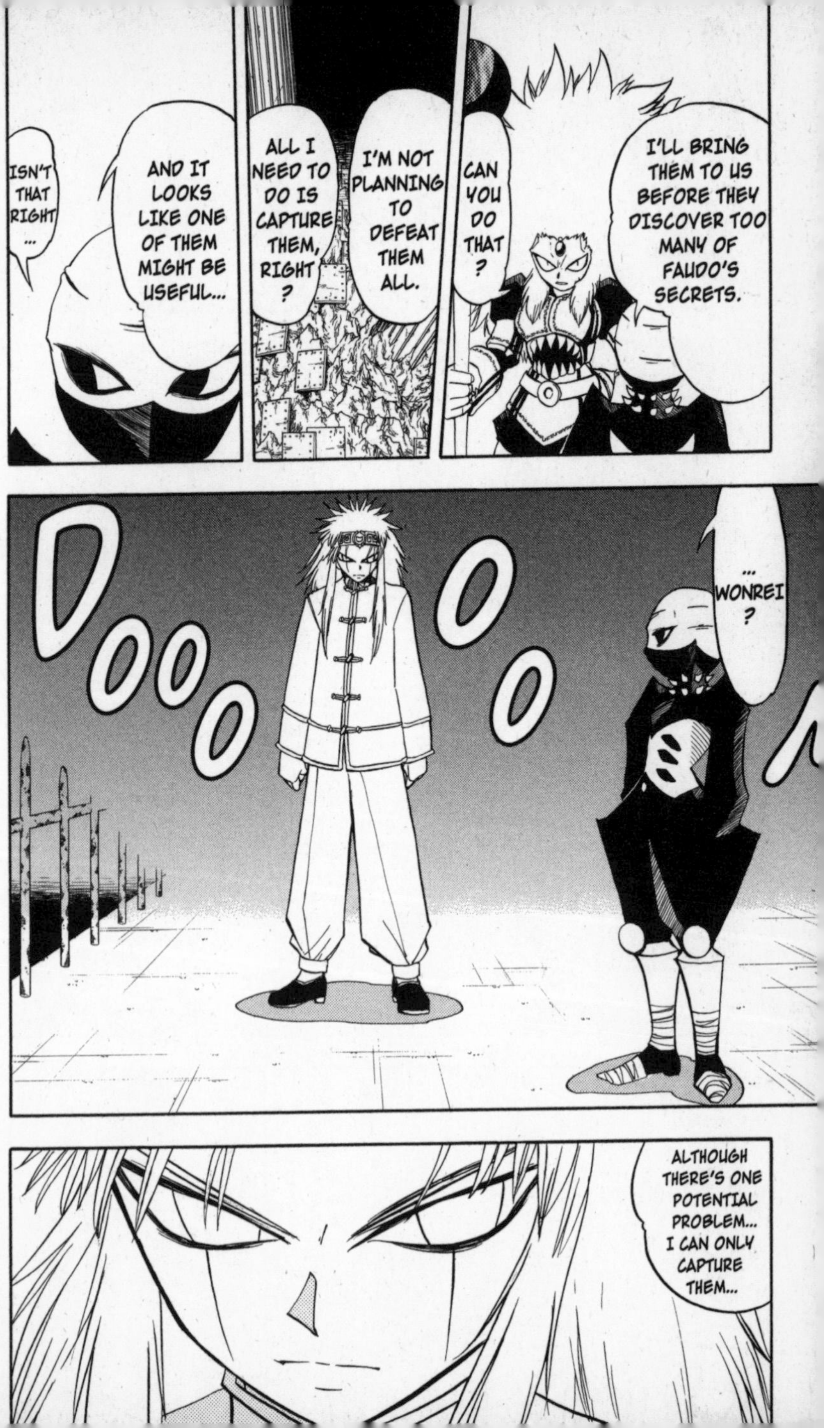
I'LL BRING THEM TO US BEFORE THEY DISCOVER TOO MANY OF FAUDO'S SECRETS.
CAN YOU DO THAT?
I'M NOT PLANNING TO DEFEAT THEM ALL.
ALL I NEED TO DO IS CAPTURE THEM, RIGHT?
AND IT LOOKS LIKE ONE OF THEM MIGHT BE USEFUL...
ISN'T THAT RIGHT...
... WONREI?
DOOOOOOO
ALTHOUGH THERE'S ONE POTENTIAL PROBLEM... I CAN ONLY CAPTURE THEM...

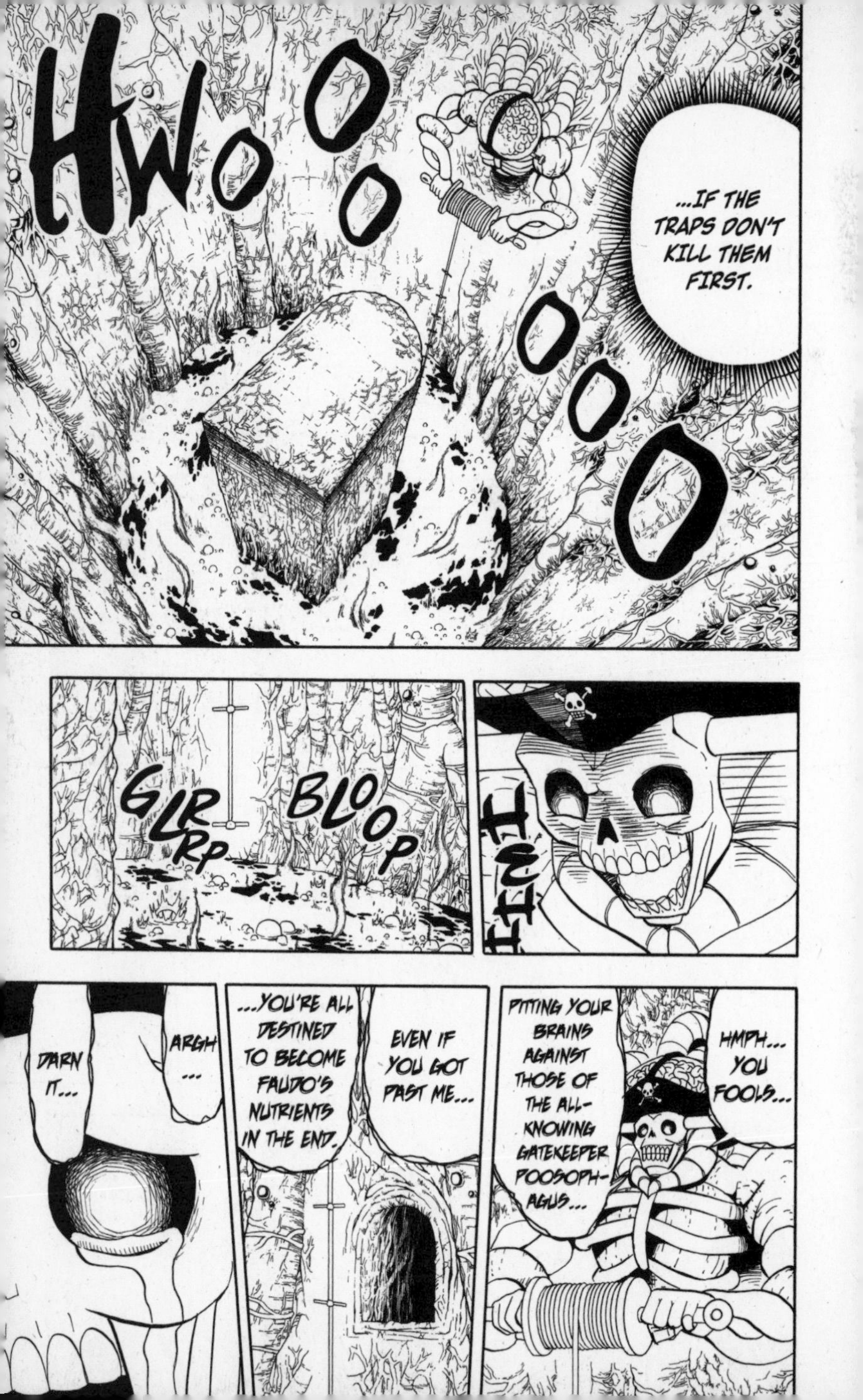
...IF THE TRAPS DON'T KILL THEM FIRST.
HWOOOOOOOO
HEH
BLOOOP
GLRLRP
HMPH... YOU FOOLS...
PITTING YOUR BRAINS AGAINST THOSE OF THE ALL-KNOWING GATEKEEPER POOSOPHAGUS...
EVEN IF YOU GOT PAST ME...
...YOU'RE ALL DESTINED TO BECOME FAUDO'S NUTRIENTS IN THE END.
ARGH...
DARN IT...

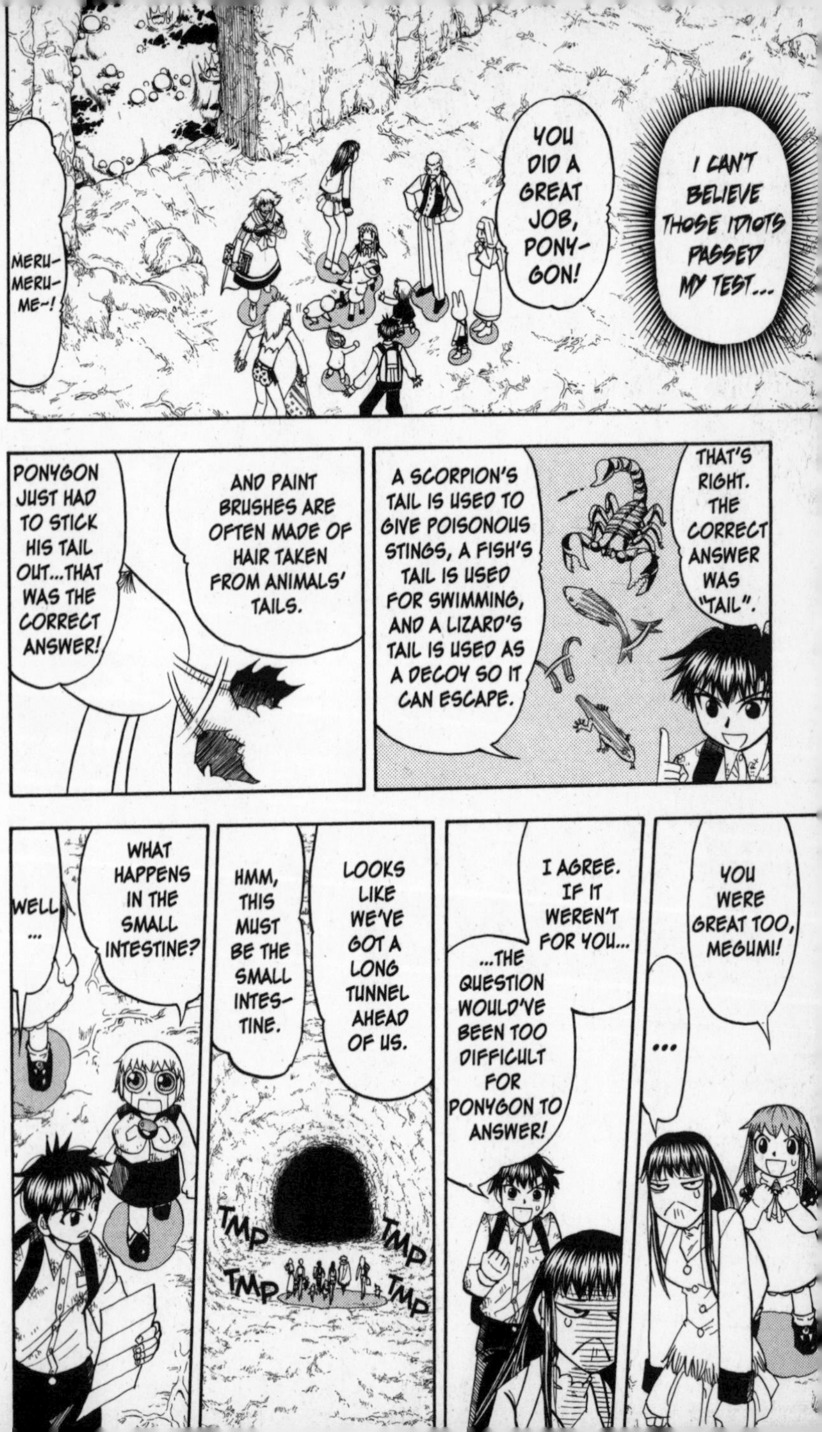
I CAN'T BELIEVE THOSE IDIOTS PASSED MY TEST...
YOU DID A GREAT JOB, PONYGON!
MERU-MERU-ME~!
THAT'S RIGHT. THE CORRECT ANSWER WAS "TAIL".
A SCORPION'S TAIL IS USED TO GIVE POISONOUS STINGS, A FISH'S TAIL IS USED FOR SWIMMING, AND A LIZARD'S TAIL IS USED AS A DECOY SO IT CAN ESCAPE.
AND PAINT BRUSHES ARE OFTEN MADE OF HAIR TAKEN FROM ANIMALS' TAILS.
PONYGON JUST HAD TO STICK HIS TAIL OUT...THAT WAS THE CORRECT ANSWER!
YOU WERE GREAT TOO, MEGUMI!
...
I AGREE. IF IT WEREN'T FOR YOU...
...THE QUESTION WOULD'VE BEEN TOO DIFFICULT FOR PONYGON TO ANSWER!
LOOKS LIKE WE'VE GOT A LONG TUNNEL AHEAD OF US.
HMM, THIS MUST BE THE SMALL INTESTINE.
TMP
TMP
TMP
TMP
WHAT HAPPENS IN THE SMALL INTESTINE?
WELL...

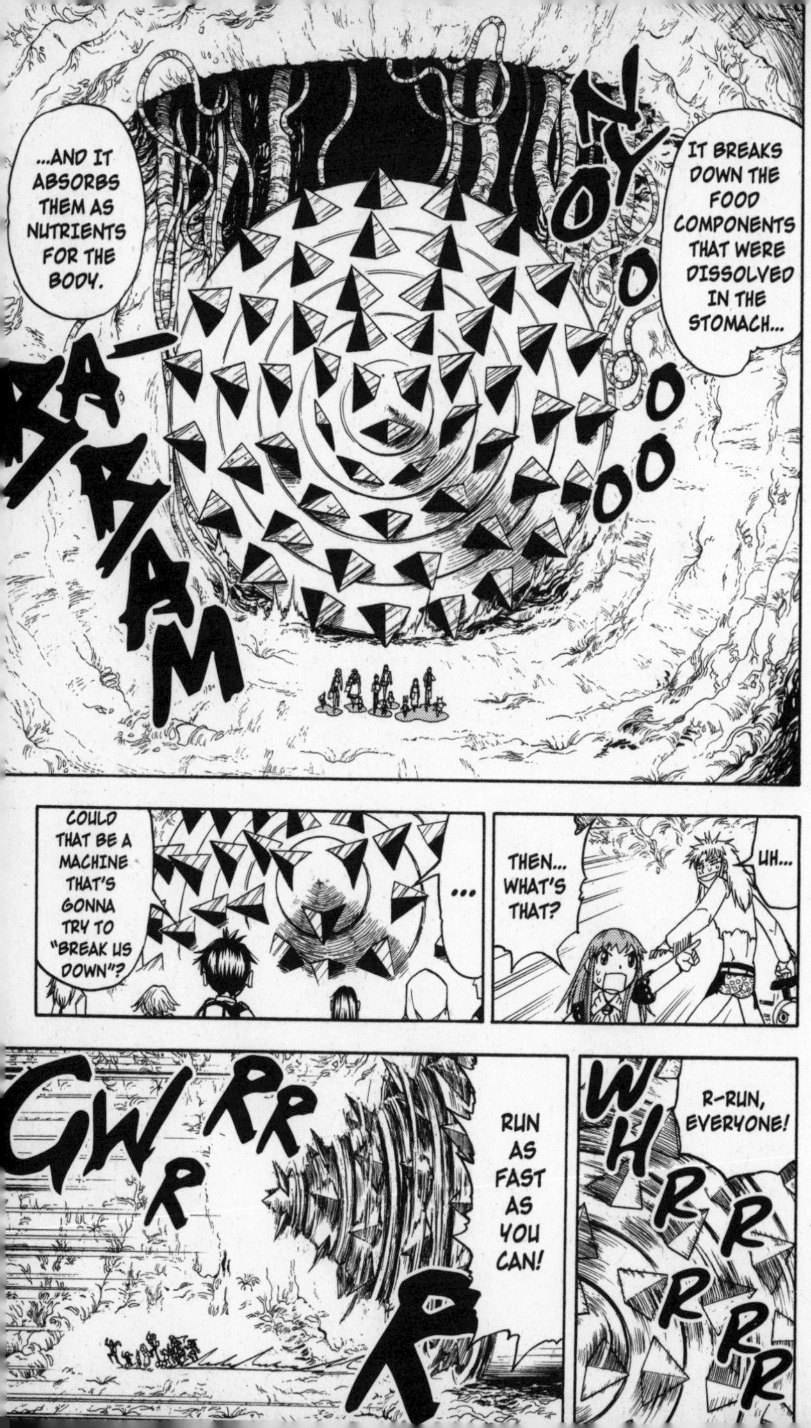

IT BREAKS DOWN THE FOOD COMPONENTS THAT WERE DISSOLVED IN THE STOMACH...
NYOOOOOO
...AND IT ABSORBS THEM AS NUTRIENTS FOR THE BODY.
BA-BRAM
UH...
THEN... WHAT'S THAT?
...
COULD THAT BE A MACHINE THAT'S GONNA TRY TO "BREAK US DOWN"?
R-RUN, EVERYONE!
WHRRRRRRR
RUN AS FAST AS YOU CAN!
GWRRRR

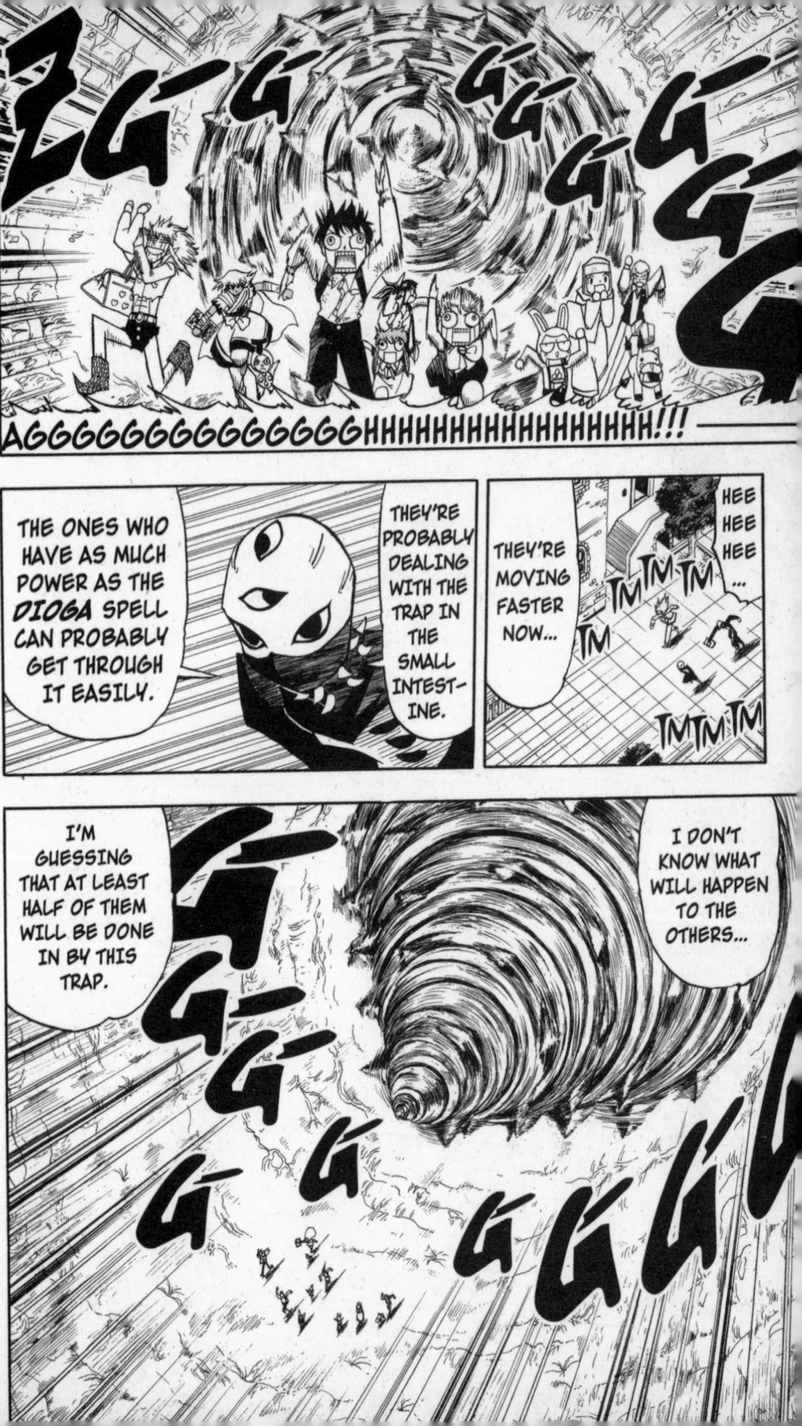
ZGGGGGGGG
AGGGGGGGGGGGGGGHHHHHHHHHHHHHHHHHH!!!
HEE HEE HEE...
TMTMTMTM
THEY'RE MOVING FASTER NOW...
TMTMTM
THEY'RE PROBABLY DEALING WITH THE TRAP IN THE SMALL INTESTINE.
THE ONES WHO HAVE AS MUCH POWER AS THE DIOGA SPELL CAN PROBABLY GET THROUGH IT EASILY.
I DON'T KNOW WHAT WILL HAPPEN TO THE OTHERS...
I'M GUESSING THAT AT LEAST HALF OF THEM WILL BE DONE IN BY THIS TRAP.
ZGGGGGGGG

# LEVEL 201: The Exit

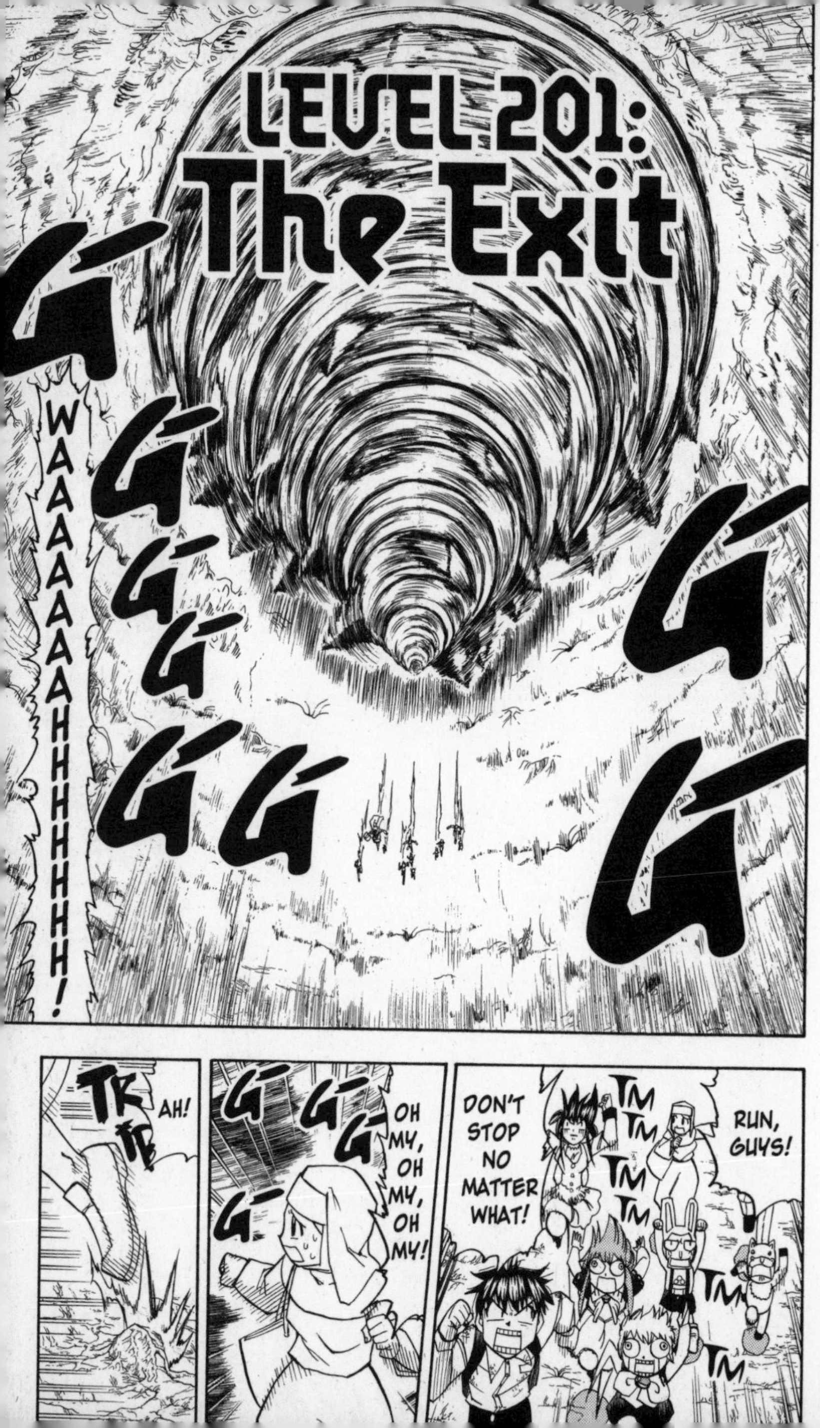
GGGGGGGGG
WAAAAAAAAAHHHHHHHHH!
RUN, GUYS!
TM TM TM TM TM TM
DON'T STOP NO MATTER WHAT!
GGGG
OH MY, OH MY, OH MY!
TR TR
AH!

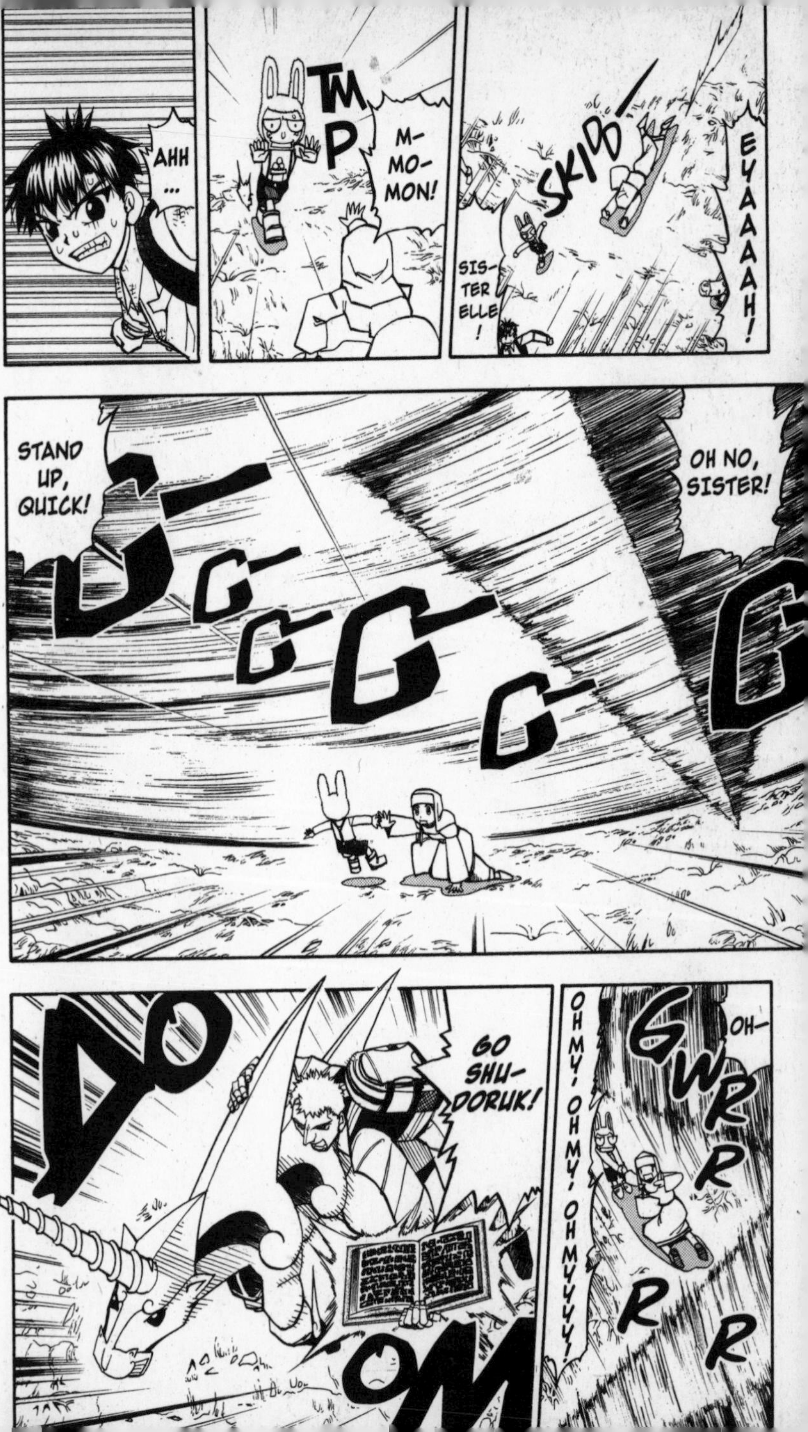
EYAAAAAH!
SKIDD
SISTER ELLE!
TMP
M-MO-MON!
AHH ...
OH NO, SISTER!
STAND UP, QUICK!
DG-G-G-G-G
OH-
GWRRRR
OH MY! OH MY! OH MYYYY!
GO SHUDORUK!
DOOM

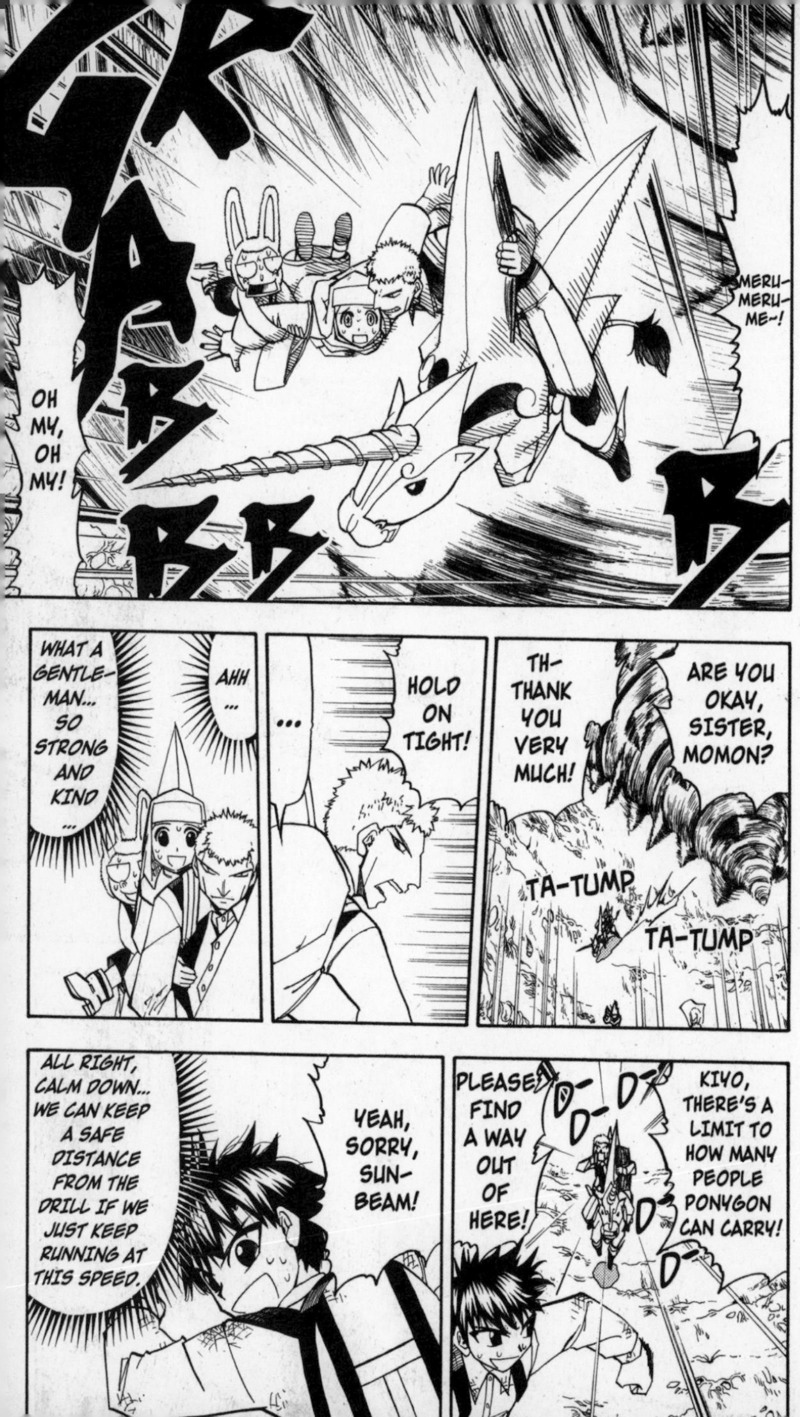
MERU-MERU-ME~!
OH MY, OH MY!
ARE YOU OKAY, SISTER, MOMON?
TH-THANK YOU VERY MUCH!
TA-TUMP
TA-TUMP
HOLD ON TIGHT!
...
AHH...
WHAT A GENTLE-MAN... SO STRONG AND KIND...
KIYO, THERE'S A LIMIT TO HOW MANY PEOPLE PONYGON CAN CARRY!
PLEASE FIND A WAY OUT OF HERE!
D- D- D- D- D-
YEAH, SORRY, SUN-BEAM!
ALL RIGHT, CALM DOWN... WE CAN KEEP A SAFE DISTANCE FROM THE DRILL IF WE JUST KEEP RUNNING AT THIS SPEED.

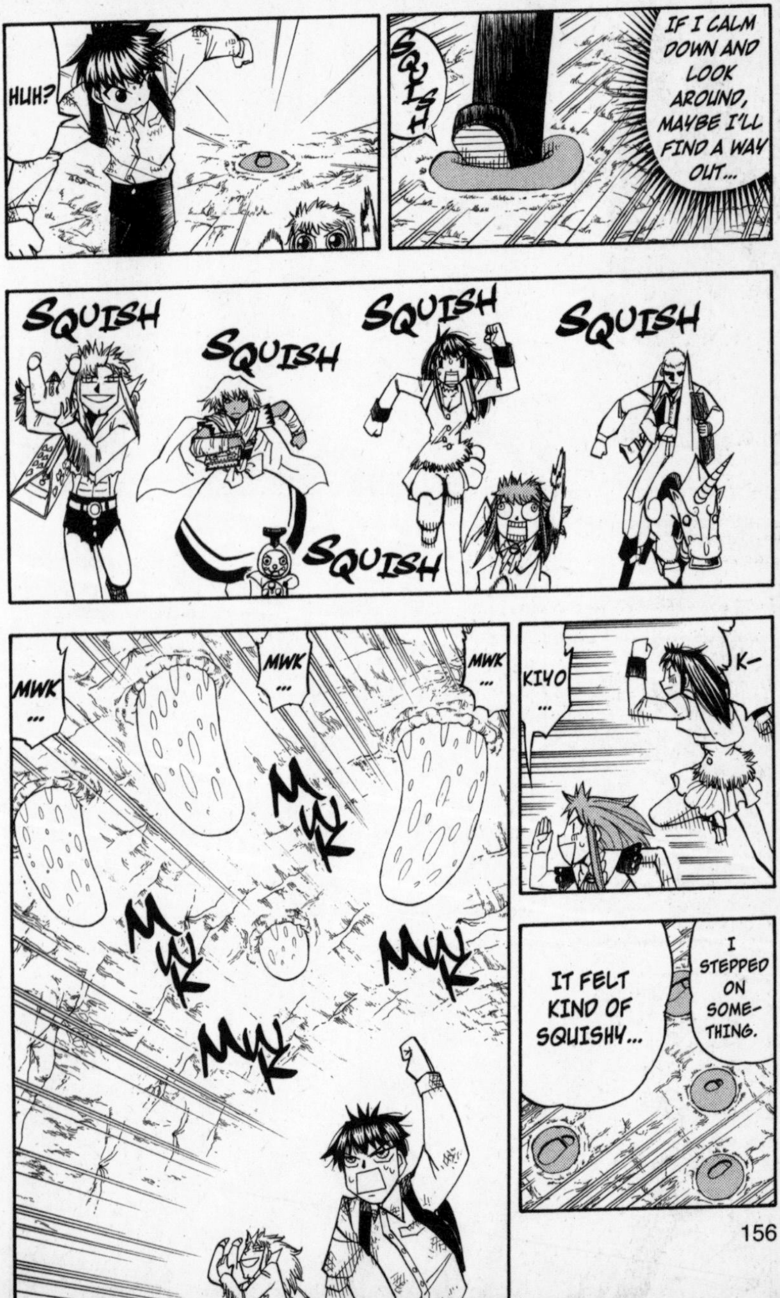
IF I CALM DOWN AND LOOK AROUND, MAYBE I'LL FIND A WAY OUT...
SQUISH
HUH?
SQUISH
SQUISH
SQUISH
SQUISH
SQUISH
K-
KIYO...
I STEPPED ON SOME-THING.
IT FELT KIND OF SQUISHY...
MWK...
MWK...
MWK...
MWK
MWK
MWK
MWK

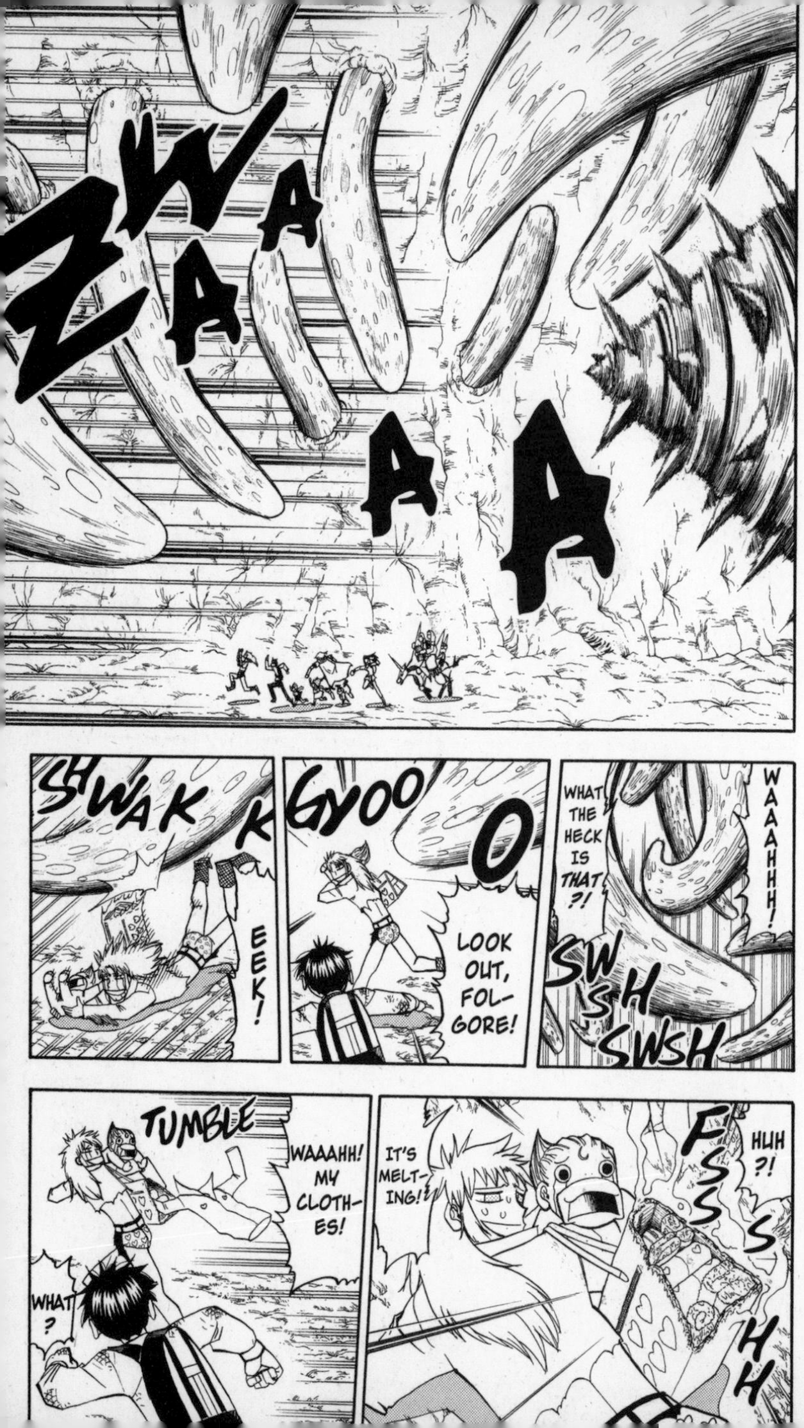
ZWA
ZAAA
WAAAAHHH!
WHAT THE HECK IS THAT?!
SWSH SWSH
GYOOO
LOOK OUT, FOLGORE!
SHWAKK
EEK!
FSSSSHH
HUH?!
IT'S MELTING!
WAAAHH! MY CLOTHES!
TUMBLE
WHAT?

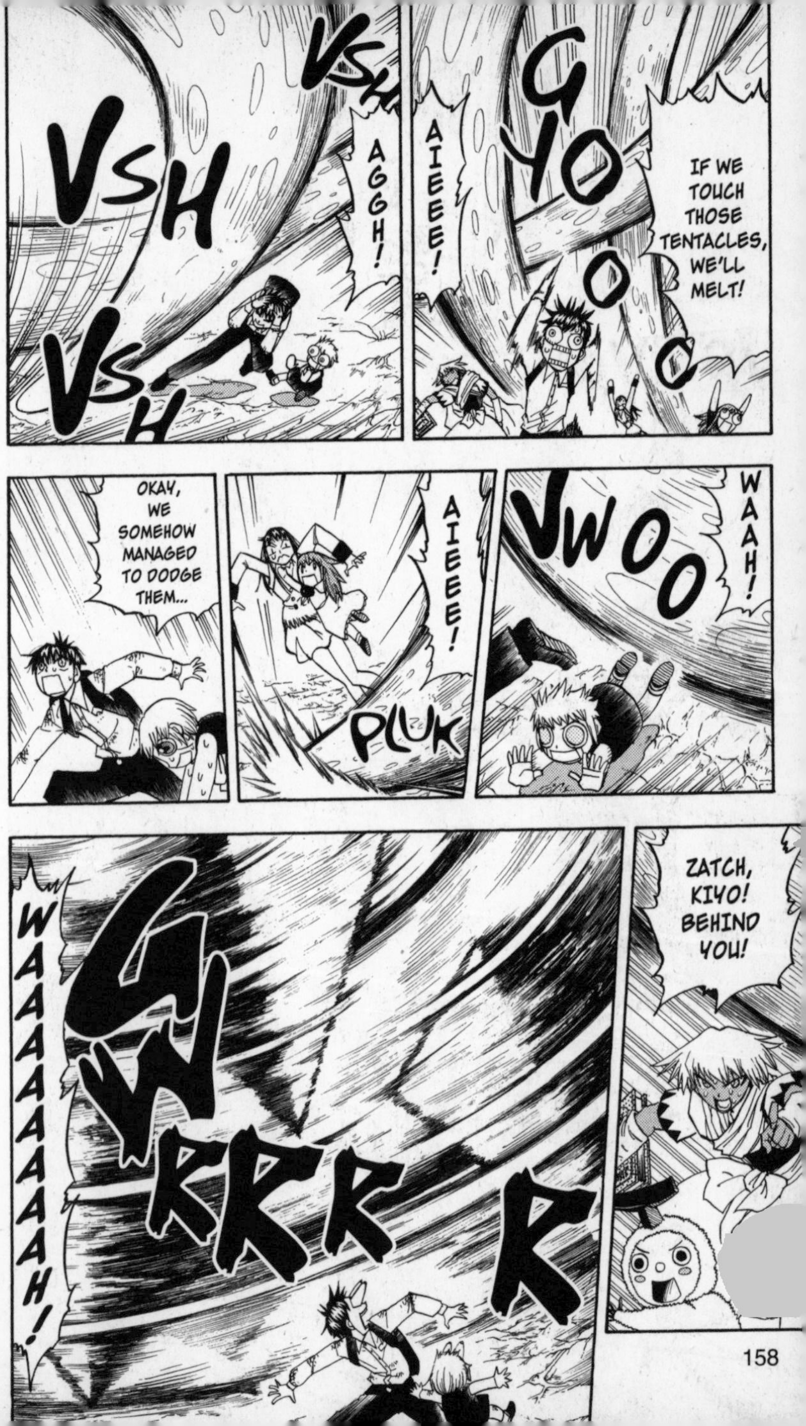

IF WE TOUCH THOSE TENTACLES, WE'LL MELT!
GYOOOC
AIEEEE!
VSH
AGGH!
VSH
VSH
WAAAH!
VWOOO
AIEEEE!
PLUK
OKAY, WE SOMEHOW MANAGED TO DODGE THEM...
ZATCH, KIYO! BEHIND YOU!
GWRRRR
WAAAAAAAAAAAAH!

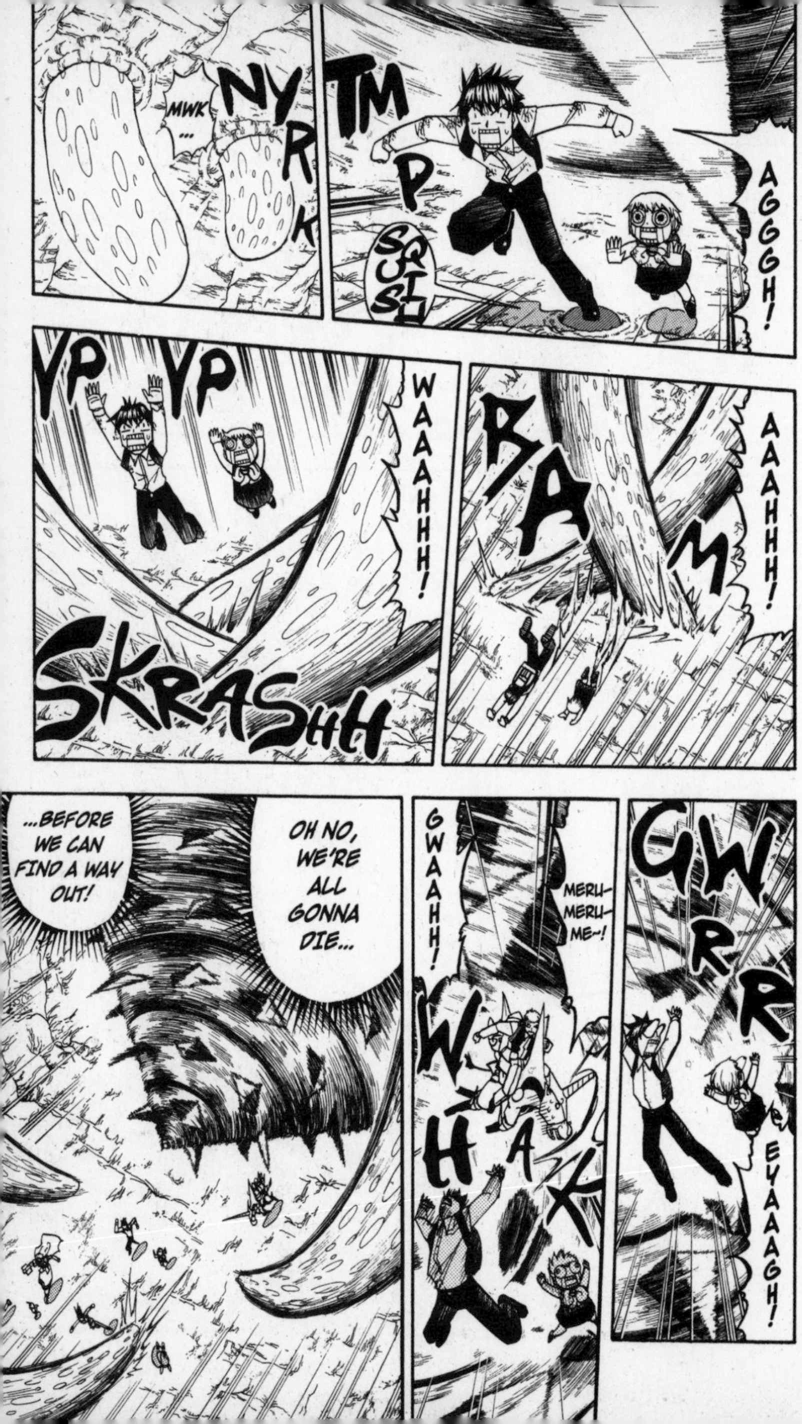
AGGGH!
TMP
SQUISH
NYRK
MWK...
AAAHHHH!
BAM
WAAAAHHH!
YP YP
SKRASHH
GWRRR
EYAAAAGH!
MERU-MERU-ME~!
GWAAAHH!
WHAK
OH NO, WE'RE ALL GONNA DIE...
...BEFORE WE CAN FIND A WAY OUT!

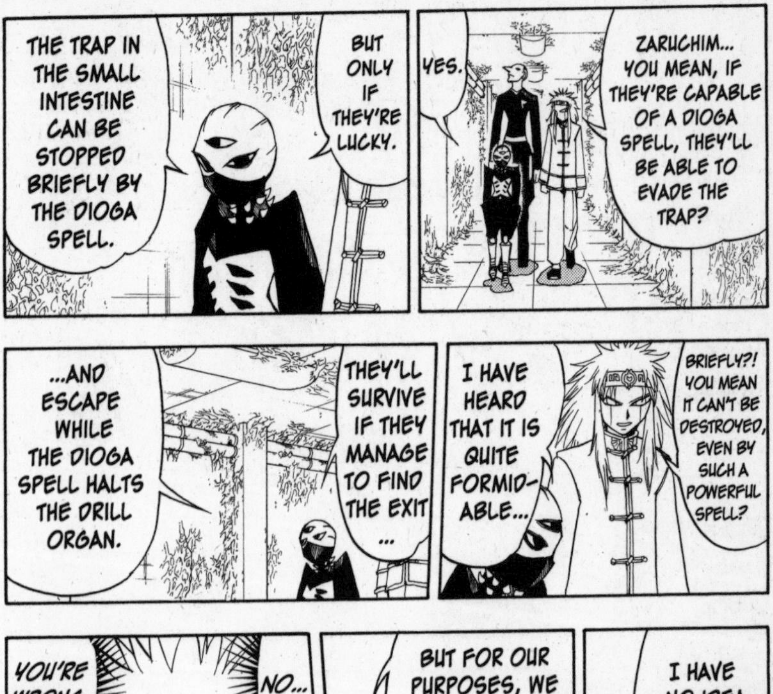

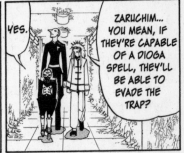

ZARUCHIM... YOU MEAN, IF THEY'RE CAPABLE OF A DIOGA SPELL, THEY'LL BE ABLE TO EVADE THE TRAP?
YES.
BUT ONLY IF THEY'RE LUCKY.
THE TRAP IN THE SMALL INTESTINE CAN BE STOPPED BRIEFLY BY THE DIOGA SPELL.
BRIEFLY?! YOU MEAN IT CAN'T BE DESTROYED, EVEN BY SUCH A POWERFUL SPELL?
I HAVE HEARD THAT IT IS QUITE FORMID-ABLE...
THEY'LL SURVIVE IF THEY MANAGE TO FIND THE EXIT ...
...AND ESCAPE WHILE THE DIOGA SPELL HALTS THE DRILL ORGAN.
I HAVE NO IDEA HOW MANY OF THEM WILL MAKE IT.
BUT FOR OUR PURPOSES, WE ONLY NEED THE ONES WHO CAN CAST DIOGA TO SURVIVE.
NO...
YOU'RE WRONG, ZARU-CHIM...

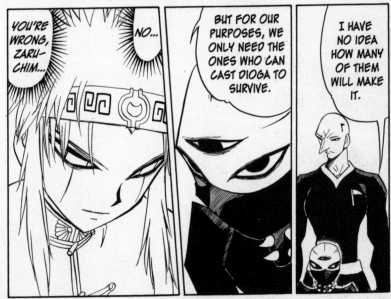

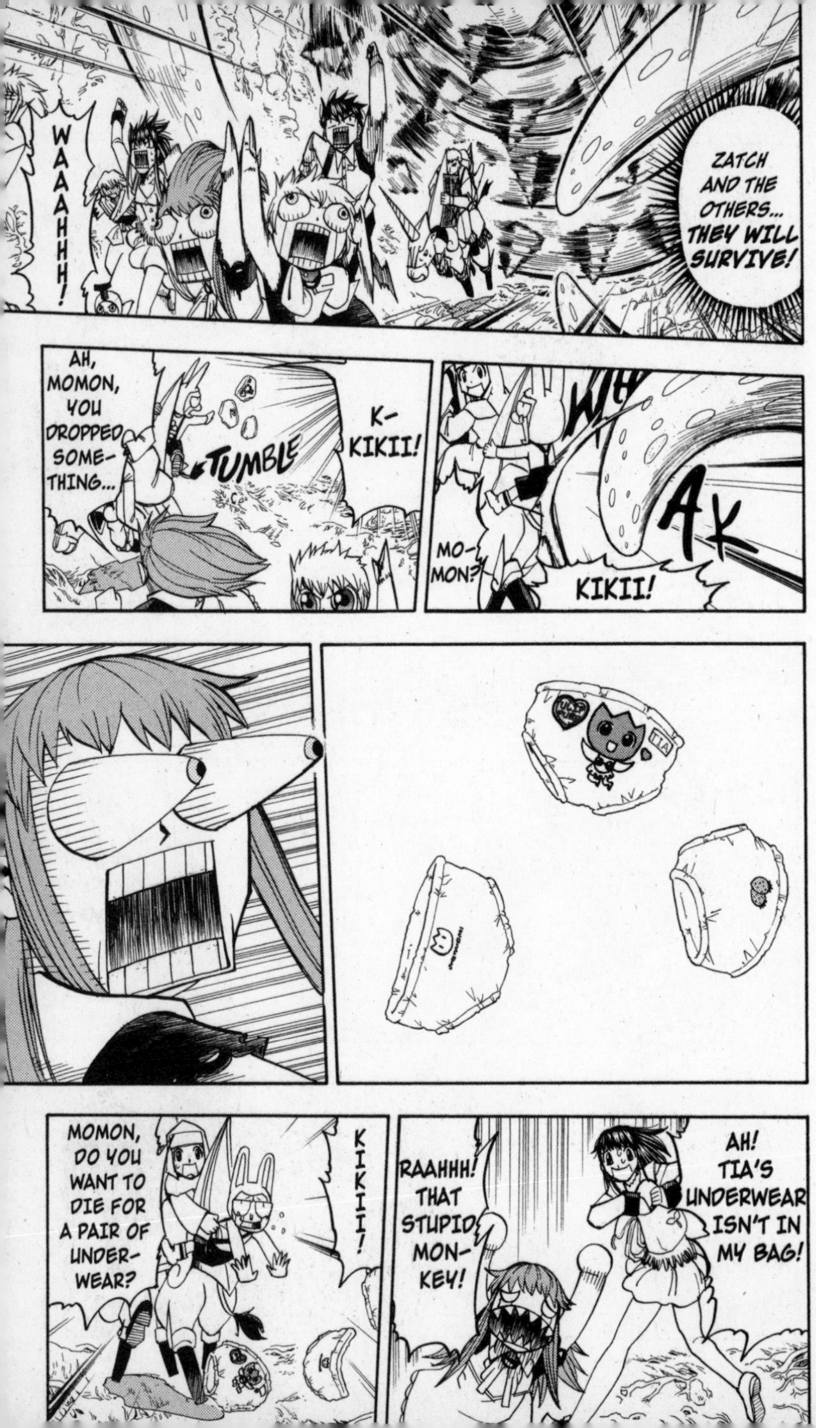
ZATCH AND THE OTHERS... THEY WILL SURVIVE!
WAAAAHHH!
WHAK
KIKII!
MO-MON?
K-KIKII!
TUMBLE
AH, MOMON, YOU DROPPED SOME-THING...
TIA
AH! TIA'S UNDERWEAR ISN'T IN MY BAG!
RAAHHH! THAT STUPID MON-KEY!
KIKII!
MOMON, DO YOU WANT TO DIE FOR A PAIR OF UNDER-WEAR?

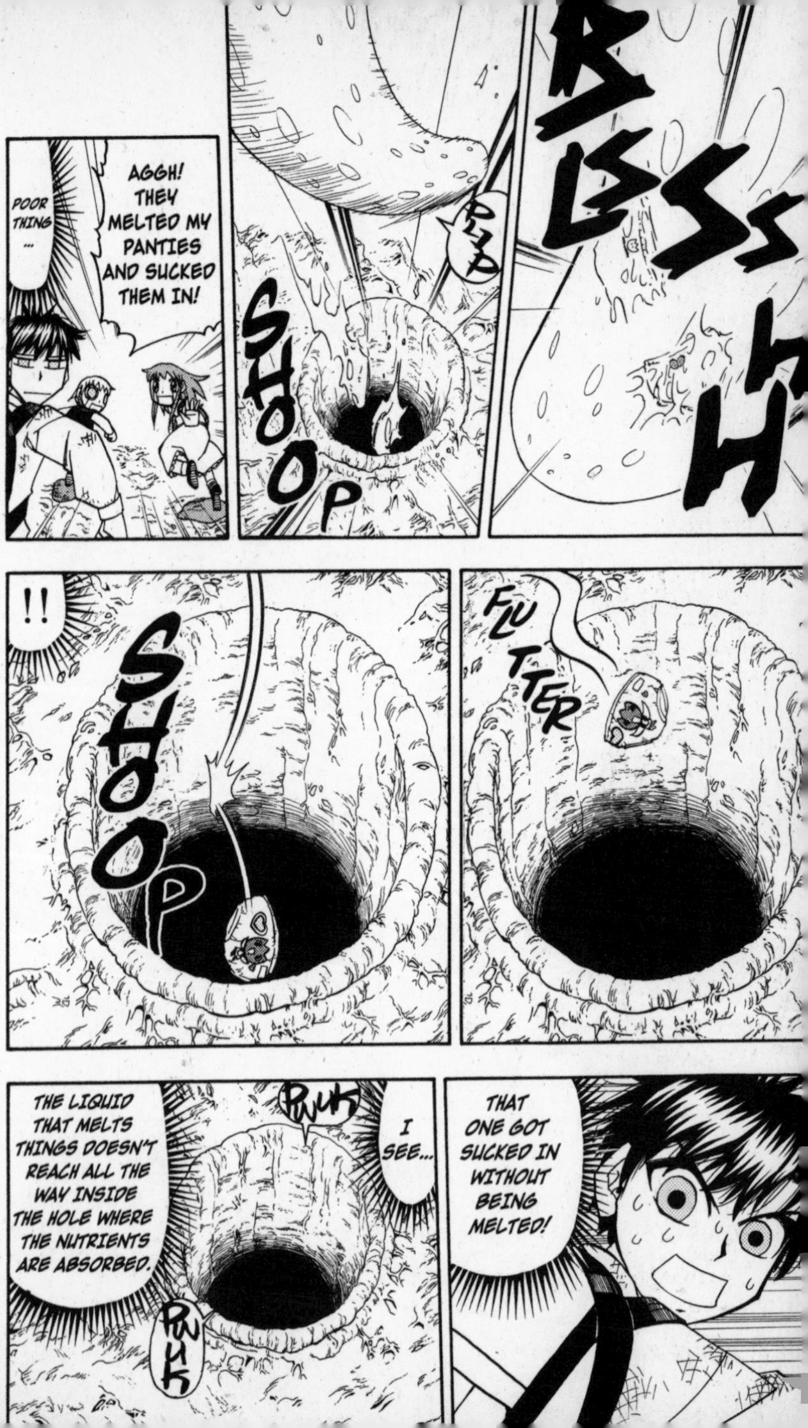
PLIP
SHOOP
AGGH! THEY MELTED MY PANTIES AND SUCKED THEM IN!
POOR THING...
FLUTTER
!!
SHOOP
THAT ONE GOT SUCKED IN WITHOUT BEING MELTED!
I SEE...
PWUK
THE LIQUID THAT MELTS THINGS DOESN'T REACH ALL THE WAY INSIDE THE HOLE WHERE THE NUTRIENTS ARE ABSORBED.
PWUK

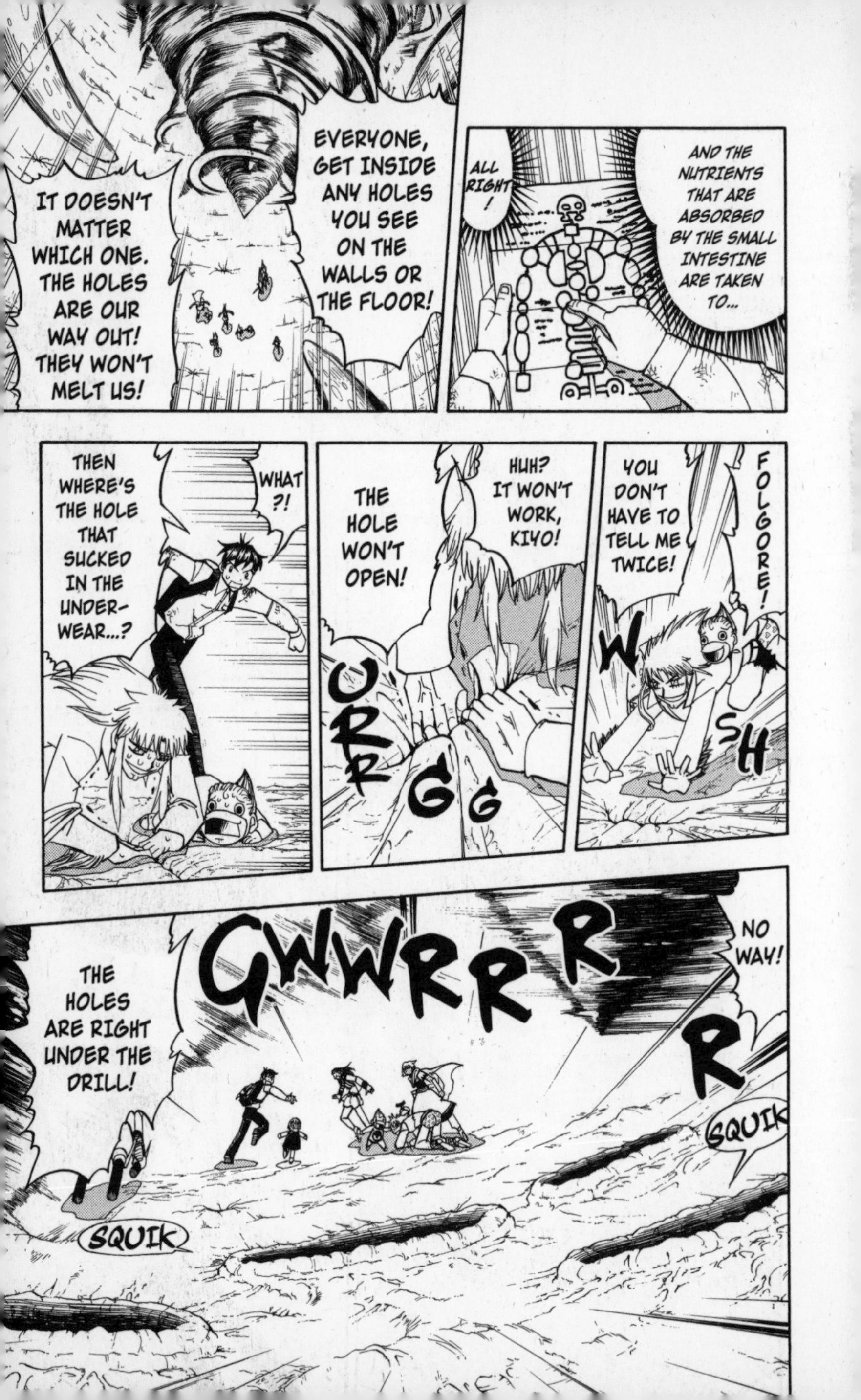
AND THE NUTRIENTS THAT ARE ABSORBED BY THE SMALL INTESTINE ARE TAKEN TO...
ALL RIGHT!
EVERYONE, GET INSIDE ANY HOLES YOU SEE ON THE WALLS OR THE FLOOR!
IT DOESN'T MATTER WHICH ONE. THE HOLES ARE OUR WAY OUT! THEY WON'T MELT US!
FOLGORE!
YOU DON'T HAVE TO TELL ME TWICE!
WSH
HUH? IT WON'T WORK, KIYO!
THE HOLE WON'T OPEN!
URRGG
WHAT?!
THEN WHERE'S THE HOLE THAT SUCKED IN THE UNDER-WEAR...?
NO WAY!
GWWRRRR
THE HOLES ARE RIGHT UNDER THE DRILL!
SQUIK
SQUIK

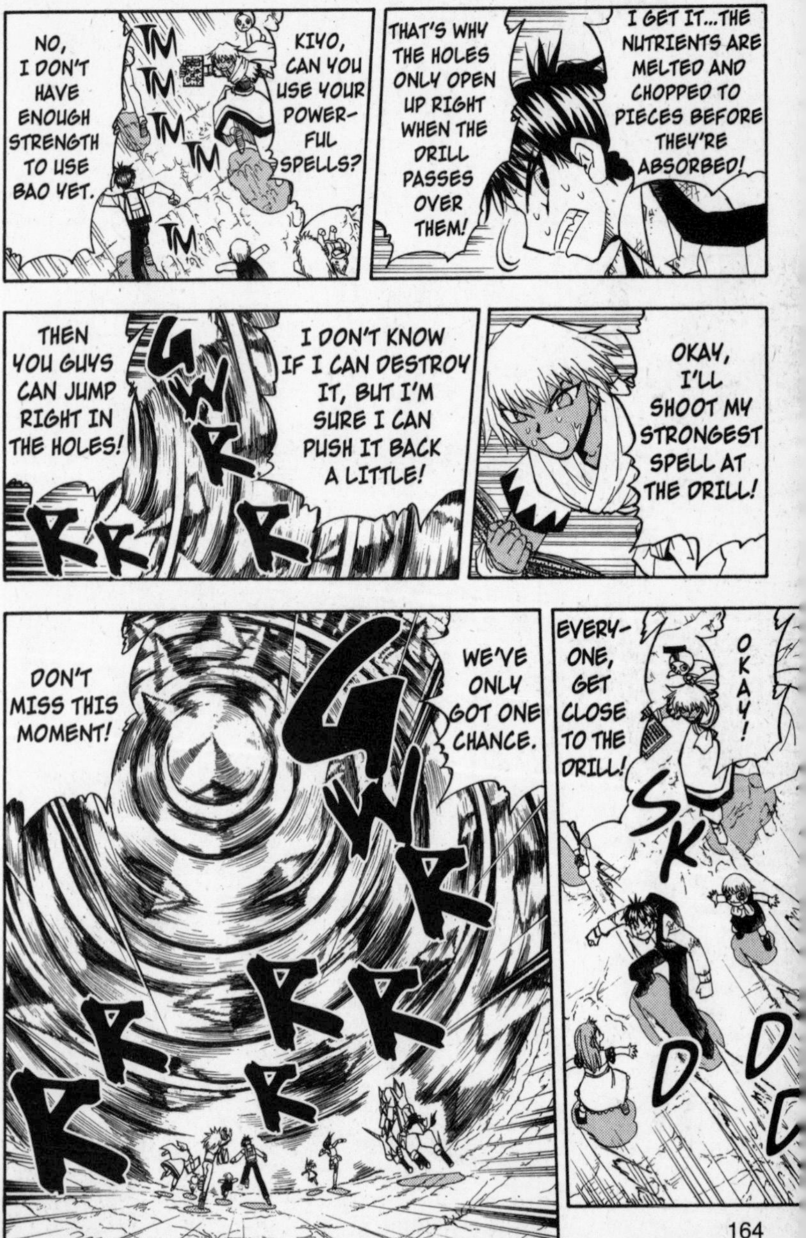
I GET IT...THE NUTRIENTS ARE MELTED AND CHOPPED TO PIECES BEFORE THEY'RE ABSORBED!
THAT'S WHY THE HOLES ONLY OPEN UP RIGHT WHEN THE DRILL PASSES OVER THEM!
KIYO, CAN YOU USE YOUR POWER-FUL SPELLS?
NO, I DON'T HAVE ENOUGH STRENGTH TO USE BAO YET.
TM TM TM TM TM
OKAY, I'LL SHOOT MY STRONGEST SPELL AT THE DRILL!
I DON'T KNOW IF I CAN DESTROY IT, BUT I'M SURE I CAN PUSH IT BACK A LITTLE!
THEN YOU GUYS CAN JUMP RIGHT IN THE HOLES!
GWRRRR
OKAY!
EVERY-ONE, GET CLOSE TO THE DRILL!
SK
DD
WE'VE ONLY GOT ONE CHANCE.
DON'T MISS THIS MOMENT!
GWRRRRRR

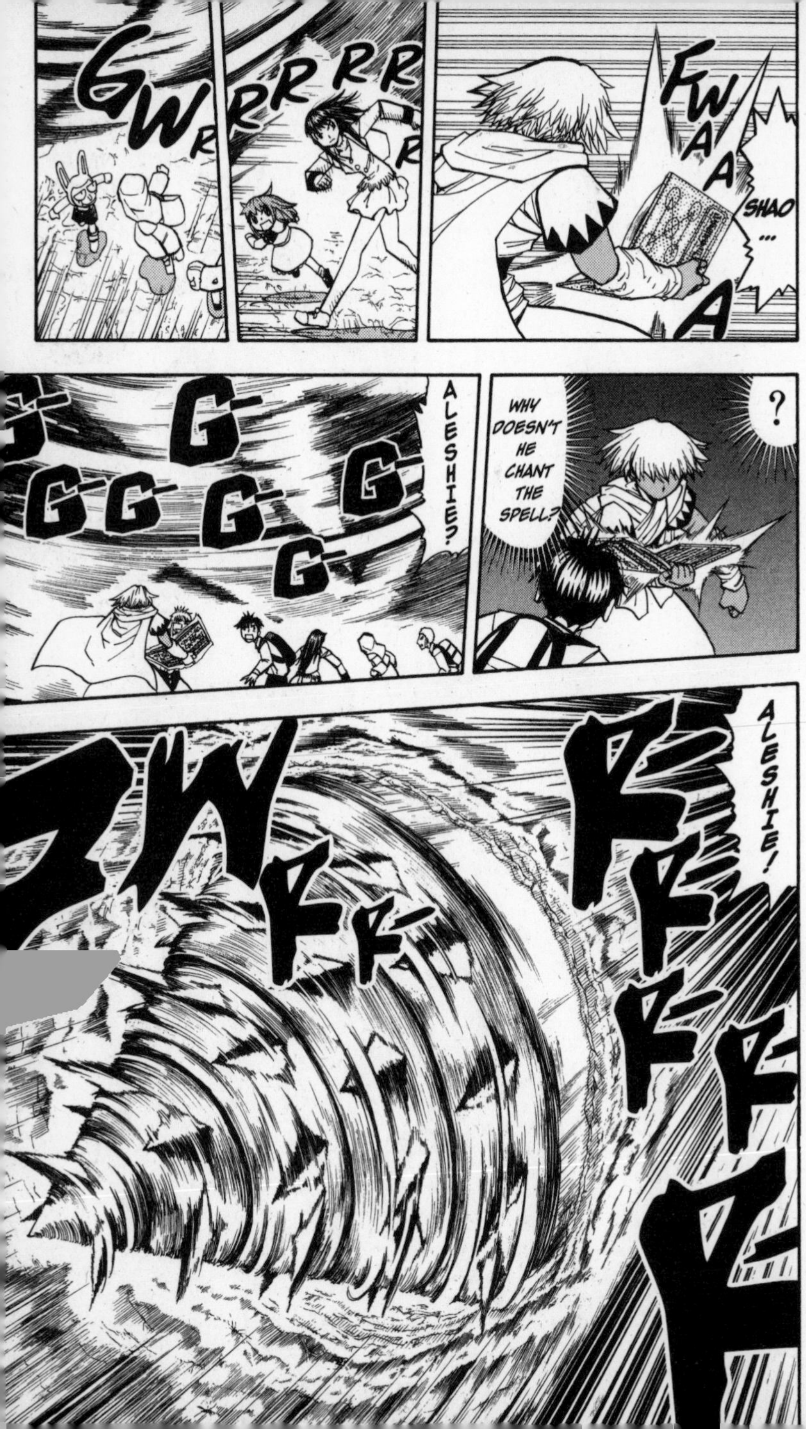
SHAO...
?
WHY DOESN'T HE CHANT THE SPELL?
ALESHIE?
ALESHIE!

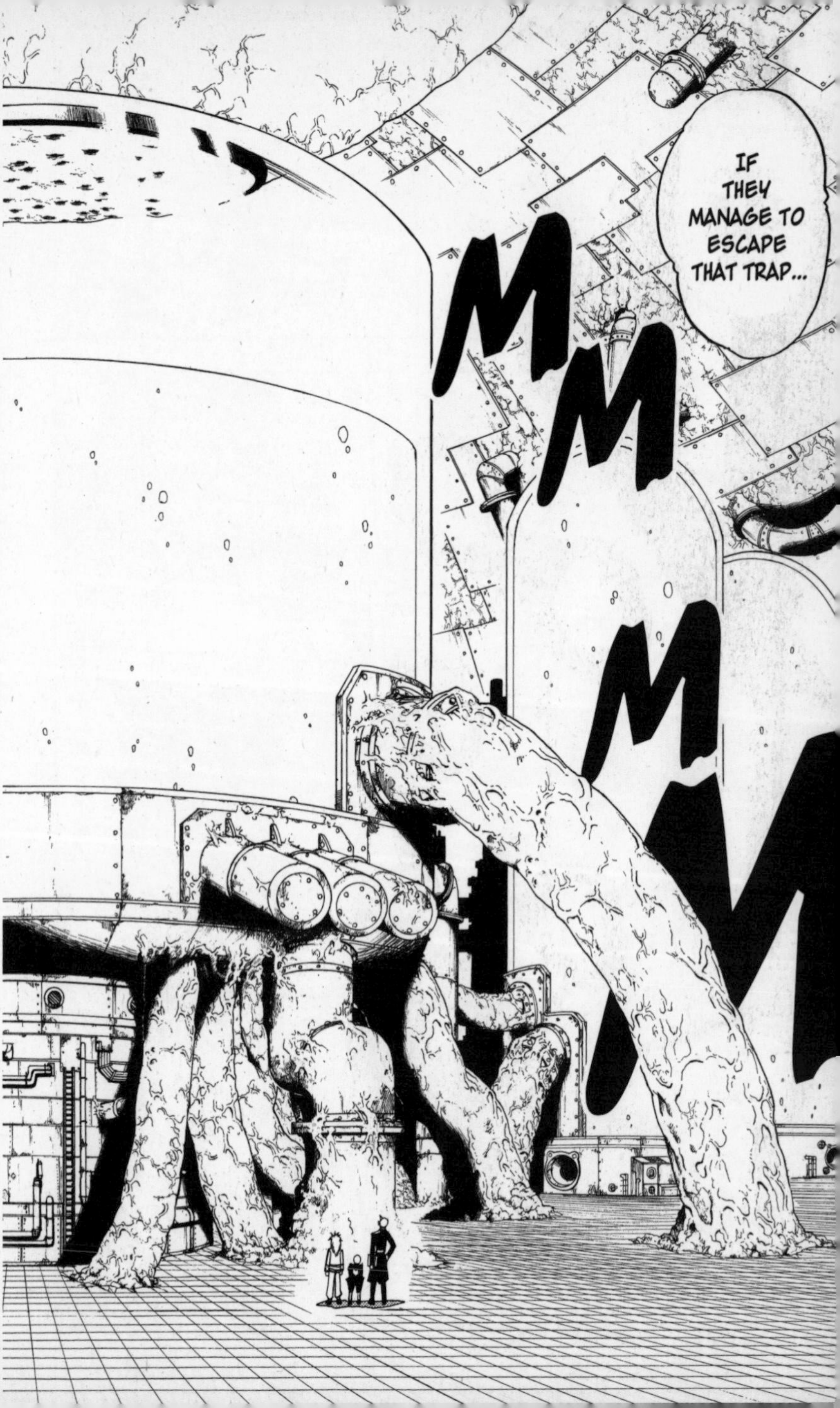
IF THEY MANAGE TO ESCAPE THAT TRAP...
MMMM

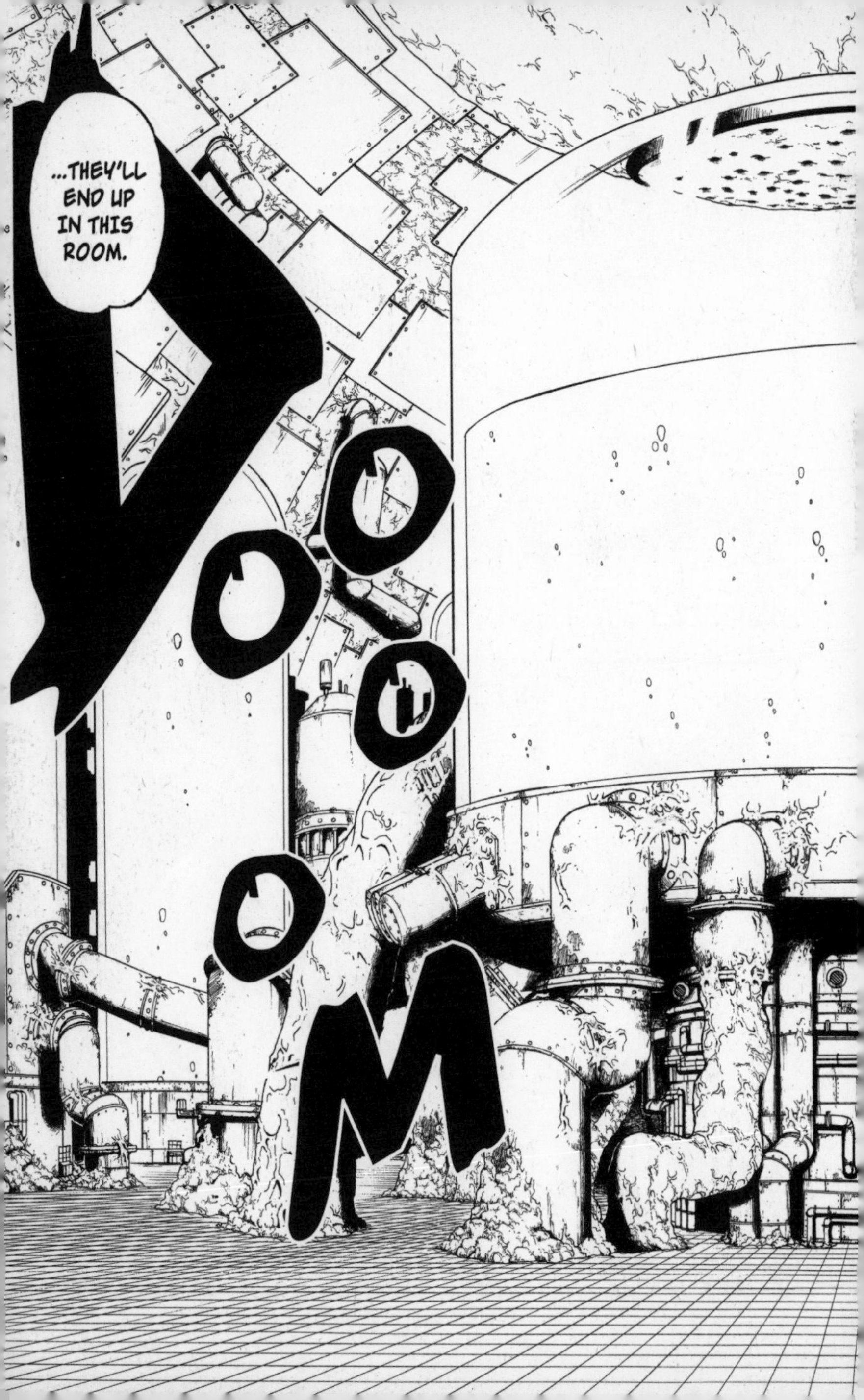
...THEY'LL END UP IN THIS ROOM.
DOOOOM

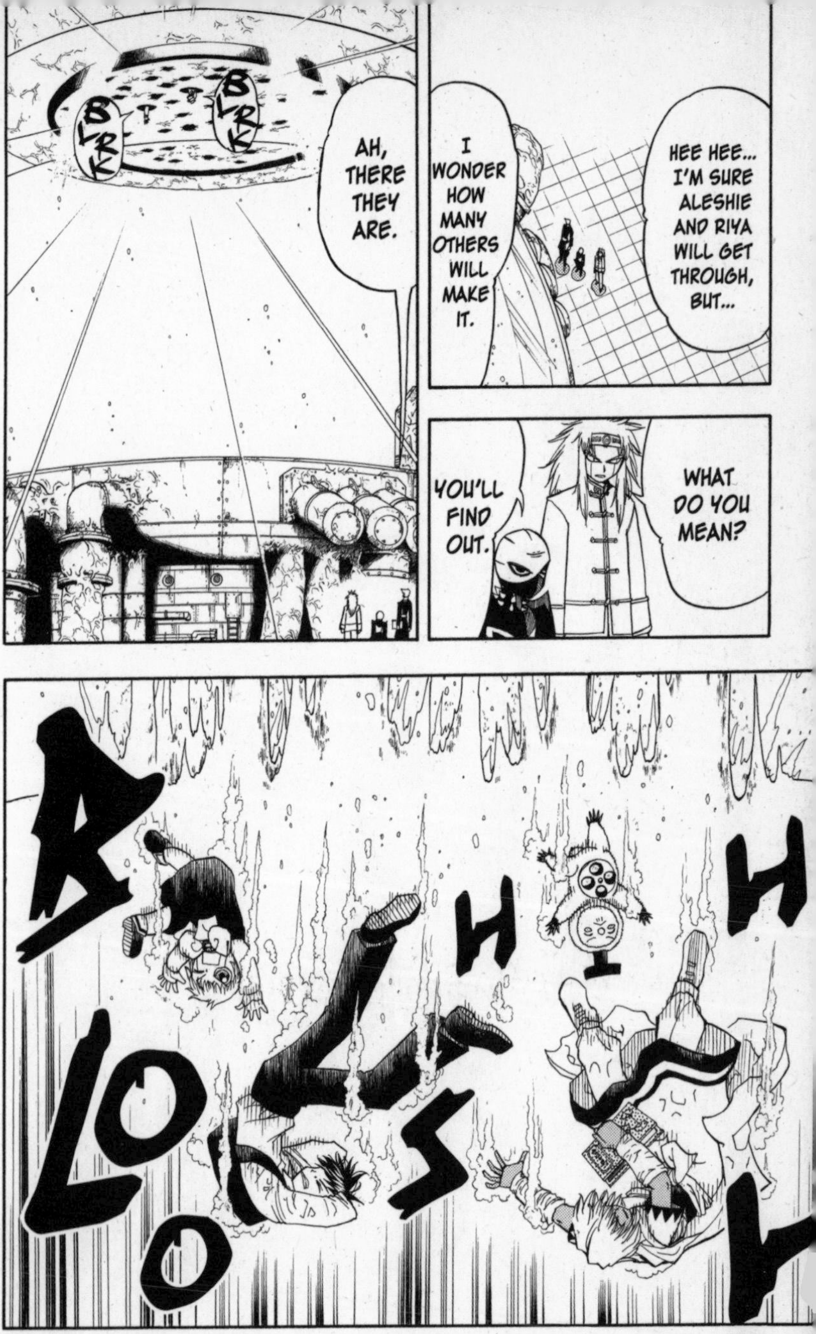
HEE HEE... I'M SURE ALESHIE AND RIYA WILL GET THROUGH, BUT...
I WONDER HOW MANY OTHERS WILL MAKE IT.
WHAT DO YOU MEAN?
YOU'LL FIND OUT.
AH, THERE THEY ARE.
BLRK
BLRK

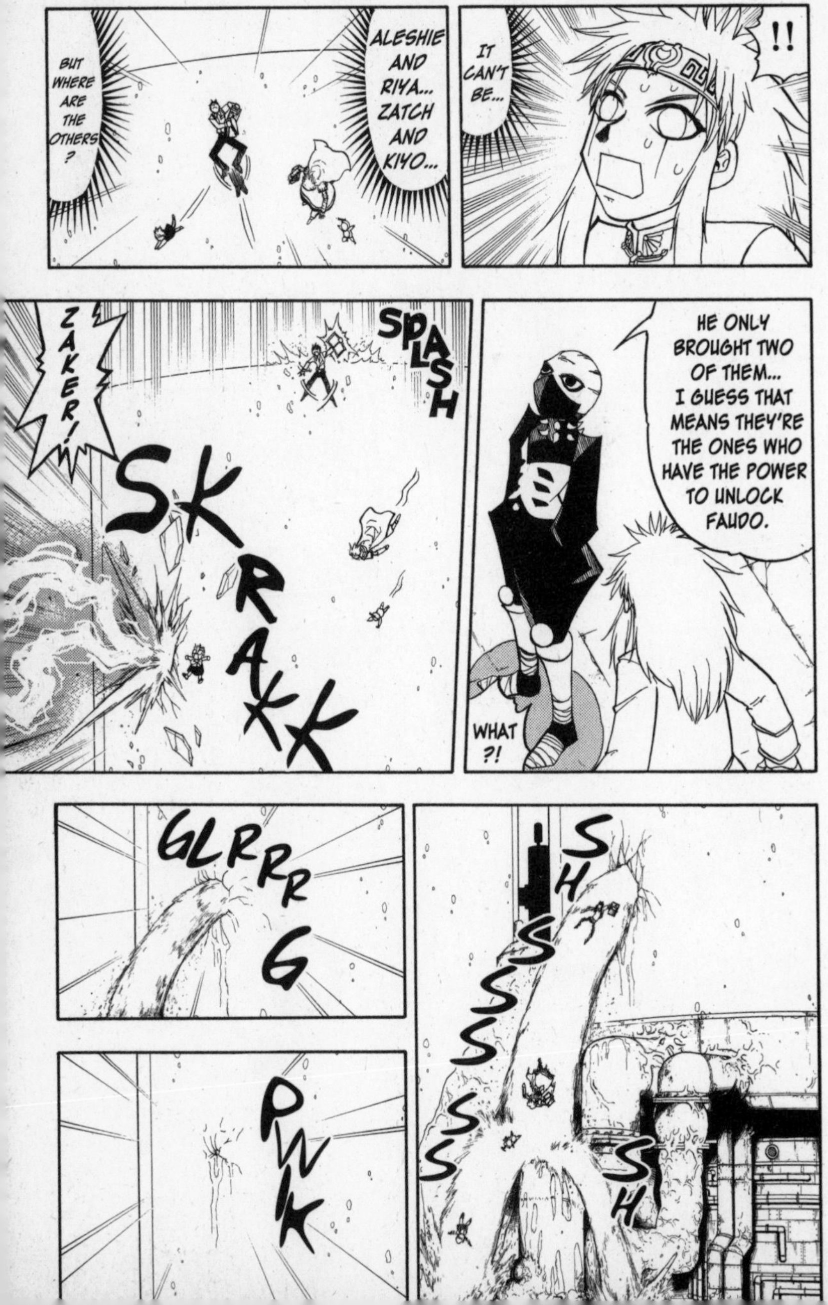
!!
IT CAN'T BE...
ALESHIE AND RIYA... ZATCH AND KIYO...
BUT WHERE ARE THE OTHERS?
HE ONLY BROUGHT TWO OF THEM... I GUESS THAT MEANS THEY'RE THE ONES WHO HAVE THE POWER TO UNLOCK FAUDO.
WHAT?!
SPLASH
ZAKER!
SKRAKK
SHSSSSSSSH
GLRRRRG
PWIK

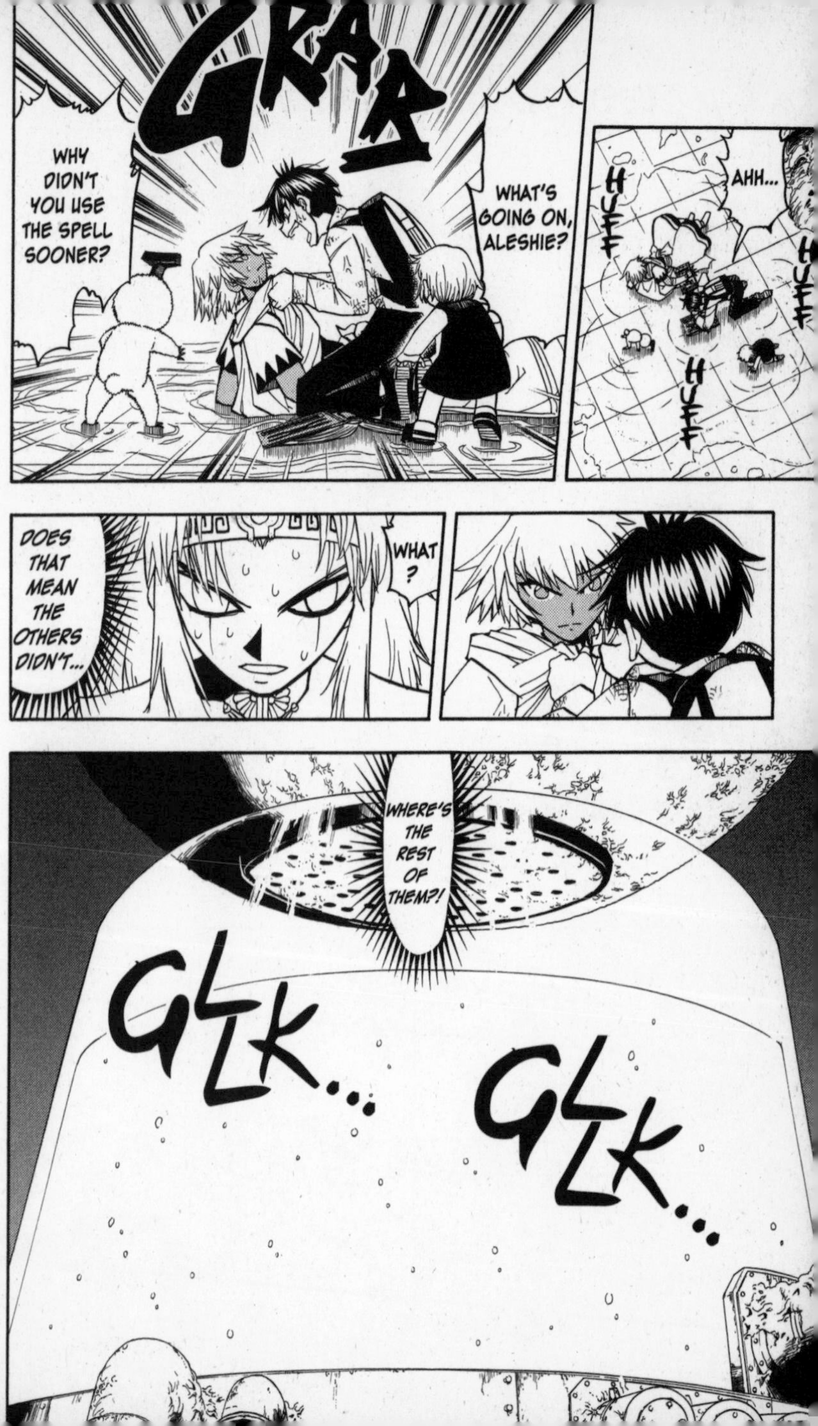
AHH...
HUFF HUFF
HUFF
GRAB
WHAT'S GOING ON, ALESHIE?
WHY DIDN'T YOU USE THE SPELL SOONER?
WHAT?
DOES THAT MEAN THE OTHERS DIDN'T...
WHERE'S THE REST OF THEM?!
GLK... GLK...

# LEVEL 202: The True Heart

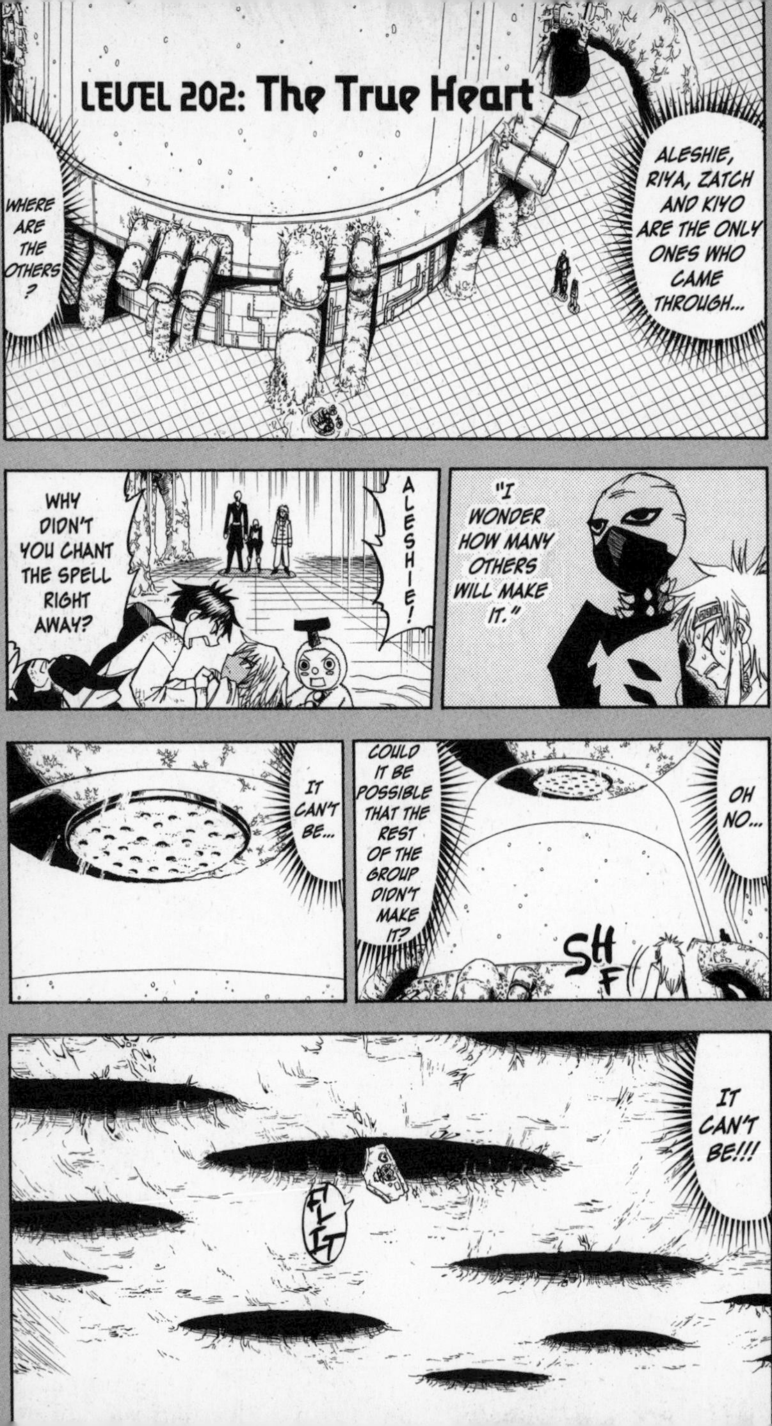

ALESHIE, RIYA, ZATCH AND KIYO ARE THE ONLY ONES WHO CAME THROUGH...
WHERE ARE THE OTHERS?
"I WONDER HOW MANY OTHERS WILL MAKE IT."
ALESHIE!
WHY DIDN'T YOU CHANT THE SPELL RIGHT AWAY?
OH NO...
SHF
COULD IT BE POSSIBLE THAT THE REST OF THE GROUP DIDN'T MAKE IT?
IT CAN'T BE...
IT CAN'T BE!!!
FLIT

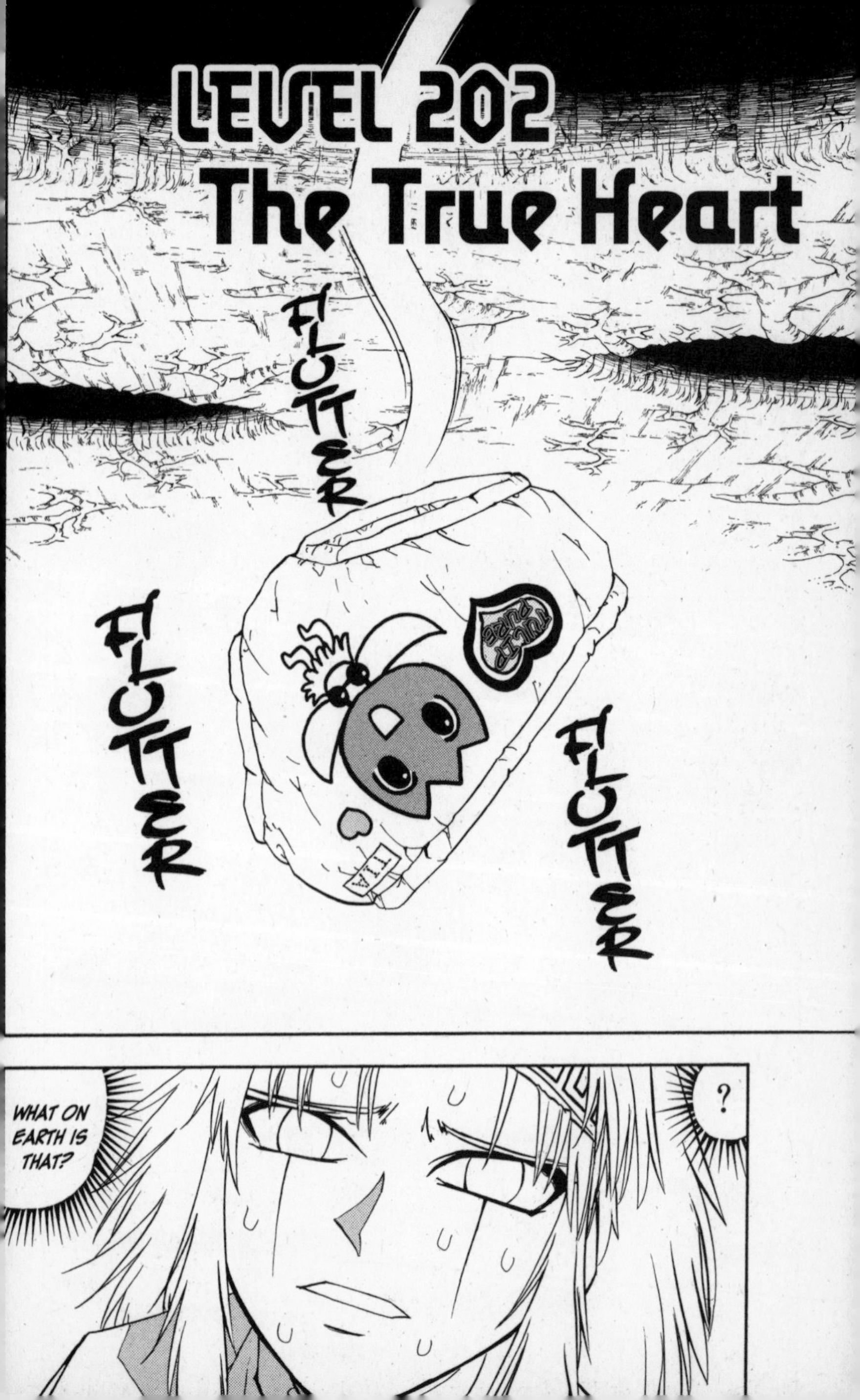
LEVEL 202
The True Heart
FLOTTER
FLOTTER
FLOTTER
?
WHAT ON EARTH IS THAT?

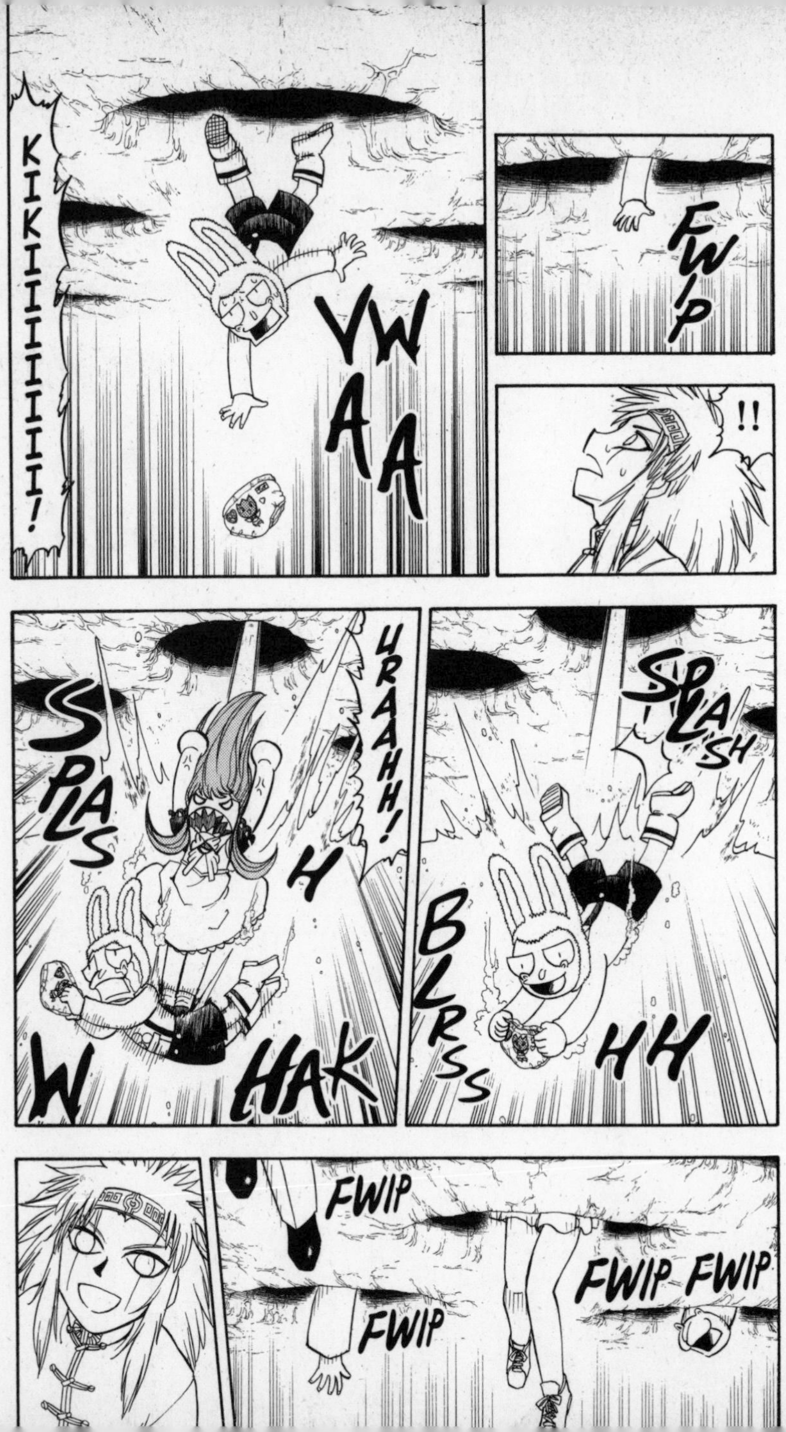
FWIP
!!
YWAAA
KIKIIIIIIIIIII!
SPLASH
BLRSS
HH
URAAHH!
SPLAS
H
W
HAK
FWIP
FWIP FWIP
FWIP

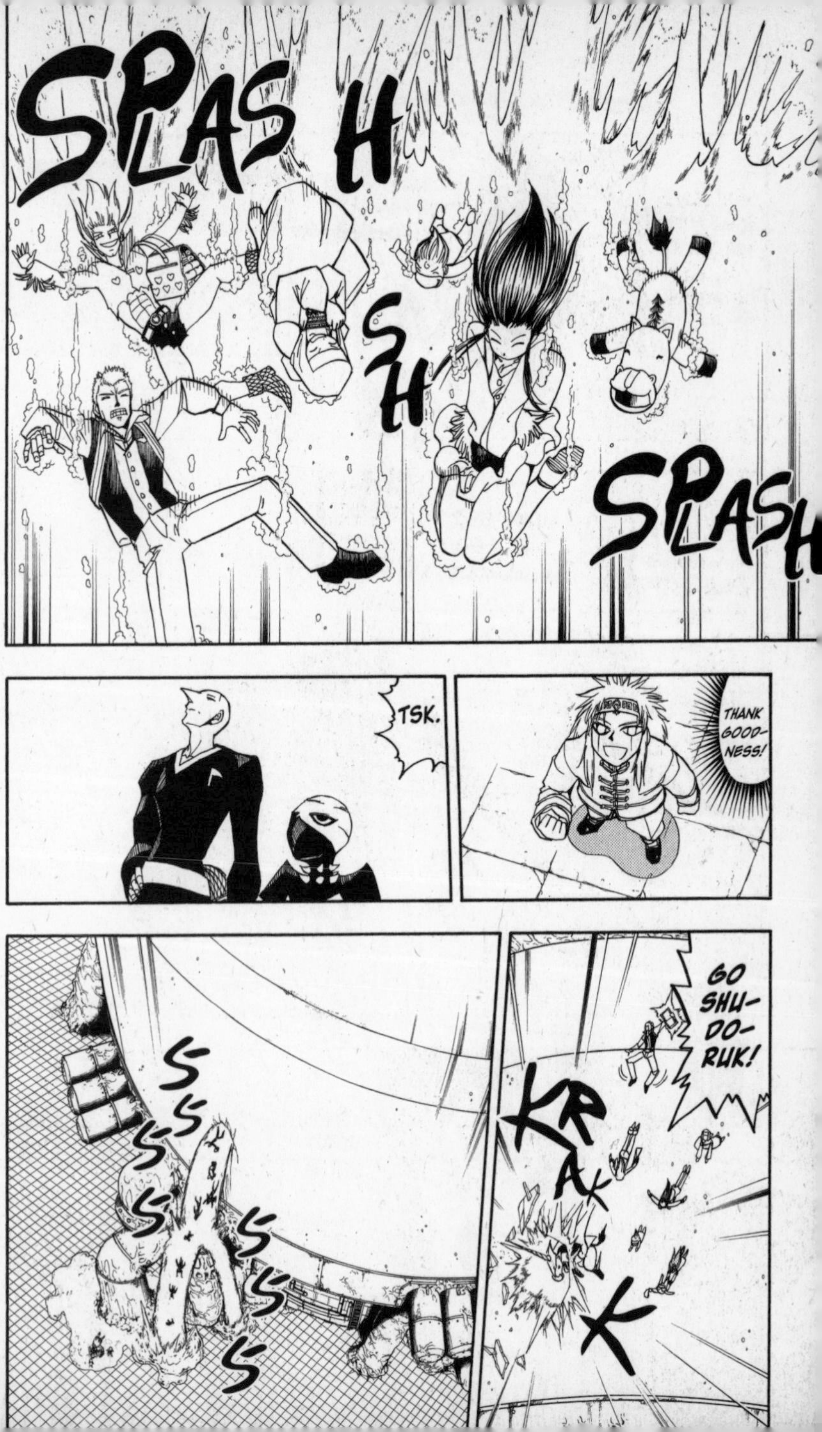
SPLASH
SH
SPLASH
THANK GOOD-NESS!
TSK.
GO SHU-DO-RUK!
KRAK
SSSSS
SSSS

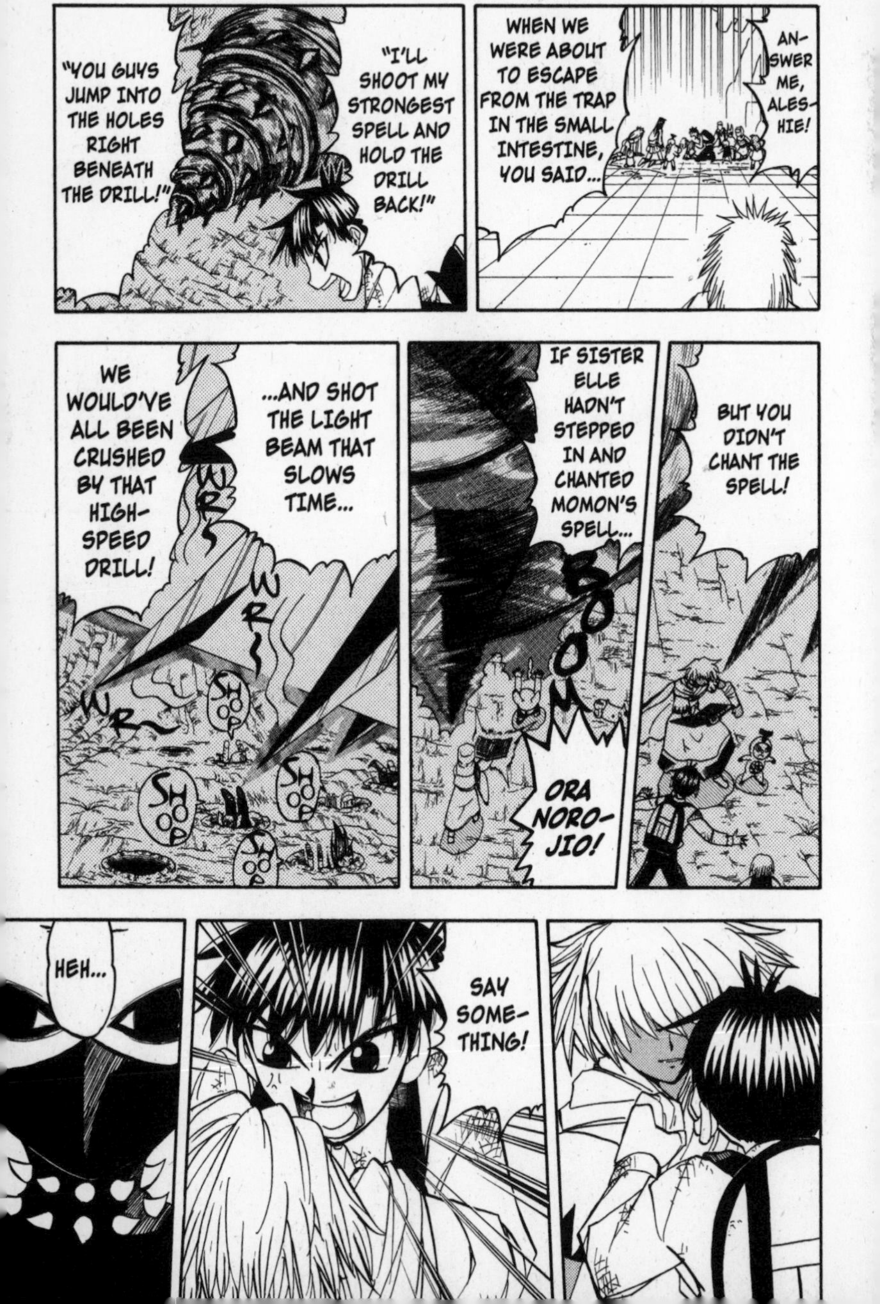
ANSWER ME, ALESHIE!
WHEN WE WERE ABOUT TO ESCAPE FROM THE TRAP IN THE SMALL INTESTINE, YOU SAID...
"I'LL SHOOT MY STRONGEST SPELL AND HOLD THE DRILL BACK!"
"YOU GUYS JUMP INTO THE HOLES RIGHT BENEATH THE DRILL!"
BUT YOU DIDN'T CHANT THE SPELL!
IF SISTER ELLE HADN'T STEPPED IN AND CHANTED MOMON'S SPELL...
BOOOM
ORA NORO-JIO!
...AND SHOT THE LIGHT BEAM THAT SLOWS TIME...
WE WOULD'VE ALL BEEN CRUSHED BY THAT HIGH-SPEED DRILL!
WRR
WRI
WR~
SHOOP
SHOOP
SHOOP
SHOOP
SHOOP
SAY SOMETHING!
HEH...

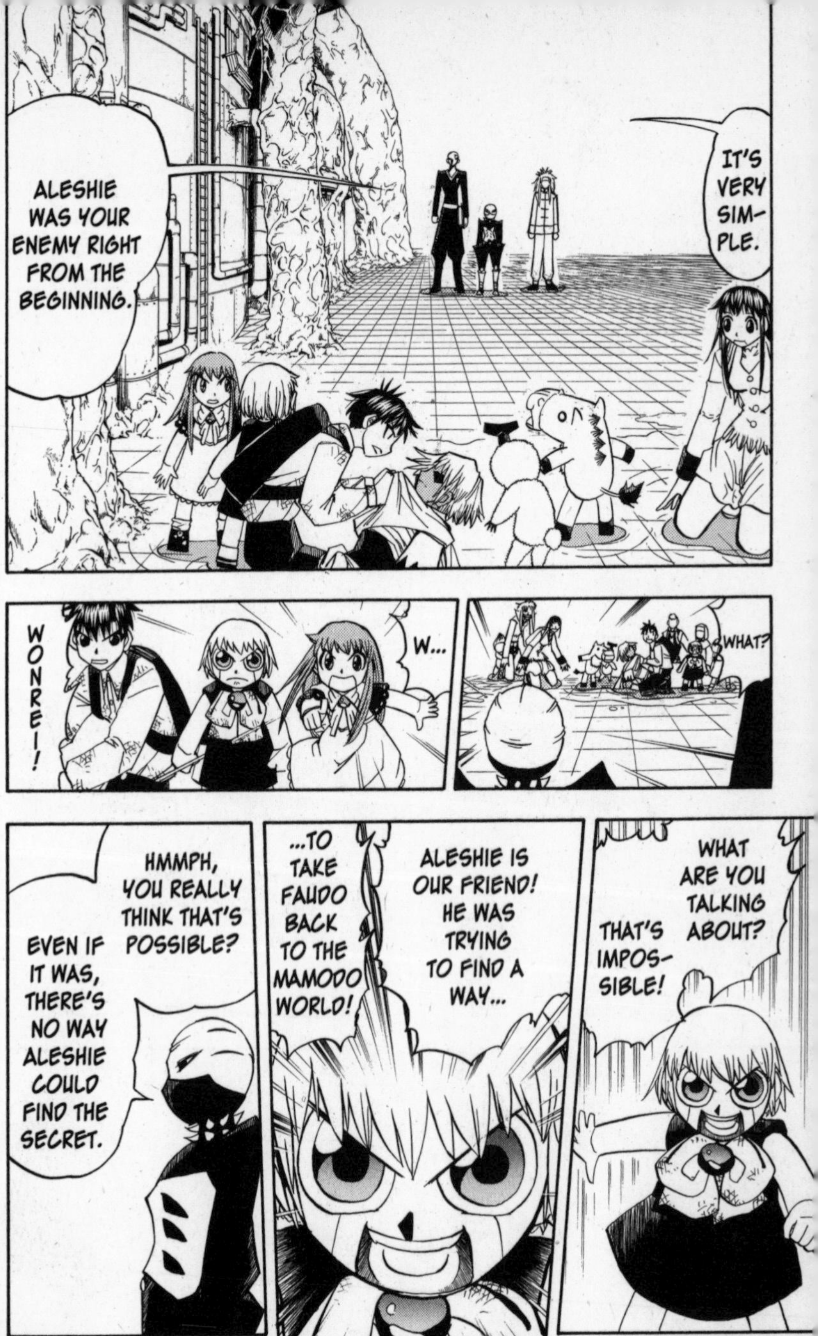
IT'S VERY SIMPLE.
ALESHIE WAS YOUR ENEMY RIGHT FROM THE BEGINNING.
WHAT?
W...
WONREI!
WHAT ARE YOU TALKING ABOUT?
THAT'S IMPOSSIBLE!
ALESHIE IS OUR FRIEND! HE WAS TRYING TO FIND A WAY...
...TO TAKE FAUDO BACK TO THE MAMODO WORLD!
HMMPH, YOU REALLY THINK THAT'S POSSIBLE?
EVEN IF IT WAS, THERE'S NO WAY ALESHIE COULD FIND THE SECRET.

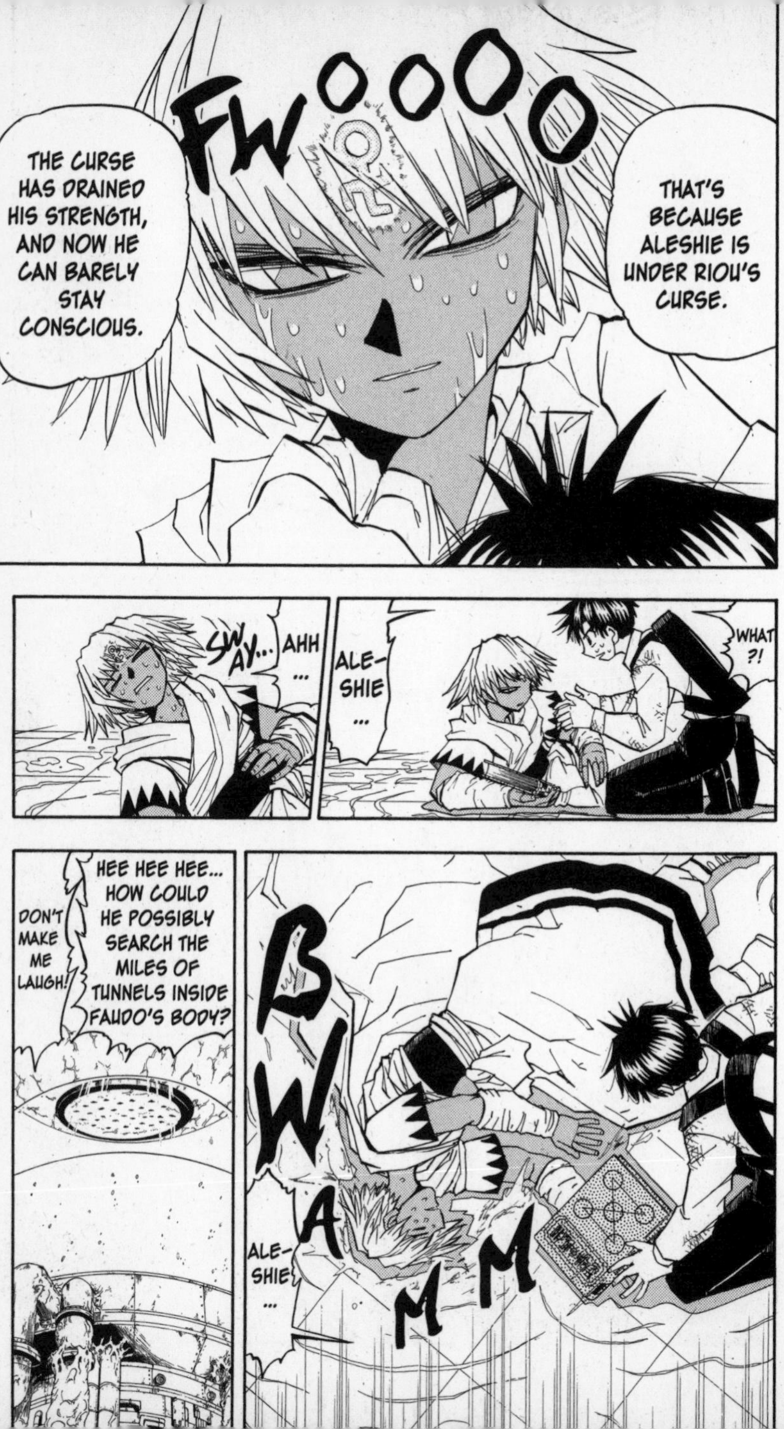
THAT'S BECAUSE ALESHIE IS UNDER RIOU'S CURSE.
FWOOOO
THE CURSE HAS DRAINED HIS STRENGTH, AND NOW HE CAN BARELY STAY CONSCIOUS.
WHAT?!
ALE-SHIE...
AHH...
SWAY...
BWAMM
ALE-SHIE...
HEE HEE HEE... HOW COULD HE POSSIBLY SEARCH THE MILES OF TUNNELS INSIDE FAUDO'S BODY?
DON'T MAKE ME LAUGH!

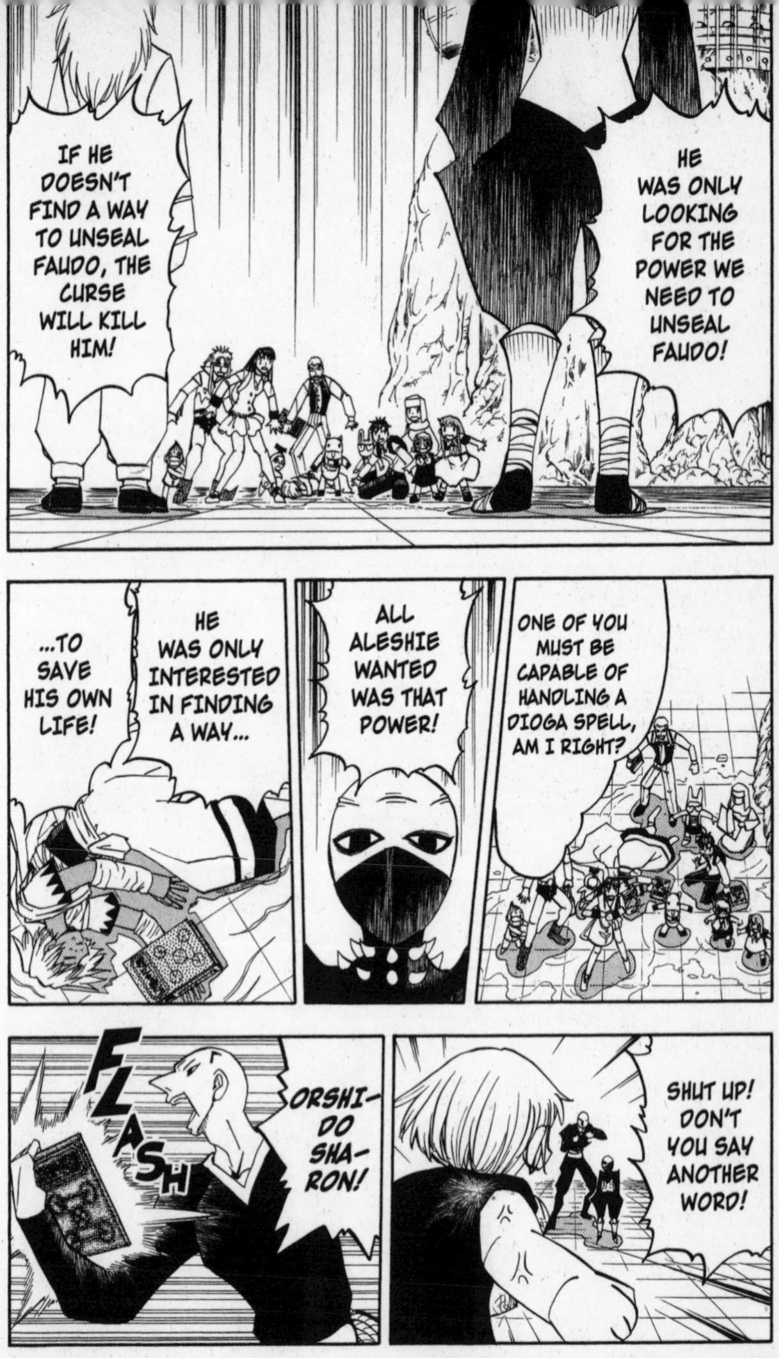
HE WAS ONLY LOOKING FOR THE POWER WE NEED TO UNSEAL FAUDO!
IF HE DOESN'T FIND A WAY TO UNSEAL FAUDO, THE CURSE WILL KILL HIM!
ONE OF YOU MUST BE CAPABLE OF HANDLING A DIOGA SPELL, AM I RIGHT?
ALL ALESHIE WANTED WAS THAT POWER!
HE WAS ONLY INTERESTED IN FINDING A WAY...
...TO SAVE HIS OWN LIFE!
SHUT UP! DON'T YOU SAY ANOTHER WORD!
FLASH
ORSHIDO SHARON!

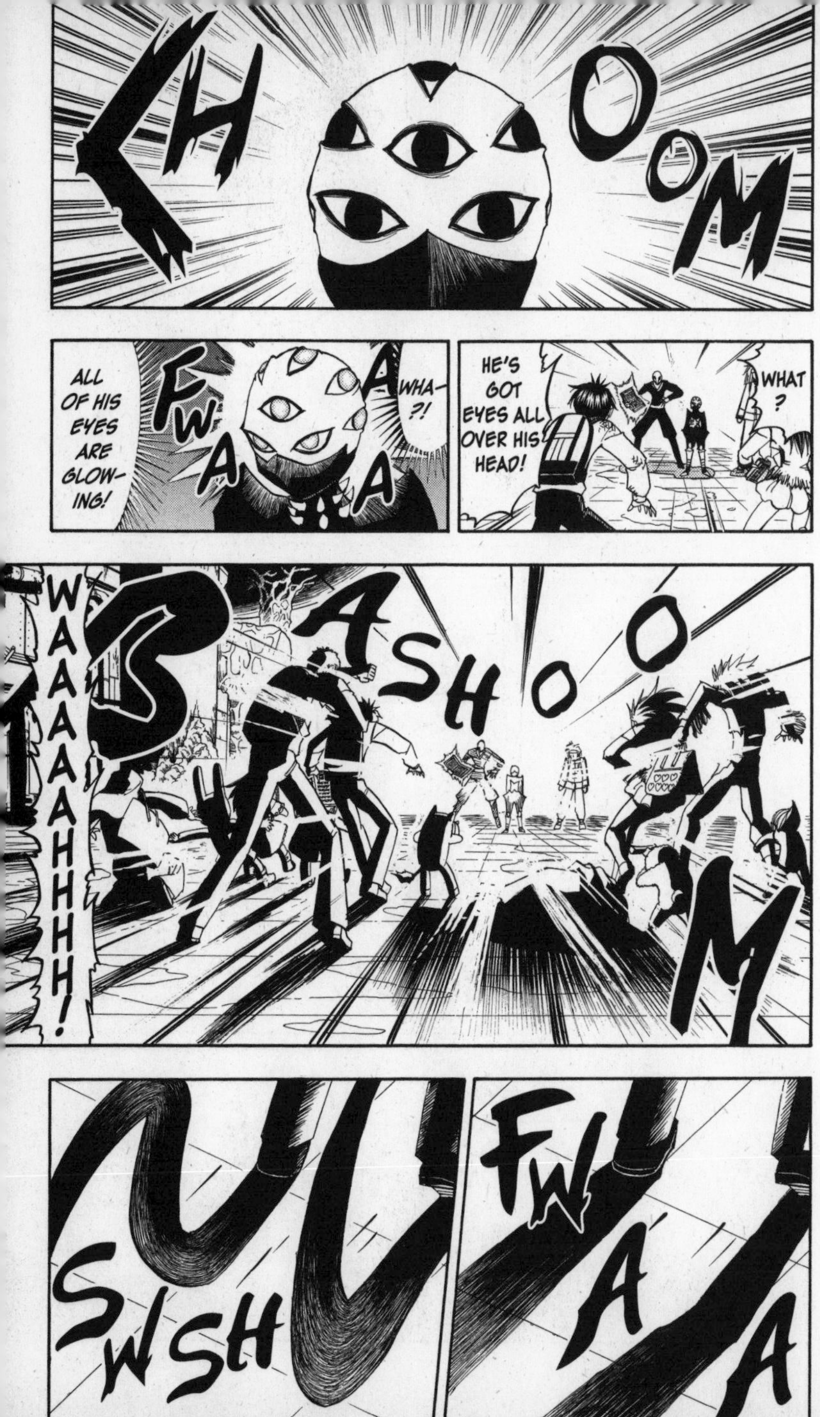
KHOOOM
WHAT?
HE'S GOT EYES ALL OVER HIS HEAD!
WHA-?!
FWAAA
ALL OF HIS EYES ARE GLOWING!
SASHOOM
WAAAAAAHHHHH!
FWAAA
SWSH

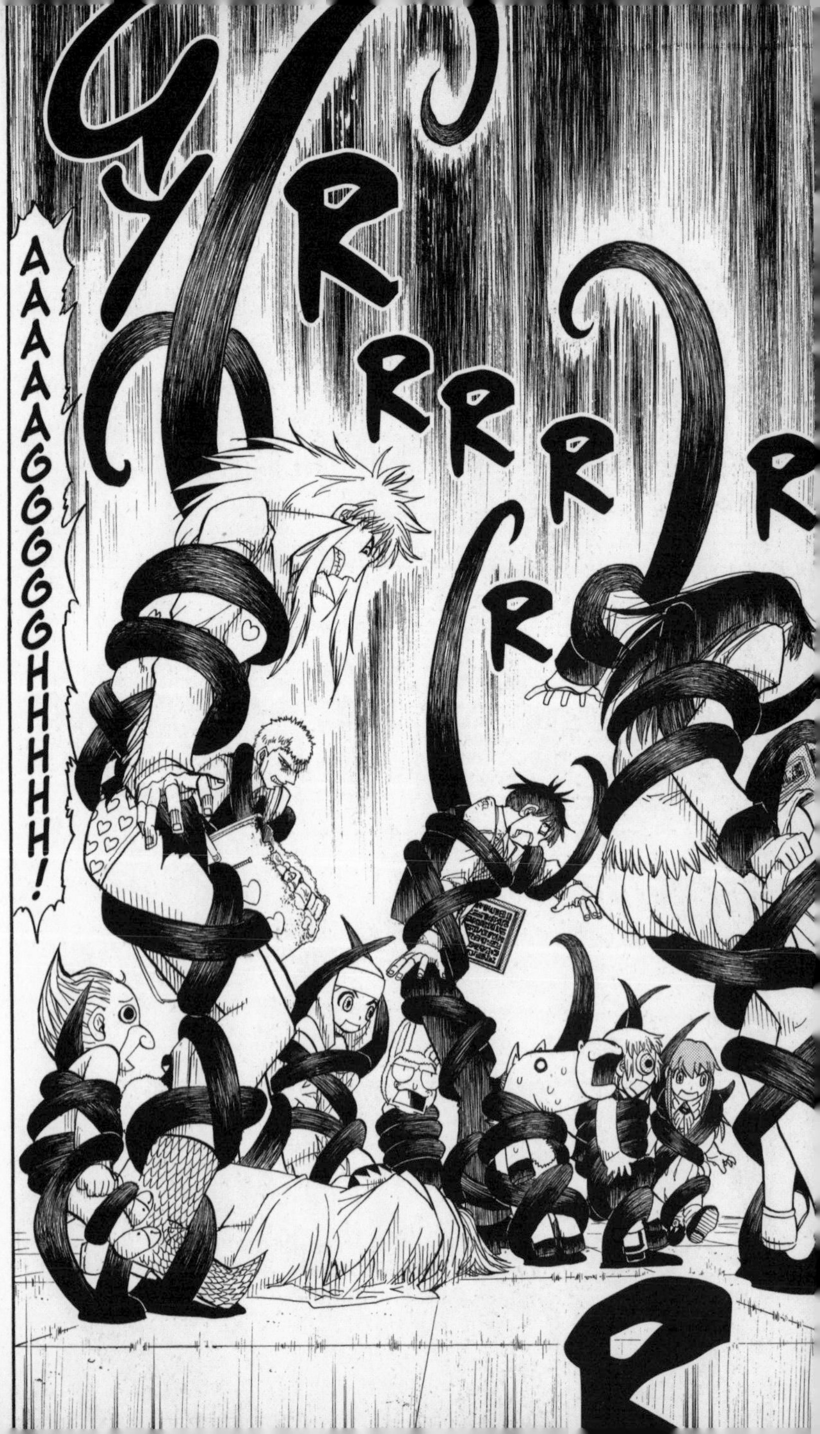

GYRRRRRRR
AAAAAAGGGGGHHHHHH!

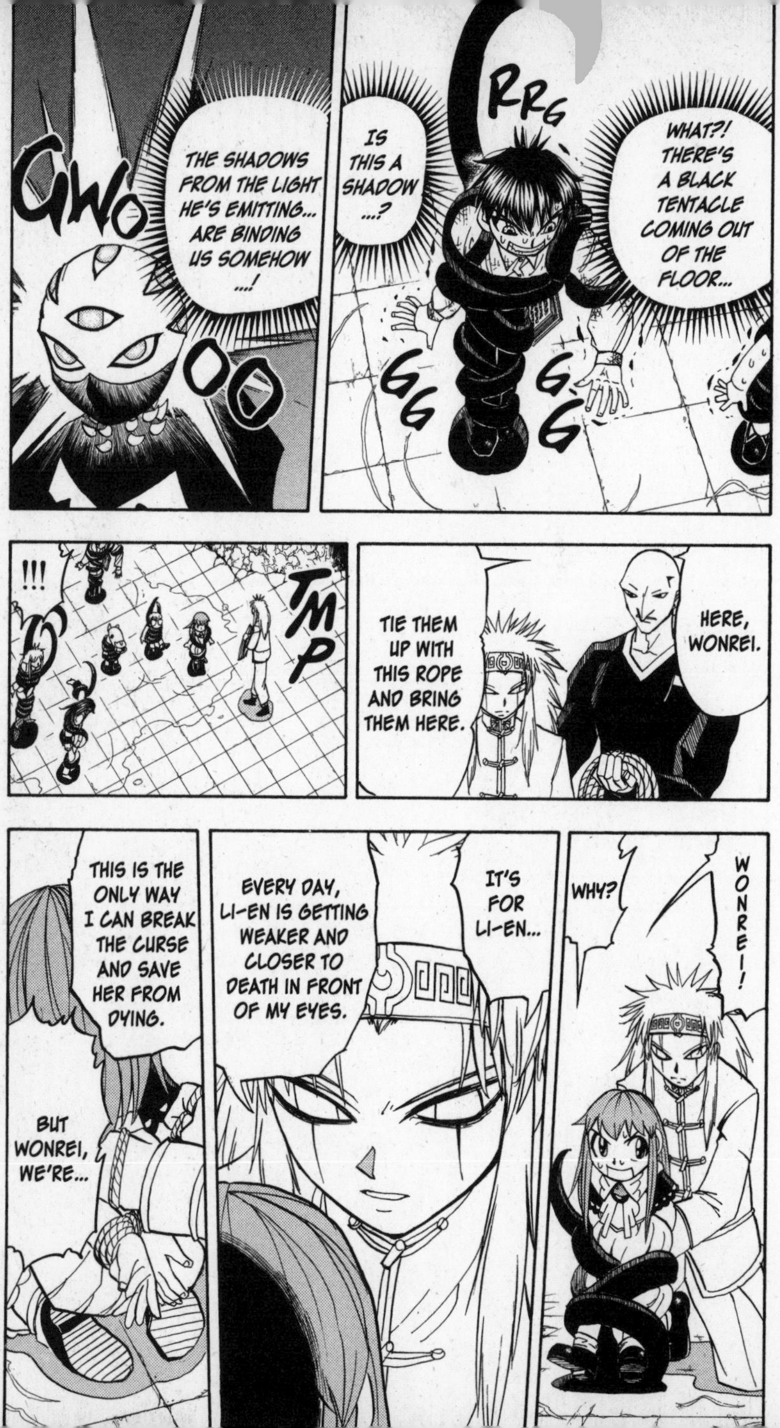
WHAT?! THERE'S A BLACK TENTACLE COMING OUT OF THE FLOOR...
RRG
IS THIS A SHADOW ...?
GG
GG
THE SHADOWS FROM THE LIGHT HE'S EMITTING... ARE BINDING US SOMEHOW ...!
GWOOOO
HERE, WONREI.
TIE THEM UP WITH THIS ROPE AND BRING THEM HERE.
TMP
!!!
WONREI!
WHY?
IT'S FOR LI-EN...
EVERY DAY, LI-EN IS GETTING WEAKER AND CLOSER TO DEATH IN FRONT OF MY EYES.
THIS IS THE ONLY WAY I CAN BREAK THE CURSE AND SAVE HER FROM DYING.
BUT WONREI, WE'RE...

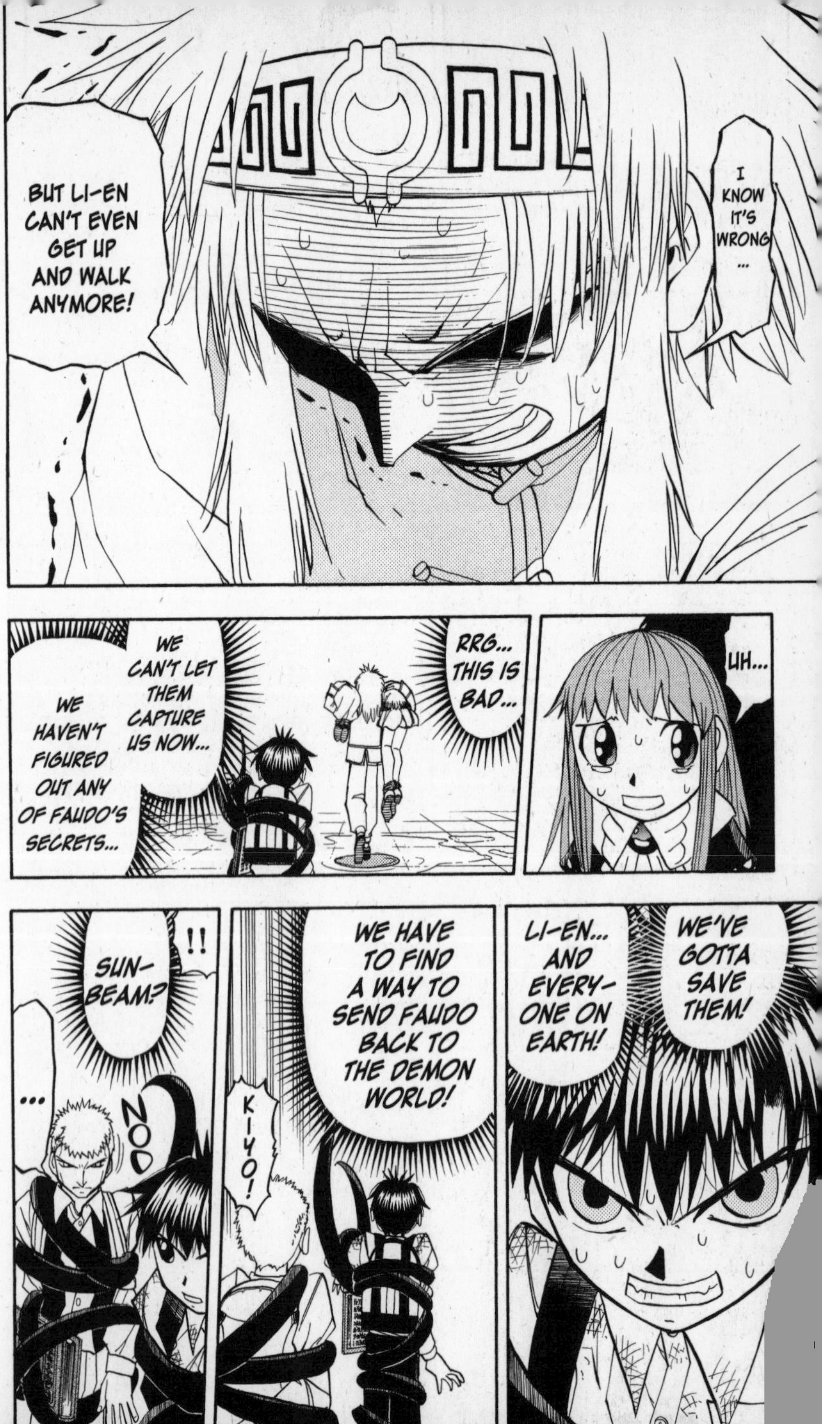
I KNOW IT'S WRONG...
BUT LI-EN CAN'T EVEN GET UP AND WALK ANYMORE!
UH...
RRG... THIS IS BAD...
WE CAN'T LET THEM CAPTURE US NOW...
WE HAVEN'T FIGURED OUT ANY OF FAUDO'S SECRETS...
WE'VE GOTTA SAVE THEM!
LI-EN... AND EVERY-ONE ON EARTH!
WE HAVE TO FIND A WAY TO SEND FAUDO BACK TO THE DEMON WORLD!
KIYO!
!!
SUN-BEAM?
NOD
...

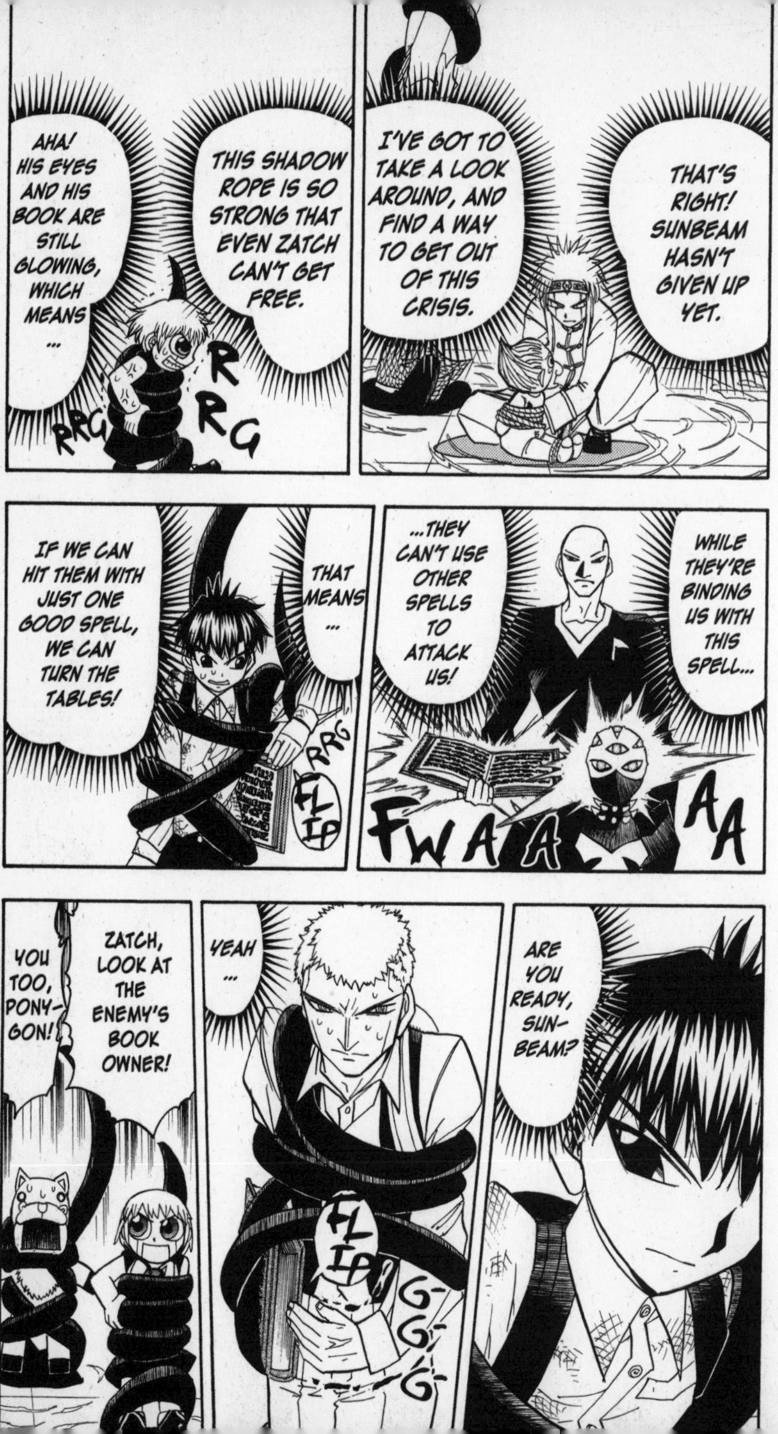
THAT'S RIGHT! SUNBEAM HASN'T GIVEN UP YET.
I'VE GOT TO TAKE A LOOK AROUND, AND FIND A WAY TO GET OUT OF THIS CRISIS.
THIS SHADOW ROPE IS SO STRONG THAT EVEN ZATCH CAN'T GET FREE.
AHA! HIS EYES AND HIS BOOK ARE STILL GLOWING, WHICH MEANS ...
R RG
RRG
WHILE THEY'RE BINDING US WITH THIS SPELL...
...THEY CAN'T USE OTHER SPELLS TO ATTACK US!
FWAAAAA
THAT MEANS ...
IF WE CAN HIT THEM WITH JUST ONE GOOD SPELL, WE CAN TURN THE TABLES!
RRG
FLIP
ARE YOU READY, SUN-BEAM?
YEAH ...
FLIP
G-G-G-
ZATCH, LOOK AT THE ENEMY'S BOOK OWNER!
YOU TOO, PONY-GON!

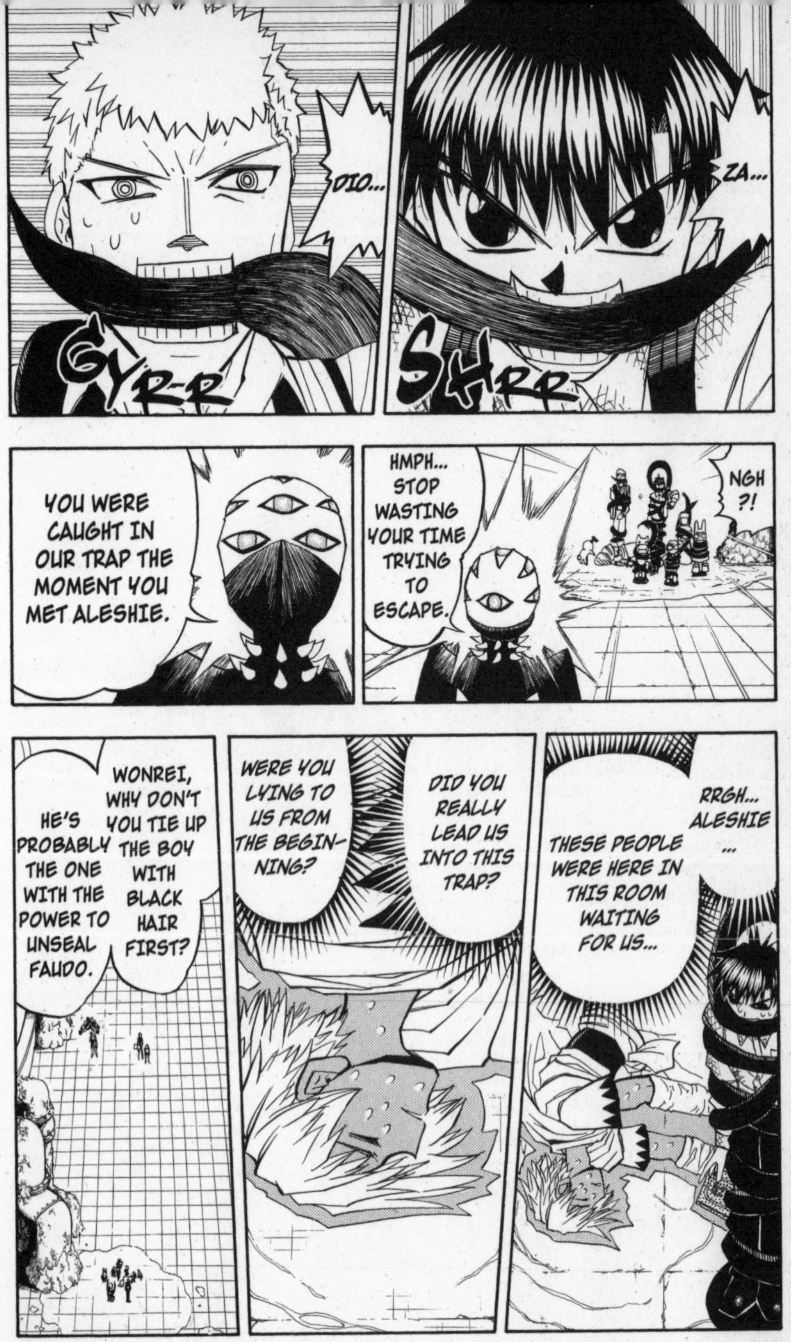
ZA...
SHRR
DIO...
GYR-R
NGH ?!
HMPH... STOP WASTING YOUR TIME TRYING TO ESCAPE.
YOU WERE CAUGHT IN OUR TRAP THE MOMENT YOU MET ALESHIE.
RRGH... ALESHIE ...
THESE PEOPLE WERE HERE IN THIS ROOM WAITING FOR US...
DID YOU REALLY LEAD US INTO THIS TRAP?
WERE YOU LYING TO US FROM THE BEGIN-NING?
WONREI, WHY DON'T YOU TIE UP THE BOY WITH BLACK HAIR FIRST?
HE'S PROBABLY THE ONE WITH THE POWER TO UNSEAL FAUDO.

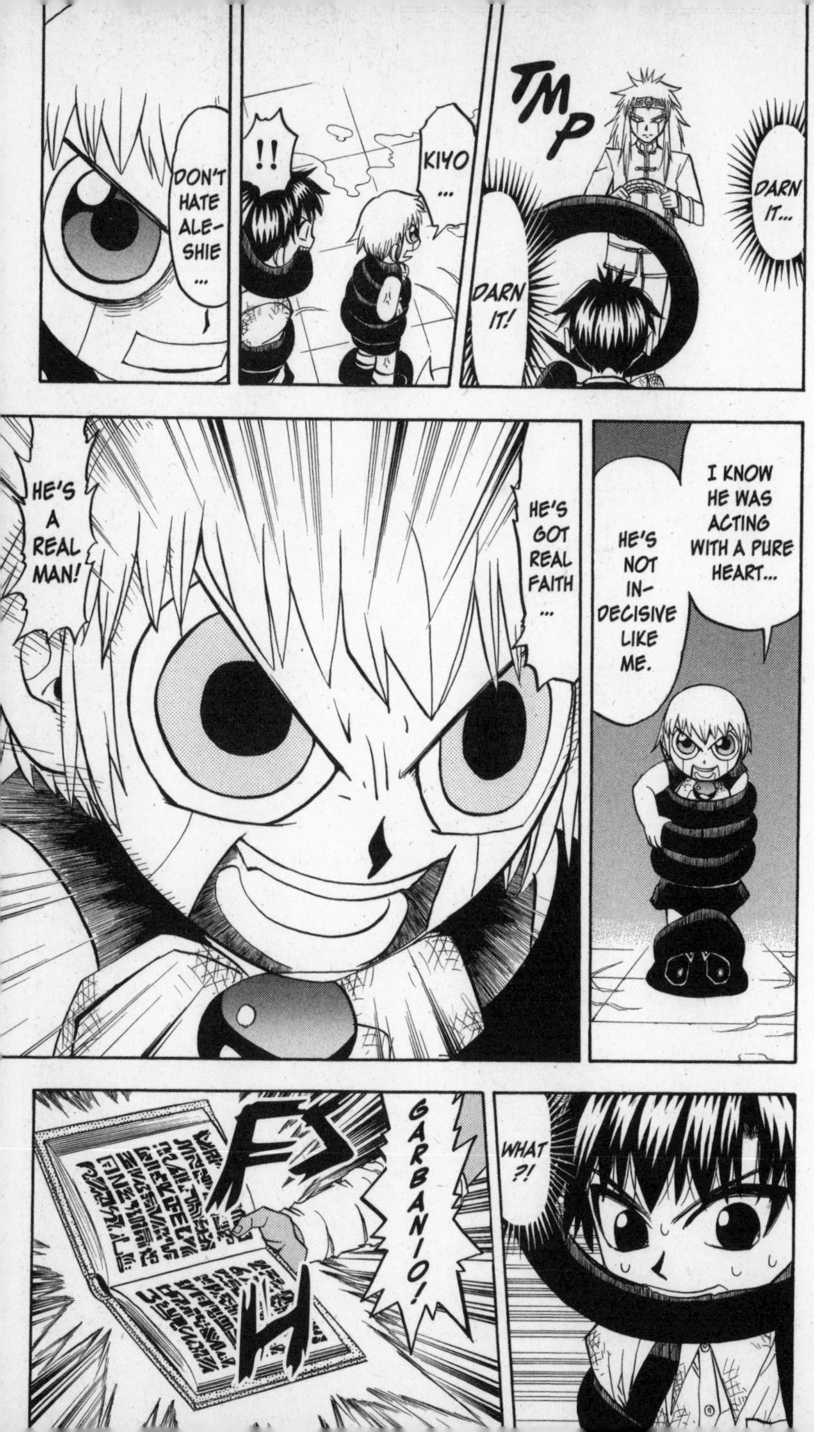
DARN IT...
TMP
DARN IT!
KIYO...
!!
DON'T HATE ALE-SHIE...
I KNOW HE WAS ACTING WITH A PURE HEART...
HE'S NOT IN-DECISIVE LIKE ME.
HE'S GOT REAL FAITH...
HE'S A REAL MAN!
WHAT?!
GARBANIO!
FSH

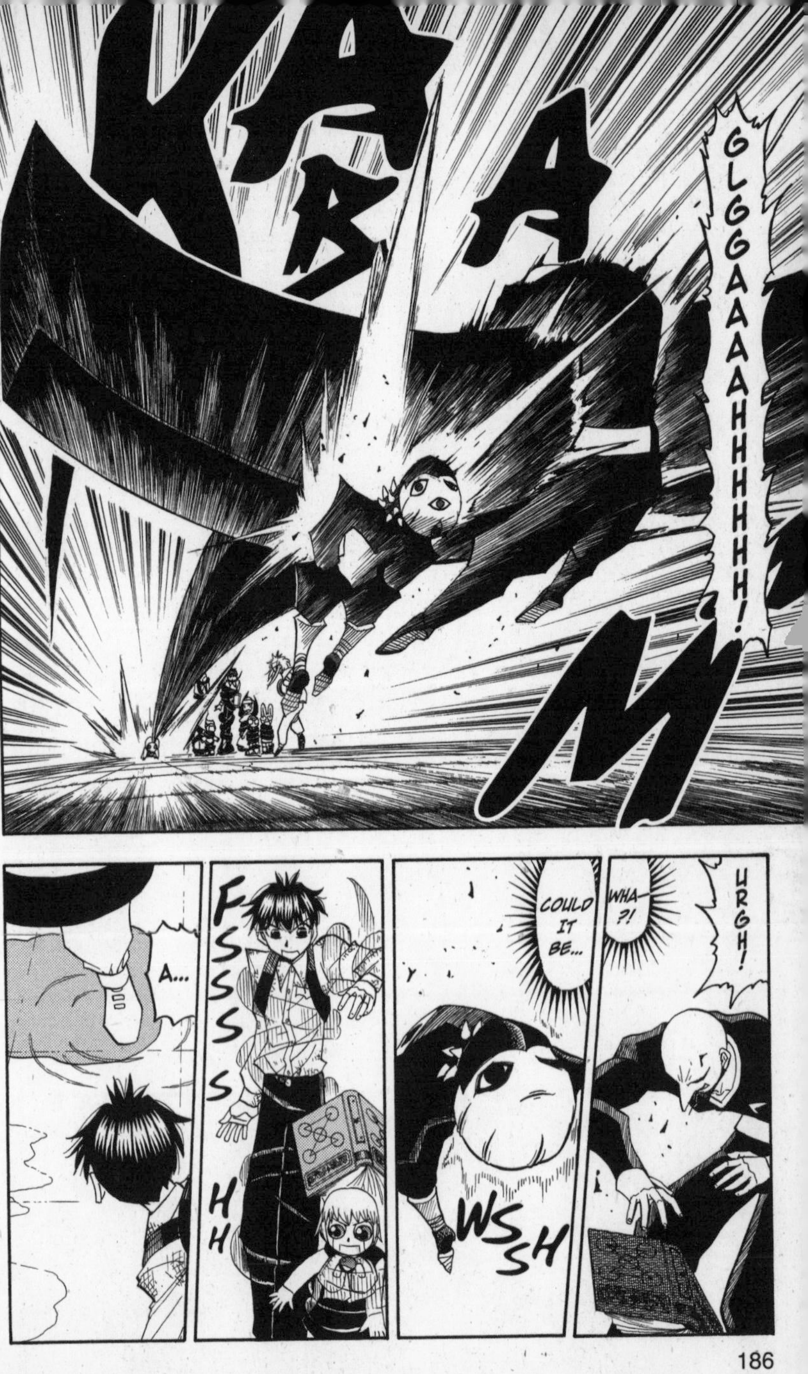

GLGGAAAAHHHHHHH!
KABAM
URGH!
WHA?!
COULD IT BE...
WSSH
FSSSSHHH
A...

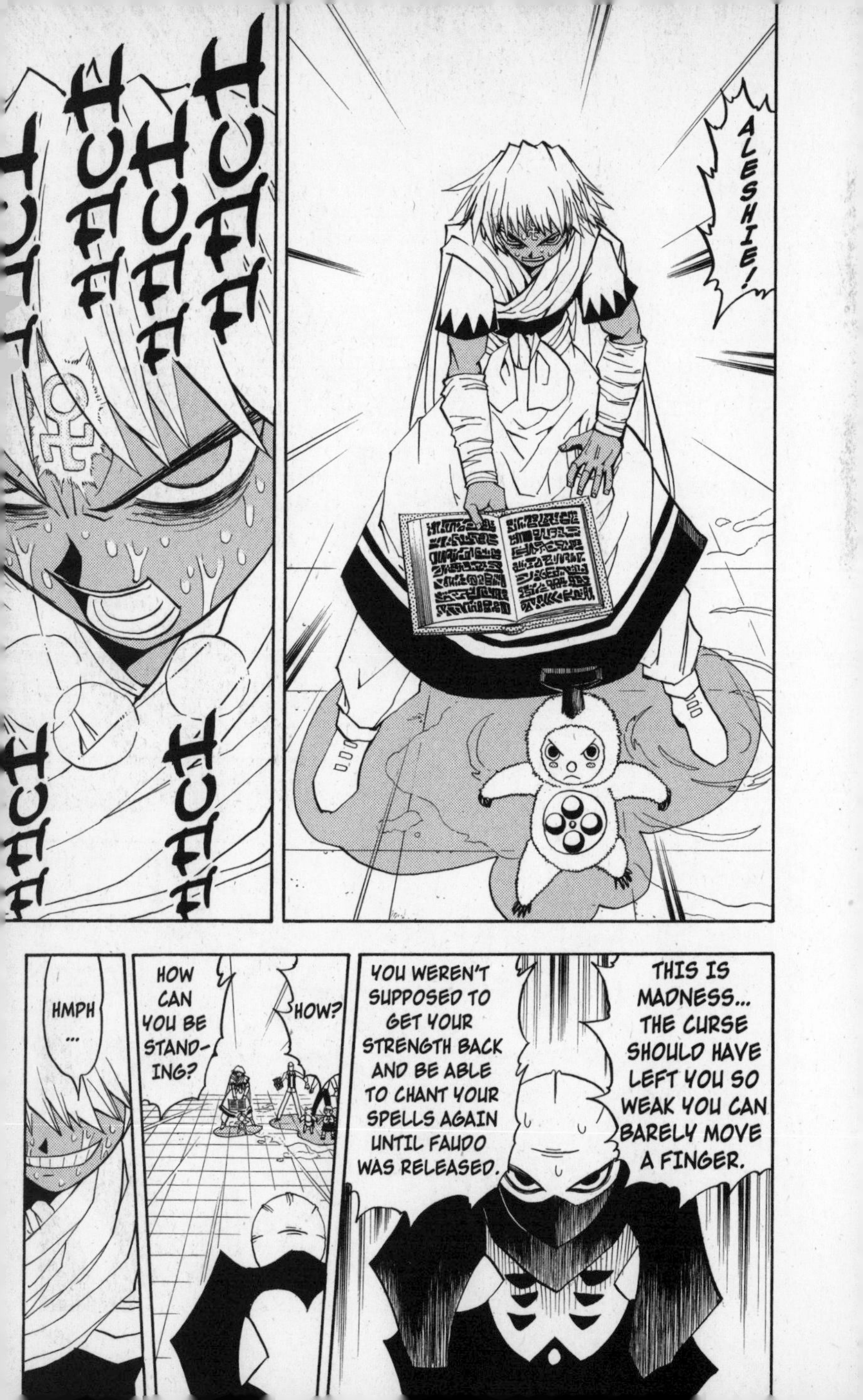
ALESHIE!
HUFF HUFF HUFF HUFF
HUFF HUFF
THIS IS MADNESS... THE CURSE SHOULD HAVE LEFT YOU SO WEAK YOU CAN BARELY MOVE A FINGER.
YOU WEREN'T SUPPOSED TO GET YOUR STRENGTH BACK AND BE ABLE TO CHANT YOUR SPELLS AGAIN UNTIL FAUDO WAS RELEASED.
HOW?
HOW CAN YOU BE STAND-ING?
HMPH ...

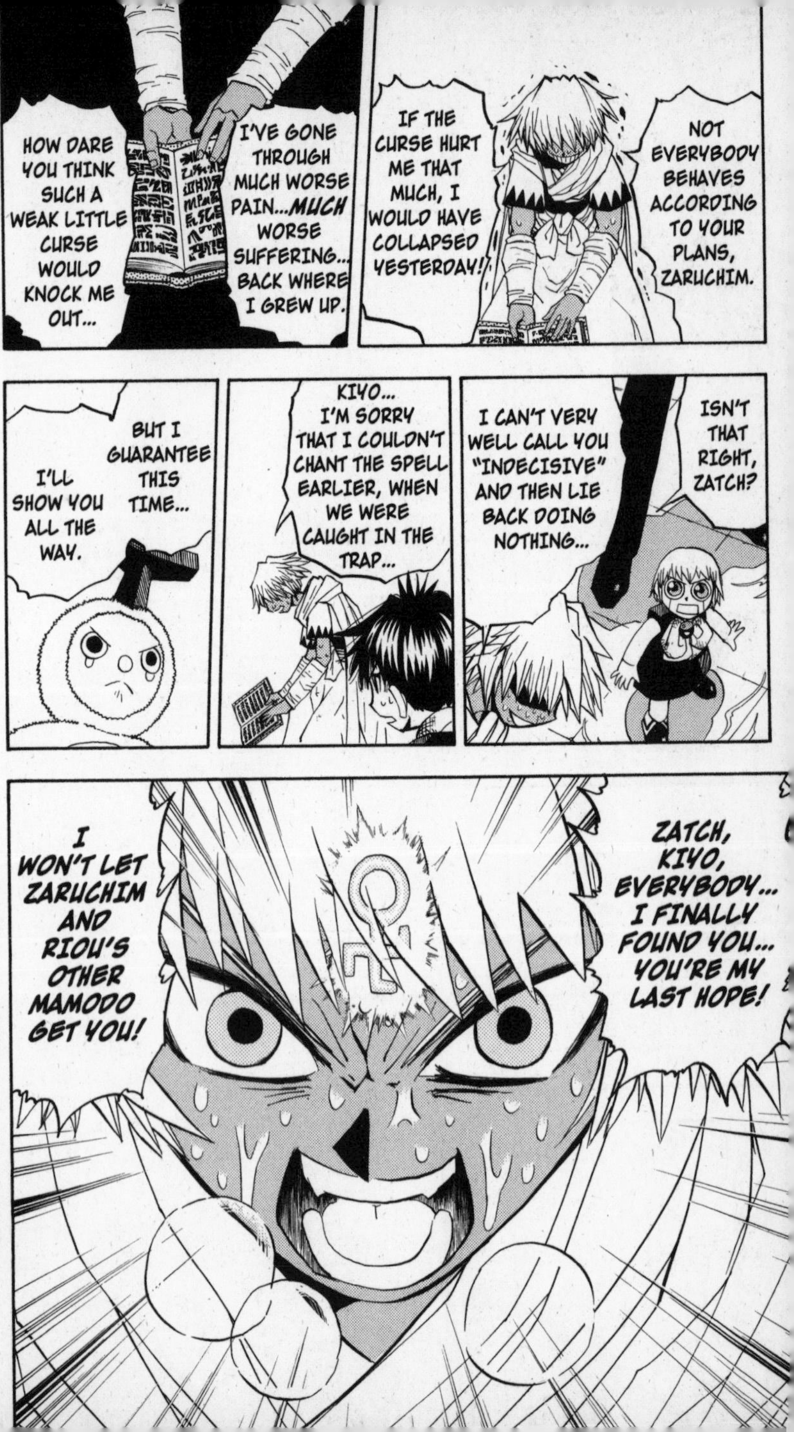

NOT EVERYBODY BEHAVES ACCORDING TO YOUR PLANS, ZARUCHIM.
IF THE CURSE HURT ME THAT MUCH, I WOULD HAVE COLLAPSED YESTERDAY!
I'VE GONE THROUGH MUCH WORSE PAIN...MUCH WORSE SUFFERING... BACK WHERE I GREW UP.
HOW DARE YOU THINK SUCH A WEAK LITTLE CURSE WOULD KNOCK ME OUT...
ISN'T THAT RIGHT, ZATCH?
I CAN'T VERY WELL CALL YOU "INDECISIVE" AND THEN LIE BACK DOING NOTHING...
KIYO... I'M SORRY THAT I COULDN'T CHANT THE SPELL EARLIER, WHEN WE WERE CAUGHT IN THE TRAP...
BUT I GUARANTEE THIS TIME...
I'LL SHOW YOU ALL THE WAY.
ZATCH, KIYO, EVERYBODY... I FINALLY FOUND YOU... YOU'RE MY LAST HOPE!
I WON'T LET ZARUCHIM AND RIOU'S OTHER MAMODO GET YOU!


TO BE CONTINUED!!

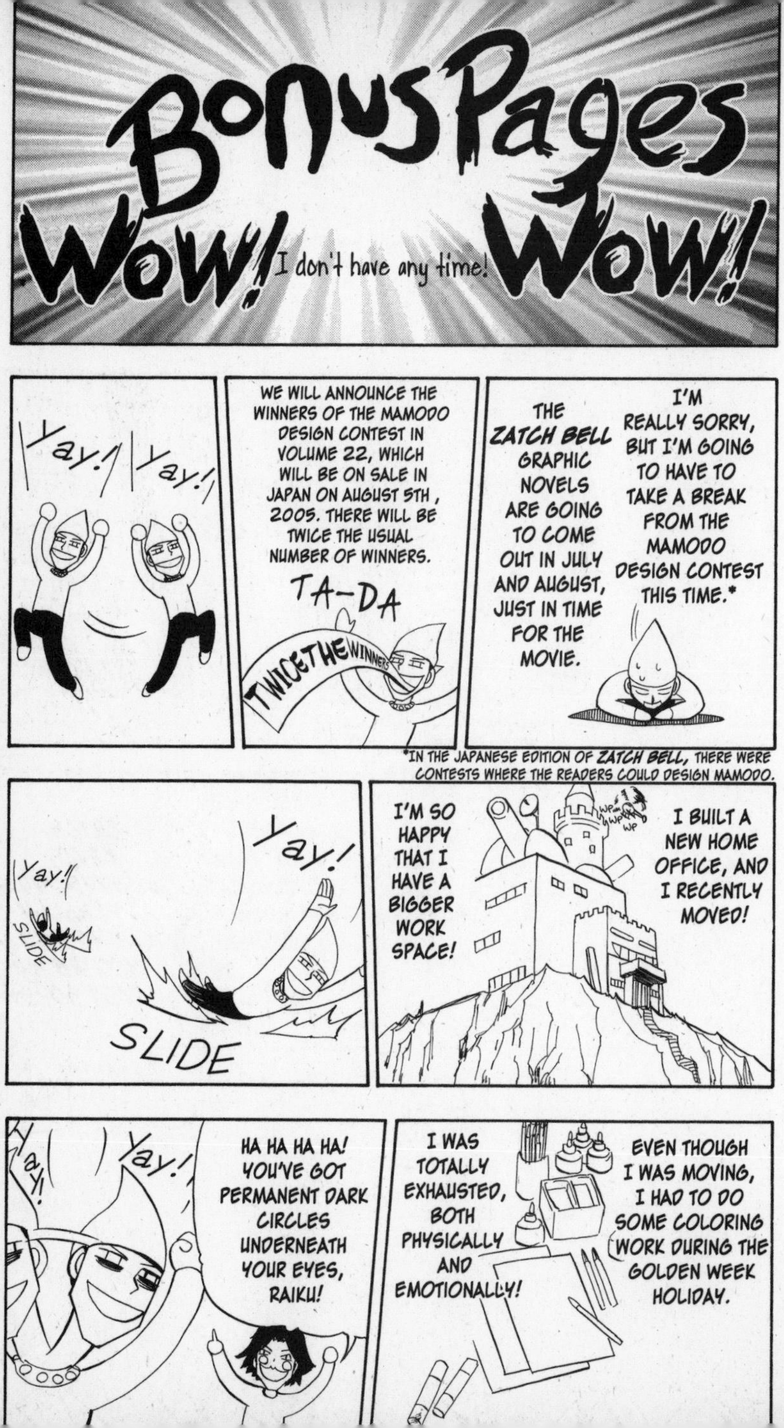
Bonus Pages
Wow! I don't have any time! Wow!
I'M REALLY SORRY, BUT I'M GOING TO HAVE TO TAKE A BREAK FROM THE MAMODO DESIGN CONTEST THIS TIME.*
THE ZATCH BELL GRAPHIC NOVELS ARE GOING TO COME OUT IN JULY AND AUGUST, JUST IN TIME FOR THE MOVIE.
WE WILL ANNOUNCE THE WINNERS OF THE MAMODO DESIGN CONTEST IN VOLUME 22, WHICH WILL BE ON SALE IN JAPAN ON AUGUST 5TH, 2005. THERE WILL BE TWICE THE USUAL NUMBER OF WINNERS.
TA-DA
TWICE THE WINNERS
Yay!
Yay!
*IN THE JAPANESE EDITION OF ZATCH BELL, THERE WERE CONTESTS WHERE THE READERS COULD DESIGN MAMODO.
I BUILT A NEW HOME OFFICE, AND I RECENTLY MOVED!
I'M SO HAPPY THAT I HAVE A BIGGER WORK SPACE!
Yay!
Yay!
SLIDE
SLIDE
EVEN THOUGH I WAS MOVING, I HAD TO DO SOME COLORING WORK DURING THE GOLDEN WEEK HOLIDAY.
I WAS TOTALLY EXHAUSTED, BOTH PHYSICALLY AND EMOTIONALLY!
HA HA HA HA! YOU'VE GOT PERMANENT DARK CIRCLES UNDERNEATH YOUR EYES, RAIKU!
Yay!
Yay!

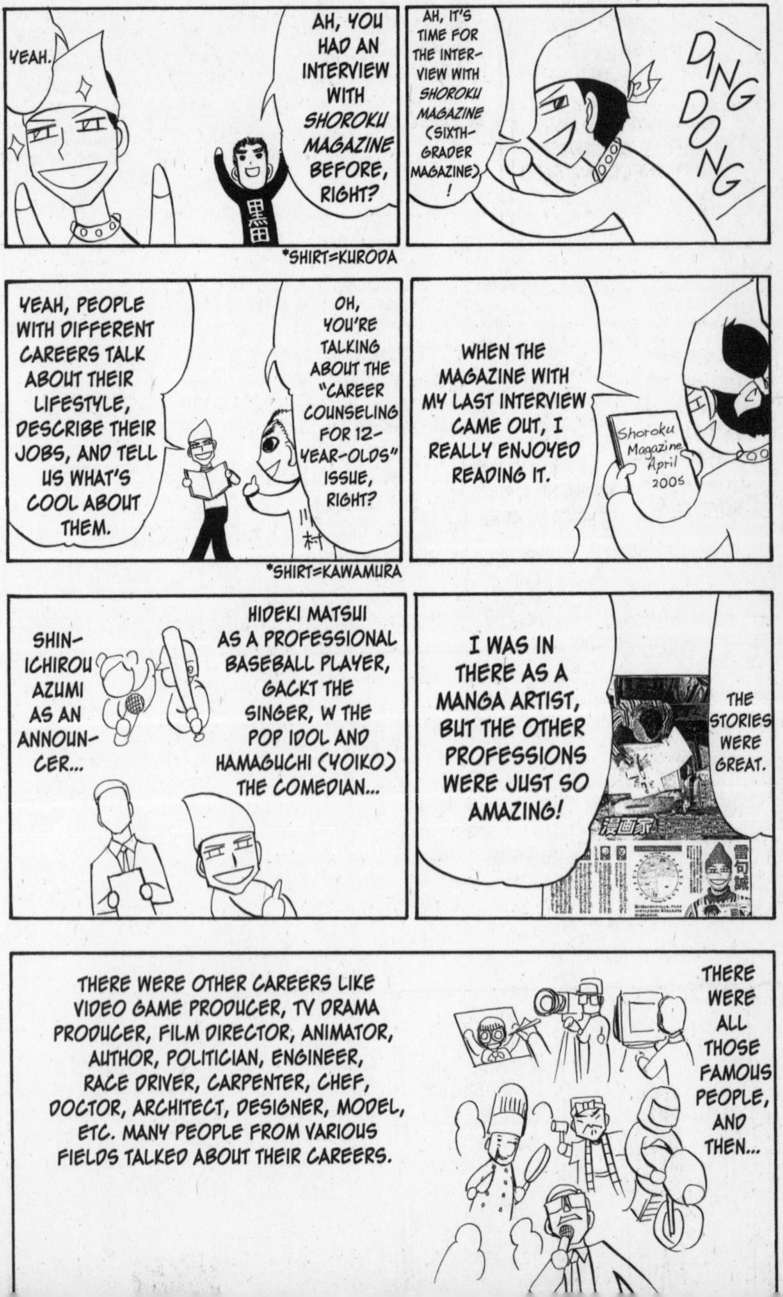
DING DONG
AH, IT'S TIME FOR THE INTERVIEW WITH SHOROKU MAGAZINE (SIXTH-GRADER MAGAZINE)!
AH, YOU HAD AN INTERVIEW WITH SHOROKU MAGAZINE BEFORE, RIGHT?
黒田
YEAH.
*SHIRT=KURODA
WHEN THE MAGAZINE WITH MY LAST INTERVIEW CAME OUT, I REALLY ENJOYED READING IT.
Shoroku Magazine April 2005
OH, YOU'RE TALKING ABOUT THE "CAREER COUNSELING FOR 12-YEAR-OLDS" ISSUE, RIGHT?
川村
YEAH, PEOPLE WITH DIFFERENT CAREERS TALK ABOUT THEIR LIFESTYLE, DESCRIBE THEIR JOBS, AND TELL US WHAT'S COOL ABOUT THEM.
*SHIRT=KAWAMURA
I WAS IN THERE AS A MANGA ARTIST, BUT THE OTHER PROFESSIONS WERE JUST SO AMAZING!
THE STORIES WERE GREAT.
漫画家
雷句誠
HIDEKI MATSUI AS A PROFESSIONAL BASEBALL PLAYER, GACKT THE SINGER, W THE POP IDOL AND HAMAGUCHI (YOIKO) THE COMEDIAN...
SHIN-ICHIROU AZUMI AS AN ANNOUNCER...
THERE WERE ALL THOSE FAMOUS PEOPLE, AND THEN...
THERE WERE OTHER CAREERS LIKE VIDEO GAME PRODUCER, TV DRAMA PRODUCER, FILM DIRECTOR, ANIMATOR, AUTHOR, POLITICIAN, ENGINEER, RACE DRIVER, CARPENTER, CHEF, DOCTOR, ARCHITECT, DESIGNER, MODEL, ETC. MANY PEOPLE FROM VARIOUS FIELDS TALKED ABOUT THEIR CAREERS.

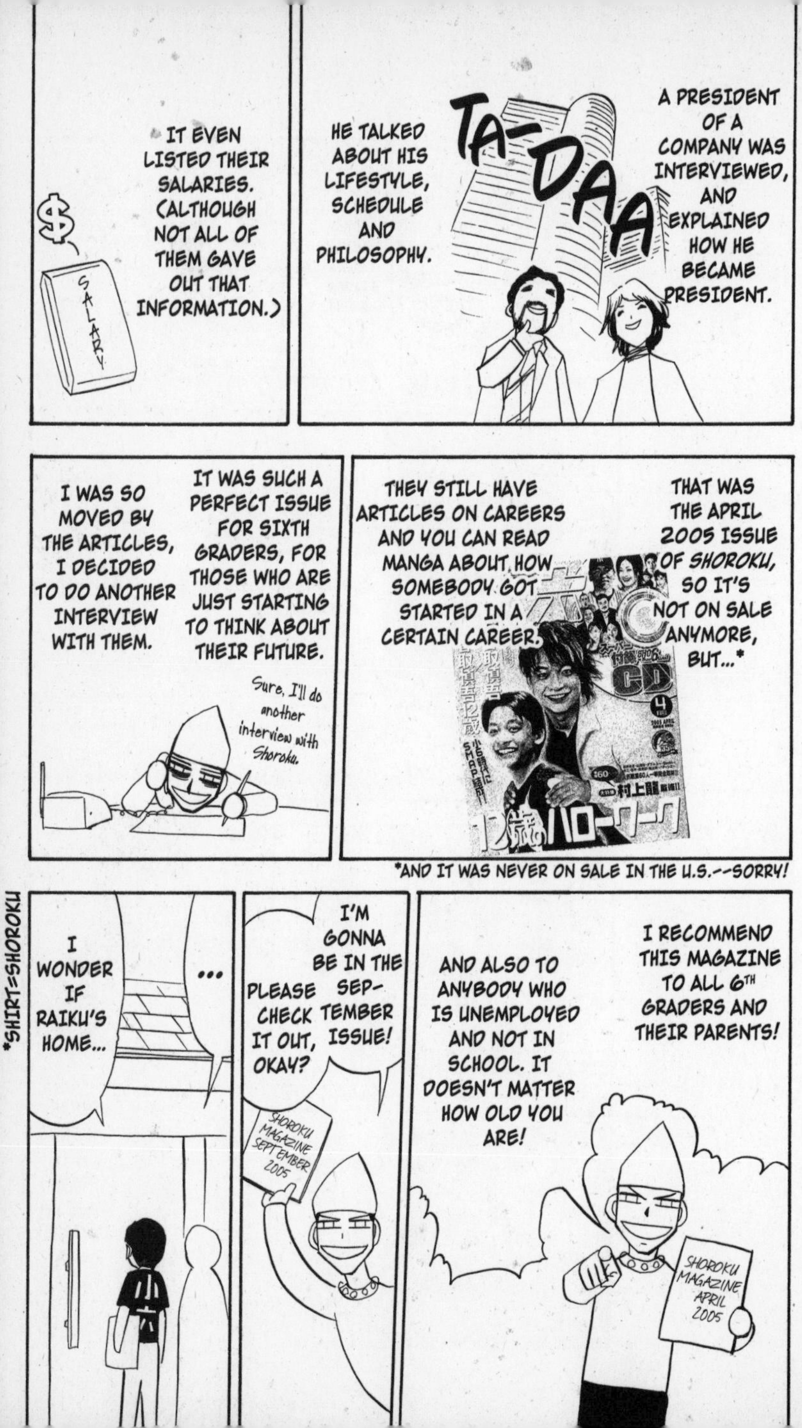
A PRESIDENT OF A COMPANY WAS INTERVIEWED, AND EXPLAINED HOW HE BECAME PRESIDENT.
TA-DAA
HE TALKED ABOUT HIS LIFESTYLE, SCHEDULE AND PHILOSOPHY.
IT EVEN LISTED THEIR SALARIES. (ALTHOUGH NOT ALL OF THEM GAVE OUT THAT INFORMATION.)
$
SALARY
THAT WAS THE APRIL 2005 ISSUE OF SHOROKU, SO IT'S NOT ON SALE ANYMORE, BUT...*
THEY STILL HAVE ARTICLES ON CAREERS AND YOU CAN READ MANGA ABOUT HOW SOMEBODY GOT STARTED IN A CERTAIN CAREER.
CD
村上龍
IT WAS SUCH A PERFECT ISSUE FOR SIXTH GRADERS, FOR THOSE WHO ARE JUST STARTING TO THINK ABOUT THEIR FUTURE.
I WAS SO MOVED BY THE ARTICLES, I DECIDED TO DO ANOTHER INTERVIEW WITH THEM.
Sure, I'll do another interview with Shoroku.
*AND IT WAS NEVER ON SALE IN THE U.S.--SORRY!
I RECOMMEND THIS MAGAZINE TO ALL 6TH GRADERS AND THEIR PARENTS!
AND ALSO TO ANYBODY WHO IS UNEMPLOYED AND NOT IN SCHOOL. IT DOESN'T MATTER HOW OLD YOU ARE!
SHOROKU MAGAZINE APRIL 2005
I'M GONNA BE IN THE SEPTEMBER ISSUE!
PLEASE CHECK IT OUT, OKAY?
SHOROKU MAGAZINE SEPTEMBER 2005
...
I WONDER IF RAIKU'S HOME...
*SHIRT=SHOROKU

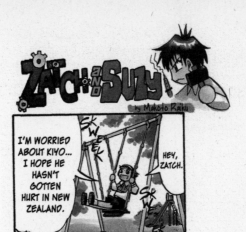

ZATCH AND SUZY
by Makoto Raiku
HEY, ZATCH.
SKWEEK
I'M WORRIED ABOUT KIYO... I HOPE HE HASN'T GOTTEN HURT IN NEW ZEALAND.
SKWEEK
DON'T WORRY, SUZY! I'M SURE KIYO IS OKAY.
AFTER ALL, I'M THERE FOR HIM.
SKWEEK
I'M SO IMPRESSED BY THE ZATCH ROBOT KIYO MADE.
SKFF
IT'S SO HIGH-LEVEL.
BUT...
SKF
BUT...
SKWEEK

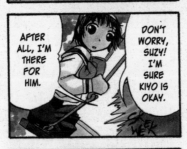

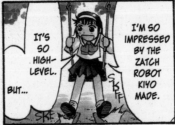

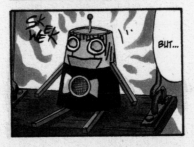

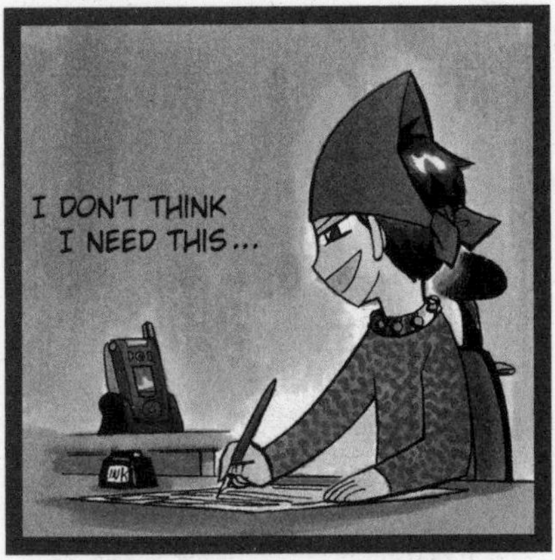
I DON'T THINK I NEED THIS...
INK

## MAKOTO RAIKU

I bought a cell phone. I wasn't able to use my home phone for a few days when I moved, so I had no choice but to buy a cell phone so that I could stay in contact with my editor. It's been three months since I moved and I haven't used my cell phone at all... I haven't gotten any calls either.
(Then again I haven't even told anybody my number yet, so...)

# ZATCH BELL!
## Vol. 21

### STORY AND ART BY
### MAKOTO RAIKU

Translation/David Ury
Touch-up Art & Lettering/Annaliese Christman
Cover Design/Courtney Utt
Interior Design/Julie Behn
Special Thanks/Jessica Villat, Miki Macaluso,
Mitsuko Kitajima, and Akane Matsuo
Editor/Jason Thompson

Editor in Chief, Books/Alvin Lu
Editor in Chief, Magazines/Marc Weidenbaum
VP, Publishing Licensing/Rika Inouye
VP, Sales & Product Marketing/Gonzalo Ferreyra
VP, Creative/Linda Espinosa
Publisher/Hyoe Narita

Printed in the U.S.A.

Published by VIZ Media, LLC
P.O. Box 77010
San Francisco, CA 94107

10 9 8 7 6 5 4 3 2 1
First printing, October 2008

www.viz.com
store.viz.com

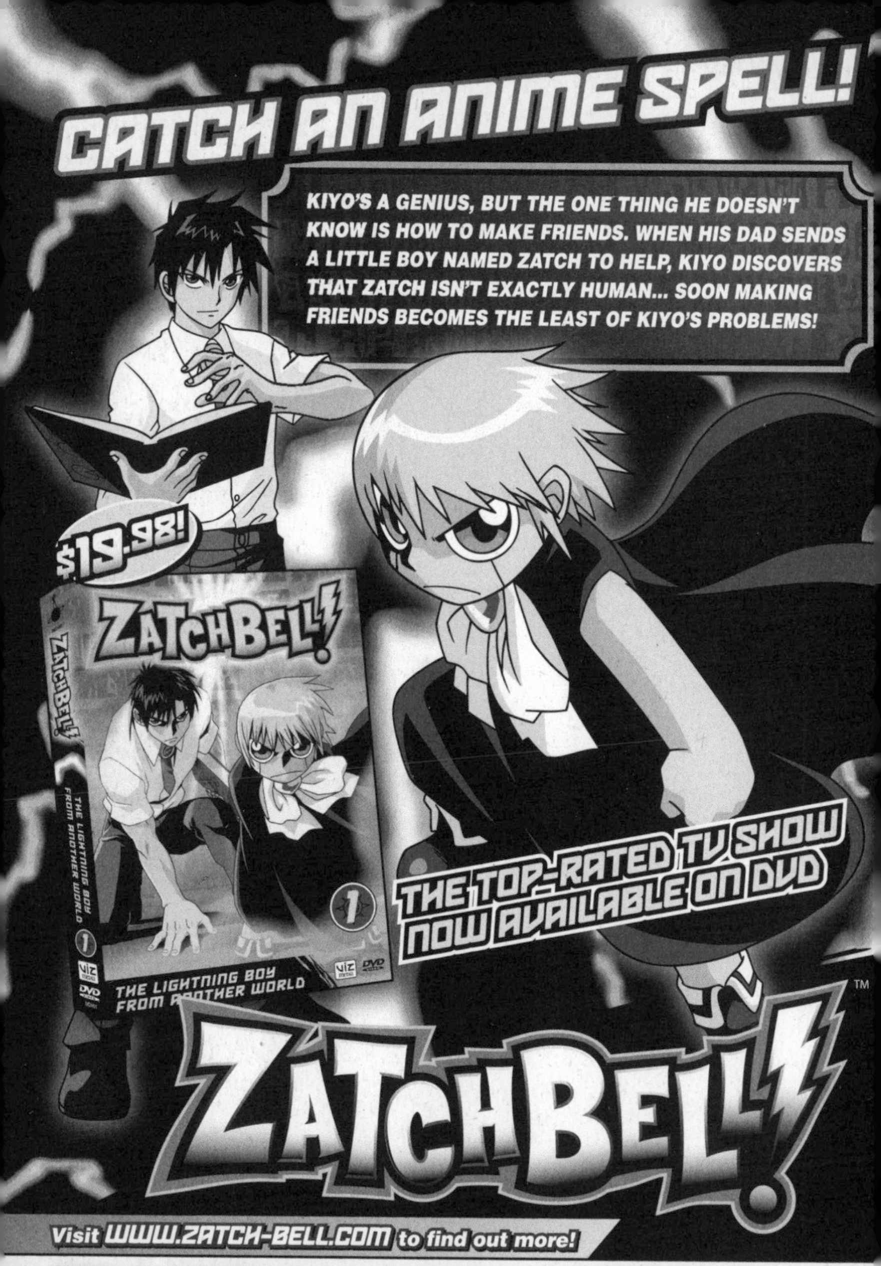
CATCH AN ANIME SPELL!
KIYO'S A GENIUS, BUT THE ONE THING HE DOESN'T KNOW IS HOW TO MAKE FRIENDS. WHEN HIS DAD SENDS A LITTLE BOY NAMED ZATCH TO HELP, KIYO DISCOVERS THAT ZATCH ISN'T EXACTLY HUMAN... SOON MAKING FRIENDS BECOMES THE LEAST OF KIYO'S PROBLEMS!
$19.98!
ZATCH BELL!
THE LIGHTNING BOY FROM ANOTHER WORLD
THE TOP-RATED TV SHOW NOW AVAILABLE ON DVD
ZATCH BELL!
Visit WWW.ZATCH-BELL.COM to find out more!
COMPLETE YOUR ZATCH BELL! COLLECTION TODAY—GRAPHIC NOVELS IN STORES NOW!

# InuYasha

Read the action from the start with the original manga series

Full color adaptation of the popular TV series

Art book with cel art, paintings, character profiles and more

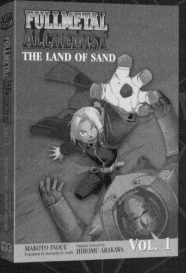

# LOVE MANGA?
## LET US KNOW WHAT YOU THINK!

# HELP US MAKE THE MANGA
# YOU LOVE BETTER!